2013

D1784522

Social Panorama
of Latin America

UNITED NATIONS

ECLAC

Alicia Bárcena
Executive Secretary

Antonio Prado
Deputy Executive Secretary

Martín Hopenhayn
Chief of the Social Development Division

Pascual Gerstenfeld
Chief of the Statistics Division

Dirk Jaspers_Faijer
Chief of the Latin American and Caribbean Demographic Centre (CELADE)-
Population Division of ECLAC

Diane Quarless
Chief of the ECLAC subregional headquarters for the Caribbean

Ricardo Pérez
Chief of the Publications and Web Services Division

The *Social Panorama of Latin America* is prepared each year by the Social Development Division and the Statistics Division of the Economic Commission for Latin America and the Caribbean (ECLAC), under the supervision of Martín Hopenhayn and Pascual Gerstenfeld, respectively, and with participation by the Latin American and Caribbean Demographic Centre (CELADE)-Population Division of ECLAC, directed by Dirk Jaspers_Faijer. The ECLAC subregional headquarters for the Caribbean, directed by Diane Quarless, was also involved in the preparation of this year's edition.

The 2013 edition was coordinated by Martín Hopenhayn, Ana Sojo and Xavier Mancero, who also worked on the preparation of the text together with Ernesto Espíndola, María Nieves Rico, Guillermo Sunkel and Pablo Villatoro. Verónica Amarante, María de la Luz Avendaño, Fabiola Fernández, Nincen Figueroa, Álvaro Fuentes, Marco Galván, Carlos Howes, Francis Jones, Tim Miller, Claudio Morris, Paulo Saad, Alejandra Silva, Vivian Milosavljevic and Natalia Yañez prepared substantive inputs and processed statistical data.

Explanatory notes:

- In this publication, the term "country" is used to refer to territorial entities, whether these are States as understood by international law and practice or simply territories for which statistical data are maintained on a separate and independent basis.
- Three dots (...) indicate that data are not available or are not separately reported.
- Two dashes and a full stop (-.-) indicate that the sample size is too small to be used as a basis for estimating the corresponding values with acceptable reliability and precision.
- A dash (-) indicates that the amount is nil or negligible.
- A blank space in a table indicates that the concept under consideration is not applicable or not comparable.
- A minus sign (-) indicates a deficit or decrease, unless otherwise indicated.
- The use of a hyphen (-) between years (e.g. 2000-2008) indicates reference to the complete number of calendar years involved, including the beginning and end years.
- A slash (/) between years (e.g. 2003/2005) indicates that the information given corresponds to one of these two years.
- The world "dollars" refers to United States dollars, unless otherwise specified.
- Individual figures and percentages in tables may not always add up to the corresponding total because of rounding.
- The boundaries and names shown on the maps of this publication do not imply official endorsement or acceptance by the United Nations.

United Nations publication
ISBN: 978-92-1-221119-0 • ISSN printed version: 1020-5160
LC/G.2580-P • Sales number: E.14.II.G.6
Copyright © United Nations, March 2014
All rights reserved
Printed in Santiago, Chile • 2013-869

Applications for the right to reproduce this work in full or in part are welcomed and should be sent to the Secretary of the Publications Board, United Nations Headquarters, New York, N.Y. 10017, U.S.A. Member States and their governmental institutions may reproduce this work without prior authorization, but are requested to mention the source and inform the United Nations of such reproduction.

Contents

Chapter IV
Landmarks in the discourse on social protection in Latin America and overview of health and pension system coverage: a synopsis

Chapter V
Recent trends in social spending as an element of public spending and household spending on health

Tables

Boxes

Introduction

The 2013 edition of *Social Panorama of Latin America* presents ECLAC official measurements for the analysis of income poverty and seeks fresh approaches to poverty and well-being, placing special emphasis on multidimensional approaches. These approaches are exploratory and therefore not comprehensive. They have nevertheless been tackled in this year's edition of *Social Panorama* because one thing is certain: the need is emerging in social policy design, in the evaluation of social development and in new demands of society for a more nuanced analysis of social progress and lags to underpin more integrated public policy design.

As in previous editions, chapter I sets out updated figures on poverty and indigence in Latin America. The 2012 data reaffirm the downtrend observed over the past 10 years, although the rate of poverty reduction, especially extreme poverty, has gradually slowed. The data also confirmed the tendency of income distribution to narrow over several years, even though income concentration edged upward in some countries in 2012.

Chapter I also examines other approaches with a view to a multidimensional measurement of poverty. In light of growing interest from the region's countries in respect of these measurements and their potential for public policy analysis, different dimensions, thresholds and forms of aggregation are analysed conceptually and empirically, in order to move forward, still in an exploratory manner, in constructing a multidimensional poverty index that is relevant and feasibly applicable in the region.

The analysis is based on a core set of non-monetary deprivation indicators, such as are traditionally used to measure unmet basic needs, and the results are shown for different multidimensional poverty indicators, along with their performance over time. The chapter then looks at the link between deprivation- and income-based poverty measurements, and sets out the results obtained from adding a measurement of monetary deprivation to the core set of indicators. It then discusses the empirical implementation of a broader definition of poverty, which includes dimensions related to the lacks in the area of social protection and institutional affiliation.

In chapter II, a method for measuring multiple deprivations through a right-based approach is used to examine trends in child poverty. This technique, used in the framework of an agreement between ECLAC and the United Nations Children's Fund (UNICEF), has shed lights on some specific features of poverty and extreme poverty in childhood. The findings call for the analysis of different levels of material deprivation and deprivation of access to public goods and services, which affect children's basic rights and add up to a situation of poverty.[1]

The above method is linked to more traditional, monetary measurements of indigence and poverty. The extent of child poverty is measured in Latin America and a group of Caribbean countries in terms of both income and deprivation, while distinguishing between the level of each deprivation and thus differentiating poverty from extreme poverty among children and adolescents. An analysis of deprivations reveals changes in their intensity, reductions in several dimensions, and their relative contributions to current poverty levels. Geographic information systems can be used to locate child poverty and deprivations, and to facilitate public policy formulation at both national and local level.

Chapter III considers the constituent dimensions of well-being, which yield an integrated and multidimensional perspective, and examines three dimensions —space, time and coexistence— which have been somewhat overlooked in the debate on well-being in Latin America.

---

[1] Because this is a joint study by ECLAC and UNICEF, the UNICEF definition of childhood is used here, i.e. referring to the population aged 0 to 17 years.

For example, in the dimension of space, a healthy environment is a prerequisite for the well-being of individuals. In recent decades, the environment in Latin America has suffered impacts of various types and intensities. Air quality deterioration is one of the main changes to have occurred in urban settings, and is a factor in rising discontent. Exposure to urban air pollution, especially particulate matter (PM10), also poses a serious health risk and causes an increase in the mortality rate.

Regarding the time dimension, a balance between paid work, unpaid domestic labour and free time is another prerequisite of well-being. The average working day in Latin America and the Caribbean is still far longer than in most European Union countries, and most employed women continue to bear the bulk of the care burden within households as well, which limits their free time to a much greater extent.

Another dimension of well-being is coexistence, which requires that people live together in a positive, democratic and non-violent setting. In this respect, the region's high homicide rate is undoubtedly a critical indicator, since it denotes a high level of violence in society. Domestic violence against women and children also remains all too common.

Chapter IV offers an up-to-date overview of health and pension coverage in Latin America, both in work and in retirement and a review of the landmarks in the discourse on social protection in Latin America.

Taking into account the positive developments in the labour market, wage employees' enrolment in health-care insurance and pensions increased in the region, albeit differing considerably in points of departure and magnitudes in different countries. Nevertheless, in some countries enrolment remains very low and is relatively stagnant, while lower enrolment reflects a higher concentration of income. Although there are wide gaps in access to social protection depending on income, education level and type of occupation, gender divides have narrowed among wage employees with better labour market integration. Enrolment in health-care insurance is generally higher than in pensions. In the labour market as a whole, enrolment is higher in the public sector than in private enterprises, while in the countries with the lowest levels of participation, the situation of workers in microenterprises is unfavourable and worsening. Non-wage earners are also at a significant disadvantage in terms of enrolment.

Pensioners enjoyed high levels of health-care coverage in the 14 countries for which measurements were available, including countries that are some way behind in terms of the overall coverage of the population. Nevertheless, most of the 16 countries reviewed had a contingent of persons aged 65 and over whose actual pensions were relatively low. Uneven income distribution is more acute in the countries with low pension coverage. The real value of pensions fluctuated according to income levels and depending on the country, with women having lower pensions owing to their employment histories and pension system provisions.

Chapter V examines recent trends in public social spending and public health spending, and looks at the effects of out-of-pocket health spending and demographic ageing on health expenditure.

Until 2011, public social spending trended upward, both in absolute amounts and as a proportion of total public expenditure and gross domestic product, albeit with different tendencies in different countries. However, new data on budget execution in the social sphere points to slower growth in social expenditure from 2012. This was intended to lower the fiscal deficits recently posted by many of the countries of the region, however the relative slowdown in the growth of social expenditure also reflects the scaling back or cancellation of social assistance programmes and other measures applied to tackle the effects of the international financial crisis of 2008-2009 (transfers, public employment schemes and fiscal stimuli to encourage private job creation).

Although unstable in the 1990s, public social spending on health strengthened along with overall public social spending during the 2000s. The financial crisis and its effects on the region's economies do not appear to have significantly impacted the sector, although growth was somewhat slower towards the end of the 2000s and at the beginning of this decade. The chapter also evaluates out-of-pocket health spending, the burden shouldered in this regard by poor and non-poor population groups, and its impact on well-being.

Consideration is likewise given to the impact of the demographic transition and its future projection in relation to health costs. Rapid population ageing, expected in many of the region's countries over the next few decades, is likely to prompt a major increase in total health spending, affecting its relative share of total social spending and as a proportion of GDP.

Summary

I. Poverty from different perspectives

Social Panorama of Latin America 2013 addresses poverty from different angles, and in particular from a multidimensional perspective. This approach enables detailed analysis not only of the magnitude of poverty, but also of its intensity and its distinctive features in different groups, while also guiding the formulation of poverty reduction policies that dovetail better with comprehensive policies in support of well-being.

A. Analysis of income poverty

Per capita GDP in Latin America and the Caribbean grew by 4.5% in 2010, 3.2% in 2011 and just 1.9% in 2012, a year in which the world economy experienced a downturn. Despite modest economic growth, employment rose on the back of job creation, absorbing the slight rise in the labour force participation rate and allowing unemployment to edge down from 6.7% to 6.4%, its lowest level in recent decades (ECLAC/ILO, 2013). The purchasing power of average wages held steady or rose in most countries with available information, in keeping with low inflation, the simple average of which fell from 7.1% in 2011 to 5.4% in 2012.

In this context, 28.2% of the population of Latin America and the Caribbean were living in poverty in 2012, with 11.3% in extreme poverty or indigence. In absolute numbers, 164 million people were poor, of which 66 million were extremely poor (see figure 1).

These figures represent a fall of about 1.4 percentage points in the poverty rate with respect to 2011 (29.6%). The extreme poverty rate varied little, with the 2012 figure just 0.3 percentage points down on 2011 (11.6%). The number of poor fell by approximately 6 million in 2012, while the number of indigents remained practically unchanged.

Poverty has fallen by 15.7 percentage points since 2002, having declined virtually across the board since 2002. Extreme poverty has also fallen significantly, by 8.0 percentage points, albeit the pace of reduction has slowed in recent years. Between 2002 and 2007, the yearly drop in the number of poor averaged 3.8% and in the number of indigent, 7.1%. But between 2007 and 2012, these rates slowed to 2.5% per year for poverty, and 0.9% per year for indigence.

Six of the 11 countries with information available in 2012 recorded falling poverty levels (see table 1). The largest drop was in the Bolivarian Republic of Venezuela, where poverty fell by 5.6 percentage points (from 29.5% to 23.9%) and extreme poverty by 2.0 percentage points (from 11.7% to 9.7%). In Ecuador, poverty was down by 3.1 percentage points (from 35.3% to 32.2%) and indigence by 0.9 percentage points (from 13.8% to 12.9%). In Brazil, poverty fell by 2.3 points (from 20.9% to 18.6%), and extreme poverty by 0.7 points (from 6.1% to 5.4%). Peru's poverty rate dropped by 2.0 points (from 27.8% to 25.8%), while in Argentina and Colombia the rate fell by just over 1 point. These three countries did not report significant changes in extreme poverty in comparison with 2011.

Figure 1
Latin America: poverty and indigence, 1980-2013 [a]
(Percentages and millions of people)

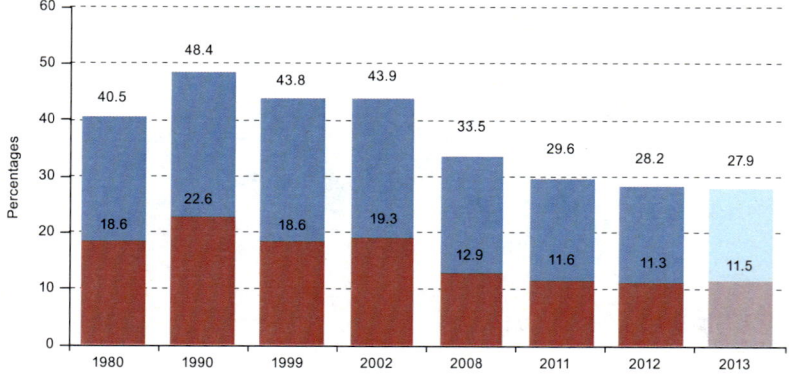

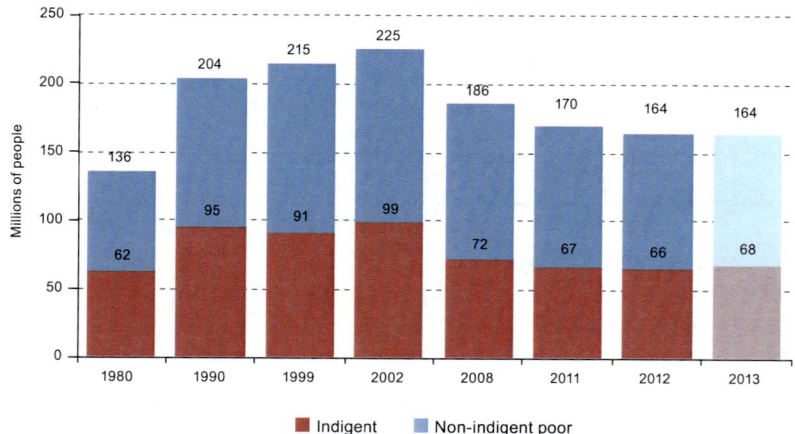

■ Indigent   ■ Non-indigent poor

Source: Economic Commission for Latin America and the Caribbean (ECLAC), on the basis of special tabulations of data from household surveys conducted in the respective countries.
[a] Estimate for 18 countries of the region plus Haiti. The figures above the bars are the percentages and total numbers of poor (indigent plus non-indigent poor). The figures for 2013 are projections.

Poverty levels in Costa Rica, the Dominican Republic, El Salvador and Uruguay remained consistent with previous estimates. Neither were there any major variations in extreme poverty in these countries, with the exception of El Salvador, where the figure decreased by 3.2 percentage points. Mexico was the only country with information available for 2012 in which poverty indicators rose, albeit marginally (poverty from 36.3% to 37.1% and indigence from 13.3% to 14.2%).

While the regional poverty rate is the result of the trends observed in each country, the changes reported in countries with larger populations weigh heavily. Poverty reductions in the Bolivarian Republic of Venezuela and Brazil significantly influenced the 2012 results, as they represented 6 million fewer poor. This poverty rise in Mexico also carried significant weight, adding about 1 million additional individuals to the numbers of poor.

No appreciable changes are expected in the Latin America's poverty and indigence levels in 2013, since growth in per capita GDP will remain similar to 2012 and no significant variations are foreseen in either employment or inflation.

Table 1
Latin America (18 countries): persons living in poverty and indigence, around 2005, 2011 and 2012 [a]
(Percentages)

Country	Around 2005			Around 2011			2012		
	Year	Poverty	Indigence	Year	Poverty	Indigence	Year	Poverty	Indigence
Argentina [b]	2005	30.6	11.9	2011	5.7	1.9	2012	4.3	1.7
Bolivia (Plurinational State of)	2004	63.9	34.7	2009	42.4	22.4	...	...	...
Brazil	2005	36.4	10.7	2011	20.9	6.1	2012	18.6	5.4
Chile	2006	13.7	3.2	2011	11.0	3.1	...	...	...
Colombia [c]	2005	45.2	13.9	2011	34.2	10.7	2012	32.9	10.4
Costa Rica [d]	2005	21.1	7.0	2011	18.8	7.3	2012	17.8	7.3
Ecuador	2005	48.3	21.2	2011	35.3	13.8	2012	32.2	12.9
El Salvador	2004	47.5	19.0	2010	46.6	16.7	2012	45.3	13.5
Dominican Republic	2005	47.5	24.6	2011	42.2	20.3	2012	41.2	20.9
Guatemala	2006	54.8	29.1	...	...	...	...	...	...
Honduras	2006	71.5	49.3	2010	67.4	42.8	...	...	...
Mexico	2006	31.7	8.7	2010	36.3	13.3	2012	37.1	14.2
Nicaragua	2005	61.9	31.9	2009	58.3	29.5	...	...	...
Panama	2005	31.0	14.1	2011	25.3	12.4	...	...	...
Paraguay	2005	56.9	27.6	2011	49.6	28.0	...	...	...
Peru [e]	2003	52.5	21.4	2011	27.8	6.3	2012	25.8	6.0
Uruguay	2005[b]	18.8	4.1	2011	6.5	1.1	2012	5.9	1.1
Venezuela (Bolivarian Republic of)	2005	37.1	15.9	2011	29.5	11.7	2012	23.9	9.7

Source: Economic Commission for Latin America and the Caribbean (ECLAC), on the basis of special tabulations of data from household surveys conducted in the respective countries.
[a] ECLAC is in the process of updating poverty estimates, the results of which will appear in Social Panorama in 2014.
[b] Urban areas.
[c] Figures from the National Administrative Department of Statistics (DANE) of Colombia.
[d] Figures for 2011 and 2012 are not strictly comparable with data from previous years.
[e] Figures from the National Institute of Statistics and Informatics (INEI) of Peru.

B. Multidimensional analysis of poverty

In this section, poverty measurement in Latin America is approached from a multidimensional perspective. This approach is exploratory by nature and is intended not to present a definitive multidimensional measurement of poverty for the region, but to complement conventional measurements. Although no consensus has yet been reached on a methodology for multidimensional poverty measurement in the region or indeed elsewhere in the world, it is useful to explore different dimensions, thresholds and forms of aggregation, in order to move towards constructing indicators that are relevant and feasible to apply in the region.

The empirical analysis is based on a core set of indicators that have traditionally formed part of the measurement of unmet basic needs (see table 2). A measurement of deprivation, based on income and certain dimensions that are not habitually included in poverty analysis, is then added. The poor are understood as those individuals suffering deprivations under at least two of the indicators considered. The aggregation of results in a synthetic index is based on the methodology proposed by Alkire and Foster (2009).

Figure 2 shows the headcount ratio (H), or the percentage of people suffering at least two deprivations, and intensity (A), which indicates the average percentage of deprivations experienced by the poor. For example, if the intensity is about 55% in Nicaragua, it means that on average, the country's poor are affected by 4.4 of the 8 deprivations included in the analysis. It may be noted that the headcount figures are dispersed over a wide range, from 2% in Chile, 10% in Uruguay and 11% in Argentina, to 71% in Nicaragua, 69% in Guatemala and 63% in Honduras.

Table 2

Dimensions, deprivation indicators and weights for poverty measurement based on traditional indicators of basic unmet needs

Dimensions	Deprivation indicators
Water and sanitation	
Lack of access to improved water sources	Urban areas: any source of water except a public system. Rural areas: unprotected wells, bottled water, mobile water sources, rivers, streams, rain and others.
Lack of toilet facility	Urban areas: no sanitation, or toilet not connected to a sewer system or septic tank. Rural areas: no sanitation, or untreated toilet system.
Energy [a]	
Lack of electricity	Households with no electricity.
Cooking fuel hazardous to health	Households that use firewood, coal or waste for cooking.
Dwelling [b]	
Makeshift housing materials	Dwellings with dirt floors, in rural and urban areas, or roof and walls made of makeshift materials.
Crowding	Three or more people per room, in rural and urban areas.
Education	
Non-attendance at school	Household has at least one child of school age (6 to 17 years old) that does not attend school.
Non-achievement of a minimum level of education	Household has nobody aged 20 or above with a minimum level of schooling. - Persons aged 20 to 59: have not completed lower secondary education. - Persons aged 60 and above: have not completed primary education.

Source: Economic Commission for Latin America and the Caribbean (ECLAC).

[a] In Argentina, only the information on fuel is available, while in the Bolivarian Republic of Venezuela and Chile, only the data on access to electricity are available. Given that fuel deprivation is usually more prevalent than that of electricity, it is likely that overall energy deprivation is underestimated in the Bolivarian Republic of Venezuela and Chile.

[b] In Brazil, information is only available on housing materials.

Figure 2

Latin America (17 countries): headcount ratio (H) and intensity (A), 2011 [a]

(Percentages)

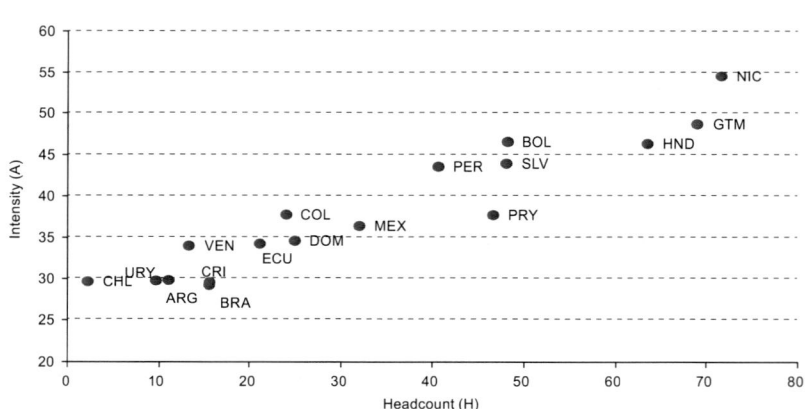

Source: Economic Commission for Latin America and the Caribbean (ECLAC), on the basis of special tabulations of data from household surveys conducted in the respective countries.

[a] Data refer to 2011, except those of El Salvador (2010), Guatemala (2010), Honduras (2010), Mexico (2010), Nicaragua (2009) and the Plurinational State of Bolivia (2009). Data for Argentina refer to urban areas.

The countries with the highest headcount ratios also usually have the highest poverty intensity. In other words, countries with the highest numbers of poor also tend to experience the most intense forms of poverty, with the poor suffering a greater number of deprivations simultaneously. There are some exceptions, however. For example, the poverty intensity figures are extremely similar for Honduras and the Plurinational State of Bolivia, and for Colombia and Paraguay, yet the headcount ratios of the respective countries are markedly different.

It is also necessary to evaluate the outcome when income poverty is included as a further dimension in the measurement of deprivations, on the understanding that monetary and multidimensional measurements cannot fully determine well-being when they are used individually and that combining them reduces possible errors of exclusion. The results show that multidimensional and monetary measurements of poverty are more complementary in countries where poverty measured through non-monetary deprivations is less prevalent. This type of measurement therefore has great potential to fill information gaps and lessen errors of omission in these countries.

Furthermore, in a number of Latin American countries, and particularly those which have seen a major improvement in living standards, poverty rates are low and are decreasing over time. Traditional indicators of unmet basic needs may not, therefore, be sufficient to identify the poor, and information on deprivation in other spheres may be needed to develop a poverty assessment that is more relevant to the situation in these countries (ECLAC, 2010). In this connection, some complementary yet previously overlooked aspects of well-being are assessed in *Social Panorama of Latin America 2013* for a group of countries in the region. These aspects include the effect of air pollution on health, the length of paid and unpaid working days, and levels of domestic and non-domestic violence (see chapter 3).

In order to include the social structure as an explicit component of this approach to poverty measurement, the study addresses two further areas of deprivation: lack of access to social protection, and institutional exclusion among young people (those not in education or paid work).

The results of this "broadened" measurement of poverty indicate that housing (crowding and makeshift materials) and energy issues (lack of electricity and cooking fuel) account for a greater share of deprivations in countries with higher rates of overall poverty. On the other hand, deprivation in relation to education (non-attendance at school and low educational achievement among adults) makes a greater contribution to poverty in countries with overall poverty rates of under 50% (see figure 3).

Figure 3
Latin America (16 countries): relative contribution to poverty
of selected dimensions, by country groupings, 2011 [a]
(Percentages)

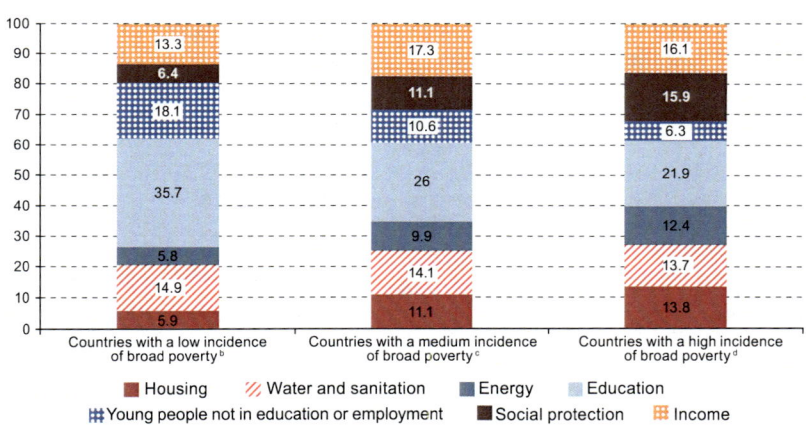

Source: Economic Commission for Latin America and the Caribbean (ECLAC), on the basis of special tabulations of data from household surveys conducted in the respective countries.
[a] The housing dimension considers aspects of materials and crowding. The energy dimension includes deprivations of electricity and cooking fuel. The social protection dimension encompasses affiliation to health-care and pension systems, and/or receipt of a pension. Data refer to 2011, except those of El Salvador (2010), Guatemala (2006), Honduras (2010), Mexico (2010) and the Plurinational State of Bolivia (2009).
[b] Countries with a low incidence of broad poverty: Argentina, Brazil, Chile, Costa Rica and Uruguay.
[c] Countries with a mid-level incidence of broad poverty: Bolivarian Republic of Venezuela, Colombia, Dominican Republic, Ecuador, Mexico and Peru.
[d] Countries with a high incidence of broad poverty: El Salvador, Guatemala, Honduras, Paraguay and Plurinational State of Bolivia.

Lack of social protection carries greater weight in countries with higher rates of deprivation-measured poverty, which may be attributable to the nature of the indicators used in the analysis, which basically measure enrolment in social protection systems. This deprivation could thus be measured more effectively by including indicators to measure the quality of accessible services in countries where social security enrolment is already high. At the same time, the fact that young people not in education or employment are increasingly contributing to overall poverty in the countries with the lowest poverty rates raises the question of whether this indicator measures actual poverty or merely vulnerability to poverty.

In short, the results show not only that the countries differ in terms of the magnitude and intensity of multidimensional poverty, but that the dimensions with the greatest impact on poverty vary as well. The shaping of policy and institutional architectures and responsibilities must therefore differ accordingly.

In sum, the renewed interest in examining poverty through a multidimensional approach offers an opportunity for debate on what is understood by poverty and which dimensions of well-being are relevant to this understanding. Although this edition of the *Social Panorama* considers only some of the basic aspects of this type of poverty measurement, these suffice to illustrate the potentials and challenges presented by multidimensional measurements. Even in their most traditional application, limited to unmet basic needs, it can be confirmed that deprivations such as lack of access to drinking water or sanitation continue to affect considerable numbers in the region. It must be asked, then, whether public policies on poverty reduction are placing enough emphasis on achieving minimum standards in core dimensions aside from income.

Lastly, multidimensional approaches to poverty imply new challenges for the region. First, the study highlights the major challenge in developing the region's information sources to enable poverty to be measured and characterized from a multidimensional perspective, in a more comprehensive and relevant way. Methodology is another significant issue. Data on income poverty are based on a long-established methodology whose results are solidly enshrined in monetary income thresholds that unequivocally delineate the poor population and, within it, the indigent population. By comparison, the multidimensional, deprivation-based approach to poverty measurement still lacks the methodological consensus enjoyed by income-based measurements, and does not support such a clear-cut interpretation of the results. Nevertheless, it complements the income approach and captures both population groups that both parameters signal as poor, and groups whose income places above the poverty line, but that suffer deprivation in relation to basic needs.

C. Income distribution

Highly uneven income distribution is one of Latin America's hallmarks. The most recent available data indicated that the poorest income quintile (i.e. the 20% of households with the lowest income) on average accounted for of 5% of total income, with the figure varying between 4% (in the Dominican Republic, Honduras and Paraguay) and 10% (in Uruguay). Meanwhile, the wealthiest income quintile accounted for an average of 47% of total income, ranging from 35% (in Uruguay) to 55% (in Brazil) (see table 3).

Table 3
**Latin America (18 countries): distribution of household income
by extreme quintiles, around 2002 and 2012**
(Percentages)

	Around 2002				Around 2012			
	Year	Share in total income *(percentages)*		Ratio of average per capita income	Year	Share in total income *(percentages)*		Ratio of average per capita income
		Poorest quintile (QI)	Richest quintile (QV)	QV / QI		Poorest quintile (QI)	Richest quintile (QV)	QV / QI
Argentina [a]	2002	5.1	55.0	20.6	2012	6.9	43.6	13.2
Bolivia (Plurinational State of)	2002	2.2	57.7	44.2	2011	4.4	42.6	15.9
Brazil	2002	3.4	62.3	34.4	2012	4.5	55.1	22.5
Chile	2003	4.9	55.1	18.4	2011	5.5	52.5	15.0
Colombia	2002	4.2	53.3	24.1	2012	4.6	49.8	19.8
Costa Rica	2002	4.2	47.3	17.0	2012	4.7	49.3	16.5
Ecuador [a]	2002	5.1	48.8	16.8	2012	6.4	43.0	10.9
El Salvador	2001	4.1	49.6	20.2	2012	6.9	41.9	10.3
Dominican Republic	2002	3.9	53.4	20.7	2012	3.9	50.8	19.4
Guatemala	2002	4.8	51.8	19.3	2006	4.3	54.7	23.9
Honduras	2002	3.8	55.2	26.3	2010	3.5	53.7	25.2
Mexico	2002	5.9	49.1	15.5	2012	6.6	46.2	14.0
Nicaragua	2001	3.7	55.5	27.3	2009	5.6	46.0	14.5
Panama	2002	3.6	52.2	25.8	2011	4.4	48.3	20.3
Paraguay	2001	4.2	51.8	23.2	2011	3.8	52.7	21.3
Peru	2001	4.5	49.6	19.3	2012	5.0	43.7	12.7
Uruguay [a]	2002	8.8	41.8	10.2	2012	10.0	34.8	7.3
Venezuela (Bolivarian Republic of)	2002	4.3	48.2	18.1	2012	6.8	39.0	9.4

Source: Economic Commission for Latin America and the Caribbean (ECLAC), on the basis of special tabulations of data from household surveys conducted in the respective countries.
[a] Urban areas.

As described in several editions of the *Social Panorama of Latin America* and numerous studies on the subject in the region, income distribution has tended to improve slowly over the past 10 years. These changes have occurred gradually and are barely noticeable from one year to the next; however they are evident in comparisons over longer periods. Taking data from around 2002 as a benchmark, the most recent figures indicate that the poorest income quintile's share of total income rose by at least one percentage point in eight countries. Conversely, in nine countries the relative share of the wealthiest income quintile fell by five percentage points or more. This quintile continued to capture over 50% of income in six countries, compared with 11 countries in 2002.

The changes noted in the top and bottom quintiles' share of total income are also reflected in variations in the inequality indexes. Of the 13 countries with information available in 2011 or 2012, 12 reported a fall in their Gini coefficient, the simple average of which fell by 1% per year. Inequality narrowed by more than 1% per year in Argentina, the Bolivarian Republic of Venezuela, Brazil, Peru and Uruguay, and by at least 0.5% per year in Chile, Colombia, Ecuador and Panama.

Inequality eased slightly more quickly in the last four years of the period reviewed, as figure 4 shows. Also apparent is the change in the Gini coefficient for the subperiods 2002-2008 and 2008-2012, taking the year 2008, when international financial crisis broke out, as the midpoint. In eight countries, inequality fell more during the second subperiod than the first. The Plurinational State of Bolivia and Uruguay posted the largest reductions, of more than 3% per year. On the other hand, inequality increased in Costa Rica, Panama and Paraguay in the second subperiod, although only Costa Rica recorded an overall increase for the entire period.

Figure 4
Latin America (15 countries): annual variation of Gini coefficient, 2002-2008 and 2008-2012 [a]
(Percentages)

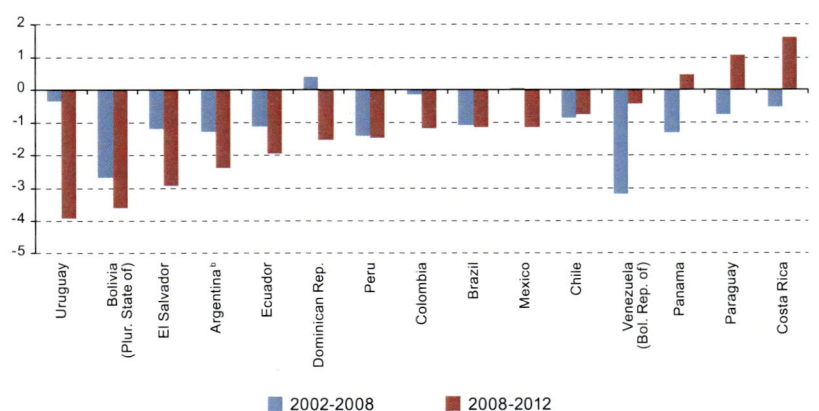

Source: Economic Commission for Latin America and the Caribbean (ECLAC), on the basis of special tabulations of data from household surveys in the respective countries.
[a] Includes only countries with data available for 2011 or 2012. Countries are ordered by variation in the second subperiod (2008-2012).
[b] Urban areas.

II. Child poverty in Latin America and the Caribbean: a multidimensional, rights-based approach

One aspect of concern relating to monetary poverty in Latin America and the Caribbean is that it has a greater impact on households with high dependency rates, which worsens the situation of children and adolescents. The mid-1990s marked the beginning of debate in the region on the juvenilization of poverty; an increasingly relevant concept given that children and adolescents are overrepresented among the poor, compared with other age groups.

A high proportion of children and adolescents face adversities that impact them directly, are detrimental to the rest of their lives and are passed on to subsequent generations. Those worst affected are usually caught in situations where insufficient household income combines with deprivation of the right to survival, shelter, education, health and nutrition, among others. In other words, they are denied the assets and opportunities to which all human beings are entitled. Poverty is also strongly associated with social exclusion and inequality.

Analysing the nature of the poverty faced by children and adolescents, and fully understanding the phenomenon of child poverty, requires a comprehensive perspective. It is therefore important to develop a multidimensional measurement that identifies deprivations that directly affect these groups in relation to the provision and quality of public goods and services, as well as in monetary terms, with a view to meeting the needs of all household members.

A. Rights-based approach and multidimensional measurement of child poverty[1]

In a joint study undertaken by ECLAC and the UNICEF Regional Office for Latin America and the Caribbean, child poverty is understood as deprivations in specific dimensions in which children and adolescents hold rights, and which are broadly recognized as constituting poverty. These dimensions are: education, nutrition, housing, drinking water, sanitation and information (ECLAC/UNICEF, 2012).

In this chapter, child poverty is measured on the basis of household surveys, through two methodological approaches: (i) direct methods which, based on the indicators proposed by the University of Bristol (2003),

---

[1] Because this is a joint study by ECLAC and UNICEF, the UNICEF definition of childhood is used here, i.e. referring to the population aged 0 to 17 years.

were adapted to measure multiple deprivations in childhood (with two thresholds defining severe and moderate deprivation in each dimension); and (ii) indirect methods, by which absolute poverty is measured by per capita household income.

In terms of methodology, the criteria adopted in this study were determined by the rights-based approach. As such, the universality of rights implies that rights, and the deprivation thereof, must be assessed in the same way for all population groups of children and adolescents, without setting different thresholds for urban and rural populations. Since human rights are indivisible and interdependent, each moderate deprivation is considered an indicator of poverty since it represents a violation or breach of at least one right, with each severe deprivation being regarded as an indicator of extreme poverty in childhood.

If poverty is measured in these terms, 40.5% of children and adolescents in Latin America are poor. This means that overall child poverty in the region affects 70.5 million individuals under the age of 18. Of this total, 16.3%, or one in six children and adolescents, is living in extreme poverty, understood as at least one severe deprivation. The scourge of extreme poverty thus affects more than 28.3 million individuals.

The situation differs significantly between groups of countries. In the countries with the highest overall child poverty (El Salvador, Guatemala, Honduras, Nicaragua, Peru and the Plurinational State of Bolivia), on average 72% of children were living in poverty. In the countries with the lowest overall child poverty (Argentina, Chile, Costa Rica, Ecuador and Uruguay) only 19.5% of children were poor (see figure 5).

Figure 5
Latin America (17 countries): rates of extreme and overall child poverty, and percentage of children in indigent and poor households (according to income method), around 2011 [a]
(Percentages)

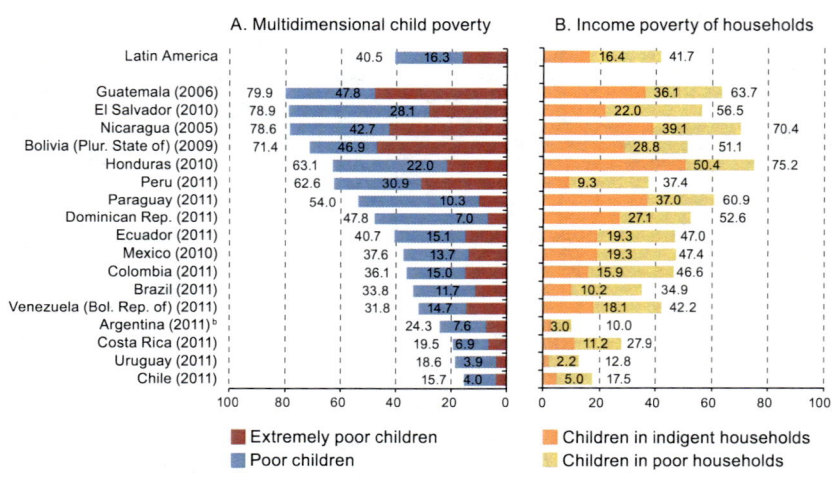

Source: Economic Commission for Latin America and the Caribbean (ECLAC), on the basis of special tabulations of data from household surveys conducted in the respective countries.
[a] Uses the UNICEF definition, which encompasses the population aged 0 to 17 years. Figures for poor children include extremely poor children, and figures for children in poor households include children in indigent households. The figures shown may differ from those in the text, which examine trends between 2000 and 2011 and only refer to 14 countries.
[b] Urban areas.

Child poverty measurements are also given from around the years 2000 and 2011. These measurements are encouraging, with all countries reporting a decrease in the percentage of children under 18 who are deprived of some basic rights (overall poverty). In the region as a whole (14 countries, comparable over time at national level), overall child poverty fell by over 14 percentage points over the period, from 55.3% of children in around 2000 to 41.2% around 2011.

Extreme poverty tends to be more intense (i.e. to involve multiple severe deprivations) where a greater percentage of children are living in extreme poverty. While the existence of a single severe deprivation is already serious for a child's development, a "syndrome" of multiple deprivations signals a sure loss of opportunities for developing a child's potentials and is at the root of the intergenerational reproduction of poverty. One in four extremely poor children suffers from a serious violation of more than one fundamental right, and one in three poor children suffers moderate deprivation of more than one need, though this deprivation may be moderate. Policy formulation must consider the interaction between deprivations, since deprivation in one dimension usually has consequences for the child's opportunity and capacity to exercise rights in one or more of the other dimensions (Gordon and others, 2003; Minujin, Delarmónica and Davidziuk, 2006; Kaztman, 2011).

In all the countries, the reduction in overall and extreme child poverty was accompanied by a reduction in its intensity (the percentage of children suffering multiple deprivations). In 2000, about 41% of extremely poor children suffered two or more severe deprivations; by 2011 this percentage was down to 28%. In 2000, about 58% of poor children had more than one of their rights infringed; falling to 42% by 2011 (see figure 6). In this analysis, the intensity of poverty is represented by the number of deprivations affecting poor (and extremely poor) children, and does not necessarily reflect their severity.

Figure 6
Latin America (14 countries): changes in the cumulative distribution of the number of severe and total deprivations, 2000 and 2011 [a]
(Percentages)

A. Cumulative distribution of the number of severe deprivations among extremely poor children

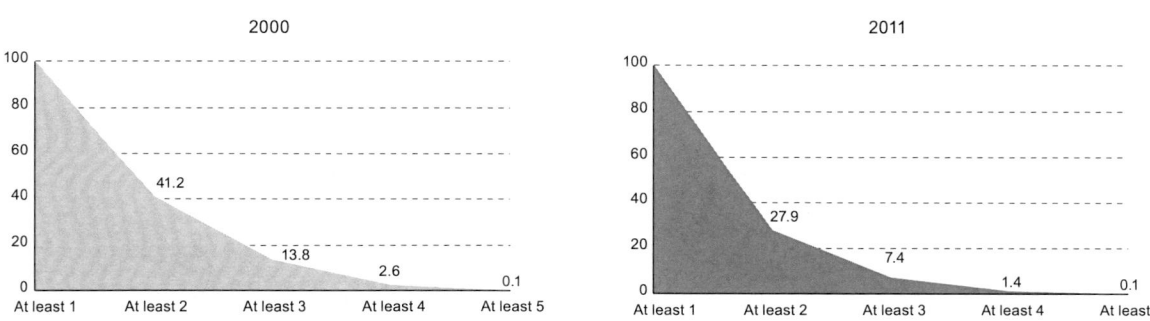

B. Cumulative distribution of the total number of deprivations among poor [b]

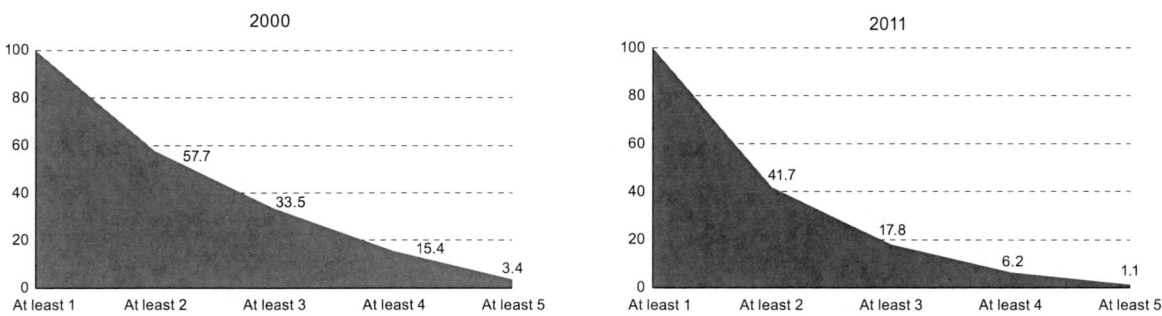

Source: Economic Commission for Latin America and the Caribbean (ECLAC) on the basis of special tabulations of data from household surveys conducted in the respective countries.
[a] Uses the UNICEF definition, which encompasses the population aged 0 to 17 years. Deprivation figures are presented cumulatively. For example, the percentage of children suffering at least three deprivations includes those with four or five deprivations. Initial values are equivalent to 100% (children suffering at least one deprivation), since the distributions are calculated from samples of poor or extremely poor children, respectively.
[b] Total number of deprivations refers to moderate and severe deprivations, including those of children living in extreme poverty.

B. Levels of deprivation in the different dimensions of poverty in Latin America and some Caribbean countries

In Latin America, levels of both severe and moderate deprivation fell sharply in all dimensions of child poverty, especially sanitation, housing and access to information, between 2000 and 2011. The smallest decreases were in education and nutrition, given that deprivation levels among the region's children were already low in these areas in the early 2000s. The general fall in deprivation across all dimensions explains the significant advances made towards easing overall and extreme child poverty, as well as in reducing its intensity (see figure 7). The three dimensions that accounted for most deprivations were sanitation facilities, housing quality and access to drinking water. The proportional contribution of these dimensions did not vary between 2000 and 2011, and in fact gained in relative terms as extreme poverty declined. This suggests that advances in education, information and nutrition had a greater bearing on reducing extreme poverty.

Figure 7
Latin America (14 countries): severe and total deprivations in the dimensions of child poverty, around 2000 and 2011 [a]
(Percentages)

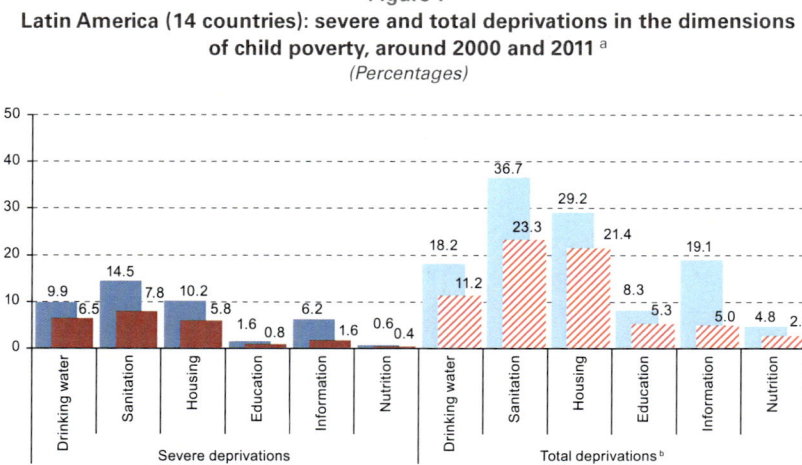

Source: Economic Commission for Latin America and the Caribbean (ECLAC), on the basis of special tabulations of data from household surveys conducted in the respective countries.
[a] Average of 14 countries with national information available in around 2000 and 2011. Uses the UNICEF definition, which encompasses the population aged 0 to 17 years.
[b] Includes moderate and severe deprivations.

Analogous data were also obtained for seven Caribbean countries: Antigua and Barbuda, Belize, Grenada, Guyana, Saint Lucia, Suriname, and Trinidad and Tobago. Where available, some deprivation figures are also shown for Jamaica. These estimates were drawn up on the basis of Multiple Indicator Cluster Surveys (MICS) and, in the case of Antigua and Barbuda, Grenada and Santa Lucia, surveys of living conditions. These surveys were conducted between 2005 and 2008. Prepared using the same methodology as was applied for Latin America, the estimates allow multidimensional child poverty in Caribbean countries to be compared with the rest of the region. This had not been possible hitherto using monetary poverty statistics, which are constructed under different methods.

The estimates revealed overall child poverty levels of between 10% and 70% in the seven Caribbean countries, and extreme child poverty levels of between 1% and 46% (see table 4). There was a marked difference between the continental countries (Belize, Guyana and Suriname) and the island countries (Antigua and Barbuda, Grenada, Jamaica, Santa Lucia and Trinidad and Tobago). Belize, Guyana and Suriname posted overall poverty rates of over 60%, and extreme poverty rates of over 35%, while in the Caribbean island countries overall poverty averaged 24% and extreme poverty, 6%. The difference is partly a reflection of high levels of rural poverty in Belize, Guyana and Suriname. In these three countries, unlike the small islands, urban and rural areas differ sharply.

Table 4
The Caribbean (8 countries): overall and extreme poverty rates in childhood[a]
(Percentages)

	Overall poverty rate in childhood	Extreme poverty rate in childhood
Antigua and Barbuda (2005)[b]	10	2
Belize (2006)	71	36
Grenada (2007/2008)[b]	32	7
Guyana (2006)	74	46
Jamaica (2005)[c]	25	16
Saint Lucia (2005)[b]	25	6
Suriname (2006)[c]	41	30
Trinidad and Tobago (2006)[d]	28	10

Source: Economic Commission for Latin America and the Caribbean (ECLAC), on the basis of special tabulations of data from the countries' Multiple Indicator Cluster Surveys and surveys of living conditions.
[a] Uses the UNICEF definition, which encompasses the population aged 0 to 17 years. The dimensions of the multidimensional child poverty estimation included are drinking water, sanitation, housing, education, information and nutrition.
[b] Does not include the dimension of nutrition.
[c] The survey contained a significant omission in the dimension of information, as a result of which deprivations relating to this dimension are underestimated.
[d] Does not include the dimension of information.

The various deprivations call for initiatives that are sectoral, but which must be coordinated under a comprehensive approach to poverty. In this regard, it should be recalled that efforts designed to improve children's quality of life often involve improving the quality of life of all family members. It should also be recalled that while initiatives in individual sectors can reduce deprivation in one dimension of child poverty, they do not necessarily safeguard children's other fundamental rights; and that in a culture of poverty, children often experience rights infringements that are not included in poverty measurements, such as child exploitation or physical and psychological violence. Comprehensive action to combat child poverty therefore involves not only coordinated efforts by States in different sectoral policies and programmes, but also psychosocial aspects and the promotion of a culture of recognition of and respect for children's rights within households.

III. Commonly overlooked aspects of well-being — space, time and coexistence

The multidimensional view of poverty set out in the preceding chapters is ultimately a reflection of the idea that well-being itself needs to be considered in a multidimensional manner. Commonly used indicators do not fully capture the complexity of poverty and well-being. GDP, for example, captures the production of goods and services, but disregards aspects such as income distribution, justice and freedom, as well as people's chances of leading a meaningful and satisfying life and the sustainability of economic progress.

In recent years various initiatives have been launched to establish a set of spheres that can be assessed to provide a more comprehensive view of well-being. One such initiative is the global project "Measuring the Progress of Societies", led by the Organisation for Economic Cooperation and Development (OECD). This project was set up to develop key economic, social and environmental indicators that could facilitate understanding of what is meant by societal well-being. It also encourages the use of indicators to promote better-informed decision-making in the public and private sectors and civil society.

Against that backdrop, chapter III proposes a group of constituent elements of well-being that, taken together, help form a comprehensive, multidimensional overview. Three main aspects —space, time and coexistence— have been overlooked in discussions on well-being in Latin America, and go beyond basic "first-generation" needs as regards health, education, working conditions, housing, or economic situation.

This proposal has particular resonance in Latin America, where three distinct factors stand out: (i) major progress in meeting global development goals, particularly a significant reduction in poverty; (ii) the persistence of widely disparate income distribution and a broad array of social inequalities; and (iii) the emergence of increasingly visible signs of societal concern in such areas as the environment, education, public transport and the entitlements of indigenous peoples.

A. Space: environmental problems in cities

Space is a fundamental material element for human life. It encompasses the environment we inhabit, including water, earth, air, objects, living beings, gender relations and intangible factors such as cultural values. A healthy space (or environment) to live in is an essential prerequisite for a decent standard of well-being.

In the past few decades the environment in Latin America has been affected in various ways, and to varying extents, by the development model. These changes have all had an impact on well-being. The deterioration in air quality is a one of the most serious issues affecting the well-being of the region's urban populations.

The countries of the region have made great strides in implementing air-quality management programmes. Yet many cities still have worrisome levels of air pollution: vast swathes of the Latin American population are still exposed to air-pollution levels exceeding the limits recommended by the World Health Organization (WHO). In 2007-2008 at least 27 cities in the region —including 10 capitals— exceeded the particulate matter (PM10) limits recommended by WHO.

Figure 8
Latin America and the Caribbean (selected cities): annual average particulate matter (PM10) pollution, around 2008-2009
(Microgrammes per cubic metre)

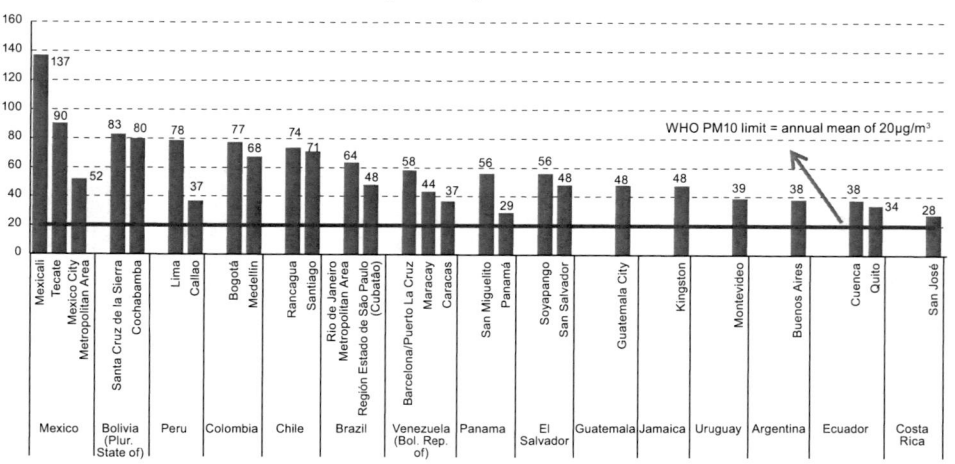

Source: Economic Commission for Latin America and the Caribbean (ECLAC), on the basis of information from the World Health Organization (WHO), "Outdoor air pollution in cities" [online] http://www.who.int/phe/health_topics/outdoorair/databases/en/.

Exposure to urban air pollution, especially PM10, poses a serious risk to human health and leads to higher rates of morbidity and mortality. At least 100 million people in Latin America and the Caribbean are said to be exposed to air pollution at levels that exceed WHO-recommended limits (Cifuentes and others, 2005). The groups most vulnerable to the effects of air pollution are children, the elderly, people with certain pre-existing health conditions and those in poverty.

Exposure to particulate matter increases the risk of contracting cardiovascular and respiratory diseases and lung cancer. In a period of around four years from 2004 to 2008, less than a third of the countries (seven of 24) were able to reduce the number of deaths from causes related to air pollution. This is starkly inconsistent with the urgency of action in response to deaths that public health and environmental strategies could have helped to avoid, especially since a reduction in PM10 from 70 to 20 microgrammes per cubic metre would reduce air-quality-related deaths by approximately 15%, according to WHO. Exposure to air pollution must be acknowledged as a major cause of mortality, on which effective public policy action is desperately needed.

B. Time: available time and paid and unpaid work

Time is another fundamental element for human life. Our well-being is greatly dependent on what we do and what we are able to do and, therefore, on the time that we can devote to our various activities. However, people's daily lives are subject to numerous restrictions on this freedom. Time is, therefore, a resource that is limited throughout life.

Time spent in gainful employment, whose purpose is to generate monetary resources to provide for a wide range of needs, is an essential part of most people's lives. The more time people spend at work, the less they have for other activities, such as family responsibilities and rest. Reductions in working hours —one of the most common demands from workers' movements for much of the twentieth century— have been made with a view to safeguarding workers' physical and mental health.

The length of the working day varies greatly according to such factors as workers' age and gender as well as the type of employment. However, average working hours in Latin America remain very long. Unlike in most European countries, where workers spend an average of 37 hours per week at work, weekly working hours in Latin American remain well above 40, and show no signs of shortening.

Remuneration is not, however, forthcoming for all the value generated by work. Much of what is produced in society is not valued in monetary terms. All forms of work carried out in the home —chiefly by women— such as cooking, cleaning and caring for others are performed without pay and with no contract to govern aspects such as wages, responsibilities and the benefits derived from the work.

Figure 9
Latin America (18 countries): working hours of the economically active population aged 15 years and over, around 2002 and 2011
(Hours per week)

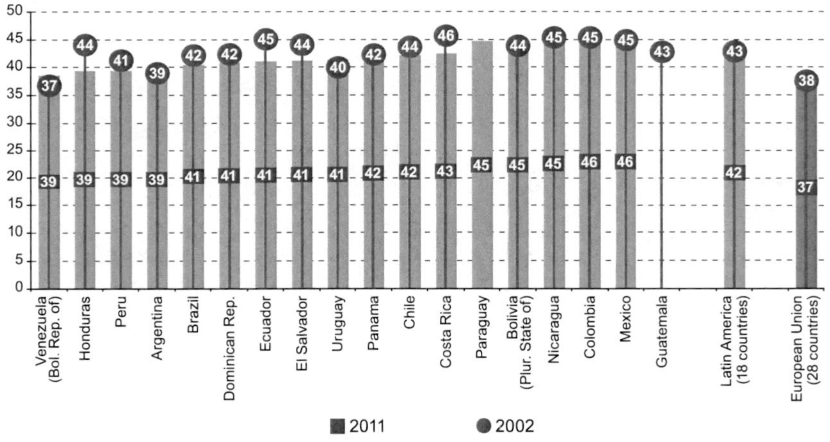

Source: Economic Commission for Latin America and the Caribbean (ECLAC), on the basis of special tabulations of data from household surveys conducted in the respective countries.

The available information shows that women spend many more hours a day performing unpaid domestic work than men. Women's increasing incorporation into the labour force has not been offset by greater participation by men in household work. Thus, in Latin America the sexual division of labour has remained partial and uneven.

The overall workload is the sum of hours spent in both paid employment and unpaid household work, including caring for children and elderly or sick family members. The data show that women in employment shoulder a greater total work burden than men. This excess burden seriously affects the well-being of employed women, particularly those living with a partner and who have preschool-aged children. Women who are heads of households also carry a high workload. All such women can be said to be "time-poor", which means that they have scant time for rest, leisure, recreation, family life and socializing.

Figure 10
**Latin America (selected countries): time spent by the employed population
in paid work, unpaid work and free time** [a]
(Hours per week)

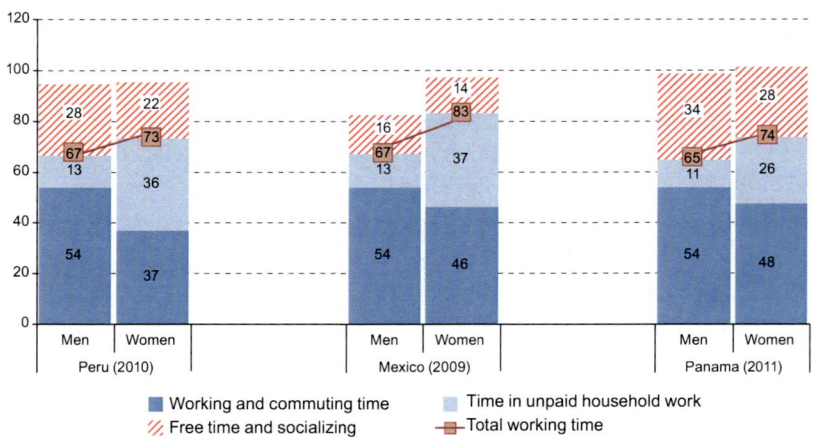

Source: Economic Commission for Latin America and the Caribbean (ECLAC), on the basis of special tabulations of data from time-use surveys conducted in Ecuador (2011), Mexico, (2009) and Panama and Peru (2011).

[a] Time-use surveys conducted in Latin America differ from country to country in terms of design and implementation. What is more, there is no standardized indicator for comparisons between surveys. Time-use surveys from Mexico, Panama and Peru have been selected as they encompass a similar range of activities, including working hours, free time, and time spent in unpaid household work, socializing, covering personal needs and volunteering.

C. Coexistence: high levels of violence in Latin America

Coexistence is another basic dimension of human life. People's well-being is contingent upon their continuing to build a life shared with loved ones that imparts a sense of belonging and security and motivates them to make life plans. Well-being therefore necessarily entails forms of positive and peaceful social coexistence that enable everyone to feel part of society.

However, the rapid processes of modernization and urbanization in Latin America in the past two decades have led to numerous problems involving coexistence. One of the most serious is violence, both in public spaces and the home.

The murder rate is one of the most important indicators of insecurity and violence in public spaces. According to the United Nations' *2011 Global Study on Homicide*, in 2010, 31% of the world's murders were committed in the Americas, a figure second only to Africa (36%) (UNODOC, 2012). The murder rate in the Americas (15.6 per 100,000 people) is more than double the global average (6.9 per 100,000).

Latin America's high average murder rate masks considerable differences from country to country. Homicide rates in the region have diverged markedly in recent years, with sharp increases in certain countries —such as Honduras, El Salvador, Peru and Mexico— and decreases in others, such as Nicaragua, Jamaica and Colombia (see figure 11).

Another prevalent form of violence is violence within the home (or in a family environment). The available statistics show that a very high percentage of women aged 15-49 suffer or have suffered at some time physical violence at the hands of an intimate partner, ranging from 33% in Colombia to 14% in Haiti.

Lastly, the phenomenon of domestic violence against children in Latin America and the Caribbean warrants special attention. The most common forms of punishment used by both parents with their children include verbal reprimands, but physical punishments, including smacking, are used against a high percentage of children, showing that physical violence towards children is an everyday reality in the region.

Figure 11
**Latin America and the Caribbean (15 countries): gross homicide rate
per 100,000 inhabitants, 2008-2011** [a]
(Number per 100,000 inhabitants)

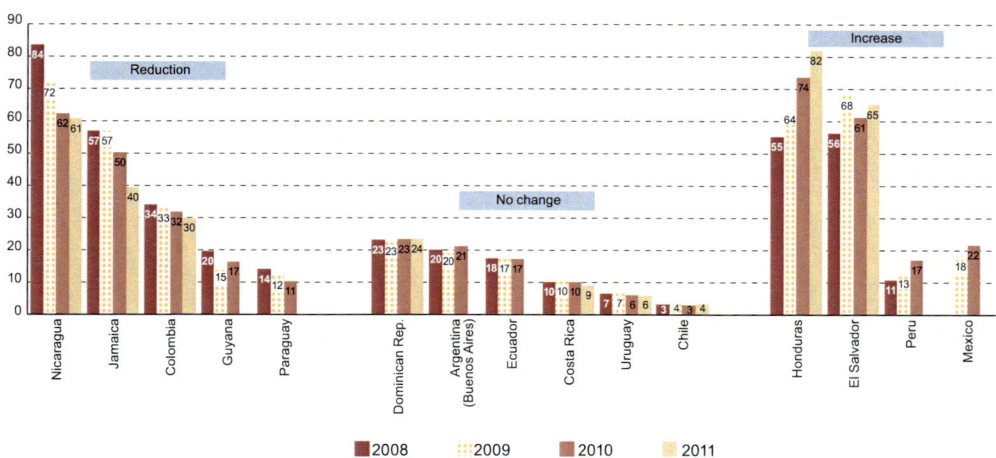

Source: Inter-American Development Bank (IDB), Regional system of standardized indicators in peaceful coexistence and citizen security (RIC) [online] http://www.
seguridadyregion.com/images/Indicadores/muertes%20por_homicidio.pdf.
[a] RIC defines homicide as "Intentional injuries caused by a person to another causing death" (deaths caused by traffic accidents or other non-intentional injuries are
not included). The figures include all cases of homicide known to the authorities occurring anywhere in the country, as well as femicides. There is no information
on Brazil as it is in the process of joining RIC.

A final reflection is the synergy between the various aspects of well-being described here. Good use of space in the framework of urban policies that address broad coexistence in spatial planning can help to reduce violence. Conversely, with lower levels of violence, citizens become more inclined to use the city in constructive and sustainable ways. A direct link is evident, as well, between spatial decongestion and decompression of time use, precisely because urban congestion leads to longer travel times, among other things. It is important, therefore, that policies be designed to build on the synergies that could be achieved by managing the various dimensions of well-being.

IV. Social protection in Latin America: an up-to-date review of membership of health and pension systems

The present and future well-being of all individuals is influenced by risks such as illness, the need to care for children and the frail or those with disabilities, periods of unemployment and underemployment, and the radical decline in (or loss of) income during old age. These factors have an impact for varying lengths of time and with varying degrees of intensity. Although asymmetrical socioeconomic circumstances are a crucial determining factor, they are, to differing degrees, beyond individuals' control. Thus, the range of risks against which persons should be protected is very wide and changes as societies evolve.

Whether social protection policies are financed using tax revenues or contributions, a crucial part of their evaluation is to determine how they respond to the dynamics of risk and its social distribution. It is vital to identify how services are provided, against which risks they offer protection, and how the benefits are specified. This section will look closely at two fundamental dimensions of social protection: health and pension system affiliation.

As proposed by ECLAC, social protection should be governed by the following principles:[2]

- **The principle of universality** dictates that all citizens, as members of society, are entitled to certain types of protection or benefits, which must have certain characteristics in terms of quantity and quality, and which are necessary for their full participation in society. In terms of insurance, this principle seeks to ensure that all members of society are guaranteed a certain level and quality of well-being, which must be the maximum permitted by economic development at any given time. This does not mean that any benefit can be made universal, but rather that society sets, on the basis of covenants, standards for quality and coverage that must be guaranteed for all its members.
- **The principle of solidarity** proposes that everyone should participate in funding social policy in accordance with their means, to help ensure universality and equity of access to social security benefits. It also assumes that, given the externalities of individual well-being, there is a close interrelationship between individual and social well-being.
- **Selectivity criteria** are understood to ensure that social services reach the poorest. In order to address the multidimensional and heterogeneous nature of poverty, universal and comprehensive policies must interact beneficially with selective and differentiated policies.

---

[2]   See ECLAC, *Shaping the Future of Social Protection: Access, Financing and Solidarity* (LC/G2294(SES.31/3)), Santiago, Chile, 2006.

- **The principle of efficiency** provides that, for greater and substantive equality, public resources should be used efficiently so as to enhance, not counteract, the principles of universality and solidarity. This principle should not be understood solely in terms of its macro and microeconomic impact; ultimately, it concerns the ability to achieve the social objectives set.

Based on the foregoing, the main challenges for social protection systems in the region are: (i) to make strides towards universal social protection and its benefits, which means promoting social covenants that prioritize them and improving capacities for their implementation; (ii) to level the playing field in the production sphere by reducing the heterogeneity of the production structure, which will lead to better financing of social protection and maximize the impact of social policies; (iii) to make progress in labour institutions, since the development of social protection has historically been associated with labour legislation and regulations governing working conditions, dismissals, collective bargaining, and training and education policies, and the capacity to monitor compliance with the regulations; and (iv) to overcome the fragmentary and segmented nature of social protection by creating an integral solidarity framework that combines contributory and non-contributory mechanisms.

A. An overview of population coverage

Affiliation to health and pension systems as reported in household surveys is a valid criterion for gauging the course of social protection, although it is not indicative of the quality or range of health services to which people have access. Surveys are, however, able to measure pensioners' income, which provides clues as to employment histories and current pension systems.

Between 2002 and 2011, wage-earner health care and pension coverage expanded, although to differing degrees and from very different starting points. In affiliation terms, this reflects positive labour market trends, in particular considering that it occurred during the most severe global financial and economic crisis since the Great Depression, which affected the region in a number of domains. Nevertheless, coverage is still very limited in some countries.

Except in Honduras, wage earners are more likely to be affiliated to health systems than pension funds (see figures 12 and 13). Given that the two forms of coverage are highly correlated, countries reporting low levels of coverage in one area tend to do so in the other, as well. Countries with the highest levels of pension scheme participation (on average, 76%) record health-care affiliation of around 90%, and in several cases their health systems are making progress towards universal provision through contributory and non-contributory mechanisms. In countries with intermediate pension coverage, levels of health-care affiliation vary widely: although the average is nearly 65%, it ranges from 49% to 75%. The great exception in this group is Colombia, where health coverage expanded from 53% in 2002 to 92% in 2011, while pension coverage underwent a significant but lesser increase (16 percentage points).

In terms of gender, coverage was more extensive among female than male wage earners at both points in time (2002 and 2011) in 16 countries in the region, and they have gained more, proportionally speaking, where access has expanded for both indicators. However, some countries buck this trend: in Argentina, Brazil, Chile, Costa Rica, the Dominican Republic, Peru and Uruguay —a group that includes some of the countries with the broadest coverage— levels of affiliation to pension schemes (but not health care, apart from in the Dominican Republic) are lower among female wage earners. Men, meanwhile, gained more in proportional terms from improvements in the two indicators in Chile, Colombia, Guatemala and Honduras.

There are striking disparities by income quintile in access to both pension and health systems. Educational level is also a source of significant gaps, but these are narrowing, especially with regard to health care. Between the two extremes (employees with a university education versus employees who did not complete primary education), the difference in affiliation to pension and health systems is 55 and 40 percentage points, respectively. In terms of access trends by age group, although affiliation to both pension and health care systems increased in all age groups, access for both indicators can be described as an inverted U-curve, because affiliation levels are lower both at the beginning and at the end of people's working lives. This is problematic because it means that young people are deferring saving for their pensions, and older persons do not have access to the full range of health services.

The distribution of the region's coverage shortfalls constitutes grounds for strengthening universal policies with supportive financing since, although clearly to a differing degree and depth, social sectors across the income spectrum lack social protection. There is a need to safeguard the efficiency and quality of social security systems and forge proper links between benefits and their funding, so as to make the benefits more attractive and therefore more highly valued.

B. Aspects of health-care affiliation in the countries

On average, affiliation to health-care systems increased by around 12 percentage points in the Latin American countries between 2002 and 2011. The exceptions are El Salvador, which registered a minor setback, and Uruguay (urban areas), where affiliation was already very high in 2002 (over 98%), and only marginal improvement was recorded. The most significant progress was made in Colombia, the Dominican Republic, Ecuador (urban areas) and Peru, where affiliation increased by between 21 and 39 percentage points.

Health-care coverage was most extensive at both points in time in Argentina (urban areas), Chile, Costa Rica, Panama and Uruguay (urban areas). Over a 10-year period, Colombia was able to expand coverage considerably, and its health-care affiliation rates are now among the region's highest. Considerable efforts were made to extend coverage in the Dominican Republic, Ecuador (urban areas), Mexico and Peru, where affiliation is at an intermediate level compared with the rest of the countries in the group; there were major increases in Argentina (urban areas) and the Plurinational State of Bolivia, and more moderate rises in the other countries. Affiliation was trending downwards in El Salvador prior to the health-care reform now under way, and has remained low and virtually unchanged in Honduras. Unfortunately, levels of health-care affiliation in Brazil could not be detected from the surveys consulted, as the country has a universal system.

On grouping the countries by high, average or low wage-earner affiliation, it is clear that as the overall affiliation among these workers falls, the relative position of those working in microenterprises or in domestic service worsens.

By employment sector, affiliation is higher in the public sector than in the private, owing to evasion issues and a lack of labour-market oversight, among other factors. Affiliation to health systems among professionals and technicians in microenterprises declined (along with pension scheme affiliation) in four of the countries with the lowest levels of affiliation. Health-care affiliation among domestic workers is greater than pension scheme affiliation but remains poor; it did, however, rise significantly in Colombia, Ecuador, Mexico and Peru, and more modestly in five other countries.

In the 15 countries in which health-care affiliation among non-wage-earners could be analysed, it is clear that this group lags far behind wage earners. The gap is smallest in Chile, Colombia, Costa Rica and Uruguay. But even though there is an obvious gap in general terms, with the exception of the countries that are furthest behind, non-wage-earner affiliation has risen in recent years, in particular in Colombia and Peru. Women are at a greater disadvantage with respect to pensions systems than health care.

The existing inequality with regard to non-wage-earners and social protection is illustrated by the socioeconomic distribution of affiliation. There are huge differences between the first and the fifth income quintile in terms of affiliation to both pension and health systems. But even among wage earners, whenever affiliation is below average, it is more concentrated by income. Gaps by income level are smaller for health-care affiliation than for pension scheme participation and are, in general, narrowing: in 2011 the difference in access between the fifth and the first quintiles was a little under 36 percentage points, while in 2002 it had been almost 44 points.

Although the gradients of non-affiliation become smaller as incomes rise, even the top income quintile contains a group that is not affiliated to any health system, just as in the other quintiles. This occurs to a somewhat lesser degree than in the case of pensions and varies considerably between the countries; it may be due to certain types of employment contracts or could reflect self-selection among those who decide not to join because they are privately insured or because they make out-of-pocket payments. If the social security system has no barriers to entry and acts as reinsurance from the private market, some people may try to transfer over when they require essential health treatment that is not covered by their insurance policies or their out-of-pocket expenses become too high.

The high rate of health-care affiliation among pensioners, meanwhile, is notable in the 14 countries that were compared, even where total population coverage is lagging far behind. With just one exception, health-care affiliation among pensioners also rose between 2002 and 2011.

Figure 12

Latin America (16 countries): affiliation to health-care systems among wage earners aged 15 years and over, around 2002 and 2011

(Percentages)

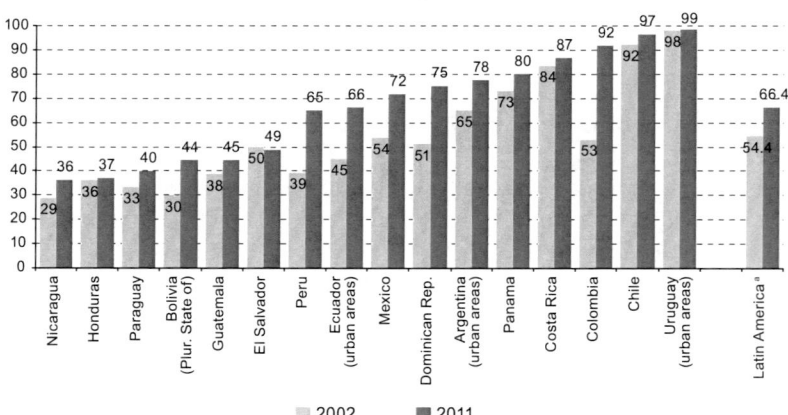

2002 2011

Source: Economic Commission for Latin America (ECLAC), on the basis of special tabulations of data from household surveys conducted in the respective countries.
a Simple average of 16 countries.

C. Aspects of pension-system affiliation in the countries

Based on current levels of wage-earner affiliation to pension systems, the countries may be divided into three groups. The first group, in which coverage is the most extensive, includes Argentina, the Bolivarian Republic of Venezuela, Brazil, Chile, Costa Rica and Uruguay (urban areas), where affiliation ranges from 68% to 85%. In the second group, comprising Colombia, the Dominican Republic, Ecuador (urban areas), El Salvador, Mexico and Peru, between 41% and 65% of employees are covered. Lastly, the lowest levels of coverage are seen in Guatemala, Honduras, Nicaragua, Paraguay and the Plurinational State of Bolivia, where affiliation ranges from 30% to 40%.

In Latin America, there was a relatively moderate increase of a little over nine percentage points in wage-earner access to pension systems between 2002 and 2011, when the figure stood at 55.4% of all employees (simple average of 16 countries). Increases were especially significant in urban areas of Argentina, in Colombia, in the Dominican Republic, in urban areas of Ecuador and in Peru, ranging from between 14 and 23 percentage points. El Salvador was the only country to record a decline (2 percentage points) and the variations were not statistically significant in Honduras, Mexico or Nicaragua (see figure 13).

Figure 13

Latin America (17 countries): affiliation to pension systems among wage earners aged 15 years and over, around 2002 and 2011

(Percentages)

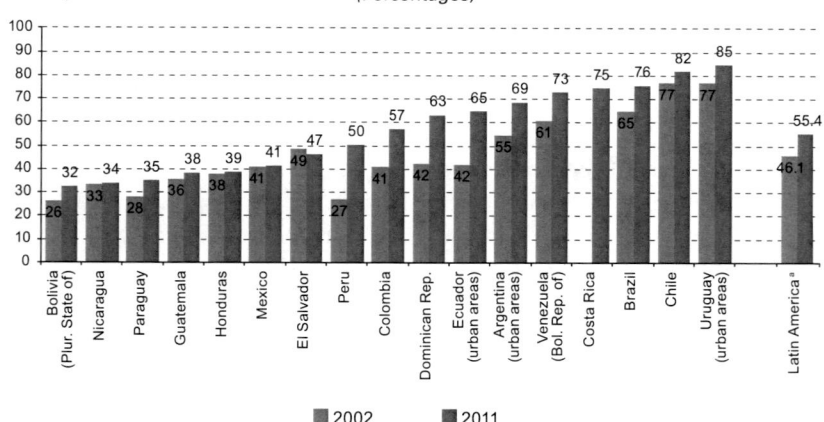

2002 2011

Source: Economic Commission for Latin America (ECLAC), on the basis of special tabulations of data from household surveys conducted in the respective countries.
a Simple average of 16 countries. Excludes countries that have no data for the two years under consideration.

The marked variation in affiliation levels depending on the labour-market position of wage earners reflects differences in employment quality. Affiliation is widespread among public-sector employees: averaging almost 88% for pension systems and a little over 90% for health systems, and these figures are relatively similar to those recorded in 2002 (albeit seven percentage points higher in both cases). Among wage earners employed in the private sector by small, medium-sized or large enterprises, affiliation falls to 66% in the case of pension systems and 73% in the case of health systems, although with some improvement between 2002 and 2011. Even lower levels were recorded among wage earners employed by microenterprises (20% and 39%, respectively), with no significant improvement between 2002 and 2011. The gap widens further for domestic workers, most of whom are women. In contrast to health-care affiliation, no significant progress has been made in pension scheme affiliation in the least secure employment categories.

In the group of countries in which the situation of non-wage-earners could be measured, there is clear evidence that women suffer exclusion and are in a worse position; nevertheless, some progress in this area was detected. The highest levels of affiliation within this segment of the population were found in Brazil, Chile, Costa Rica and Uruguay. Male affiliation rates in Peru increased substantially.

As may be expected, there are glaring disparities in access to both pension and health systems by income quintile. In 2011, the gap in wage earner pension affiliation between the fifth and first income quintiles, as an average for the Latin American countries, was almost 49 percentage points, having widened slightly since 2002.

However, the changes reveal that the socioeconomic distribution of pension scheme affiliation has become a little less regressive in several countries, including El Salvador and Mexico. Costa Rica, with Uruguay some way behind, reports the highest percentage of low-income workers affiliated to a pension system. Other countries have also experienced a significant relative expansion in coverage within low-income sectors: this is true of Argentina, Brazil, Chile, the Dominican Republic, Ecuador and Peru. In Ecuador, the increases were spread more evenly across the quintiles, while in the Plurinational State of Bolivia, the first quintile's share also increased relative to that of the wealthiest quintile. Nevertheless, inequality rose in six countries.

Albeit with great variations among countries, the top quintile shows individuals not affiliated with any pension system. There is also evidence of some limitations on access in the second, third and fourth quintiles, but while protection shortfalls vary considerably by socioeconomic status, in no case are they comparable to those of the first income quintile.

Pension system affiliation has become less regressive in Argentina, Chile, Colombia, the Dominican Republic, El Salvador, Mexico, Peru and the Plurinational State of Bolivia; in Costa Rica and Ecuador it has risen fairly evenly across the income quintiles, as it has in the Dominican Republic, where the top and bottom quintiles show most progression. In Colombia, Ecuador, Paraguay, Peru and the Plurinational State of Bolivia there have been significant increases in the access enjoyed by the intermediate sectors. Guatemala and Uruguay saw a drop in participation in the bottom income quintile.

D. Determinants of employee pension affiliation: a multivariate analysis

Both as a subject for research and as a reference for public policy, it is important to identify the determinants of pension system affiliation. An exercise was thus carried out to identify the effect of a range of explanatory variables on the affiliation of workers aged between 15 and 64 years, considered together using estimates from selection bias-corrected probit models.

Analysis of the determinants of worker affiliation to pension systems shows common patterns among countries, but also disparities. In general terms, the nature of the job is decisive. The informal sector, part-time work, own-account employment and domestic service all show a lower probability of affiliation than employment in the formal sector.

Clear patterns also emerge in relation to different branches of activity: in most countries, workers in construction, commerce and agriculture show a significantly lower probability of affiliation than industrial workers (which was used as the omitted category). In several Central American countries, employment in the services sector also shows a negative effect.

As to the personal characteristics of workers, no clear pattern of differences between men and women was found (after controlling for other personal characteristics and for type of job). The likelihood of affiliation is considerably lower in the youngest age group (aged 15 to 29 years) than in workers aged 45 years and over in almost every country. Lastly, there is a clearly positive association between likelihood of affiliation and educational attainment (the higher the level of schooling, the greater the probability of affiliation) in most countries, but the magnitude and significance of the effect varies.

E. Actual access to pensions and pension levels

In most of the 16 countries analysed, the proportion of people aged 65 years and older who receive a pension is relatively low, and varies from country to country. Honduras is at the lower end of the spectrum, whereas this population enjoys the most protection in Argentina, Brazil, Chile, Costa Rica and Uruguay, with Panama in an intermediate position. Distribution is also unequal by income quintile, and this is much sharper in the countries where pensioners are least likely to be covered. At more advanced ages, the percentage of pensioners covered usually rises.

As for the pension received, measured in 2005 dollars, in the poorest quintile this rose most in Brazil, the Dominican Republic, Ecuador and Uruguay, but fell in six other countries. The declines seen in the wealthiest quintile in Chile and the Dominican Republic were particularly striking, and were perhaps attributable to the exposure to financial risk of individual capitalization schemes; in Chile pensions were also adversely impacted in the second, third and fourth quintiles, a systematic trend not observed in any other country.

Women receive lower pensions than men, because they are disadvantaged both by their labour trajectories and by the way pension systems are designed. For example, actuarial calculations based on women's longer life expectancies reduce the replacement rate of their pensions.

Figure 14
Latin America (16 countries): persons aged 65 and over receiving contributory or non-contributory pensions and average monthly pension, by sex, around 2011
(Percentages and dollars at constant 2005 prices)

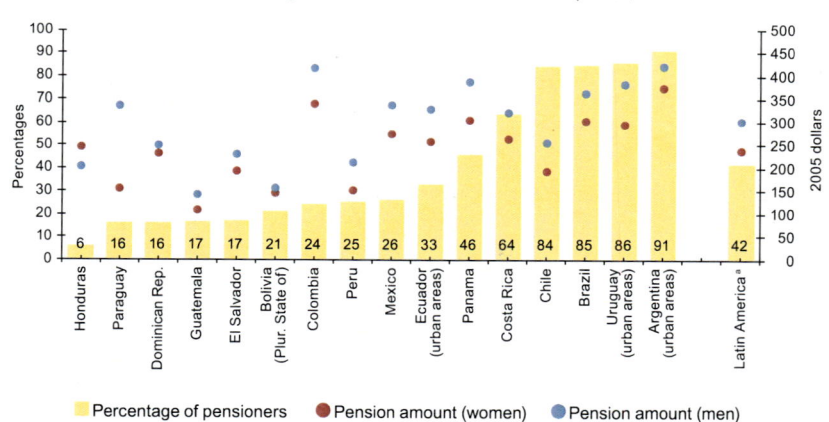

Source: Economic Commission for Latin America (ECLAC), on the basis of special tabulations of data from household surveys conducted in the respective countries.
[a] Simple average of 14 countries with information for 2002 and 2011.

V. Recent trends in social spending and economic, social and demographic considerations for health spending

A. Public social spending in Latin America and the Caribbean

Until the mid-2000s, public social spending was strongly procyclical. In the second half of the decade, several countries undertook systematic efforts to strengthen social programmes, particularly those aimed at combating poverty, which marked a first turning point in the evolution of social spending. This trend began to take root to some extent in the mid-1990s, when certain countries departed from the prevailing orthodoxy on measures to reduce fiscal spending promoted by the Washington Consensus (mainly Brazil and Mexico).

The faster pace of growth in social spending in the second half of the 2000s was mostly driven by policies that were applied to offset various external shocks: the sharp increase in food and fuel prices in 2008; the commodity export boom that began in 2003; the global financial crisis, the manifestations and consequences of which were most strongly felt between late 2008 and 2009; and the more recent external uncertainty caused by the global economic slowdown, which continues to be reflected in a very low growth rate in the countries of the European Union and the ongoing use of stimulus measures by the United States Federal Reserve pending a reduction in the unemployment rate.

Figure 15
Latin America and the Caribbean (21 countries): social public spending as a share of total public spending, and total public spending as a share of GDP, 1992-1993 to 2010-2011 [a]
(Percentages of GDP and total public spending)

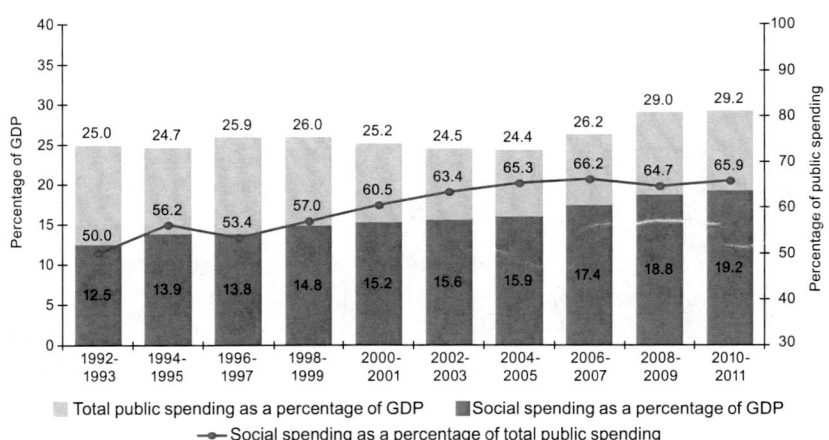

■ Total public spending as a percentage of GDP   ■ Social spending as a percentage of GDP
──●── Social spending as a percentage of total public spending

Source: Economic Commission for Latin America and the Caribbean (ECLAC), social expenditure database.
[a] Weighted average for the countries.

These three moments in time shaped fiscal and social policy to varying degrees. In addition to strengthening some major social programmes (to combat poverty and strengthen the social safety net, primarily its non-contributory pillar), measures were adopted to redirect spending (and taxes) to offset the regressive effects of rising commodity prices, mainly in 2007 and 2008. When the financial crisis hit, the governments took various steps to stabilize internal demand, by increasing public non-social spending (investment in infrastructure) and especially social spending.

Since the early 1990s, the fiscal priority of social spending as a share of total public spending has been climbing, from 50% in 1992-1993 to 60.5% in 2000-2001 and 65.9% in 2010-2011. However, some fluctuations and increases in the fiscal priority of social spending have had more to do with contractions in non-social public spending and thus relative declines in total public spending, primarily between 1999 and 2004.

Since 2010, several countries have embarked on fiscal reforms, on both the revenue and spending sides, to consolidate their public finances, because after approximately five years (2003-2008) of primary surpluses and shrinking public debt, measures involving public spending increases were taken that led to deficits in the public accounts. Although the 2010 figures show that the countercyclical trend of increased spending continued that year, there was a larger increase in social public spending and in several cases declines in non-social public spending.

The figures for 2011 and the very limited data for 2012 (mostly budget, not execution, data) already suggest a relative declining trend in social spending, but this would not necessarily translate into an absolute decrease in the funds allocated to the social sectors.

B. Trends in public spending on health

During the 1990s, public spending on health, as with most components of social public spending —with the sole exception of spending on social security— was affected by large fluctuations associated with the highly volatile growth that characterized much of the decade.

A good part of these fluctuations, which meant that for a group of 21 countries in the region one third of budgets came in below the previous year's (45 episodes of spending decreases and 90 of absolute spending increases between 1993 and 2000), were associated with swings in the countries' economic cycles. Although not every case involved a decline in gross domestic product, but rather slower growth, it is clear that public spending on health was closely tied to the economic cycle in the 1990s. Thus, in cases where public spending on health declined or stagnated, it was because the sector was used to tighten the budget. The cuts did not affect current spending (such as payroll or supplies) so much as the investment component (construction and maintenance of hospitals and clinics, purchases of new technology, etc.).

Although on balance for the 1990s, the macroeconomic priority of public spending on health at the regional level (that is, as a percentage of GDP) increased from 2.7% in 1992-1993 to 3.1% in 2000-2001, there was a significant decline in the period 1996-1997 (from 3% of GDP in 1994-1995 to 2.8%), as illustrated in figure 16. These regional declines occurred even as total public spending held steady or grew, with health spending shrinking as a share of total spending on several occasions (that is, its fiscal priority diminishing). These declines were not fundamentally associated with reductions in social public spending, which means that health spending as a share of social spending lost significant ground even, in some cases, as other types of social spending, such as education and social security, rose (see figure 16).

Since the mid-2000s, coincident with a widespread push to increase social spending as well as protect it from cyclical swings, public spending on health has been gaining stability (becoming less procyclical) and becoming more fixed, mainly in countries with larger tax yields, higher total spending, and by extension, higher social spending. Since the early 2000s, the macroeconomic priority of health spending has been rising, to 3.9% of GDP in 2010-2011. This increase has made it possible, to a certain extent, to stabilize health spending as a share of both total spending and social spending.

Figure 16

**Latin America and the Caribbean (21 countries): public spending on health as a share of GDP,
of total public spending, and of social public spending, 1992-1993 to 2010-2011** [a]

(Percentages)

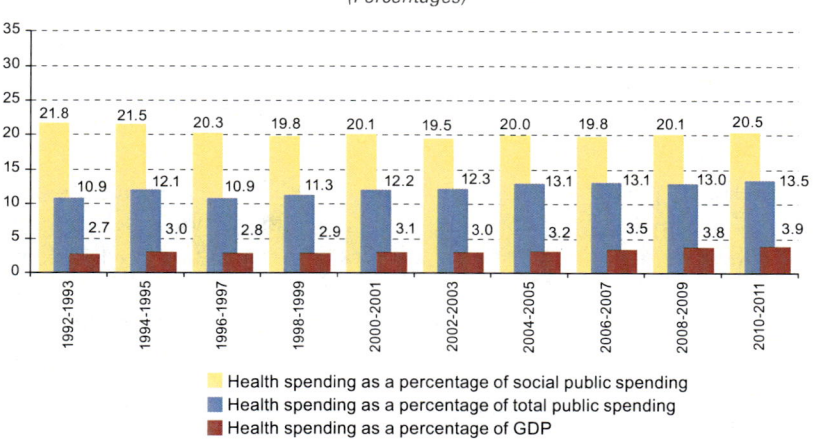

■ Health spending as a percentage of social public spending
■ Health spending as a percentage of total public spending
■ Health spending as a percentage of GDP

Source: Economic Commission for Latin America and the Caribbean (ECLAC), social expenditure database.
[a] Weighted average for the countries.

Against the backdrop of the financial crisis and its impact on the real economies of the region, the public health sector was not heavily cut (only 10 instances of budget cuts out of a total of 53 in the 21 countries between 2008 and most recent data available). Although it did not benefit from an injection of resources as part of an explicit countercyclical policy (for example, job creation through increased investment spending in the sector), it was protected to the extent that it even increased its share of both GDP and public spending.

However, despite that increase, spending levels vary greatly from one country to another. Annual average health spending was around US$ 226 per capita in 2011 for the region as a whole, but in countries that spend large amounts on health (over US$ 300 per capita), such as Argentina, Chile, Costa Rica, Cuba, Panama, Trinidad and Tobago and Uruguay, the figure was US$ 413. For countries with intermediate levels of spending (between US$ 100 and US$ 300 per capita), such as the Bolivarian Republic of Venezuela, Brazil, El Salvador, Mexico and Peru, the per capita average was around US$ 175, whereas countries with low levels of spending (under US$ 100 per capita) allocated on average just US$ 55 per capita on health (Colombia, Dominican Republic, Ecuador, Guatemala, Honduras, Jamaica, Nicaragua, Paraguay and Plurinational State of Bolivia). While the group of countries with the lowest levels of per capita spending on health increased their spending in this area by 4.1% annually between 2000 and 2011 and the intermediate group saw theirs go up by 4% annually, per capita health spending in the countries with the highest levels of spending jumped up by 7.4% annually. This resulted in a wider gap between the countries in terms of per capita public spending on health (see figure 17).

Figure 17

Latin America and the Caribbean (21 countries): per capita spending on health, 1992-2011

(Dollars at constant 2005 prices)

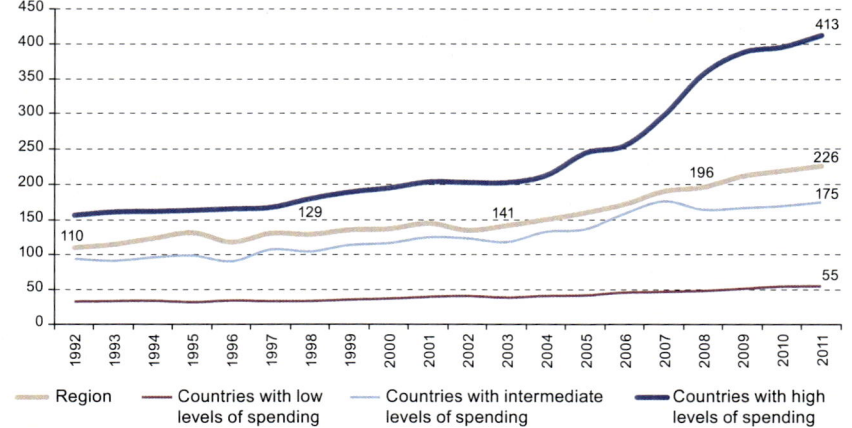

── Region ── Countries with low levels of spending ── Countries with intermediate levels of spending ── Countries with high levels of spending

Source: Economic Commission for Latin America and the Caribbean (ECLAC), social expenditure database.

C. Out-of-pocket health expenses and the effects on well-being

According to the definition used by the Pan American Health Organization, household spending on health services encompasses two types of expenditure. Direct expenditures are known as out-of-pocket health expenses and include household outlays on health-related items such as hospitalizations, out-patient procedures and medications, and are net payments, that is, separate from any reimbursements that might be received from the health-care system or insurance. Indirect expenses are outlays for prepaid medical care plans, private medical insurance or contributions to public insurance.

Households make these direct payments as the need arises, generally to the service provider, which means they depend on each individual's ability to pay and are thus antithetical to the notion of shared responsibility or risk diversification. Therefore, they are one of the least fair ways to finance health care. The population is vulnerable to varying degrees to incurring out-of-pocket health expenses that adversely affect their socioeconomic position. This vulnerability is a function of both the magnitude of the outof-pocket expense in question and household spending capacity.

A look at out-of-pocket health spending as a percentage of the household budget and its relative composition, as well as the comparisons between income groups, offers important information on the spending options of households and sheds light on this phenomenon in countries with very different health systems. The analysis of how these spending patterns are related to the various forms of financing is still relatively unexplored terrain.

Surveys give an idea of the uneven capacity of households to meet expenses not covered by insurance in cases of acute or chronic morbidity. At any given moment, out-of-pocket health spending can plunge families into poverty; this reality is measured in the chapter.

Another useful indicator for elucidating the relationship between socioeconomic conditions and out-of-pocket health spending has to do with the inability to make out-of-pocket payments in poor households. There are many different reasons—positive and negative—why households might not spend on health: good health coverage through public or private systems; no cases of morbidity recorded during the period in question; or insufficient income and lack of access to credit, which prevent households from spending during episodes of morbidity even when they do not have adequate coverage. If a household has limited spending options owing to insufficient funds, the value that would indicate their actual need for health spending cannot be observed.

Figure 18
Latin America (18 countries): poverty rate among households with and without out-of-pocket spending
(Percentages)

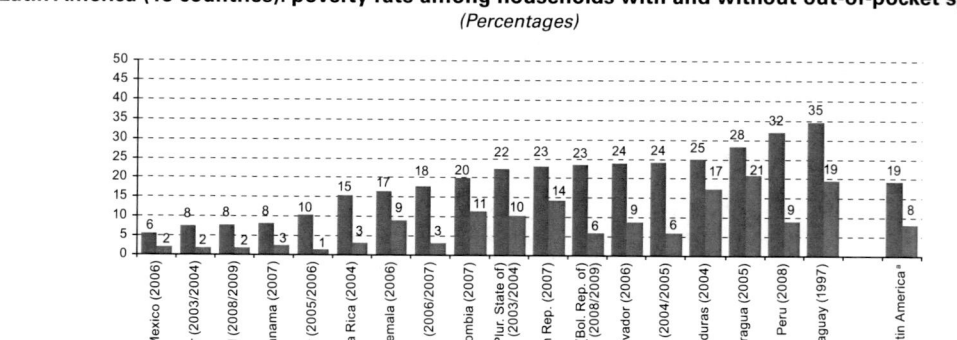

Source: Economic Commission for Latin America and the Caribbean (ECLAC), on the basis of special tabulations of data from income and expenditure surveys conducted in the respective countries.
a Simple average for the countries.

It is noteworthy, then, that the incidence of poverty (measured against the subsistence line) is higher among households without out-of-pocket spending, especially in countries with low health insurance coverage. Since the adverse socioeconomic conditions of these households mean that they are not typically part of a particularly healthy population, this would seem to suggest that a contingent of the poor has limited capacity to incur out-of-pocket expenses.

Because out-of-pocket health expenses are antithetical to the notion of shared responsibility or risk diversification, detrimental to well-being and in some cases potentially inefficient (for example, the expense incurred as a result of high prices for medications in certain markets), efforts to reduce them must be seen as one of the challenges to be tackled on the path to a more universal social safety net based on shared responsibility.

D. Population ageing and the future of health spending

In Latin America, the population ageing process began later than in Europe but has proceeded at a faster pace. At the same time, the region's countries are experiencing a comparatively high rate of growth, which means that health spending can be increased for everyone, but especially for the older population.

The national transfer accounts are a disaggregation of the national accounts by age, sex and socioeconomic status, which help to measure flows between population groups and to determine the role that the market, State and families play in these economic relationships. Using this methodology, a look at the amounts being spent and that will be spent by age group shows that the ageing of the population will clearly put upward pressure on health spending, which in turn will increase the share of health spending.

Figures 19 and 20 show some worrying projections in this regard. In countries which are fairly well advanced in the demographic transition, such as Brazil, Chile and Mexico, the proportion of the population aged over 60 will be larger in 2060 than it is today in Germany and Spain, which are considered to be on the ageing "frontier" (see figure 19). The implications of this for potential spending on health in these three Latin American countries by 2060 are significant: virtually double the percentage of GDP projected in 2015 (see figure 20).

Figure 19
**Latin America and Europe (selected countries): projections for the proportion
of the population aged 60 years and over, 2010-2060**
(Percentages)

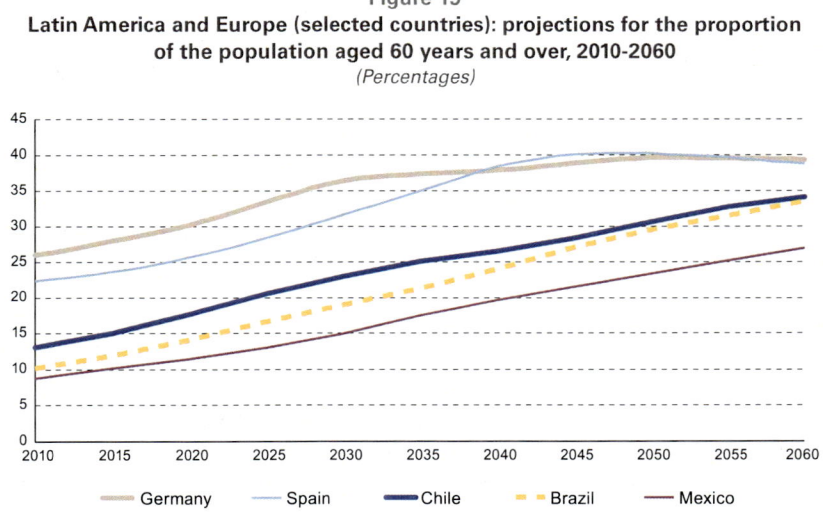

Source: Latin American and Caribbean Demographic Centre (CELADE)-Population Division of ECLAC, on the basis of United Nations, *World Population Prospects: The 2012 Revision*, New York, 2012

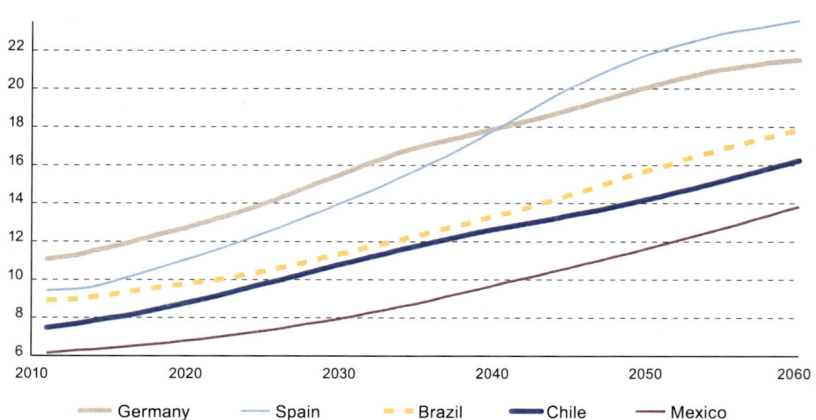

Figure 20
Latin America and Europe (selected countries): projected health spending as a proportion of GDP, 2015-2060
(Percentages)

Source: Economic Commission for Latin America and the Caribbean (ECLAC), on the basis of the findings of the model constructed using the method developed by R. Lee and A. Mason (eds.), *Population Aging and the Generational Economy: a Global Perspective*, Cheltenham, Edward Elgar Publishing, 2011.

Bibliography

Alkire, Sabine and James Foster (2009), "Counting and multidimensional poverty measurement. Revised and updated", *OPHI Working Paper*, No. 32 [online] http://www.ophi.org.uk/working-paper-number-32.

Cifuentes, L. and others (2005), *Urban Air Quality and Human Health in Latin America and the Caribbean*, Washington, D.C., Pan American Health Organization (PAHO).

ECLAC/ILO (Economic Commission for Latin America and the Caribbean/International Labour Organization) (2013), "Advances and challenges in measuring decent work", *The Employment Situation in Latin America and the Caribbean*, No. 8 (LC/L.3630), Santiago, Chile, May.

ECLAC/UNICEF (Economic Commission for Latin America and the Caribbean/United Nations Children's Fund) (2012), "Pobreza infantil en pueblos indígenas y afrodescendientes", *Project Documents*, No. 477 (LC/W.477), Santiago, Chile.

___(2010), "Pobreza infantil en América Latina y el Caribe" (LC/R.2168), Santiago, Chile, December.

Gordon, David and others (2003), *Child Poverty in the Developing World*, Bristol, The Policy Press.

Kaztman, Ruben (2011), "Infancia en América Latina: privaciones habitacionales y desarrollo de capital humano", *Project Documents*, No. 431 (LC/W.431), Santiago, Chile, Economic Commission for Latin America and the Caribbean (ECLAC).

Minujin, Alberto, Enrique Delamónica and Alejandra Davidziuk (2006), "Pobreza infantil. Conceptos, medición y recomendaciones de políticas públicas", *Cuaderno de Ciencias Sociales*, No. 140, San José, Latin American Faculty of Social Sciences (FLACSO).

UNICEF (United Nations Children's Fund) (2005), *The State of the World's Children 2005: Childhood under Threat*, New York. United Nations publication, Sales N° E.05.XX.1.

UNODC (United Nations Office on Drugs and Crime) (2011), *Global Study on Homicide 2011. Context, Trends, Data*, Vienna.

Chapter I

Different approaches to poverty measurement

A. Income poverty

Continuing with the trend observed in the region for a decade, the year 2012 saw a decline in the poverty rate across the region. The change in the indigence rate has been slower, so that there has been practically no variation in recent years in the number of persons living in extreme poverty.

1. Economic context

The year 2012 was marked by deterioration in the world economy, caused by the recession in Europe, particularly in the eurozone, a slowdown in the Chinese economy and moderate growth in the United States. Against this backdrop, growth in output stood at 3,0% in Latin America, admittedly a lower figure than in the two previous years but still higher than the world average, which was 2.2%. This performance was due to robust domestic demand, which helped to offset the decline in exports (ECLAC, 2012b).

Per capita GDP grew by 1.9%, way below the rates recorded in 2010 (4.5%) and 2011 (3.2%), which marked a recovery from the 3.0% contraction recorded in 2009. This performance was due mainly to the slowdown in Argentina and Brazil, where per capita growth fell from 7.9% and 1.9%, respectively, in 2011 to 1.0% and 0.1% in 2012. Indeed, if these two countries are not included, regional per capita GDP growth would have been barely 0.3 of a percentage point lower than the 2011 rate without those two countries (ECLAC, 2012b).

Thirteen countries recorded higher per capita GDP rates than the regional average, the most notable being Panama (8.8%), Peru (5.1%), Chile (4.6%) and the Bolivarian Republic of Venezuela (4.0%). In addition, per capita output increased by 3.0% or more in Costa Rica, Cuba, Ecuador, Nicaragua, Plurinational State of Bolivia and Uruguay. The only country that experienced a decline in its per capita output was Paraguay (-2.8%), while less than 1% was recorded in Brazil (0.1%) and Guatemala (0.5%).

Although economic growth was moderate, labour-market indicators have not worsened. Job creation resulted in an increase in the employment rate (from 55.4% to 55.8%), which absorbed the slight increase in participation in economic activity (0.2 of a percentage point), bringing the unemployment rate down from 6.7% to 6.4%, its lowest level for decades (ECLAC/ILO, 2013). The variation in the unemployment rate was mixed. Nine countries showed variations of 0.5 of a percentage point or more, downward variations in the case of Brazil, Chile, Honduras, Panama and Peru, and upward variations in Cuba, Dominican Republic, Guatemala and Paraguay.

According to the information available, the purchasing power of average wages remained constant or increased in most countries. The greatest increase was recorded in the Bolivarian Republic of Venezuela (6%), followed by Brazil, Guatemala and Uruguay (4%), and Chile and Panama (3%). Only in El Salvador was there a fall in the real average wage.

These results are consistent with the low levels of inflation, which in most countries of the region were below those of 2011. Inflation (simple average) declined from 7.1% to 5.3%, and the number of countries with inflation below 5% increased from 6 to 12 between 2011 and 2012. The reduction was particularly marked in the Bolivarian Republic of Venezuela (from 29.0% to 19.5%), despite the fact that this country recorded the highest inflation in the region. The rise in food prices slowed although not as sharply as in the case of other products. As a result, food price inflation was higher than headline inflation in 15 countries, notably Chile, Dominican Republic and Mexico.

In 2013 per capita GDP growth is expected to stand at around 2.0%, a similar level to that of 2012. In keeping with the variation in indicators up to the first half of the year, no significant variations in employment are expected and inflation may rise slightly (ECLAC, 2013b).

Table I.1
Latin America (20 countries): selected socioeconomic indicators, 2000-2012
(Percentages)

Country and year	Per capita GDP (average annual growth rate) [a]	Unemployment (simple average for the period) [b]	Real average wage [c] (average annual growth rate)	Consumer price index [d] (average annual growth rate)	Country and year	Per capita GDP (average annual growth rate) [a]	Unemployment (simple average for the period) [b]	Real average wage [c] (average annual growth rate)	Consumer price index [d] (average annual growth rate)
Argentina					**Haiti**				
2000-2010	2.9	12.5	...	9.1	2000-2010	-1.3	...	...	13.6
2011	7.9	7.2	...	9.5	2011	4.3	...	...	8.3
2012	1.0	7.2	...	10.8	2012	1.5	...	...	7.6
Bolivia (Plurinational State of)					**Honduras**				
2000-2010	1.9	7.7	-0.5	5.0	2000-2010	2.2	5.8	...	7.7
2011	3.6	5.8	-1.3	6.9	2011	1.7	6.8	...	5.6
2012	3.6	...	...	4.5	2012	1.3	5.6	...	5.4
Brazil					**Mexico**				
2000-2010	2.3	9.1	-0.6	6.6	2000-2010	0.9	4.8	2.0	4.9
2011	1.9	6.0	2.4	6.5	2011	2.7	6.0	0.9	3.8
2012	0.1	5.5	3.7	5.8	2012	2.7	5.9	0.2	3.6
Chile					**Nicaragua**				
2000-2010	2.8	9.0	1.9	3.3	2000-2010	1.8	9.0	0.7	9.3
2011	4.9	7.1	2.5	4.4	2011	4.0	...	0.1	8.6
2012	4.6	6.4	3.2	1.5	2012	3.7	...	0.4	7.1
Colombia					**Panama**				
2000-2010	2.4	14.7	1.4	5.7	2000-2010	4.0	11.9	-0.3	2.6
2011	5.2	11.5	9.2	3.7	2011	9.0	5.4	0.1	6.3
2012	2.6	11.2	-7.2	2.4	2012	8.8	4.8	3.4	4.6
Costa Rica					**Paraguay**				
2000-2010	2.3	6.3	1.1	10.1	2000-2010	1.0	9.4	0.6	8.0
2011	3.0	7.7	5.7	4.7	2011	2.6	6.5	2.7	4.9
2012	3.7	7.8	1.4	4.5	2012	-2.8	6.1	0.7	4.0
Cuba					**Peru**				
2000-2010	5.1	2.6	4.8	2.6	2000-2010	4.1	8.8	1.1	2.4
2011	2.8	3.2	0.3	1.3	2011	5.7	7.7	...	4.7
2012	3.0	3.8	0.3	2.0	2012	5.1	6.8	...	2.6
Dominican Republic					**Uruguay**				
2000-2010	3.8	5.8	...	11.6	2000-2010	2.7	12.0	0.1	8.4
2011	3.1	5.8	...	7.8	2011	6.2	6.6	4.0	8.6
2012	2.6	6.5	...	3.9	2012	3.6	6.7	4.2	7.5
Ecuador					**Venezuela (Bolivarian Republic of)**				
2000-2010	1.9	8.8	...	12.2	2000-2010	1.4	11.9	-2.5	21.9
2011	5.7	6.0	...	5.4	2010	2.6	8.3	3.0	29.0
2012	3.3	4.9	...	4.2	2012	4.0	8.1	5.8	19.5
El Salvador									
2000-2010	1.5	6.4	-1.3	3.4					
2011	1.4	6.6	-2.9	5.1					
2012	1.1	6.2	-2.8	0.8					
Guatemala					**Latin America**				
2000-2010	0.9	5.0	-0.5	6.6	2000-2010	2.0	9.2	...	7.8
2011	1.7	3.1	0.4	6.2	2011	3.2	6.7	...	7.1
2012	0.5	4.0	4.0	3.4	2012	1.9	6.4	...	5.3

Source: Economic Commission for Latin America and the Caribbean (ECLAC), on the basis of official figures.
[a] Based on per capita GDP in dollars at constant 2005 prices.
[b] For 2000-2010, the only data available for Guatemala were for the triennium 2002-2004 and for 2010. For Honduras, the data for the period 2000-2010 consist of data from 2001. Unemployment data for Peru relate to the city of Lima.
[c] Generally speaking, the coverage of this index is very limited. In most countries, it refers only to formal industrial-sector workers.
[d] Year-on-year variations taking December as the reference month. The regional aggregate corresponds to the simple average of the variations.

2. Recent poverty trends

In 2012, the poverty rate in Latin America stood at 28.2%, while the indigence or extreme poverty rate was 11.3%. In terms of numbers of persons, these percentages represent 164 million poor people, including 66 million living in extreme poverty (see figure I.1).

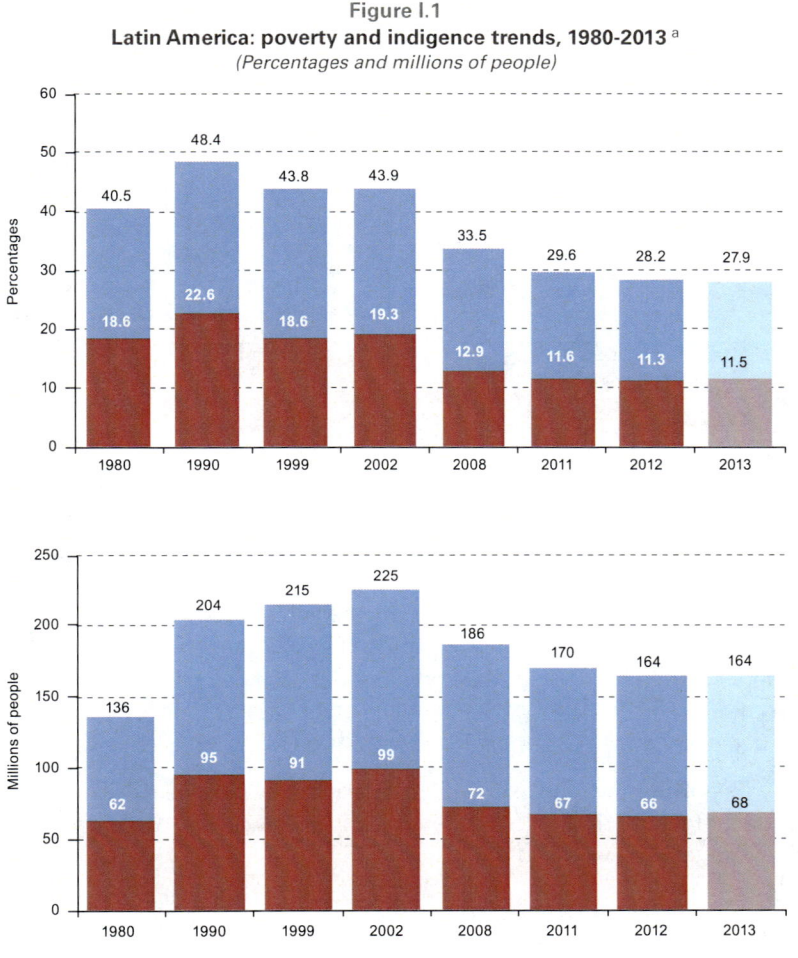

Figure I.1
Latin America: poverty and indigence trends, 1980-2013 [a]
(Percentages and millions of people)

■ Indigents   ■ Non-indigent poor

Source: Economic Commission for Latin America and the Caribbean (ECLAC), on the basis of special tabulations of data from household surveys conducted in the relevant countries.
[a] Estimate for 18 Latin American countries plus Haiti. The figures appearing above the bars are percentages (in the graph on the left) and total numbers of poor people (indigents plus non-indigent poor) (in the graph on the right). The 2013 figures are projections.

These values indicate a 1.4 percentage-point decrease (approximately) in the poverty rate compared with 2011. No appreciable change has been observed in extreme poverty, since the figure recorded for 2012 is scarcely 0.3 of a percentage point below the 2011 rate. This implies that the number of poor persons fell by approximately 6 million in 2012, while the number of indigents remained practically constant.

Thus, in cumulative terms, poverty has diminished by 15.7 percentage points since 2002, owing almost without exception to reductions in the past 10 years. Extreme poverty also fell appreciably (by 8.0 percentage points) since 2002, although in this case, the rate of reduction has slowed in recent years, owing mainly to a steeper rise in food costs than in headline inflation.

Figure I.2 identifies two subperiods in the trajectory of poverty and indigence since the early years of the decade of the 2000s. The first, between 2002 and 2007, began with high poverty levels, which fell rapidly; the number of poor persons decreased at a rate of 3.8% per year and the number of indigent persons at a rate of 7.1% per year. The second subperiod, which started in 2007, shows a slowdown in the rate of reduction of the number of income-poor persons, which fell to 2.5% per year in the case of poverty and to 0.9% per year in the case of indigence.

Figure I.2
Latin America: non-indigent poor and indigents and per capita GDP, 2000-2012
(Millions of persons and constant 2005 dollars)

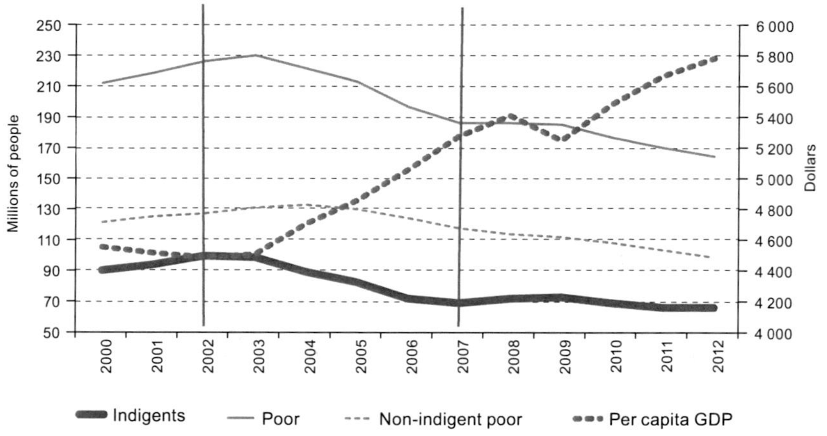

Indigents — Poor --- Non-indigent poor ••• Per capita GDP

Source: Economic Commission for Latin America and the Caribbean (ECLAC).

The slowdown in the process of poverty reduction is closely linked to the region's macroeconomic performance. Per capita GDP increased by 3.3% per year, between 2002 and 2007 and by 1.8% per year between 2007 and 2012.

Even though growth was slower in the second subperiod, the fall in poverty per percentage point of growth was slightly steeper. Between 2002 and 2007, cumulative per capita GDP growth stood at 17.6% and the number of poor persons in the region decreased by 17.4%, which implies that each percentage point of growth lifted 1% of the population out of poverty. Between 2007 and 2012, cumulative per capita GDP growth amounted to 9.6% and the number of poor persons decreased by 12.0%, meaning that the growth elasticity of poverty was 1.3.

Unlike the situation with poverty, the ratio of growth to the variation in indigence shows an obvious deterioration in the second subperiod. Growth-elasticity, which in the first subperiod was 1.7, even higher than in the case of total poverty, diminished to 0.4 in the subperiod 2007-2012.

As shown on previous occasions, the difficulty in obtaining a further reduction in indigence is due largely to the difference between the increase in food prices and that of prices of other goods and services. While sharper differences were recorded in 2007 and 2008, when prices for food rose 2.3 times as fast as those of non food items, since then, there has normally been a gap between food inflation and non-food inflation. In 2012, the difference was 1.5 times (considering the simple average of variations in each country's price indices).

As regards forecasts for 2013, the fact that per capita GDP growth will be similar to that of 2012 and that no significant variations in employment or in inflation are expected, no appreciable changes are anticipated in the levels of poverty and indigence at the regional level.

Six of the eleven countries for which information relating to 2012 is available are seen to have recorded decreases in poverty levels. The Bolivarian Republic of Venezuela showed the sharpest poverty reduction: by 5.6 percentage points (from 29.5% to 23.9%) in the case of poverty and by 2.0 percentage points (from 11.7% to 9.7%) in the case of extreme poverty. In Ecuador, poverty fell by 3.1 percentage points (from 35.3% to 32.2%), while indigence fell by 0.9 percentage points (from 13.8% to 12.9%). In Brazil, poverty diminished by 2.3 percentage points (from 20.9% to 18.6%), while extreme poverty declined by 0.7 of a percentage point (from 6.1% to 5.4%). Peru recorded a 2.0 percentage-point decrease in its poverty rate, while in Argentina and Colombia, the reduction was slightly above 1 percentage point. In these three countries, extreme poverty did not show any appreciable variation compared with the 2011 levels (see figure I.3).

Figure I.3
Latin America (11 countries): variation in poverty and indigence rates, 2011-2012
(Percentage points)

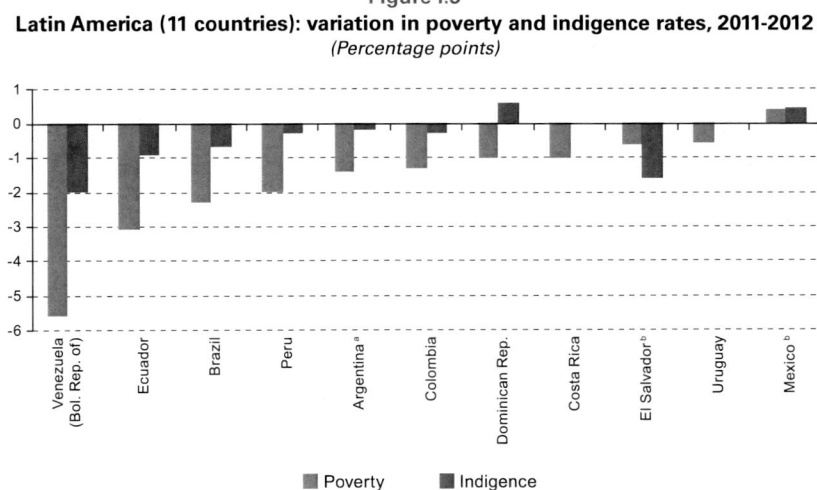

■ Poverty　　■ Indigence

Source: Economic Commission for Latin America and the Caribbean (ECLAC), on the basis of special tabulations of data from household surveys conducted in the respective countries.
[a] Urban areas.
[b] Annual variation between 2010 y 2012.

Poverty levels in Costa Rica, Dominican Republic, El Salvador and Uruguay remained constant compared with the previous estimate. In most of these countries, extreme poverty did not show significant variations either, except in the case of El Salvador, where this indicator diminished by 1.6 percentage points per year (since 2010). Mexico is the only country with information available for 2012; poverty indicators increased in this country, but the variations are minor (from 36.3% to 37.1% in the case of poverty and from 13.3% to 14.2% in the case of extreme poverty).

While the poverty rate at the regional level is the result of the trend observed in each of the countries, the changes registered in countries with larger populations have a significant impact. In 2012, the falls observed in the Bolivarian Republic of Venezuela and Brazil had a major impact as the number of poor persons diminished by approximately 6 million, while in Mexico, the increase noted meant that about 1 million additional persons were counted as poor.[1]

The poverty gap index and the gap-squared index may be used in order to obtain a more comprehensive assessment of the monetary poverty trend. The poverty gap index is calculated by taking into account the difference between the mean income of the poor sector of the population and the poverty line (weighted by the percentage of poor people), while the poverty gap squared index also takes into consideration the way income is distributed among the poor (see box I.2 and annex table I.A-1).

The movements in the three poverty indices (expressed as a percentage variation) have tended to be similar in each country. The percentage variations between 2011 and 2012 are practically identical in Colombia, Dominican Republic, Ecuador, and Peru. In Argentina, Bolivarian Republic of Venezuela, Costa Rica and Uruguay, the complementary indices diminished slightly less than the poverty rate, bearing in mind that the average gap between the income of the poor and the poverty line tended to increase; while in Brazil, El Salvador and Mexico, the opposite occurred (see figure I.4).

If the variations for a longer period (2008-2011) are considered, in general, the poverty gap and gap-squared indices are observed to have reduced slightly more than the headcount index, particularly in those countries with greater poverty reductions. This indicates that the poverty reduction has occurred following an improvement in the relative situation of all the persons that are below the poverty line, rather than as a result of an increase in income only of persons situated closer to this threshold.

---

[1]　Since no data are available for Mexico for 2011, the regional estimate applies a linear projections between the data of 2010 and 2012 for this country, so that impact of the variation observed is distributed over two years.

Box I.1
Methodology used for measuring poverty

According to the approach used in this report for arriving at poverty estimates, a person is classified as poor when the income of that person's household is below the poverty line, which is placed at the minimum level of income needed to meet a person's basic needs. Poverty lines, expressed in each country's currency, are calculated from the cost of a basket of goods and services using the cost of basic needs method.

The basic food basket that is used to measure poverty contains the goods required to cover people's nutritional needs, taking into account consumption habits, the actual availability of foodstuffs and their prices, for each country and geographic area. In most cases, data on the structure of household consumption patterns for both foodstuffs and other goods and services are derived from national household budget surveys carried out in the 1980s.

This figure is referred to as the indigence line. The total value of the poverty line is calculated by taking this figure and then adding the amount that households require in order to meet their basic non-food needs. In order to carry out this calculation, the indigence line is multiplied by a factor that differs for urban and rural areas. For poverty estimates up until 2006, a factor of 2 was used for urban zones and a factor of 1.75 was used for rural areas.[a] The factors applied since 2007 vary depending on the differentials between trends in the prices for foodstuffs and for other goods and services.

Indigence lines and poverty lines are updated each year to reflect cumulative changes in the consumer price index (CPI). For the estimates calculated prior to December 2006, the same rate of variation was applied to both lines. Since 2007, the indigence line is updated on the basis of the CPI for food products, while the portion of the poverty line corresponding to expenditure on non-food goods is updated using the non-food CPI.

Household income data have been taken from household surveys conducted in the respective countries in the years corresponding to the poverty estimates presented in this edition. In line with standard ECLAC practice, the data have been corrected to account for the non-response rate for some income-related questions from wage earners, the self-employed and retirees and to mitigate probable underreporting biases. This latter operation is carried out by comparing the responses to income-related questions in the survey with estimates based on the household income and expenditure accounts included in each country's application of the System of National Accounts. These estimates are calculated using official information.

The income figures used for this purpose refer to total current income, i.e. income from wage labour (in both money and kind), self-employment (including self-supply and the consumption value of products generated by the household), property income, retirement and other pensions, and other transfers received by households. In most countries, household income also includes an imputed rental value for owner-occupied dwellings.

ECLAC is currently in the process of updating the poverty estimates, the results of which will appear in *Social Panorama of Latin America 2014*.

Source: Economic Commission for Latin America and the Caribbean (ECLAC).
[a] The sole exceptions to this general rule are the calculations for Brazil, Colombia and Peru. For Brazil, this study has used the indigence lines estimated by the Brazilian Geographical and Statistical Institute (IBGE), the Brazilian Institute of Applied Economic Research (IPEA) and ECLAC as a joint effort in the late 1990s. For Colombia, the thresholds proposed by the Colombian Mission for the Linkage of Employment, Poverty and Inequality Series (MESEP) were used. For Peru, indigence and poverty lines were estimated by the National Institute of Statistics and Informatics (INEI).

Box I.2
Poverty indicators

The poverty indicators used in this study belong to the family of parametric indices proposed by Foster, Greer and Thorbecke (1984) and have been obtained from the following formula:

(1)
$$FGT_\alpha = \frac{1}{n}\sum_{i=1}^{q}\left(\frac{z-y_i}{z}\right)^\alpha$$

where n represents population size, q denotes the number of people with incomes below the poverty or indigence line (z) and the parameter $\alpha > 0$ assigns differing levels of shortfall between the income (y) of each poor or indigent individual and the poverty or indigence line.

When α takes a value of 0, then formula (1) corresponds to the headcount ratio (H), which indicates the percentage of people with incomes below the poverty or indigence line:

(2)
$$H = \frac{q}{n}$$

When α equals 1, the expression yields the poverty gap (PG) (or indigence gap), which weights the percentage of poor (or indigent) people by how far their incomes fall short of the poverty (or indigence) line:

(3)
$$PG = \frac{1}{n}\sum_{i=1}^{q}\left[\frac{z-y_i}{z}\right]$$

Lastly, when α has a value of two, a greater relative weight is assigned in the final result to those who fall furthest below the poverty (or indigence) line by squaring the relative income deficit:

(4)
$$FGT_2 = \frac{1}{n}\sum_{i=1}^{q}\left(\frac{z-y_i}{z}\right)^2$$

Source: Economic Commission for Latin America and the Caribbean (ECLAC), on the basis of James Foster, Joel Greer and Erik Thorbecke, "A class of decomposable poverty measures", *Econometrica*, vol. 52, No. 3, 1984.

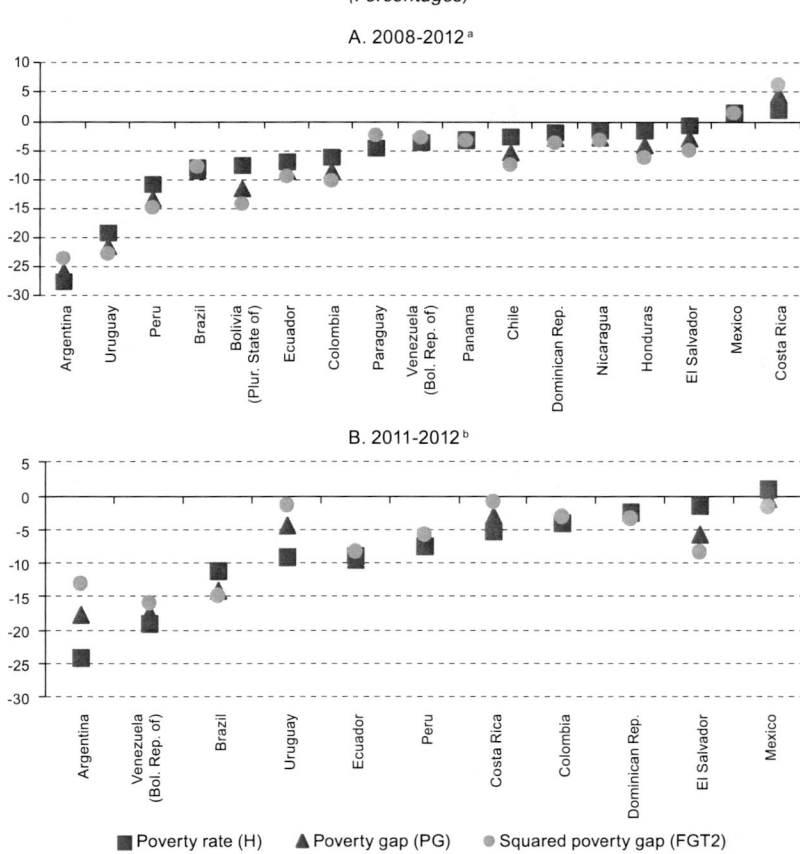

Figure I.4
Latin America (17 countries): annual change in poverty indicators
(Percentages)

A. 2008-2012 [a]

B. 2011-2012 [b]

■ Poverty rate (H) ▲ Poverty gap (PG) ● Squared poverty gap (FGT2)

Source: Economic Commission for Latin America and the Caribbean (ECLAC), on the basis of special tabulations of data from household surveys conducted in the respective countries.
[a] Corresponds to the period 2008-2012, except in Argentina (2009-2012), Chile (2009-2011), El Salvador (2004-2012), Honduras (2006-2010), Nicaragua (2005-2009), Panama (2008-2011) and Plurinational State of Bolivia (2009-2011).
[b] Corresponds to the period 2011-2012, except in El Salvador and Mexico (2010-2012).

3. Characteristics of changes in poverty

In order to determine which factors impacted on poverty in 2012, the variations in the different sources of household income for the subset of the population that was living in poverty a year earlier are analysed.

Labour income (that is, salaries or wages or income earned through independent work) is the main source of income for households. In the countries for which information is available for 2012, this source accounted for between 58% (in México) and 84% (in the Bolivarian Republic of Venezuela) of the income of households living in poverty. In keeping with its high share of total income, labour income tends to account for a significant share of poverty variations.

This fact is corroborated in 2012, in accordance with the information presented in figure I.5. In practically all the countries where poor households have recorded the most substantial increases in income, 75% or more of the increase in total income came from labour income and of this the greater part corresponded to wages and salaries. The Bolivarian Republic of Venezuela presented the greater increase in total real income, of the order of 11%, of which almost 7 percentage points came from the increase in salaries and wages and nearly 2 points from the remunerations of independent workers.[2] Brazil, Colombia, El Salvador and Peru are also examples of reductions in poverty that are linked mainly to the increase in income from employment. Ecuador is the only country where poverty levels fell

---

[2]   The notable increase in labour income stems from the appreciable increase in the minimum wage and some benefits connected with labour income (for example the food bonus), at a time when inflation eased considerably in relation to 2011.

significantly in 2012 and the contribution of labour income was less than 60%.[3] In some countries, such as Costa Rica, Mexico and Uruguay, where poverty rates did not vary appreciably, the lack of change was linked to a decline in salaries and wages, which counteracted the increase in other sources of income.

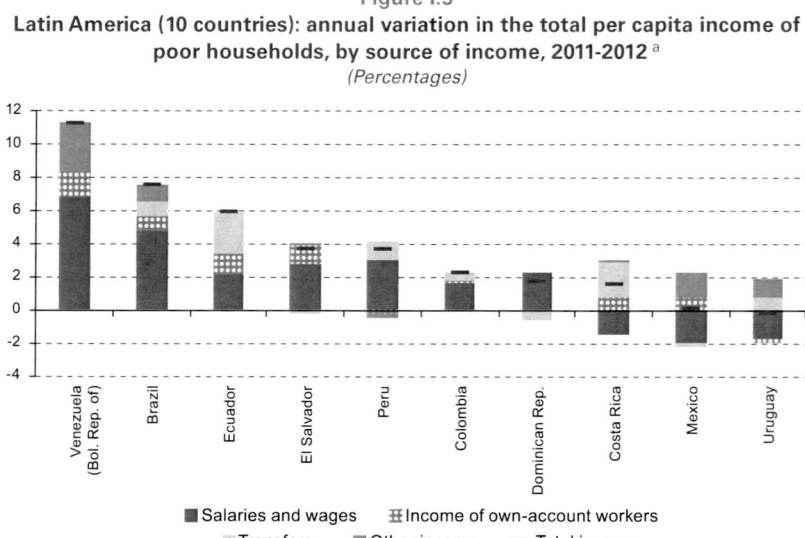

Figure I.5
Latin America (10 countries): annual variation in the total per capita income of poor households, by source of income, 2011-2012 [a]
(Percentages)

Source: Economic Commission for Latin America and the Caribbean (ECLAC), on the basis of special tabulations of household surveys conducted in the respective countries.
[a] The percentage of population examined is the same in both periods and corresponds to the 2011 poverty rate (except in the case of El Salvador and Mexico, where it corresponds to the 2010 rate).

The labour income received by households may be obtained as the product of the income per employed member and the number of employed household members. During the period 2011-2012, the greatest increases in labour income stemmed mainly from a rise in labour income per employed person, since the percentage of occupied persons did not vary significantly except in El Salvador. This variable increased more sharply in Mexico, although the fall in labour income per employed person caused a contraction in per capita labour income.

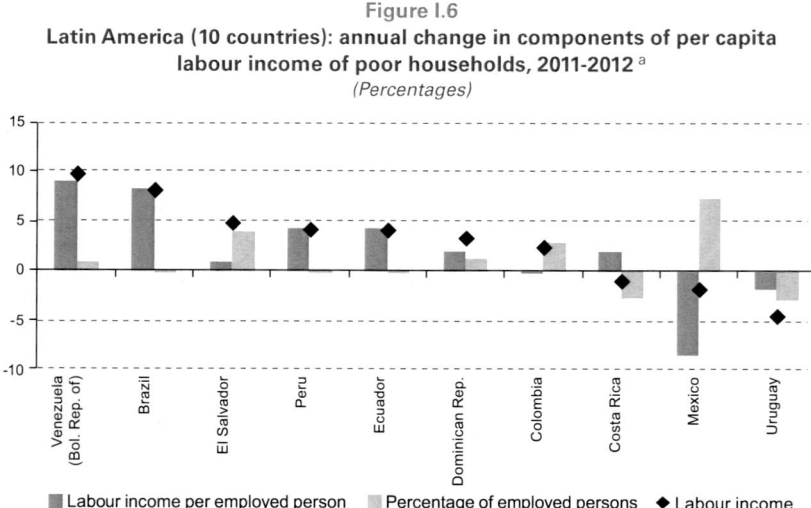

Figure I.6
Latin America (10 countries): annual change in components of per capita labour income of poor households, 2011-2012 [a]
(Percentages)

Source: Economic Commission for Latin America and the Caribbean (ECLAC), on the basis of special tabulations of data from household surveys conducted in the respective countries.
[a] The percentage of population analysed is the same in both periods and corresponds to the 2011 poverty rate (except in the case of El Salvador and Mexico, where it corresponds to the 2010 rate).

---

[3] In this case the transfers both of pensions and benefits such as the Human Development Bonus played a significant role, accounting for 2.5 of the 6.0 percentage points of the increase in the income of poor households.

From a different perspective, variations in poverty rates may be analysed in terms of the contribution of two elements: growth in the mean income of persons (growth effect) and changes in the way in which this income is distributed (distribution effect).

As regards poverty rate variations that occurred in 2012, the growth effect was dominant. In three of the six countries that recorded reductions of at least one percentage point in their poverty rates, the growth effect accounts for practically the entire poverty reduction, particularly in those with the most notable reductions; in turn, the distribution effect predominated only in the country with the lowest poverty reduction.

The relative weight of the growth and distribution effects is a bit different when one looks at the period 2008-2012 as a whole. While the growth effect predominated in practically all the countries which recorded an appreciable decline in poverty, the contribution of the distribution effect was over 50% in two countries and over 25% in six others.

Figure I.7
Latin America (13 countries): changes in poverty rates and the impact of the growth and distribution effects [a]

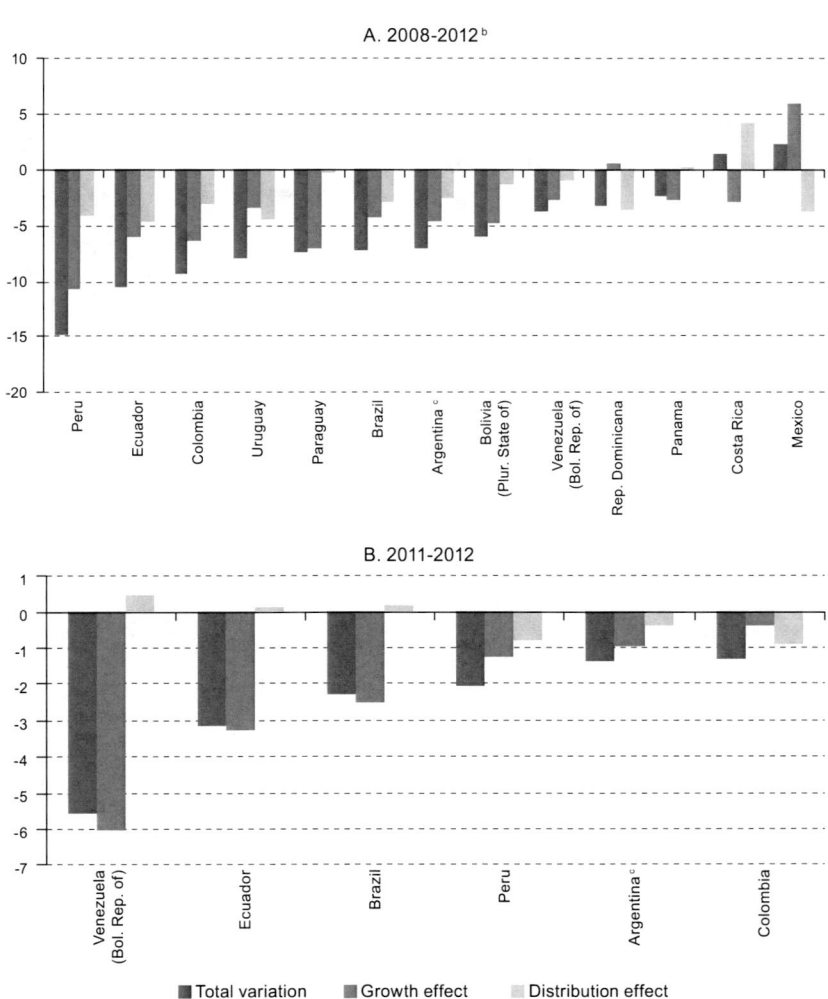

Source: Economic Commission for Latin America and the Caribbean (ECLAC), on the basis of special tabulations of data from household surveys conducted in the respective countries.
[a] Corresponds to the countries with statistically significant variations in poverty rates in the periods under consideration.
[b] Relates to the period 2008-2012, except in Argentina (2009-2012) and Panama, Paraguay and Plurinational State of Bolivia (2008-2011).
[c] Urban areas.

4. Poverty in different population groups

As indicated on various occasions, poverty affects people differently depending on their personal characteristics (see ECLAC, 2013a, for an analysis of probabilities of poverty by personal characteristics). In order to supplement the characterization of income poverty in Latin America, updated results are presented for some population groups that are relevant to the poverty analysis.

One of the most obvious regular empirical features in the countries of the region is that the poverty rate among children is considerably higher than for the rest of the population. Poverty rates among children under the age of 15 may be between 1.1 and 2.0 times higher than for the total population,[4] with the most notable differences recorded in countries with lower poverty levels. While there are several exceptions, in many countries the poverty rate tends to be inversely proportionate to the age of the person. Thus, in most countries, poverty among the 55 and over age group tends to be lower than the average (see figure I.8).

Figure I.8
Latin America (16 countries): difference in poverty rates by population characteristic, 2012 [a]

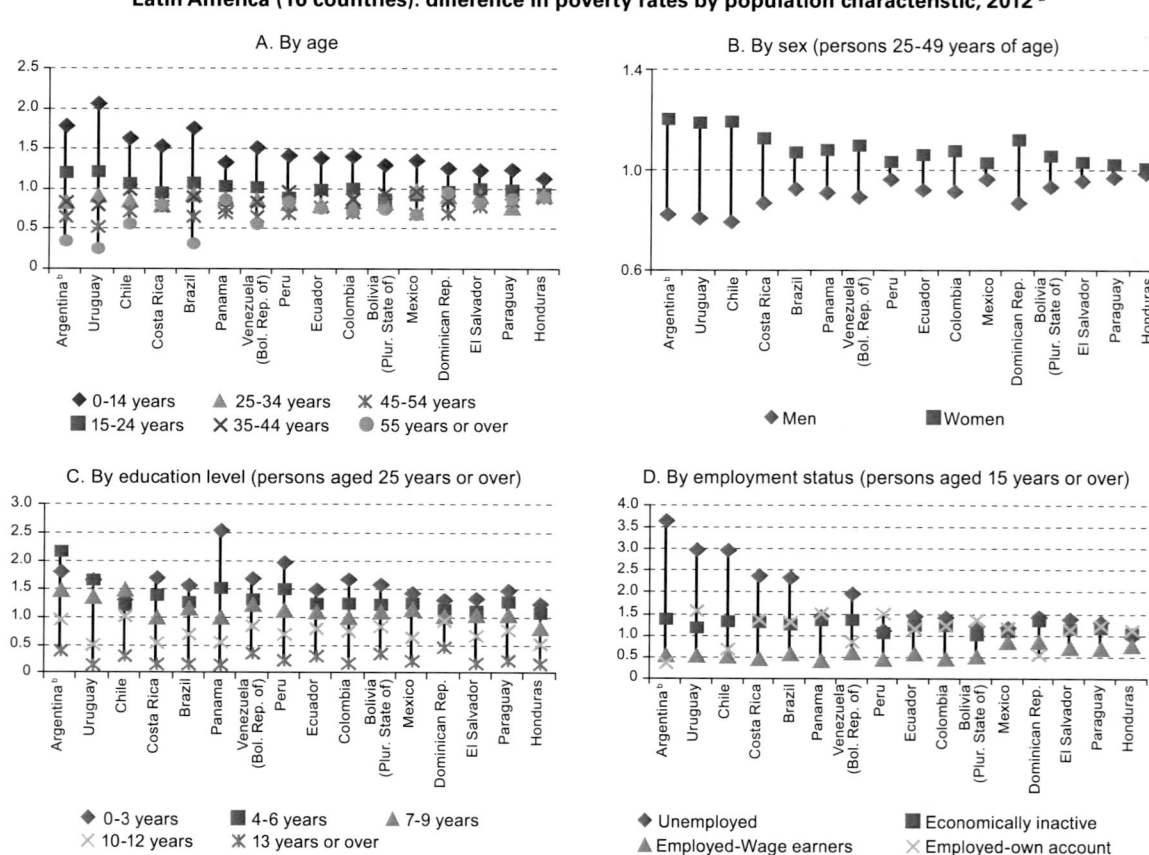

Source: Economic Commission for Latin America and the Caribbean (ECLAC), on the basis of special tabulations of data from household surveys conducted in the respective countries.
[a] Corresponds to the year 2012, except in Chile (2011), Honduras (2010), Panama (2011), Paraguay (2011) and Plurinational State of Bolivia (2011).
[b] Urban areas.

Another feature that has been examined in detail is the higher incidence of poverty among women. Even though poverty rates do not differ significantly between men and women when the comparison is made for the total population, the result is different when the comparison is made for adults with the highest probability of participating in the labour market. In practically all the countries of the region, the poverty rate is higher for women than for men.

---

[4] For a detailed analysis of child poverty, see chapter II.

There is also a close link between low levels of education and poverty. The poverty incidence is highest for persons who have had no more than three years of schooling and it diminishes gradually as the number of years of schooling of the population increases. Persons with between seven and nine years of schooling have a poverty rate similar to the average.

Lastly, the employment status of working age persons also has an impact on the poverty incidence. Predictably, the percentage of poor persons is higher among the unemployed than among the employed and the economically inactive. Moreover, among the employed, the poverty rate is lower for wage earners than for own-account workers, who in several countries have a similar poverty rate to that of the economically inactive population.

B. Multidimensional poverty analysis

A multidimensional measurement of poverty limited to unmet basic needs shows that deprivations such as lack of access to drinking water or to a proper sanitation system still affects a substantial number of people in the region. This raises the question of whether the public policies for poverty alleviation are placing sufficient emphasis on the achievement of minimum standards. A broader look at poverty, including deficiencies in spheres such as social protection and income, explores the relationship between different dimensions of deprivation.

This section discusses a multidimensional approach to poverty measurement in Latin America. In particular, it explores conceptually and empirically different dimensions, thresholds and ways of adding dimensions in order to advance towards the construction of a relevant multidimensional poverty index that can be applied throughout the region. An effort is also made to identify difficulties in availability and quality of information, for contributing to the generation of better data for the multidimensional measurement of poverty. Therefore, the indices presented here in this section are basically exploratory in nature and are not presented as a definitive multidimensional measurement of poverty in the region.

The section is organized as follows: first, arguments are presented that justify moving towards a multidimensional poverty measurement. Next, different dimensions and thresholds are considered, bearing in mind the selection of those that are most relevant and feasible for measurement in the regional context. Then, an empirical analysis is presented using part of the methodology proposed by Alkire and Foster (2007 and 2011). The analysis begins with an index based on a core set of indicators of critical deficiencies or unmet basic needs (UBN), continues by adding to this core a measurement of deprivation due to income insufficiency, and is supplemented with the addition of some dimensions not usually included in the poverty analysis.

1. Preliminary concepts

In recent years, the States in the region have manifested a growing interest in multidimensional poverty measurements as instruments for public policy analysis. This interest was prompted by the dissemination of new conceptual frameworks on development and well-being, such as the rights-based approach and the capabilities approach. These approaches have been fully assumed by ECLAC, which has declared that "living in poverty does not involve just not having the income necessary to cover basic needs; being poor also means suffering social exclusion", which prevents one from participating fully in society. "Ultimately, poverty is not being entitled to rights, the negation of citizenship." (Bárcena (2010, p.2).

The use of multidimensional poverty indicators may also be justified by the fact that measurements based on income insufficiency provide an incomplete assessment of the standard of living. Indeed, income insufficiency is a proxy for individuals' consumption capacity through the market and does not properly reflect access to goods not acquired through income, which results in an erosion of the correlation between income and well-being. Thus, poverty measurement is fundamental for monitoring public policies and, since these initiatives do not just provide monetary transfers but also educational, health, labour and social protection services, the monetary indicators provide insufficient information for capturing the impact of policies.

A widely debated issue relating to multidimensional measurement methodologies is whether it is appropriate to incorporate information provided by the different poverty indicators in a synthetic index. For example, it has been pointed out that procedures for adding information may result in information losses and that the choice of an aggregation mechanism for handling information in a system of indicators may be arbitrary (Maurizio, 2010). However, a system of indicators does not solve the problem of identification, that is, of selecting those that may be classified as poor and those that may not. Moreover, a synthetic index facilitates the joint analysis of shortcomings, allowing for a comprehensive system (Santos, 2013), fosters communication by summing up a high number of dimensions and, consequently, facilitates decision-making (Maurizio, 2010; Santos, 2013).

Thus, new methodologies developed in recent years have overcome some of the obstacles to the addition of different dimensions in a poverty index (see Bourguignon and Chakravarty, 2003, and Alkire and Foster, 2007, 2011); these methodologies create better conditions for making these measurements, even if they do not overcome the political complexities and the data constraints that affect this type of exercise. International agencies and States have stepped up efforts to propose new multidimensional poverty indices,[5] based on the implementation of these new methodologies (for further details see box I.3).

The conduct of a multidimensional poverty measurement exercise calls for an evaluation of whether individuals attain minimum thresholds of well-being in each of the dimensions considered. This means that the dimensions and indicators must be selected, minimum thresholds set for each dimension and lastly the results obtained in the different dimensions must be combined in a synthetic indicator. Thus, a set of arguments must be formulated and spelled out to justify the selection of dimensions and indicators for identifying poor people. This does not imply reaching a concept of poverty that is set in stone but of adopting criteria that guide decision-making in the different phases of measurement.

Box I.3
Multidimensional poverty measurement: recent applications

Recent years have seen accelerated development in the many areas related to multidimensional poverty measurement. These processes have led to a gradual increase in the number of dimensions under consideration, moving from the meeting of basic needs to a broader approach that is generally related to functionings and capabilities. The renewed interest in producing synthetic measures, which address the challenges of aggregating dimensions into a single indicator in the best way possible, has given rise to various types of indices and methodologies. The proposals that have gained the widest acceptance are those that link the axiomatic tradition with deprivation counting approaches, and include those by Bourguignon and Chakravarty (2003) and Alkire and Foster (2008 and 2011). Based on these approaches, practical applications for the multidimensional measurement of poverty have been developed at both regional and international level. Some recent official applications are described below:

The multidimensional poverty index (MPI) used by the United Nations Development Programme (UNDP) was prepared by the Oxford Poverty and Human Development Initiative (OPHI) in collaboration with UNDP. This index, which applies the methodology devised by Alkire and Foster (2008), is a measure of acute poverty that reflects deprivations in access to basic services and in key functionings of education, health and living standards among the populations of 104 countries, including some in Latin America. The unit of analysis is the household, with individuals identified as poor when they reside in households subject to three or more deprivations.

Dimensions are aggregated with equal weighting (Alkire and Santos, 2010).

In simplified terms, the following steps were taken in constructing the MPI: (i) selection of dimensions or indicators that will be used in measurement; (ii) determination of cut-offs for each indicator or dimension; (iii) application of cut-offs to determine whether individuals or households are deprived in each indicator; (iv) definition of weights for each of the dimensions or indicators; (v) determination of the multidimensional poverty cut-off (k), i.e. the proportion of weighted indicators in which a person is deprived in order to be identified as multidimensionally poor; (vi) calculation of the deprivation count for each individual, and determination, based on the comparison of said score with the value of k, of whether he or she is multidimensionally poor; (vii) determination of the proportion of multidimensionally poor individuals in the population (this is the headcount, or incidence, of multidimensional poverty (H)); (viii) determination of poverty intensity (A), calculated by obtaining the weighted deprivation count of poor people in all dimensions and dividing this number by the total number of poor people, and (ix) estimate of M0 (the adjusted headcount ratio) (Alkire and Santos, 2013).

While the MPI gives estimates of acute poverty that are generally low for the region (Latin America appears as the second least-poor region, after Central and Eastern Europe), Roche and Santos (2013) explore alternative ways of making the MPI more relevant to the region, by capturing a 'second layer' of poverty (beyond the acute one).

---

[5] For a review of the regional experience with multidimensional poverty measurement, see Santos (2013).

Box I.3 (concluded)

Dimensions, indicators, cut-offs and weights of the multidimensional poverty index of the United Nations Development Programme (UNDP) and the Oxford Poverty and Human Development Initiative (OPHI)

Dimensions	Indicators	Cut-offs A person is deprived if…	Relative weight (percentages)
Education	Years of schooling	No household member has completed five years of education.	16.7
	Child school attendance	At least one school-aged child (up to eighth grade) is not attending school.	16.7
Health	Nutrition	At least one household member is undernourished.	16.7
	Infant mortality	One or more children have died in the family.	16.7
Standard of living	Electricity	The household has no electricity.	5.6
	Sanitation	The household does not have access to adequate sanitation.	5.6
	Water	The household does not have access to drinking water.	5.6
	Floor	The household has a dirt floor.	5.6
	Cooking fuel	The household uses a polluting fuel (dung, wood or charcoal) for cooking.	5.6
	Assets	The household does not have a car, truck or other motorized vehicle, and only has one of: bicycle, motorcycle, radio, refrigerator, telephone or television.	5.6

Source: Sabina Alkire and María Emma Santos, *Acute Multidimensional Poverty: A New Index for Developing Countries*, 2010 [online] http://www.fundacionpobreza.cl/biblioteca-archivos/acute_multidimensional_poverty.pdf.

Another example is the multidimensional poverty index for Colombia (IPM-Colombia), developed in 2011 by the National Planning Department (DNP). The IMP-Colombia includes 5 dimensions and 15 variables, related to the household's educational conditions, childhood and youth, health, work, access to basic services and living conditions. As with the global MPI, the unit of analysis is the household. Five or more deprivations are required for a household to be considered poor. Dimensions are aggregated through equal weighting, a mechanism that is also used in the aggregation of indicators within each dimension. Poverty indices are calculated on the basis of the Alkire-Foster methodology (2008) (Angulo, Yadira and Pardo, 2013).

On the other hand, the multidimensional poverty index used by Mexico since 2010 adopts a perspective similar to that of the traditional two-dimensional method, using unmet basic needs (UBN) and monetary poverty indicators in tandem. Two dimensions are considered: rights (deprivations) and well-being (income). Rights are measured through six indicators: the education gap, access to health care, access to social security, quality of living spaces, basic services at home and access to food. Premised on the indivisibility of social rights, a person is deemed to be deprived in this dimension if he or she registers at least one of the six social deprivations. The two dimensions are aggregated through cross-tabulation (CONEVAL, 2010).

Mexico: typology of poverty based on the multidimensional poverty index

Rights and well-being	Households with deprivations	Households without deprivations
Households that are income poor	Multidimensionally poor	Income vulnerable
Households that are not income poor	Vulnerable in terms of social deprivations	Not poor and not vulnerable

Source: National Council for the Evaluation of Social Development Policy (CONEVAL), *Informe de pobreza multidimensional en México 2008*, 2010 http://www.coneval.gob.mx/cmsconeval/rw/resource/coneval/med_pobreza/Informe_pobreza_multidimensional/Informe_de_Pobreza_Multidimensional_en_Mexico_2008_.pdf?view.

Source: Economic Commission for Latin America and the Caribbean (ECLAC).

The first question refers to what should be measured and responses differ depending on the approach used. From a rights perspective, the poor are not persons who are deprived or needy but rather citizens and rights-holders (chapter II, which discusses the multidimensional measurement of child poverty, expands on this perspective). From the perspective of capabilities, poverty measurement based solely on resources is inadequate, since it does not provide information on the things that people can do or actually do with these abilities. From this perspective, the capabilities that individuals have for achieving certain functionings should be measured, for example, their capability to be well nourished or to live without humiliation or shame (Sen, 1985, 1997).

The option chosen here is to incorporate elements from the rights approach, the capabilities approach and the unmet basic needs approach. This integration is based on the idea that these traditions should be seen as complementary (rather than opposing) approaches, which cover different aspects of deprivation. The rights-based approach describes the institutional means or guarantees for achieving well-being, while needs are a way of conceptualizing the ends (or the content) of well-being.[6] In other words, the exercise of rights enables people to satisfy their basic needs and achieve basic functionings. If unable to satisfy their basic needs or to enjoy the freedom to function, people will not be in a position to demand their rights, and this will deepen and reproduce poverty.

---

[6] Consideration should be given not only to the legal aspects of rights but also to the institutional mechanisms that come into play in order to make them a reality.

While the notions of rights, capabilities and basic needs may be viewed as different ways of conceptualizing well-being, given the instruments available, it is not usually possible to make quantitative distinctions. The available information on the surveys of households make reference mainly to lack of resources or deprivation, many of which may be interpreted simultaneously as proxies for infringements of rights, constraints on meeting needs or obstacles to the achievement of functionings. A direct measurement of these concepts would require information which often cannot be adequately obtained through surveys or which, when they can be, are generally not available (for example, the nutritional status of the population or actual food consumption) (Santos and others, 2010).

In the regional context, the starting point that appears most advisable is the set of core indicators of critical deficiencies in living conditions (see box I.4), whether because these indicators are available in the surveys or because they constitute relatively well-established poverty measures. This subset of indicators can be used to explore other deprivations that can help to identify the poor, such as those relating to insufficient monetary resources and those that point to deficiencies in social participation or in linkages with institutions.

Box I.4
A pioneering experience: the unmet basic needs approach

In the early 1980s, ECLAC introduced the unmet basic needs (UBN) methodology in Latin America in order to make use of census information in the identification and characterization of poverty. The aim of this approach was to directly evaluate whether households could meet a set of basic needs.

The types of need that could be studied were limited according to the information available in censuses, meaning that some important aspects of well-being had to be excluded.

In initial studies, unmet needs were assessed on the basis of certain housing characteristics —such as the type of materials used in construction, access to drinking water, the availability of waste disposal systems and the number of rooms— as well as demographic features such as the number of household members, children's school attendance, and the age, education and employment status of the head of household.

Basic needs, dimensions and variables

Basic needs	Dimensions	Census variables
Housing	Dwelling quality	Construction materials used in the floor, walls and roof
	Crowding	Number of persons and rooms in the household
Sanitation	Availability of drinking water	Water supply in the dwelling
	Waste disposal system	-Toilet availability -Waste disposal system
Education	School attendance among children	Attendance of children in an educational establishment
Economic capacity	Probability of insufficient household income	-Age of household members -Highest education level attained -Number of household members -Employment status

Source: Juan Carlos Feres and Xavier Mancero, "El método de las necesidades básicas insatisfechas (NBI) y sus aplicaciones en América Latina", *Estudios Estadísticos y Prospectivos series*, No. 7 (LC/L.1491-P), Santiago, Chile, Economic Commission for Latin America and the Caribbean (ECLAC), 2001. United Nations publication, Sales No. S.01.II.G.31.

Under the UBN method, poor people were identified according to their deprivation count. Households that experienced at least one deprivation were classified as poor. The rationale behind this process, described in literature as the union approach, is that needs must be met in all dimensions as a prerequisite for overcoming poverty.

Subsequently, the UBN method began to be used as a means of complementing monetary poverty measurements. Just as the poverty line method does not account for access to free public services or other needs that are not met through spending, the UBN approach does not recognize the possibility of meeting needs through the private consumption of goods and services. It was therefore considered that the poverty line method was better suited to identifying recent or situational poverty, while the UBN method was more appropriate for gauging structural or long-term poverty.

Following these arguments, some researchers proposed two-dimensional methods based on combining the results generated by the UBN and poverty line methods (Beccaria and Minujin, 1985; Kaztman and Gerstenfeld, 1988). This cross-tabulation identifies four possible situations (set forth in the table below).

Combination of unmet basic needs (UBN) and poverty line methods

	Households with UBN	Households without UBN
Poor households	Chronically poor households (total)	Recently impoverished households (situational)
Non-poor households	Households with inertial deprivations (structural deprivations)	Socially integrated households

Source: Rubén Kaztman and Pascual Gerstenfeld, "La heterogeneidad de la pobreza: Una aproximación bidimensional" (LC/MDV/R.12 (Sem.44/7)), Montevideo, ECLAC office in Montevideo, 1988.

Box I.4 (concluded)

Conversely, Boltvinik (1990 and 1992) devised a method to avoid the duplication of information between the two methods, by removing the consumption capacity indicator from the UBN index. Under this proposal, UBN indicators would be able to account for access to goods provided through public investment, while income indicators would measure private consumption. This method attempted to determine the extent of deprivation in each dimension in order to establish gaps, as is the case with the poverty line. The UBN score would be added to the income poverty score to obtain an aggregate poverty score, which would be compared with the overall poverty threshold in order to determine who should be classified as poor.

Despite its use of the UBN method, this approach was criticized because of its inability to establish the intensity of deprivations, because it permitted discretion in defining the number of deprivations that a household should suffer in order to be identified as poor, and because of the lack of a theoretical basis for the weights assigned to the different evaluated needs (giving rise to a problem with the comparability of dimensions).

Source: Economic Commission for Latin America and the Caribbean (ECLAC).

The unit of analysis that will be used is the household, this being the basic entity where the most important decisions are taken for satisfaction of needs and the achievement of functionings. Nevertheless, for the time being, the significance of asymmetries within households (not all household members are affected in the same way by lack of resources or are able to function with the same degree of freedom) will not be taken into account owing to methodological difficulties and problems with data.

2. Multidimensional poverty measurement based on a core set of traditional indicators of unmet basic needs

The indicators most frequently used in multidimensional poverty measurements in Latin America are those that determine deficiencies in living conditions (overcrowding and material deprivation), in basic services (water and sanitation) and in education. This is the case not only because of the importance of these indicators for identifying the poor, but also because they are the most readily available indicators in surveys conducted in the region. Admittedly, a more comprehensive multidimensional poverty measurement requires data on other aspects, such as nutritional status, state of health and employment status of persons (for a proposal on the aspects of well-being that should be captured in a multidimensional poverty measurement, see Santos, 2013), but this information is not available for a sufficient number of countries in the region.

As regards the *housing* dimension, deprivation occurs when the dwelling does not provide its occupants with a minimum level of habitability. This means, on the one hand, that the dwelling does not provide protection against various environmental factors (for example, rain, humidity, etc.) and on the other, that it does not provide privacy and convenience for the basic biological and social activities. Thus, a dwelling is observed to be deficient when it does not guarantee sufficient insulation against natural and social elements.

The housing unit's ability to insulate individuals against the natural elements usually is assessed by looking at the construction materials used in the roof, walls and floor. Information on the materials used in the construction of housing units is usually obtained differently in different country surveys, partly because of the features peculiar to those contexts (Feres and Mancero, 2001).

The capacity of the housing unit to provide social insulation is established through the indicator of overcrowding, the usual standard being three or more persons per room for rural and urban areas. The divisions counted as "rooms" differ between countries. Generally speaking, any area other than bathrooms, the kitchen, passages, garages, and business areas count as rooms, although in some country surveys, the kitchen and/or bathrooms are not excluded. In order to minimize the effect of differences in the definition of rooms on the comparability of estimates, some adjustments were made on the basis of the methodology used by Kaztman (2011).

The importance of water and sanitation to well-being has been amply recognized. In 2010, the United Nations General Assembly affirmed the human right to water and sanitation, since both are essential for preventing mortality, undernutrition and gastrointestinal diseases (Taccari and Stockins, 2013). The international standard defines as appropriate access to improved water sources that each individual should have access to at least 20 litres of clean water per day from a source situated less than one kilometre from the home.[7]

Current survey information does not allow us to measure directly the lack of access to improved water sources, as defined in the international standard, a constraint that is especially serious in rural areas. Under international standards, unimproved water is that obtained from vendors, water trucks, unprotected wells or watersheds, and bottled water; rainwater is classified as an improved source (UNICEF/WHO, 2012), which means a modification in the standards used in earlier measurements applied in the region (see for example ECLAC, 2011).

These recommendations may be adopted except in the case of rainwater, since the availability of this source cannot be guaranteed throughout the year.[8] Another information problem concerns identification of types of wells, since in most surveys, no information is obtained as to whether a well is protected or not. In any event, several surveys ascertain whether or not the well has a pump, which makes it feasible to consider as an evaluation criterion the effort made to obtain water in accordance with international standards.[9]

An improved sanitation installation is one which allows for the hygienic separation of faeces from human contact (Taccari and Stockins, 2013). The lack of such systems results in a higher incidence of child mortality, among other health problems (Kaztman and Gerstenfeld, 1988). As in the case of water sources, a usual practice in the evaluation of improved sanitation is consideration of the features of the surroundings. For example, in some rural settings, households, irrespective of their poverty status, would not have access to a sewerage system or to mains water.

Lack of electricity and the use of toxic fuels for cooking are considered to be the basis for the notion of energy poverty, which identifies situations in which households have an insufficient endowment of modern energy services or where the energy consumption of households does not meet their daily requirements and the fuel used is harmful to health (Nussbaumer and others, 2011).[10] The resources of households have been linked to the level of toxicity and the efficiency of the fuel that they use, with the worst fuels being waste matter, wood and charcoal, in that order[11] (see Dufflo, Greenstone and Rema, 2008).

The lack of appropriate systems for the elimination of garbage should also be included in a multidimensional evaluation of poverty, not only because of its sanitary and environmental implications, but also because of its harmful effects in terms of the dignity of persons. However, there are not enough countries with data and there are difficulties in determining thresholds. For example, it is not clear whether the burning or burial of rubbish in rural areas should be considered as a lack. Burning can produce emissions containing dioxins and metals, but this depends on the type of waste, and the effectiveness of burial depends on the depth, the lining and the sealing of the excavation (World Bank, 2005, 2012).

Education is essential in order to build the competencies and skills that people need in order to participate properly in productive and social life. Lack of education is also a huge obstacle to escaping from poverty and can contribute to reproduction of poverty.

The indicator of school attendance has been used traditionally in multidimensional poverty measurements in the region. It is usually calculated for the population aged 6 to 14 years, but given the high rates of school attendance in most countries in the region, the age bracket has been expanded on this occasion to 6 to 17 years. As regards data problems, in some countries, the population under 7 years of age is excluded and also in some surveys, enrolment is used as the criterion instead of actual attendance.

Given that the indicator of school attendance is not sufficient to establish the educational situation of all the members of the household, an indicator on completion of education is also included for the members of the household aged 20 years or over, the household being understood to be lacking in this area if none of its members have reached a given threshold. Usually, this threshold is completion of primary education, but owing to the growing levels of

[7] See the website of the World Health Organization, http://www.who.int/water_sanitation_health/mdg1/en /.
[8] The climate change scenario makes this situation even more uncertain.
[9] For a recent review of the gaps and discrepancies in water and sanitation indicators, as well as in other Millennium Development Goal indicators, see Taccari and Stockins (2013).
[10] See [online] http://practicalaction.org/energy-poverty-2.
[11] No differentiated thresholds have been set for urban and rural areas in relation to the use of cooking fuel, since the very harmful effects of the use of toxic fuels are believed to take precedence over cultural differences or differences in resources.

completion of this level in the Latin American population (see ECLAC, 2013a), the threshold now used for persons aged 20-59 years is completion of lower secondary school.

Table I.2 shows the dimensions, thresholds and weightings used in the multidimensional poverty measurement based on classical UBN indicators. In line with the usual practice in the research used in the multidimensional approach (see boxes I.3 and I.5), the same weighting is assigned for the dimensions used in this exercise, since no agreement was reached on whether to assign them more or less importance.

Table I.2
Dimensions, indicators of deprivations and weightings for measuring poverty based on classical unmet basic needs indicators

Dimensions	Indicators of deprivations	Weighting
Water and sanitation		1/4
Lack of access to improved water sources	Urban areas: any source of water except the public mains Rural areas: unprotected well, bottled water, mobile water sources, river, water course, rain and others	1/8
Lack of a waste disposal system	Urban areas: not having a toilet or waste disposal system connected to a sewerage system or a sceptic tank Rural areas: not having a toilet or having an evacuation system without treatment of waste matter	1/8
Energy [a]		1/4
Lack of electric power	Households that do not have electricity	1/8
Cooking fuel that is unsafe for health	Households that use wood, charcoal or waste for cooking purposes	1/8
Housing [b]		1/4
Substandard housing materials	Housing with a dirt floor, or substandard roofing or wall materials	1/8
Overcrowding	Three or more persons per room, rural and urban areas	1/8
Education		1/4
Non-attendance at school	In the household, at least one child of school age (6-17 years of age) does not attend school	1/8
Non-attainment of a minimum level of education	In the household, no person 20 years or over has achieved a minimum level of education -Persons aged 20 to 59 years: have not completed secondary schooling -Persons aged 60 or over: have not completed primary education	1/8

Source: Economic Commission for Latin America and the Caribbean (ECLAC).
[a] Data for Argentina relate only to fuel; for Bolivarian Republic of Venezuela and Chile, data are available only on access to electric power. Thus, these indicators have a weighting of ¼ in the relevant countries. Given that lack of fuel is usually more widespread than lack of electric power in the countries in the region, the total lack under the energy dimension may be underestimated for Bolivarian Republic of Venezuela and Chile.
[b] For Brazil, no information is available on the floor of the housing.

Hereinafter, the analysis is carried out on the basis of the methodology proposed by Alkire and Foster (2008, 2011). In this approach, two types of threshold are used: (i) thresholds by dimension, which makes it possible to determine whether the households/individuals are lacking in each of the dimensions assessed and (ii) a multidimensional threshold (denoted by the letter k), which expresses the proportion of deprivations that a household has to have in order to be identified as poor. In this method, the main indicators that are taken into account are: the headcount ratio (H), or the percentage of the population that is multidimensionally poor, the intensity of poverty (A), or the average quantity of deficiencies experienced by the poor and the adjusted headcount ratio (M0), which combines information on the incidence (H) and the intensity of poverty (A) by multiplying the two indicators (for further details, see box I.5).

Before selecting the multidimensional threshold and proceeding to identify the poor population, it must be determined whether the estimates provided by the poverty index are sufficiently robust. One way of determining the robustness of the index is to verify whether the ordering of the countries tends to be similar for different values of k (multidimensional poverty threshold).

Figure I.9 shows the values of the adjusted headcount ratio (M0) for different values of k. Generally speaking, the positions of the countries do not change substantially when the value of k varies, and non-parametric tests show acceptable levels of consistency and correlation between positions obtained by the countries.[12] Thus, irrespective of the value of k, Nicaragua, Guatemala and Honduras show the highest adjusted poverty ratio level (M0) and Chile the lowest. In any event, some overlaps are seen in the order of countries such as those existing between Guatemala and Honduras (k=70%) and between Peru and Paraguay (k=20%).

---

[12] When values of M0 are analysed in relation to different values of k, Kendall's Tau fluctuates between 0.786 and 0.967, while Spearman's Rho fluctuates between 0.88 and 0.997. When this procedure is replicated for H (the gross headcount ratio), Kendall's Tau can be seen to vary between 0.723 and 0.982, while Spearman's Rho ranges between 0.849 and 0.997.

Box I.5
The Alkire-Foster Method

The Alkire-Foster method links the counting tradition, which identifies the poor according to the number of deprivations that affect them, with the axiomatic tradition, which sets out a group of desirable properties that poverty measures must satisfy at the identification and aggregation stages. The Alkire-Foster approach proposes: (i) an identification method ρk, which links and extends traditional intersection and union approaches, and (ii) a class of poverty measures $M\alpha$, which are extensions of the traditional measures proposed by Foster, Greer and Thorbecke (the FGT index), but adjusted for multidimensionality and which satisfy a variety of axioms. This method of identification and aggregation, and the basic measures that result from both steps (the headcount ratio, intensity and the adjusted headcount ratio), are highly suited to ordinal data.

The identification function ρk classifies an individual i as poor when the number of dimensions j in which he experiences deprivation is at least k. Since ρk is dependent on both the within-dimension cut-off line zj and the across-dimension cut-off line k, therefore ρk is a dual cut-off method of identification. Even where the method does not require a specific value for k, the authors propose an intermediate cut-off level, which would be somewhere between the union ($k = 1$) and intersection methods (k = the sum of all analysed deprivations).

The basic input for the Alkire-Foster methodology is a deprivations matrix, $g0 = [gij0]$, where each individual or dimension is assigned the value of zero when there is no deprivation in that dimension, and the value of one when there is ($yij < zj$). The matrix is then censored ($g0k$), which means that the deprivations of the non-poor are excluded (they are assigned a value equal to zero). Individuals' deprivation counts are then constructed based on the (weighted) sum of deprivations suffered in the different dimensions.

The basic indicators calculated using the Alkire-Foster method are the poverty headcount ratio (H), poverty intensity (A) and the adjusted headcount ratio (M0). These indicators are defined below:

The headcount ratio (H) refers the proportion of individuals identified as poor. ($H=q/n$) where q is the number of poor people and n is the total population.

Poverty intensity (A): is the (weighted) average of the deprivations suffered by people identified as poor ($A=\sum Ci (k)/dq$).

To estimate A, it is necessary to calculate the proportion of deprivations experienced by individuals, taking the censored vector of deprivation counts ($Ci(k)/d$, discounting deprivations among the non-poor) as a benchmark. This value is then divided by the total number of poor people (q).

The adjusted headcount ratio (M0) is the result of multiplying H by A.

The measures H, A and M0 satisfy the axiom of dimensional monotonicity, meaning that if a poor person suffers an additional deprivation, then the poverty measure rises. They also satisfy the deprivation focus axiom (an adaptation of the poverty focus axiom), meaning that the poverty measure does not vary if deprivations increase or decrease in the non-poor population, and the property of "decomposability", which requires that overall poverty be the weighted average of subgroup poverty levels.

However, H, A and M0 are not sensitive to the depth of deprivation and therefore do not satisfy the monotonicity axiom, which dictates that if the deprivations suffered by an individual become more severe, then the poverty measure must increase. To satisfy this axiom, we must consider a censored matrix of normalized gaps $g1(k)$ and estimate an average poverty gap G. M1 is then calculated, where M1 = HAG. Nevertheless, the increase in a deprivation has the same impact no matter whether the person is very slightly deprived or acutely deprived in that dimension, meaning that the transfer axiom is not satisfied. To resolve this problem, the average severity of deprivations (S) is calculated. M2 is then estimated, where M2=M0*S.

Ideally M1 and M2 require cardinal data. Where this is not available, suggested alternatives include a hybrid deprivation matrix, and reweighting.

Source: Economic Commission for Latin America and the Caribbean (ECLAC), on the basis of Sabina Alkire and James Foster, "Counting and multidimensional poverty measurement", *OPHI Working Paper*, No. 7, Oxford, Oxford Poverty & Human Development Initiative (OPHI), 2008 [online] http://www.ophi.org.uk/wp-content/uploads/ophi-wp7.pdf; and "Counting and multidimensional poverty measurement", *Journal of Public Economics*, vol. 95, No. 7-8, Amsterdam, Elsevier, 2011.

Figure I.9
Latin America (17 countries): adjusted headcount ratio (M0) of extreme poverty with different thresholds (k), 2011 [a]

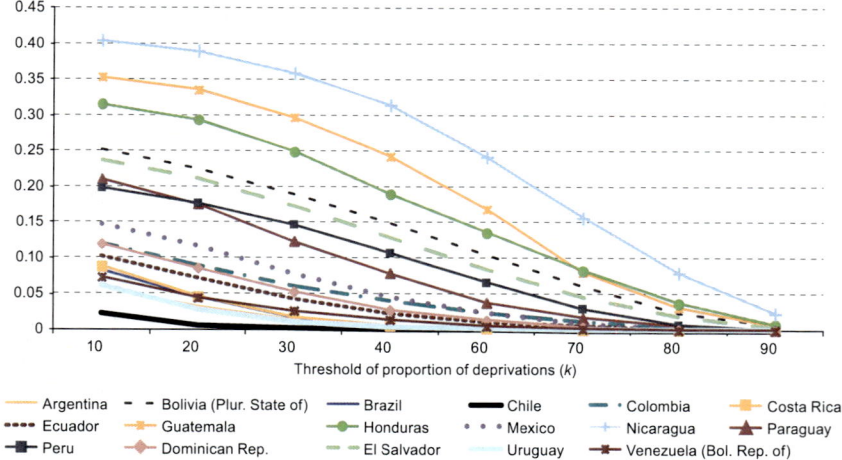

Source: Economic Commission for Latin America and the Caribbean (ECLAC).
[a] The data for Argentina relate to urban areas; those for El Salvador, Guatemala, Honduras and Mexico to 2010; and those for Nicaragua and Plurinational State of Bolivia to 2009.

The selection of the proportion or number of deprivations used to determine multidimensional poverty (threshold k) is particularly important. Under the UBN approach (see box I.4), the aggregation methodology used is the union methodology, which classifies as poor even persons who suffer a single deprivation. However, this increases the probability of an error of inclusion, since a household may suffer deprivations in a particular dimension for reasons unrelated to poverty. On the other hand, the method of intersection, which requires persons/households to be deprived in all dimensions, raises sharply the probability of an error of exclusion.

In terms of opting to diminish (or reduce to a greater extent) one type of error (inclusion or exclusion) as opposed to the other, the latter was preferred bearing in mind how significant it is in the current context of public policies (for a discussion, see Ocampo, 2008). Accordingly, the value of k was set at 20%, which means that households with two or more deprivations are considered to be poor.[13]

Table I.3 presents the incidence, intensity and adjusted headcount ratio by country, with a multidimensional poverty threshold set at $k = 20\%$. The countries with the highest poverty incidences are Nicaragua (71.4%), Guatemala (68.8%) and Honduras (63.4%), and those with lowest incidences are Chile (2.2%), Uruguay (9.6%) and Argentina (11.0%). The highest intensities were observed in Nicaragua, Guatemala and the Plurinational State of Bolivia and the lowest in Chile, Brazil and Costa Rica. With respect to M0, the countries with the highest and lowest values are the same as for the poverty incidence.

Table I.3
Latin America (17 countries): headcount ratio (H), intensity (A) and adjusted poverty ratio (M0) by country, 2011[a]
(Percentages)

Country	H	A	M0
Chile	2.2	29.8	0.6
Uruguay	9.6	29.9	2.9
Argentina	11.0	29.9	3.3
Venezuela (Bolivarian Republic of)	13.2	34.1	4.5
Brazil	15.5	29.3	4.5
Costa Rica	15.5	29.7	4.6
Ecuador	21.0	34.4	7.2
Dominican Republic	24.8	34.7	8.6
Colombia	23.9	37.9	9.0
Mexico	31.9	36.5	11.6
Paraguay	46.6	37.8	17.6
Peru	40.5	43.7	17.7
El Salvador	48.0	44.1	21.1
Bolivia (Plurinational State of)	48.1	46.7	22.5
Honduras	63.4	46.4	29.4
Guatemala	68.8	48.8	33.6
Nicaragua	71.4	54.6	39.0

Source: Economic Commission for Latin America and the Caribbean (ECLAC).
[a] The data for Argentina relate to urban areas; those for El Salvador, Guatemala, Honduras and Mexico to 2010; and those for Nicaragua and Plurinational State of Bolivia to 2009.

In general, the countries with the highest non-adjusted incidences have the highest poverty intensity index (see figure I.10). However, there are exceptions: for example, the Plurinational State of Bolivia has a much lower headcount ratio (H) than Honduras (48.1% versus 63.4%), but the two countries have a very similar reading of intensity of poverty (46.7% and 46.4%, respectively). Meanwhile, Paraguay has a much higher headcount index (46.6%) than Colombia (23.9%), but in terms of the intensity of poverty, these two countries are very similar. In addition, the

---

[13] López Calva and Ortíz Juárez (2009) observed a wide variability in the magnitude of the error of exclusion depending on the criterion selected for identifying households as poor (union versus intersection). This exercise was realized on the basis of a measure of insufficient income.

incidence of poverty in Paraguay is 6.1 percentage points above that of Peru, but the poverty intensity is greater in Peru than in Paraguay, which means that the adjusted headcount ratio is almost the same in the two countries. For its part, Chile has a lower poverty incidence but a very similar level of poverty intensity to that observed in Argentina, Brazil, Costa Rica and Uruguay.

Figure I.10
Latin America (17 countries): incidence (H) and intensity (A) of multidimensional poverty, 2011[a]
(Percentages)

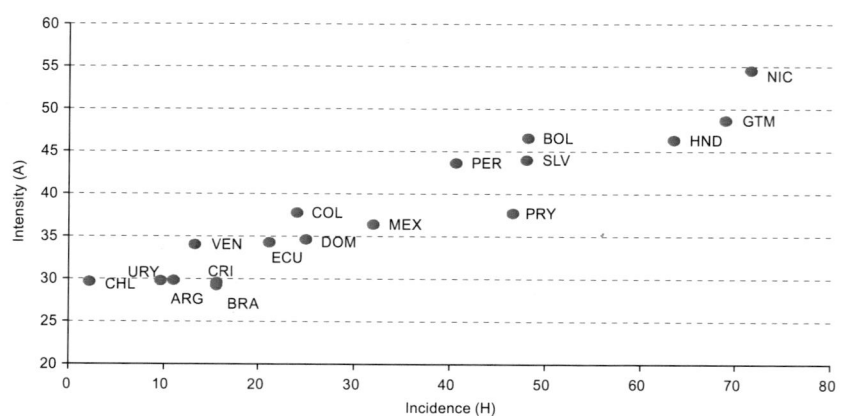

Source: Economic Commission for Latin America and the Caribbean (ECLAC).
[a] The data for Argentina relate to urban areas; those for El Salvador, Guatemala, Honduras and Mexico to 2010; and those for Nicaragua and Plurinational State of Bolivia to 2009.

Multidimensional poverty tends to be greater among those who reside in rural areas and among persons classified as indigenous or Afro-descendants, but not much difference in terms of gender is noted (see figure I.11). As regards the area of residence, the values of M0 are higher in rural areas of Guatemala, Nicaragua and Peru, while in terms of ethnicity, the highest values for M0 are found among the indigenous population of Guatemala, Paraguay and Peru.

Figure I.11
Latin America: adjusted headcount poverty ratio (M0) by sex, geographical area and recognition as belonging to indigenous peoples or Afro-descendent peoples, 2011[a]
(Proportions)

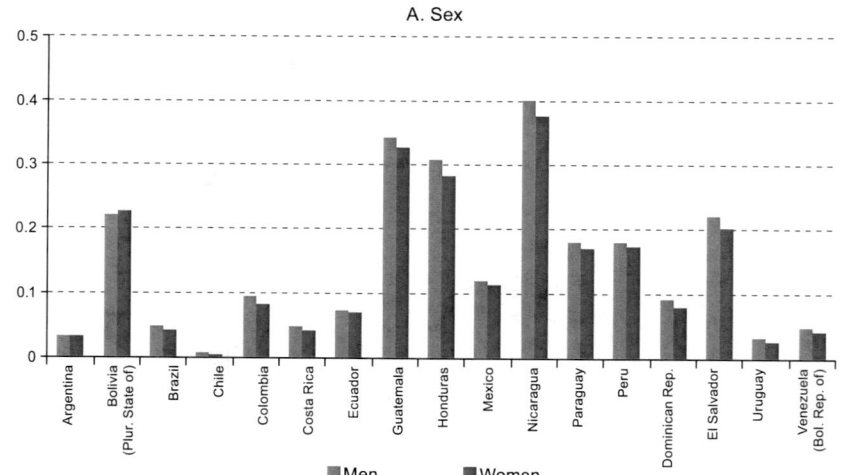

Figure I.11 (concluded)

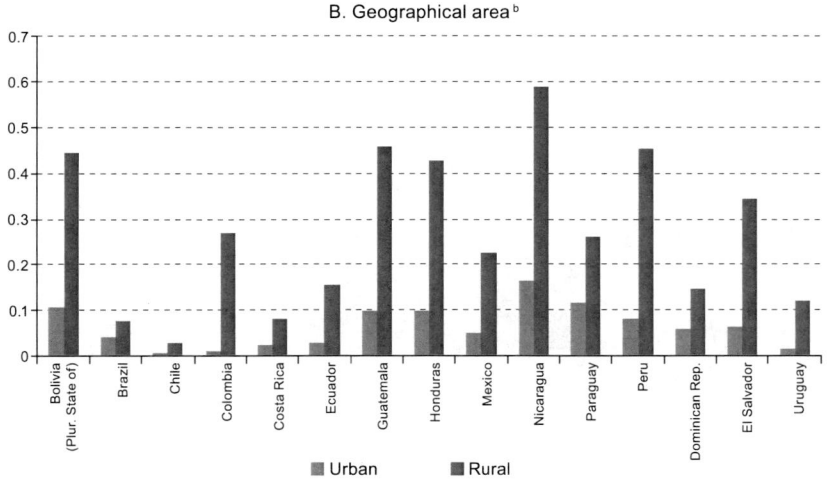

B. Geographical area[b]

■ Urban   ■ Rural

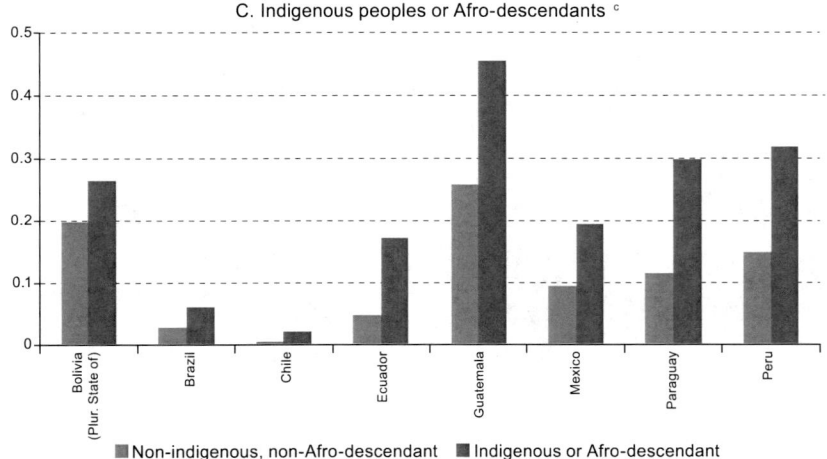

C. Indigenous peoples or Afro-descendants [c]

■ Non-indigenous, non-Afro-descendant   ■ Indigenous or Afro-descendant

Source: Economic Commission for Latin America and the Caribbean (ECLAC).
[a] Corresponds to 2011 except in the case of El Salvador (2010), Guatemala (2010), Honduras (2010), Mexico (2010) Nicaragua (2009) and Plurinational State of Bolivia (2009).
[b] The urban areas correspond to Bogotá in Colombia, metropolitan urban areas in Guatemala, Central District in Honduras, Managua in Nicaragua; San Salvador in El Salvador and Montevideo in Uruguay.
[c] In Brazil, includes Afro-descendants and persons of mixed race.

The least disparity in the incidence of poverty depending on whether or not one is of indigenous or Afro-descendent background can be seen in the Plurinational State of Bolivia, where the adjusted headcount ratio is 1.3 times as high in the indigenous population as in the non-indigenous population. The widest disparities occur in Chile (4.3 times), Ecuador (3.4 times) and Paraguay (2,6 times).

As regards the trend in multidimensional poverty, measured on the basis of the traditional UBN, a sharp fall in the incidence of multidimensional poverty in terms of the headcount index was observed between 2002 and 2011 in almost all countries in the region, with the exception of Uruguay (where it remained unchanged) and Mexico, which experienced a slight increase (see figure I.12).

Figure I.12
Latin America (17 countries): trend in the headcount index (H), 2002 and 2011[a]

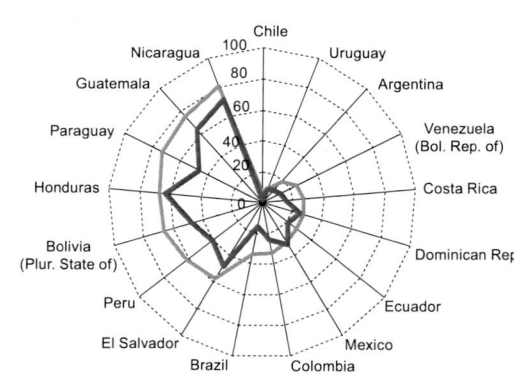

——— 2002 ——— 2011

Source: Economic Commission for Latin America and the Caribbean (ECLAC).
[a] Data for urban areas in Argentina. Corresponds to 2011 except in the case of El Salvador (2010), Guatemala (2010), Honduras (2010), Mexico (2010), Nicaragua (2009) and Plurinational State of Bolivia (2009).

The countries that saw the most substantial improvements were Paraguay, Peru, Plurinational State of Bolivia and Brazil, in that order, with absolute declines in the multidimensional poverty incidence of between 26 and 18 percentage points. A second group of countries (Argentina, Bolivarian Republic of Venezuela, Colombia, Costa Rica, Ecuador, El Salvador, Guatemala and Nicaragua) showed absolute falls of between 12 and 7 percentage points, approximately. Lastly, a third group of countries recorded declines of less than 5% (Chile, Dominican Republic and Honduras).[14]

3. Multidimensional poverty measurement with inclusion of the monetary index

The usual practice in Latin America has been to construct separate indices for monetary and non-monetary deprivations. Currently, different countries in the region have a measurement based on the UBN (see for example Calvo and others, 2013), which on occasions is crossed with the monetary index in a contingency table, as used to be done with the traditional bidimensional method. The UBN indicators have normally been selected on the basis of their correlation with income and the availability of data (Battistón and others, 2013).

The justification for measuring monetary and non-monetary poverty separately dates back several decades. The initial empirical evidence for the region, based on the bidimensional method, showed that the income measure and the UBN index identified different segments of the population as poor (see box I.4). Thus, the poverty measure based on UBN and the income-based poverty measure were viewed as two different but complementary types of poverty measure.

In recent years, some authors have affirmed the need to integrate the two types of measure into a multidimensional index. This is because the two measures are thought to be incomplete proxies for well-being and also have low correlations with each other, which could give rise to errors of exclusion when only one of them is used to identify the poor (Santos and others, 2010; Battistón and others, 2013). This argument appears to be especially valid for countries that exhibit the lowest incidences of poverty by both methods since in these countries, the discrepancies between the population identified as poor through the monetary measurement and that identified as poor using the UBN measurement are very high[15] (see figure I.13).

---

[14] The time comparison of the indicators presents constraints due to the way the survey questionnaires have evolved. Uruguay, for example, had to reweight the aggregate indicator of deprivations in 2002, since the questionnaire did not include the dimension "housing materials". Other countries where differences in categories had been observed at one time or another had to modify their definitions in an attempt to make them more comparable.

[15] Reference is made to the weight or relative incidence of discrepancies. In the countries with the highest poverty incidences, although the relative incidence of the discrepancies is lower, these can cover a significant segment of the population.

Figure I.13

Latin America (18 countries): comparison between income-based poverty and poverty on the basis of unmet basic needs, 2011[a]

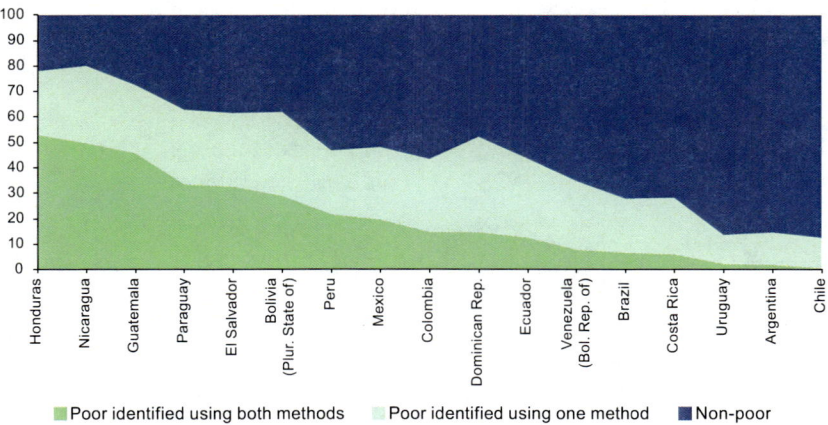

■ Poor identified using both methods   ■ Poor identified using one method   ■ Non-poor

Source: Economic Commission for Latin America and the Caribbean (ECLAC).
[a] Total monetary poverty is taken into consideration. Corresponds to 2011 except in El Salvador (2010), Guatemala (2006), Honduras (2010), México (2010), Nicaragua (2009) and Plurinational State of Bolivia (2009).

Thus, the addition of a monetary measure to a poverty index constructed on the basis of traditional UBN indicators would be justifiable because they would facilitate identification of the poor. Following this line of argument, Santos and others (2010) analysed multidimensional poverty in six countries of Latin America using a hybrid methodology, which added the World Bank measurement of US$ 2.15 per capita to a set of UBN indicators.

In this section, the hybrid methodology is applied to analyse the incidence of multidimensional poverty in 16 Latin American countries. The indicator of income below the indigence line is added to the core set of UBN indicators in order to determine how much this monetary measure contributes to the identification of poor people in different countries. This is done (i) by comparing the differences in the multidimensional estimates of poverty that result from adding a monetary dimension and an index based on traditional UBN indicators; and (ii) through a redundancy analysis of the monetary dimension and the non-monetary dimensions in the different countries.

Table I.4

Dimensions, indicators of deprivations and weightings for multidimensional poverty measurement using the hybrid methodology

Dimensions	Indicators of deprivations	Weighting
Water and sanitation		1/5
Lack of access to improved water sources	Urban areas: any source of water other than the mains Rural areas: an unprotected well, bottled water, mobile sources of water, river, water course, rain and others	1/10
Lack of a waste disposal system	Urban areas: not having a toilet or a waste disposal system connected to the sewerage system or to a sceptic tank Rural areas: not having a toilet or having a system for disposal of untreated waste	1/10
Energy [a]		1/5
Lack of electrical power	Households that do not have electricity	1/10
Cooking fuel that is harmful to human health	Households that use wood, charcoal or waste for cooking	1/10
Housing [b]		1/5
Substandard housing materials	Housing with a dirt floor, or substandard roofing or wall materials	1/10
Overcrowding	Three or more persons per room, rural and urban areas	1/10
Education		1/5
Non-attendance at school	In the home, at least one child of school age (6 to 17 years) does not attend school	1/10
Non attainment of a minimum level of education	In the household, no one aged 20 and over has attained a minimum level of education -Persons aged 20 to 59: have not completed lower secondary school -Persons 60 or over: have not completed primary school	1/10
Income [c]		1/5
	The household does not have sufficient income to pay for a basic food basket	1/5

Source: Economic Commission for Latin America and the Caribbean (ECLAC).
[a] The information concerns only fuel in the case of Argentina, and only electricity in the case of the Bolivarian Republic of Venezuela and Chile. This is why the indicators have a weighting of 1/5 in the relevant countries. Given that in general, deprivation of fuel is more widespread than deprivation of energy, total deprivation in the energy dimension may be underestimated for Bolivarian Republic of Venezuela and Chile.
[b] Brazil does not have information on the types of floor used in housing units.
[c] In Peru the official government estimate is used. The remainder are ECLAC estimates.

The indigence indicator was preferred partly because the total monetary poverty measurement could increase the possibility of double counting, given that part of the income poverty measurement that does not correspond to indigence is a proxy for the capability of households to satisfy non-food needs, including housing and education (Feres and Mancero, 2001), which are already covered by the core UBN indicators. Indigents for their part have a high probability, given their low income, of not meeting their nutritional needs, since these are a very important dimension of well-being, for which there is no information available in the surveys.[16]

The analysis of the ranking of countries based on different thresholds of deprivation show that aggregation of income does not reduce the robustness of the index, since, in general, the ranking remains constant for different values of k (although there are some minor changes in the order of the countries).

In order to make an accurate assessment of the impact of the inclusion on the dimension of income insufficiency, the value of the multidimensional threshold (k) was maintained at 20%. With this threshold, a person living in a household with two or more deprivations will still be identified as poor. In this regard, it should be noted that: (i) the probability of a person having two or more deprivations is higher than in the case of the exercise limited to UBN indicators, owing to the increase in the number of dimensions; and (ii) the intensity of poverty should fall (generally speaking), as a result of the lower weight of dimensions and indicators, which could "cushion" the increase in the adjusted headcount ratio (M0) that an additional dimension is expected to bring.

Table I.5 shows that in absolute terms, with the addition of income, the regional simple mean of the headcount ratio goes up by 4 percentage points (32.4% without income versus 36.4% with income), while the intensity of poverty decreases from 0.37 to 0.34. In relative terms, the regional mean increase in the headcount ratio amounts to 24.3%, while the intensity of poverty falls by as much as 8.7%. The adjusted headcount ratio (M0) increases by 12.7%, which seems to be due to the greater relative variation in the non-adjusted headcount ratio (H) than in the intensity of poverty (A).

Table I.5
Latin America (16 countries): changes in the multidimensional poverty index with and without income, 2011 [a]

Country	Incidence (H)			Intensity (A)			Adjusted incidence (M0)		
	Without income	With income	Percentage variation	Without income	With income	Percentage variation	Without income	With income	Percentage variation
Chile	2.2	5.1	134.9	0.298	0.243	-18.3	0.006	0.012	92.1
Uruguay	9.6	10.2	6.5	0.299	0.250	-16.3	0.029	0.026	-10.8
Argentina	11.0	12.3	11.8	0.299	0.249	-16.7	0.033	0.031	-6.1
Venezuela (Bolivarian Republic of)	13.2	20.9	58.4	0.341	0.302	-11.4	0.045	0.063	40.3
Brazil	15.5	18.4	19.0	0.293	0.262	-10.7	0.045	0.048	6.3
Costa Rica	15.5	19.9	28.7	0.297	0.274	-7.6	0.046	0.055	18.9
Ecuador	21.0	28.4	35.1	0.344	0.315	-8.3	0.072	0.089	23.9
Colombia	23.9	27.9	16.7	0.379	0.346	-8.8	0.090	0.096	6.5
Dominican Republic	24.8	36.7	47.8	0.347	0.315	-9.3	0.086	0.116	34.1
Mexico	31.9	35.4	10.9	0.365	0.344	-5.8	0.116	0.122	4.5
Peru	40.5	40.8	0.6	0.437	0.379	-13.3	0.177	0.155	-12.7
Paraguay	46.6	52.1	12.0	0.378	0.386	2.0	0.176	0.201	14.2
El Salvador	48.0	50.3	4.9	0.441	0.405	-8.1	0.211	0.204	-3.6
Bolivia (Plurinational State of)	48.1	53.0	10.3	0.467	0.430	-8.0	0.225	0.228	1.5
Honduras	63.4	68.6	8.3	0.464	0.474	2.1	0.294	0.325	10.5
Guatemala	63.6	65.9	3.6	0.437	0.429	-1.9	0.278	0.283	1.6
Nicaragua	71.4	73.7	3.1	0.546	0.506	-7.4	0.390	0.373	-4.5
Simple average	**32.4**	**36.4**	**24.3**	**0.378**	**0.348**	**-8.7**	**0.137**	**0.143**	**12.7**

Source: Economic Commission for Latin America and the Caribbean (ECLAC).
[a] Corresponds to 2011 except in the case of El Salvador (2010), Guatemala (2006), Honduras (2010), Mexico (2010), Nicaragua (2009) and Plurinational State of Bolivia (2009).

---

[16] It is understood, however, that the availability of resources for food consumption does not necessarily mean actual consumption of these (nor does it guarantee that the individuals are well nourished).

The impact of the aggregation of income tends to be less in countries that have a higher incidence and intensity of poverty in the measurement that includes only UBN indicators, and is greater in countries in the opposite situation. Thus, in countries with headcount ratios (H) that take into account only UBN indicators above 30%, the impact of introducing income never exceeds 12% (percentage variation), while in countries where this ratio is below 30%, the mean increase is 40%, although Argentina and Uruguay should be treated as exceptions (percentage variations below 12%).

An alternative way of determining how much the incorporation of a monetary dimension contributes to an index of non-monetary deprivations is the P test, which measures similarity or the strength of consistencies between two dimensions used for measuring poverty.[17] In terms of interpretation, a very high value for P means that the two indicators tend to identify the same population as poor, while a very low value means that they tend to identify different people as poor.

Thus, the degree of similarity (P) is calculated for income and the different non-monetary dimensions considered in the index based only on UBN indicators. Table I.6 shows that in general, the redundancy of income with non-monetary dimensions tends to be low. In only 13.5% of combinations (18 out of 133 cells with information), the value of P exceeds 70%.

Table I.6
Latin America (16 countries): similarity between indigence and non-monetary deprivations, 2011[a]
(Value P of similarity, percentages[b])

	Housing	Overcrowding	Water	Sanitation	Electricity	Fuel	Educational attainment	Attendance at school	Average
Chile	7	24	7	7	12	-	25	6	13
Uruguay	9	19	3	12	2	7	75	25	19
Argentina	9	22	19	24	-	6	32	7	17
Venezuela (Bolivarian Republic of)	32	34	25	35	28	-	48	21	32
Brazil	26	18	15	35	30	22	67	12	28
Costa Rica	35	25	15	13	48	24	75	16	31
Ecuador	33	38	27	36	30	39	62	26	36
Colombia	37	36	24	34	35	49	68	20	38
Dominican Republic	38	49	39	33	43	36	47	27	39
Mexico	38	49	31	35	52	50	80	26	45
Peru	88	31	55	32	47	95	72	10	54
Paraguay	66	68	35	43	69	77	60	52	59
El Salvador	46	53	32	45	40	64	83	32	49
Bolivia (Plurinational State of)	49	37	58	52	53	56	63	30	50
Honduras	78	62	66	62	79	84	86	62	73
Guatemala	67	74	47	40	59	14	95	46	55
Nicaragua	59	54	47	76	51	86	76	42	61
Simple average	42	41	32	36	42	47	66	27	41

Source: Economic Commission for Latin America and the Caribbean (ECLAC).
[a] Corresponds to 2011 except in the case of El Salvador (2010), Guatemala (2006), Honduras (2010), Mexico (2010), Nicaragua (2009) and Plurinational State of Bolivia (2009).
[b] When P =0.10, it indicates that 10% of persons who suffer a deprivation in the indicator with the lowest gross incidence also suffer deprivation in the other indicator.

On average, the most redundant non-monetary dimension is the educational attainment of adults (66%), and the least consistent dimensions are attendance at school (27%), water (32%) and sanitation (36%).

Figure I.14 verifies that income redundancy with respect to non-monetary dimensions, measured as a regional simple average is greater in countries whose headcount ratios that contemplate only UBN indicators are higher (Spearman's Rho non-parametric correlation =0,953).

---

[17] For further details on the similarity index, see Alkire, Ballón and Vaz (2013).

Figure I.14
**Latin America (17 countries): correlation between the headcount ratio (H)
without income and average redundancy of income, 2011** [a]
(Percentages)

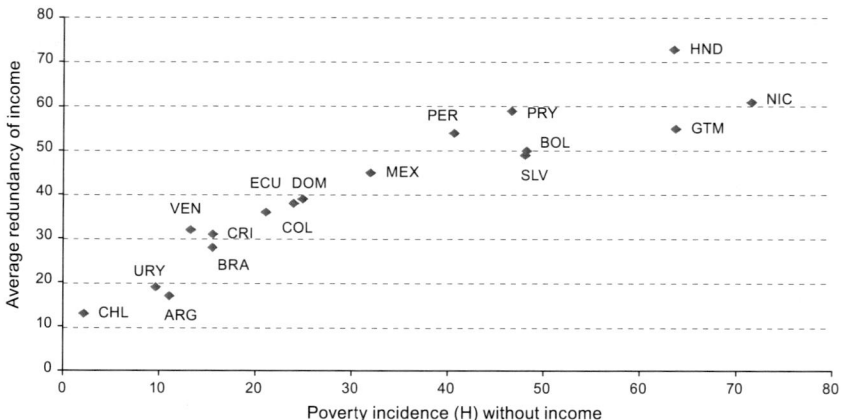

Source: Economic Commission for Latin America and the Caribbean (ECLAC).
[a] Corresponds to 2011 except in the case of El Salvador (2010), Guatemala (2010), Honduras (2010), Mexico (2010), Nicaragua (2009) and Plurinational State of Bolivia (2009).

To sum up, the redundancy between income and non-monetary dimensions is low, which indicates that the aggregation of a monetary dimension to a multidimensional poverty index has the potential to reduce information vacuums and reduce exclusion errors. This potential is greater in the countries where poverty measured using a multidimensional index based on traditional UBN indicators is less prevalent.

4. Poverty measurement with addition of indicators of exclusion or vulnerability

In the previous sections of this chapter, it has been shown that some countries in the region have multidimensional incidences of poverty that are low and decrease over time. This may indicate that the traditional UBN indicators, treated separately or together with a monetary measure of extreme deprivation are losing the capacity to identify the poor, especially in countries where the living conditions of the population have improved significantly. Thus, it has been proposed that information on deprivations should be incorporated in other areas in order to have a poverty measurement more appropriate to the reality in these countries (ECLAC, 2011).

One option is to include deprivations that reflect exclusion from institutions. Expanding on the idea put forward by Kaztman (2001), this approach would make it possible to integrate social structure as an explicit element of poverty measurement.

The outcome of the segmentation of the production structure is that the poor obtain informal jobs and do not have access to social protection (ECLAC, 2012a). Even though measures of social security membership and access (health insurance, membership in a social security system and receipt of a pension) have not been used by ECLAC in its poverty measurements, they have been taken into account in the multidimensional exercises conducted by Mexico and Colombia.

Another indicator that may be estimated on the basis of available information concerns young people neither in paid employment nor in education or training (NEETs). The greater the delinkage from institutions that provide structure in the transition from youth to adulthood, the greater the risk of poverty and exclusion (ECLAC, 2011). An alternative measure to institutional non-membership is long-term unemployment, but this indicator could be inappropriate for the region, given the way the labour market functions in Latin America.[18]

---

[18] An empirical study of this indicator resulted in very low incidences.

In any event, aspects of social structure should also be gauged in relative terms. The receipt of poor quality education and social protection and the fact of living in segregated areas may be interpreted as indicators of poverty, especially in a society dominated by mercantilism where the quality of services received by people or the neighbourhood of the city where they reside is measured by their capacity to pay (Kaztman, 2010). However, the available information is too scant to allow measurements of this type for a sufficient number of countries in the region.

Including deprivations relating to institutional coverage goes beyond the conventional notion of poverty and it may be assumed that the addition of such indicators would increase the number of errors of inclusion. This risk decreases, however, when using an aggregation scheme in which the presence of one deprivation is not sufficient for identifying a person as poor. Furthermore, some of the indicators included here serve as a proxy, albeit an imperfect one, for health and employment dimensions, which were not measured in the two indices analysed in the foregoing sections and which are relevant aspects of well-being.

There are some difficulties in measuring young people who are neither in paid employment nor in education or training and the lack of affiliation to social protection. In the first case, the presence of at least one young person in the household who was neither in education or paid employment was taken as a threshold of deprivation because, with the alternative options (half or all), the more young people in the household, the less feasible it would be to classify a household as deprived. In addition, the indicators of membership in a social protection scheme is not measured in the same way in the different countries, thus the comparability is impaired.

Table I.7
Dimensions, indicators of deprivation and weightings for measuring poverty in the broad sense

Dimensions	Indicators of deprivations	Weighting
Water and sanitation		1/6
Lack of access to improved water sources	Urban areas: any source of water except a public system Rural areas: an unprotected well, bottled water, running water sources, river, water course, rain or other	1/12
Lack of a human waste disposal system	Urban areas: not having a toilet or waste disposal system connected to a sewerage system or sceptic tank Rural areas: not having a toilet or having an untreated waste disposal system	1/12
Energy [a]		1/6
Lack of electrical power	Households that have no electricity	1/12
Cooking fuel that is harmful to human health	Households that use wood, charcoal or waste matter as cooking fuel	1/12
Housing [b]		1/6
Substandard housing materials	Housing unit with a dirt floor, or substandard materials for roofing or walls	1/12
Overcrowding	Three or more persons per room, rural and urban areas	1/12
Education		1/6
Non-attendance at school	At least one child of school age (6-17 years of age) in the household who does not attend school	1/12
Non-attainment of a minimum education level	In the household, no one aged 30 or over has attained a minimum level of education Individuals 30- 59 years of age: have not completed lower secondary school Individuals 60 years or over: have not completed primary school	1/12
Income [c]		1/6
Insufficient income	The household does not have sufficient resources to buy a basic food basket	1/6
Exclusion or vulnerability		1/6
Young people neither in employment nor in education or training	At least one young person aged 18 to 29 in the household is neither in paid employment or in education or training	1/12
Lack of social protection [d]	In the household, at least two of the following situations are observed: i) No one in a health risk group has health insurance. Risk groups: children under the age of five, women aged 15- 49 and older persons aged 60 or over ii) No employed person in the household has membership in a pension fund iii) No older person in the household has a pension or retirement benefit. Older persons: men aged 65 or over; women aged 60 or over	1/12

Source: Economic Commission for Latin America and the Caribbean (ECLAC).
[a] For the Bolivarian Republic of Venezuela and Chile, information is provided for electrical power only, while for Argentina, the information is for fuel only. This is why these indicators have a weighting of 1/5 in these countries. Given that in general, deprivation of fuel is more widespread than deprivation of energy, total deprivation in the energy dimension may be underestimated for Bolivarian Republic of Venezuela and Chile. Argentina is a special case since deprivation of fuel is very low in that country.
[b] In Brazil information is available only for housing materials.
[c] In the case of Peru, the estimate for indigence is the national estimate. The remainder are ECLAC estimates.
[d] In the Bolivarian Republic of Venezuela, information was available for two of the indicators. Two deprivations were used as an indicator. In Brazil, no enquiry is made as to health insurance, but since there is universal health coverage, the entire at-risk population is assumed to be covered.

As in the previous cases, an equal weighting is assigned to all the different dimensions, which means providing a lower weight to indicators of vulnerability or exclusion in comparison with the added weighting of the remaining dimensions.

Hereinafter, the new index, which includes the traditional UBN indicators, the indigence measure and the two additional indicators will be referred to as the "broad poverty index". (poverty in the broad sense of the term). As regards the robustness of the new index, in general the order of countries tends to be maintained even when the values of k vary.

Unlike the earlier indices, in this case, a threshold k equal to 10% is used, since the value of 20% does not guarantee that subjects suffering deprivation in two or more areas will be classified as poor. While this new threshold ensures comparability with the earlier exercises in relation to the minimum number of deprivations that a subject must experience in order to be identified as poor, the increase in the number of dimensions and indicators raises the probability of a member of the population being classified as poor.

Tables I.8 and I.9 reveal the impact of the inclusion of additional dimensions, considering the poverty incidence (H) and the adjusted headcount ratio (M0). When the broad poverty measure is compared with the index constructed solely on the basis of the traditional UBN indicators, the headcount ratio increases by 16.4 percentage points. The difference between the incidence of broad poverty and the incidence based on the index including UBN indicators and the indigence measure is 12 percentage points.

Table I.8
Latin America (16 countries): impact of the inclusion of additional dimensions on the poverty incidence (H), 2011 [a]
(Percentages)

Country	Unmet basic needs (UBN) only (1)	Hybrid methodology (2)	Broad poverty indicator (3)	Percentage variation (3/1)	Percentage variation (3/2)
Chile	2.2	5.1	11.2	419.2	119.6
Uruguay	9.6	10.2	15.5	61.3	52.0
Argentina	11.0	12.3	24.2	120	96.7
Venezuela (Bolivarian Republic of)	13.2	20.9	30.4	130.8	45.5
Brazil	15.5	18.4	26.1	69.1	41.8
Costa Rica	15.5	19.9	29.9	93.3	50.3
Ecuador	21.0	28.4	45.1	114.8	58.8
Colombia	23.9	27.9	39.4	64.9	41.2
Dominican Republic	24.8	36.7	53.0	113.4	44.4
Mexico	31.9	35.4	48.5	52.0	37.0
Peru	40.5	40.8	53.1	30.9	30.1
Paraguay	46.6	52.1	70.3	50.9	34.9
El Salvador	48.0	50.3	66.8	39.3	32.8
Bolivia (Plurinational State of)	48.1	53.0	65.6	36.4	23.8
Honduras	63.4	68.6	80.6	27.2	17.5
Guatemala	63.6	65.9	79.0	24.2	19.9
Simple average	29.9	34.1	46.2	90.5	46.6

Source: Economic Commission for Latin America and the Caribbean (ECLAC).
[a] Corresponds to 2011 except in the case of El Salvador (2010), Guatemala (2010), Honduras (2010), Mexico (2010), Nicaragua (2009) and Plurinational State of Bolivia (2009).

When the different country scores are obtained using the broad poverty index and the UBN indicators, the absolute increase is highest in the Dominican Republic (28.2 percentage points), Ecuador (24.1 percentage points) and Paraguay (23.7 percentage points), and the lowest absolute increases are seen in Uruguay and Chile. However, the latter country is the one that shows the highest relative change (419%). Other substantial relative increases occur in Bolivarian Republic of Venezuela (131%), Argentina (120%), Ecuador (114%) and Dominican Republic (113%). There tends to be a greater relative increase in the countries with very low poverty rates based solely on UBN indicators. This situation also occurs when the incidence of broad poverty is compared with the rates obtained using critical deprivations, coupled with insufficient income.

Table I.9
**Latin America (16 countries): impact of the inclusion of additional dimensions
on the adjusted headcount ratio (M0), 2011** [a]

Country	Unmet basic needs (UBN) only (1)	Hybrid methodology (2)	Broad poverty indicator (3)	Percentage variation (3/1)	Percentage variation (3/2)
Chile	0.6	1.2	2.3	251.4	87.9
Uruguay	2.9	2.6	3.2	12.5	24.1
Argentina	3.3	3.1	5.5	66.7	77.4
Venezuela (Bolivarian Republic of)	4.5	6.3	7.7	72.1	22.8
Brazil	4.5	4.8	5.7	26.9	19.8
Costa Rica	4.6	5.5	7.0	52.0	27.1
Ecuador	7.2	8.9	12.4	71.6	39.1
Colombia	9.0	9.6	11.3	24.5	29.0
Dominican Republic	8.6	11.6	15.0	73.6	17.3
Mexico	11.6	12.2	14.3	23.0	17.4
Peru	17.7	15.5	17.2	-2.9	24.0
Paraguay	17.6	20.1	24.9	41.6	11.0
El Salvador	21.1	20.4	24.6	16.4	20.6
Bolivia (Plurinational State of)	22.5	22.8	24.3	8.2	6.6
Honduras	29.4	32.5	36.2	22.8	11.3
Guatemala	27.8	28.3	31.6	13.5	11.5
Simple average	**12.1**	**12.8**	**15.2**	**48.4**	**27.9**

Source: Economic Commission for Latin America and the Caribbean (ECLAC).
[a] Corresponds to 2011 except in the case of El Salvador (2010), Guatemala (2010), Honduras (2010), Mexico (2010), Nicaragua (2009) and Plurinational State of Bolivia (2009).

As regards M0, the trends are similar to those observed for the headcount ratio (H), but nuanced owing to the fall in poverty intensity (A) associated with the use of more dimensions and indicators. Some cases warrant special attention: for example Peru, where M0 for the broad poverty measure is lower than that obtained for the measure limited to UBN indicators. This is partly because of the sharp fall in poverty intensity in this country (relative variation of -26%), when the results of the broad poverty measure are compared with those based on UBN alone. This fall is due mainly to the low contribution of the monetary dimension to the increase in the total poverty incidence, since in Peru, almost the entire difference between the headcount ratio (H) of broad poverty and the index based on UBN alone is estimated to be attributable to dimensions of social exclusion.

As regards policy design, one of the most important applications of the methodology of Alkire y Foster (2007, 2011) is a breakdown that reveals the contribution (in relative and absolute terms) of each dimension to the adjusted headcount ratio (M0). This breakdown was used for the broad poverty index because this index is more comprehensive in terms of policies and sectors involved than the indices discussed in the previous sections.

As shown in table I.10 and figure I.15, the added contribution of the dimensions of housing (overcrowding and materials used), energy (electricity and cooking fuel) and water and sanitation tends to be greater in countries with the highest incidences of broad poverty. For example, the simple average of the relative contribution of housing dimensions, energy and water and sanitation in countries with headcount ratios above 60% amounts to 39.8% of total broad poverty, while in the countries with broad poverty ratios below 30%, the simple average of the contribution of these dimensions is 26.6%. These differences by groups of countries are basically attributable to the dimensions of housing and energy. Nevertheless, caution must be exercised in interpreting the differences in energy, since in three of the five countries included in the group with a low poverty rate, only one of the two indicators included in the energy dimension was covered, which may imply an under-estimation of the deprivation associated with that dimension.

Table I.10

Latin America (16 countries): relative contribution of each of the dimensions to total broad poverty measurement (M0) by country, 2011 [a]

(Percentages)

Country	Housing materials	Over-crowding	Water	Sanitation	Electricity	Fuel	Income	Educational attainment	School attendance	NEETs	Social protection
Argentina	1.7	8.3	11.1	13.1	-	1.0	5.6	19.6	4.8	17.4	17.4
Bolivia (Plurinational State of)	7.7	6.4	10.6	10.6	4.3	7.2	15.5	13.8	7.6	4.4	11.9
Brazil	0.8	4.8	8.2	16.4	0.2	4.4	14.6	29.1	5.5	15.3	0.7
Chile	1.2	1.5	6.1	2.2	3.9		23.1	27.0	4.9	23.8	6.2
Colombia	5.4	4.0	7.0	5.6	2.3	12.0	15.8	22.6	6.1	11.3	7.8
Costa Rica	1.5	3.3	8.0	0.9	0.9	8.7	17.4	30.3	7.3	15.6	6.0
Dominican Republic	1.4	1.3	13.6	6.9	1.3	6.1	22.6	18.6	2.9	10.9	14.4
Ecuador	3.6	4.3	8.2	4.5	1.9	3.5	18.6	22.4	5.0	8.4	19.6
El Salvador	7.0	8.0	5.9	8.2	2.5	9.5	11.2	18.2	4.8	7.3	17.4
Guatemala	9.5	11.3	3.8	5.8	4.8	0.8	15.3	17.7	7.9	7.0	16.0
Honduras	4.9	6.6	2.8	3.9	4.9	13.7	19.9	15.4	6.0	6.6	15.4
Mexico	2.8	10.1	4.2	5.8	0.7	9.6	15.2	23.4	7.0	10.5	10.6
Paraguay	4.2	3.4	6.8	9.9	0.5	13.8	18.7	14.5	3.2	6.4	18.6
Peru	15.5	4.9	10.3	7.3	5.1	16.2	6.2	16.2	1.9	6.3	10.1
Uruguay	1.4	4.7	4.6	4.1	2.8	7.0	5.6	34.8	15.1	18.5	1.5
Venezuela (Bolivarian Republic of)	5.6	7.5	5.0	6.5	0.7		25.2	22.0	7.6	16.0	4.0

Source: Economic Commission for Latin America and the Caribbean (ECLAC).

[a] The percentages add up to 100 in each of the rows (countries). Correspond to 2011 except in El Salvador (2010), Guatemala (2010), Honduras (2010), Mexico (2010), Nicaragua (2009) and Plurinational State of Bolivia (2009).

Figure I.15

Latin America (15 countries): relative weight of selected dimensions of the total broad poverty measure (M0), 2011 [a]

(Percentages)

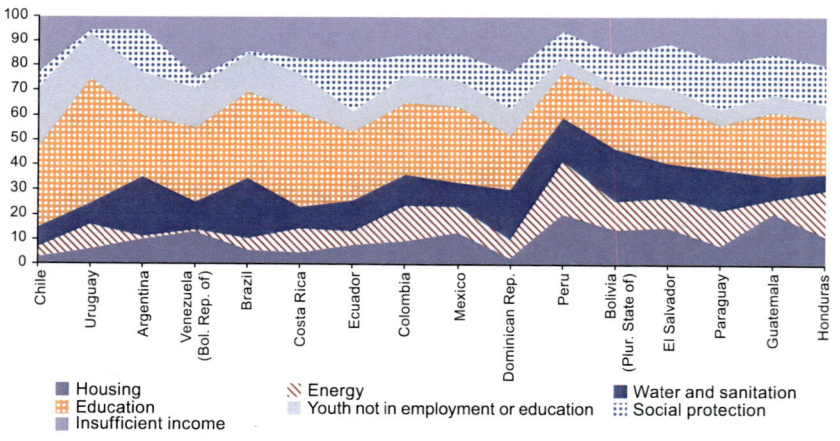

Source: Economic Commission for Latin America and the Caribbean (ECLAC).

[a] Housing: includes the sum of contributions of the subdimensions of materials and overcrowding. Energy: electricity and cooking fuel. Education: includes attendance at school by children and adolescents and educational attainment of adults. Protection: membership in a health insurance system and in a pension fund and receipt of some retirement benefit or pension. Corresponds to 2011 except in the case of El Salvador (2010), Guatemala (2010), Honduras (2010), Mexico (2010), Nicaragua (2009) and Plurinational State of Bolivia (2009).

When the added contribution of the dimensions of housing, energy and water and sanitation are broken down, these dimensions are shown to have a greater weight in total poverty in Peru (59.3%), Plurinational State of Bolivia (46.7%) and El Salvador (41.1%), and much less impact in Chile (14.9%), Costa Rica (23.3%) and Uruguay (24.6%).

The contribution of education (school attendance by children and educational attainment of adults) to total broad poverty tends to be greater in countries where the poverty rate is below 30%. The education factor is seen to represent a greater contribution to total poverty in Uruguay (49.9%) and in Costa Rica (37.6%). The greater part of the weight of education is attributable to non-attainment of the threshold of educational achievement among adults. The contribution of school attendance among children and adolescents is much lower.

The income factor has a greater impact on total poverty in Bolivarian Republic of Venezuela (25.2%) and Chile (23.1%), but less in Argentina (5.6%), Uruguay (5.6%) and Peru (6.2%). There do not appear to be substantial differences in the contribution of income to total poverty based on the poverty rate of the countries.

Membership in or access to social protection systems has a greater impact on total poverty in countries with broad poverty rates above 60% (simple average of 15.9%) and less in countries with headcount ratios below 30% (simple average of 6.4%). The opposite occurs with young people neither in paid employment nor in education or training whose impact on total poverty is much greater in countries with poverty rates below 30% (18.1%) than in countries with poverty rates above 60% (6.3%).

Thus, the social protection dimension carries greater weight in countries with the highest broad poverty rates, which may be attributed to the nature of the indicators included in the analysis, which measure basically membership in social protection systems. This highlights the need to include indicators that reflect the quality of the services to which the population has access in countries that already have high levels of affiliation. The fact that young people neither in paid employment nor in education or training account increasingly for overall poverty in countries with lower rates raises the question of whether poverty or vulnerability to fall into poverty is being effectively measured by this indicator.

In short, the results of the analysis indicate that not only are there differences in the extent and intensity of multidimensional poverty between countries, but also the dimensions that have the greatest impact on overall poverty are different. The latter means that the policy configurations and the architectures and institutional responsibilities should be different.

5. Final remarks

In conclusion, given the renewed interest in using a multidimensional approach to poverty, it is an opportune moment to redefine what is understood by poverty and to decide which dimensions of well-being are essential for identifying the poor.

Even though the studies presented in this edition of the *Social Panorama of Latin America* consider only some of the basic elements for a measurement of this type, these elements are sufficient for illustrating the potential and the challenges posed by multidimensional measures. Even in its most traditional application, limited to unmet basic needs, it can be demonstrated that deprivations such as lack of access to drinking water or sanitation continue to affect a significant number of people in the region, which raises the question as to whether public policies for overcoming poverty are placing sufficient emphasis on achieving minimum standards and not just on monetary transfers.

The results of the study carried out support the idea that the traditional UBN indicators provide a basis for advancing towards the preparation of a broader multidimensional index for identifying the poor based on a more comprehensive and all-embracing notion of well-being. The aggregation of a monetary measure of deprivation to a multidimensional index based on UBNs can be useful for filling information gaps especially in countries that have lower income-based and UBN-based headcount ratios.

Since traditional UBN indicators and monetary measures of extreme deprivation seem to be progressively less able to identify the poor in countries with better standards of living in the region, the answer may be to research new dimensions and indicators. A different approach (one not used in this study) may be to test more demanding thresholds for the indicators already available. As stated previously, all this calls for discussions and agreements on the definition of poverty and its dimensions, in the light of a more comprehensive notion of well-being.

The region clearly faces a major challenge in terms of developing its information sources in order to obtain a more thorough measurement and characterization of poverty from a multidimensional perspective. Whatever the conceptual and methodological approach used, one basic condition for a more thorough multidimensional measure is to increase the availability of data and to improve their quality.

C. Income distribution

The gap in income distribution continued to narrow, prolonging a trend first observed a decade ago. Indeed, in several countries the reductions noted between 2008 and 2012 have been sharper than those observed between 2002 and 2008.

The sharp inequality in income distribution is one of the features of Latin America in the international context. The most recent data available indicate that the poorest quintile (that is, the 20% lowest-income households) receive on average 5% of total income, with shares that vary between less than 4% (in the Dominican Republic, Honduras and Paraguay) and 10% (in Uruguay), while the share of total income in the richest quintile averages 47%, ranging from 35% (in Uruguay) to 55% (in Brazil) (see figure I.16).

Figure I.16
Latin America (17 countries): share of total income of the poorest and richest quintiles, 2002-2012
(Percentages)

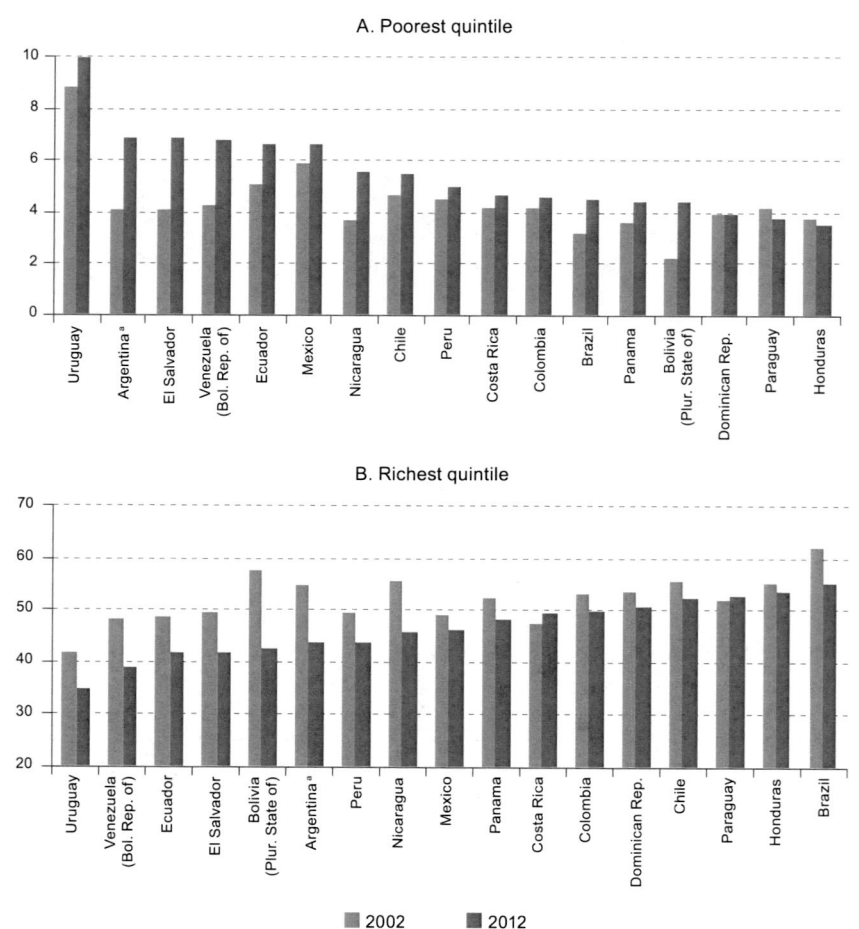

A. Poorest quintile

B. Richest quintile

■ 2002   ■ 2012

Source: Economic Commission for Latin America and the Caribbean (ECLAC), on the basis of special tabulations of data from household surveys conducted in the relevant countries.
ᵃ Urban areas.

As shown in various editions of the *Social Panorama of Latin America* and illustrated in numerous studies on income distribution in the region, this indicator has shown improved over the past 10 years. These changes have occurred gradually and are scarcely perceptible in year-on-year variations, but they are evident in a comparison over longer periods. If 2002 information is used as a reference, the most recent figures show that in eight countries the poorest quintile saw its share of total income increase by at least one percentage point. Meanwhile in nine countries, the relative share of the richest quintile declined by 5 or more percentage points. This group's share continues to be more than 50% in five countries, compared with 2002, when this applied to 10 countries.

The changes observed in the extreme quintiles' share of total income were also reflected in the variations in the inequality indices. Of the 13 countries for which information was available for 2011 or 2012, 12 recorded a simple average reduction in the Gini coefficient of 1% per year. The rate of reduction of inequality was more than 1% per year in Argentina, Bolivarian Republic of Venezuela, Brazil, Peru, and Uruguay, and was at least 0.5% per year in Chile, Colombia, Ecuador and Panama.

As illustrated in figure I.17, the trend towards a reduction in inequality has been a little more pronounced in the last four years of the period under review. This shows the percentage variation in the Gini, Theil and Atkinson indices (with an inequality aversion parameter equal to 1.5) for the subperiods 2002-2008 and 2008-2012, considering as the mid-point the year 2008, when the international financial crisis unfolded. Indeed, eight countries showed sharper declines in the inequality indices in the second subperiod than in the first. Of these, the Plurinational State of Bolivia and Uruguay had the most significant reductions, of around 4% per year in the case of the Gini coefficient. This group also included Brazil, Ecuador and Mexico, which along with the Bolivarian Republic of Venezuela saw a slight increase in their inequality coefficients in 2012 (see annex table I-A3). Costa Rica, Panama and Paraguay also experienced an increase in their inequality index in the second subperiod, although only in Costa Rica does the final figure show an increase.

It should be noted that the three inequality indices show a high degree of consistency in the trends described with just a few exceptions. If the countries are ranked by order of magnitude of the reduction in inequality during the second subperiod, Mexico is placed in a better position on the Theil and Atkinson index than on the Gini index, while the opposite occurs with Brazil.

Lastly, movements in the distribution of labour income should be examined since this is the primary source of household funds and, as such, has a significant impact on overall income distribution. The Gini coefficient of total household income and the labour income of employed persons (aged 15 years or over) are seen to follow a similar pattern. Indeed, the simple correlation between the variations in the two variables is 0.89 in the period 2002-2012 and 0.93 in the period 2008-2012 (see figure I.18).

Figure I.17
Latin America (selected countries): annual variation in inequality indices,[a] 2002-2008 and 2008-2012
(Percentages)

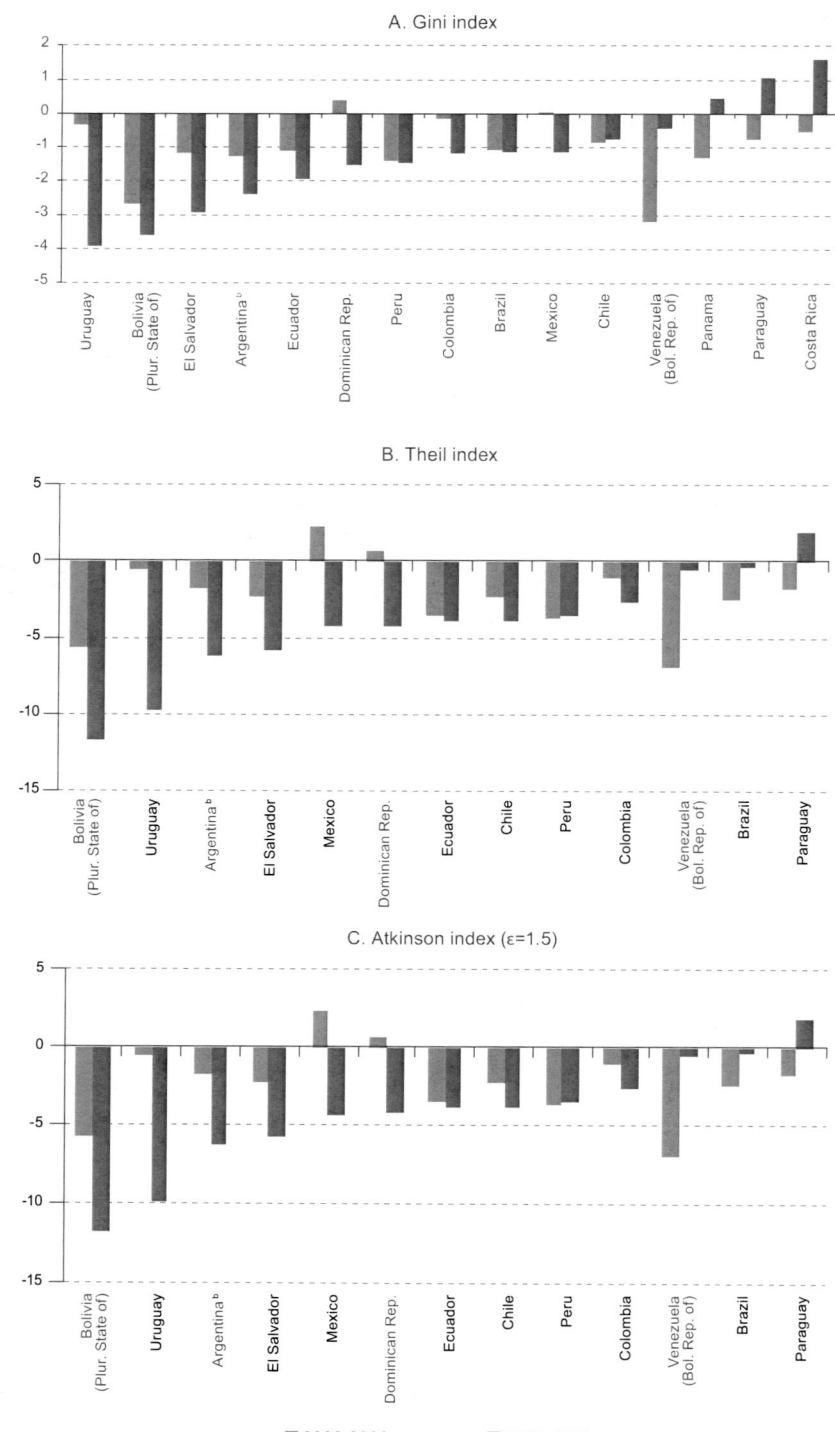

A. Gini index

B. Theil index

C. Atkinson index (ε=1.5)

■ 2002-2008   ■ 2008-2012

Source: Economic Commission for Latin America and the Caribbean (ECLAC), on the basis of special tabulations of data from household surveys conducted in the relevant countries.
[a] Includes only countries with information available up to 2011 or 2012. The countries are ranked according to the variation in the second subperiod (2008-2012).
[b] Urban areas.

Figure I.18
Latin America (15 countries): annual variation in the Gini coefficient of total income and labour income
(Percentages)

A. 2002-2012

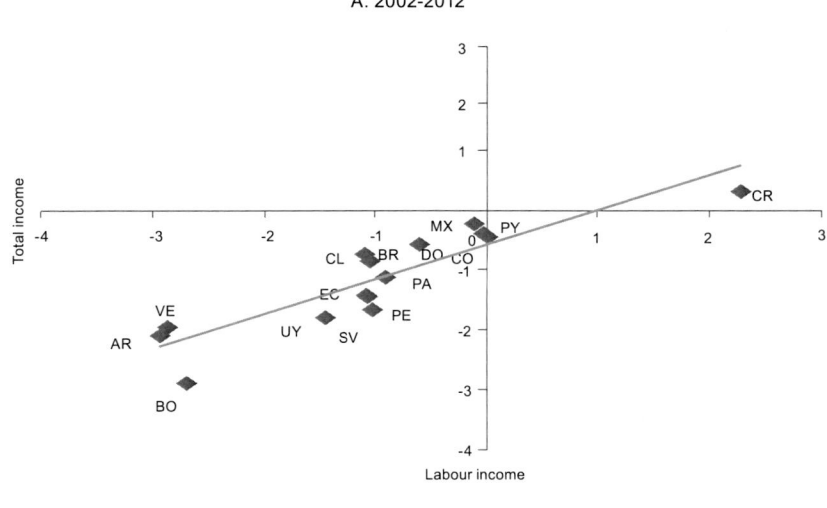

B. 2008-2012

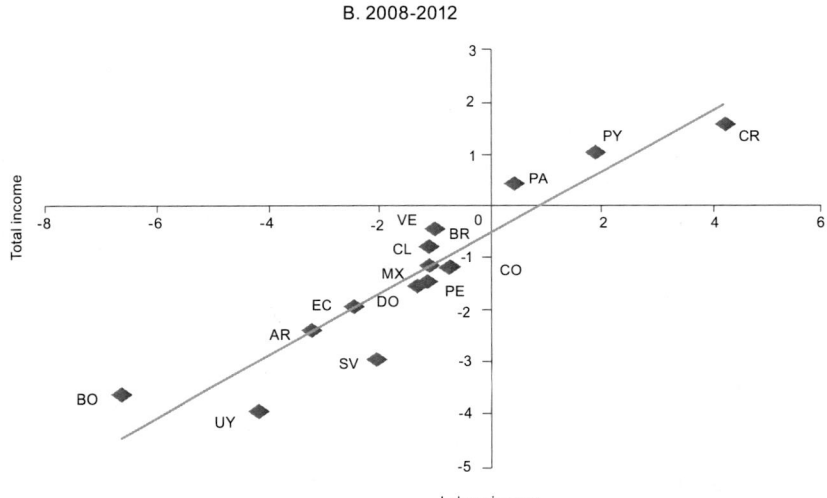

Source: Economic Commission for Latin America and the Caribbean (ECLAC), on the basis of special tabulations of data from household surveys conducted in the respective countries.

Bibliography

Alkire, Sabina and María Emma Santos (2013), "Measuring acute poverty in the developing world: robustness and scope of the multidimensional poverty index", *OPHI Working Paper Series*, No. 59, Oxford, Oxford Poverty & Human Development Initiative (OPHI).

___(2010), *Acute Multidimensional Poverty: A New Index for Developing Countries* [online] http://www.fundacionpobreza. cl/biblioteca-archivos/acute_multidimensional _poverty.pdf.

Alkire, Sabina, Paola Ballón and Ana Vaz (2013), *Asociación y similitud*, Managua [online] http://www.ophi.org.uk/ wp-content/uploads/Asociacion-y-similitud.pdf.

Alkire, Sabina and James Foster (2008), "Counting and multidimensional poverty measurement", *OPHI Working Paper*, No. 7, Oxford, Oxford Poverty & Human Development Initiative (OPHI) [online] http://www.ophi.org.uk/ wp-content/uploads/ophi-wp7.pdf.

___(2011), "Counting and multidimensional poverty measurement", *Journal of Public Economics*, vol. 95, No. 7-8, Amsterdam, Elsevier.

Angulo, Roberto, Beatriz Yadira and Renata Pardo (2013), *Multidimensional Poverty in Colombia, 1997-2010* [online] https://www.iser.essex.ac.uk/publications/working-papers/iser/2013-03.pdf.

Bárcena, Alicia (2010), "Palabras de señora Alicia Bárcena, Secretaria Ejecutiva de la CEPAL, en la inauguración del Seminario Internacional "Medición Multidimensional de la Pobreza en América Latina" [online] http://www.eclac. cl/prensa/noticias/discursossecretaria/2/39502/13y14de_mayo2010DiscursoSeminarioInternMedimultidiPobrAL.pdf.

Battistón, Diego and others (2013), "Income and beyond: multidimensional poverty in six Latin American countries", *Social Indicators Research*, vol. 112, No. 2, Springer.

Beccaria, Luis and Alberto Minujín (1985), "Métodos alternativos para medir la evolución del tamaño de la pobreza", *Documentos de trabajo*, No. 6, Buenos Aires, National Institute of Statistics and Censuses.

Boltvinik, Julio (1992), "El método de medición integrada de la pobreza. Una propuesta para su desarrollo", *Comercio Exterior*, vol. 42, No. 4, Mexico City, D.F., Banco Nacional de Comercio Exterior (BANCOMEXT).

___(1990), *Pobreza y necesidades básicas, conceptos y métodos de medición*, Caracas, UNDP Regional Project for Overcoming Poverty, United Nations Development Programme (UNDP).

Bourguignon, Francois and Satya Chakravarty (2003), "The measurement of multidimensional poverty", *Journal of Economic Inequality*, vol. 1, No. 1, Springer.

Calvo, Juan and others (2013), *Atlas sociodemográfico y de la desigualdad del Uruguay. Las necesidades básicas insatisfechas a partir del Censo 2011*, Montevideo, Trilce.

CONEVAL (National Council for the Evaluation of Social Development Policy) (2010), *Informe de pobreza multidimensional en México 2008* [online] http://www.coneval.gob.mx/rw/resource/coneval/med_pobreza/ Informe_pobreza_multidimensional/Informe_de_Pobreza_Multidimensional_en_Mexico_2008_.pdf.

Duflo, Esther, Michael Greenstone and Hanna Rema (2008), "Indoor air pollution, health and economic well-being", *SAPIENS*, vol. 1, No. 1 [online] http://sapiens.revues.org/130.

ECLAC (Economic Commission for Latin America and the Caribbean) (2013a), *Social Panorama of Latin America 2012* (LC/G.2557-P), Santiago, Chile. United Nations publication, Sales No. E.13.II.G.6.

___(2013b), *Economic Survey of Latin America and the Caribbean 2013* (LC/G.2574-P), Santiago, Chile. United Nations publication, Sales No. E.13.II.G.3.

___(2012a), *Structural Change for Equality: An Integrated Approach to Development* (LC/G.2524(SES.34/3)), Santiago, Chile.

___(2012b), *Preliminary Overview of the Economies of Latin America and the Caribbean 2012* (LC/G.2555-P), Santiago, Chile. United Nations publication, Sales No. E.13.II.G.2.

___(2011), *Social Panorama of Latin America 2010* (LC/G.2481-P), Santiago, Chile. United Nations publication, Sales No. E.11.II.G.6.

ECLAC/ILO (Economic Commission for Latin America and the Caribbean/International Labour Organization) (2013), "Advances and challenges in measuring decent work", *The Employment Situation in Latin America and the Caribbean*, No. 8, Santiago, Chile, May.

Feres, Juan Carlos and Xavier Mancero (2001), "El método de las necesidades básicas insatisfechas (NBI) y sus aplicaciones en América Latina", *Estudios Estadísticos y Prospectivos series*, No. 7 (LC/L.1491-P), Santiago, Chile, Economic Commission for Latin America and the Caribbean (ECLAC). United Nations publication, Sales No. S.01.II.G.31.

Kaztman, Rubén (2011), *Infancia en América Latina: Privaciones habitacionales y desarrollo de capital humano* (LC/W.431), Santiago, Chile, Economic Commission for Latin America and the Caribbean (ECLAC)/United Nations Children's Fund (UNICEF).

___(2010), "The spatial dimension of social cohesion in Latin America", *Social Cohesion in Latin America. Concepts, Frames of Reference and Indicators* (LC/G.2420), Santiago, Chile.

___(2001), "Seduced and abandoned: the social isolation of the urban poor", *CEPAL Review*, No. 75 (LC/G.2150-P), Santiago, Chile, Economic Commission for Latin America and the Caribbean (ECLAC).

Kaztman, Rubén and Pascual Gerstenfeld (1988), "La heterogeneidad de la pobreza: Una aproximación bidimensional" (LC/MDV/R.12 (Sem.44/7)), Montevideo, ECLAC office in Montevideo.

López-Calva, L.F. and E. Ortiz-Juárez (2009), "Medición multidimensional de la pobreza en México: Significancia estadística en la inclusión de dimensiones no monetarias", *Estudios Económicos*, special issue, Mexico City, Centro de Estudios Económicos, El Colegio de México.

Maurizio, Roxana (2010), "The feasibility of constructing a synthetic index of social cohesion in Latin America", *Social Cohesion in Latin America. Concepts, Frames of Reference and Indicators* (LC/G.2420), Santiago, Chile, Economic Commission for Latin America and the Caribbean (ECLAC).

Nussbaumer, Patrick and others (2011), "Measuring energy poverty: focusing on what matters", *OPHI Working Paper*, No. 42, Oxford, Oxford Poverty & Human Development Initiative (OPHI) [online] http://www.ophi.org.uk/measuring-energy-poverty-focusing-on-what-matters/.

Ocampo, José Antonio (2008), "Las concepciones de la política social: universalismo versus focalización", *Nueva Sociedad*, No. 215, May/June [online] http://www.nuso.org/upload/articulos/3521_1.pdf

Roche, José M. and María Emma Santos (2013), "In search of a multidimensional poverty index for Latin America" [online] http://www.ecineq.org/ecineq_bari13/FILESxBari13/CR2/p170.pdf.

Santos, María Emma (2013), "Measuring multidimensional poverty in Latin America: previous experience and the way forward", *OPHI Working Paper*, No. 66, Oxford, Oxford Poverty & Human Development Initiative (OPHI) [online] http://www.ophi.org.uk/wp-content/uploads/ophi-wp-66.pdf.

Santos, María Emma and others (2010), "Refining the basic needs approach: a multidimensional analysis of poverty in Latin America", *Studies in Applied Welfare Analysis: Papers from the Third ECINEQ Meeting*, John Bishop (ed.), Bingley, Emerald Group Publishing Limited.

Sen, Amartya (1997), "From income inequality to economic inequality", *Southern Economic Journal*, vol. 64, No. 2.

___(1985), "Well-being, agency and freedom: the Dewey Lectures 1984", *The Journal of Philosophy*, vol. 82, No. 4, New York, Journal of Philosphy Inc.

Taccari, Daniel and Pauline Stockins (2013), "Tipologías de discrepancias y medidas de conciliación estadística de los indicadores ODM. Marco general y aplicación en áreas temáticas e indicadores seleccionados", *Estudios Estadísticos series*, No. 81 (LC/L.3686), Santiago, Chile, Economic Commission for Latin America and the Caribbean (ECLAC).

UNICEF/WHO (United Nations Children's Fund/World Health Organization) (2012), *Progress on Drinking Water and Sanitation. 2012 Update* [online] http://www.unicef.org/media/files/JMPreport2012.pdf.

World Bank (2012), "What a waste. A global review of solid waste management", *Urban Development Series*, No. 15 [online] http://www-wds.worldbank.org/external/default/WDSContentServer/WDSP/IB/2012/07/25/000333037_20120725004131/Rendered/PDF/681350WP0REVIS0at0a0Waste20120Final.pdf.

___(2005), "Guidance on waste management", *Dissemination Notes*, No. 66, January [online] http://siteresources.worldbank.org/INTPOPS/Publications/20486437/DisseminationNote66GuidanceWasteManagement2005.pdf.

Annex

Table I.A.1
Latin America (18 countries): poverty and indigence indicators, 1990-2012 [a]
(Percentages)

Country	Year	Poverty [b]				Indigence			
		Households	Population			Households	Population		
		Incidence (H)	Incidence (H)	Gap (PG)	Gap-squared (FGT2)	Incidence (H)	Incidence (H)	Gap (PG)	Gap-squared (FGT2)
Argentina [c]	1990 [d]	16.2	21.2	7.2	3.5	3.5	5.2	1.6	0.8
	1999	16.3	23.7	8.6	4.4	4.3	6.7	2.2	1.1
	2002	34.9	45.4	21.1	12.8	13.9	20.9	8.4	4.6
	2011	4.3	5.7	2.3	1.5	1.8	1.9	1.1	0.8
	2012	3.4	4.3	1.9	1.3	1.7	1.7	1.0	0.8
Bolivia (Plurinational State of)	1989 [e]	48.9	52.6	24.5	15.0	21.9	23.0	9.8	6.2
	1999	54.7	60.6	33.9	24.1	32.6	36.5	20.3	14.7
	2002	55.5	62.4	34.4	23.8	31.7	37.1	19.5	13.5
	2009	36.3	42.4	19.8	12.7	18.2	22.4	11.0	7.3
	2011	31.2	36.3	15.5	9.4	15.6	18.7	8.1	4.9
Brazil	1990	41.4	48.0	23.5	14.7	18.3	23.4	9.7	5.5
	1999	29.9	37.5	17.0	10.2	9.6	12.9	5.3	3.3
	2001	30.0	37.5	17.4	10.7	10.0	13.2	5.8	3.8
	2011	16.2	20.9	8.8	5.4	5.2	6.1	3.1	2.3
	2012	14.5	18.6	7.6	4.6	4.8	5.4	2.8	2.0
Chile	1990	33.3	38.6	14.9	8.0	10.7	13.0	4.4	2.3
	1998	17.8	21.7	7.5	3.8	4.6	5.6	2.0	1.1
	2003	15.3	18.7	6.3	3.2	3.9	4.7	1.7	1.0
	2009	9.8	11.5	4.0	2.2	3.3	3.6	1.6	1.0
	2011	9.2	11.0	3.6	1.9	3.0	3.1	1.3	0.9
Colombia	1994	47.3	52.5	26.6	17.5	25.0	28.5	13.8	9.1
	1999	48.7	54.9	25.6	15.7	23.2	26.8	11.2	6.9
	2002 [f]	42.2	49.8	21.9	12.8	14.3	17.8	6.8	3.7
	2011 [f]	27.7	34.2	13.5	7.3	8.4	10.7	3.8	2.0
	2012 [f]	26.7	32.9	12.9	7.1	8.2	10.4	3.8	2.1
Costa Rica	1990	23.6	26.3	10.7	6.5	10.0	10.1	4.8	3.4
	1999	18.2	20.3	8.1	4.8	7.6	7.8	3.5	2.3
	2002	18.6	20.3	8.4	5.2	7.7	8.2	3.9	2.7
	2011 [g]	16.0	18.8	7.1	4.0	6.3	7.3	3.0	1.9
	2012 [g]	15.4	17.8	6.9	4.0	6.3	7.3	3.1	1.9
Dominican Republic	2002	42.2	47.1	20.9	12.6	18.2	20.7	8.8	5.3
	2011	38.7	42.2	18.4	10.8	18.9	20.3	7.9	4.5
	2012	37.9	41.2	18.0	10.4	19.2	20.9	8.2	4.6
Ecuador [c]	1990	55.8	62.1	27.6	15.8	22.6	26.2	9.2	4.9
	1999	58.0	63.6	30.1	18.2	27.2	31.3	11.5	6.3
	2002	42.6	49.0	20.8	11.8	16.3	19.4	6.9	3.7
	2011	27.9	32.4	11.4	5.7	9.0	10.1	3.3	1.7
	2012	24.6	28.8	10.1	5.1	8.5	9.9	3.2	1.6
El Salvador	1995	47.6	54.2	24.0	14.3	18.2	21.7	9.1	5.6
	1999	43.5	49.8	22.9	14.0	18.3	21.9	9.4	5.8
	2001	42.9	48.9	22.7	14.0	18.3	22.1	9.5	5.8
	2010	40.2	46.6	18.8	10.0	13.3	16.7	5.2	2.3
	2012	38.9	45.3	16.7	8.4	10.9	13.5	3.9	1.7
Guatemala	1989	63.0	69.4	35.9	23.1	36.7	42.0	18.5	11.2
	1998	53.5	61.1	27.3	15.4	26.1	31.6	10.7	5.1
	2002	52.8	60.2	27.0	15.4	26.9	30.9	10.7	5.5
	2006	46.7	54.8	25.5	15.2	22.7	29.1	11.3	5.9
Honduras	1990	75.2	80.8	50.2	35.9	53.9	60.9	31.5	20.2
	1999	74.3	79.7	47.4	32.9	50.6	56.8	27.9	17.5
	2002	70.9	77.3	45.3	31.2	47.1	54.4	26.6	16.2
	2010	61.2	67.4	36.6	24.2	37.0	42.8	20.1	12.1

Table I.A.1 (concluded)

Country	Year	Poverty[b] Households	Poverty[b] Population			Indigence Households	Indigence Population		
		Incidence (H)	Incidence (H)	Gap (PG)	Gap-squared (FGT2)	Incidence (H)	Incidence (H)	Gap (PG)	Gap-squared (FGT2)
Mexico	1989	39.0	47.7	18.7	9.9	14.0	18.7	5.9	2.8
	1998	38.0	46.9	18.4	9.4	13.2	18.5	5.3	2.2
	2002	31.8	39.4	13.9	6.7	9.1	12.6	3.5	1.4
	2010	29.3	36.3	12.8	6.3	9.8	13.3	4.1	1.9
	2012	29.9	37.1	12.7	6.1	10.4	14.2	4.2	1.8
Nicaragua	1993	68.1	73.6	41.9	29.3	43.2	48.4	24.3	16.2
	1998	65.1	69.9	39.4	27.3	40.1	44.6	22.6	15.1
	2001	63.0	69.4	37.1	24.5	36.5	42.5	19.2	12.0
	2009	52.0	58.3	26.1	15.2	25.1	29.5	11.7	6.3
Panama	1991[c]	26.1	31.0	12.8	7.6	9.5	10.8	5.0	3.3
	1999[c]	15.8	19.5	7.0	3.8	4.6	5.5	2.2	1.3
	2002	30.0	36.9	16.8	10.2	14.4	18.6	7.6	4.3
	2010	19.4	25.8	10.6	5.9	8.9	12.6	4.6	2.3
	2011	19.8	25.3	10.4	5.9	9.4	12.4	4.7	2.5
Paraguay	1990[h]	36.8	43.2	16.1	8.0	10.4	13.1	3.6	1.5
	1999	50.3	59.0	29.1	18.4	25.0	31.8	14.1	8.6
	2001	50.7	59.7	28.7	18.0	25.2	31.3	13.7	8.3
	2010	48.0	54.8	25.4	15.5	26.0	30.7	12.9	7.6
	2011	43.8	49.6	23.5	14.5	23.9	28.0	12.2	7.3
Peru	1997	40.4	47.5	20.7	12.0	20.3	25.0	10.1	5.6
	1999	42.3	48.6	20.6	11.7	18.7	22.4	9.2	5.1
	2001[i]	48.7	54.7	24.7	14.5	20.4	24.4	9.6	5.2
	2011[i]	24.8	27.8	9.9	4.9	5.5	6.3	1.8	0.8
	2012[i]	23.1	25.8	9.2	4.6	5.2	6.0	1.8	0.8
Uruguay[c]	1990	11.8	17.9	5.3	2.4	2.0	3.4	0.9	0.4
	1999	5.6	9.4	2.7	1.2	0.9	1.8	0.4	0.2
	2002	9.3	15.5	4.5	1.9	1.3	2.5	0.6	0.2
	2011	4.5	6.7	1.8	0.7	0.9	1.1	0.3	0.1
	2012	3.9	6.1	1.7	0.7	0.8	1.2	0.3	0.1
Venezuela (Bolivarian Republic of)	1990	34.2	39.8	15.7	8.5	11.8	14.4	5.0	2.5
	1999	44.0	49.4	22.6	13.7	19.4	21.7	9.0	5.5
	2002	43.3	48.6	22.1	13.4	19.7	22.2	9.3	5.7
	2011	25.3	29.5	10.5	5.5	10.0	11.7	4.2	2.4
	2012	20.2	23.8	8.6	4.6	8.3	9.7	3.6	2.1
Latin America[j]	1990	41.0	48.4	...	...	17.7	22.6	...	...
	1999	35.4	43.8	...	...	14.1	18.6	...	...
	2002	36.1	43.9	...	...	14.6	19.3	...	...
	2011	23.3	29.6	...	...	8.9	11.6	...	...
	2012	22.2	28.2	...	...	8.7	11.3	...	...

Source: Economic Commission for Latin America and the Caribbean (ECLAC), on the basis of special tabulations of data from household surveys conducted in the respective countries.
[a] H = headcount ratio; PG = Poverty gap; FGT2 = Foster, Greer and Thorbecke index.
[b] Includes households (persons) living in indigence or extreme poverty.
[c] Urban areas.
[d] Greater Buenos Aires.
[e] Eight departmental capitals plus the city of El Alto.
[f] Figures provided by the National Administrative Department of Statistics (DANE) of Colombia, not comparable with those of previous years.
[g] Figures not comparable with those of previous years, owing to a change in the survey used.
[h] Metropolitan area of Asunción.
[i] Figures of the National Institute of Statistics and Informatics of Peru. Figures not comparable with those of previous years.
[j] Estimate for 18 countries in the region plus Haiti.

Table I.A.2
Latin America (18 countries): income distribution of households, 1990-2012 [a]

Country	Year	Average income [b]	Share of total income (percentages)				Ratio of average per capita income (times) [c]	
			40% poorest	Next 30%	20% below the richest 10%	Richest 10%	D10 / D(1 a 4)	Q5 / Q1
Argentina [d]	1990 [e]	10.6	14.9	23.6	26.7	34.8	13.5	13.5
	1999	11.3	15.9	22.1	25.3	36.7	16.2	16.6
	2002	7.3	14.3	20.4	24.6	40.7	19.0	20.6
	2011	20.6	17.3	24.9	27.2	30.6	13.5	14.7
	2012	22.8	18.2	26.1	26.9	28.8	11.9	13.2
Bolivia (Plurinational State of)	1989 [f]	7.7	12.1	21.9	27.9	38.1	17.1	21.4
	1999	5.6	9.3	24.1	29.6	37.0	26.7	48.1
	2002	6.1	9.5	21.4	28.3	40.8	30.3	44.2
	2009	6.5	13.9	27.1	28.4	30.6	14.9	19.8
	2011	7.2	15.6	28.3	29.7	26.4	12.1	15.9
Brasil	1990	9.4	9.5	18.6	28.0	43.9	31.2	35.0
	1999	11.3	10.1	17.3	25.5	47.1	31.9	35.6
	2001	11.0	10.2	17.5	25.5	46.8	32.1	36.9
	2011	12.3	14.1	20.9	25.4	39.6	19.2	22.0
	2012	13.3	14.0	20.4	24.6	41.0	20.2	22.5
Chile	1990	9.5	13.2	20.8	25.3	40.7	18.2	18.4
	1998	13.7	13.0	20.4	26.6	40.0	19.1	19.7
	2003	13.6	13.8	20.8	25.6	39.8	18.8	18.4
	2009	14.5	14.4	21.2	26.0	38.4	16.3	15.9
	2011	14.1	15.0	21.6	25.9	37.5	15.1	15.0
Colombia	1994	7.7	10.0	21.3	26.9	41.8	26.8	35.2
	1999	6.7	12.3	21.6	26.0	40.1	22.3	25.6
	2002 [g]	7.2	13.0	22.5	26.6	37.9	22.0	24.1
	2011 [g]	8.3	13.9	23.6	26.9	35.6	18.7	20.5
	2012 [g]	8.3	14.2	24.4	26.9	34.5	17.5	19.8
Costa Rica	1990	9.5	16.7	27.4	30.2	25.7	10.1	13.1
	1999	11.4	15.3	25.7	29.7	29.3	12.6	15.3
	2002	11.7	14.5	25.6	29.7	30.2	13.7	17.0
	2011 [h]	11.3	14.0	24.5	29.8	31.7	15.2	16.8
	2012 [h]	11.5	14.0	24.3	29.3	32.4	14.7	16.5
Dominican Republic	2002	6.9	12.7	22.7	26.9	37.7	17.8	20.7
	2011	7.8	11.3	21.6	28.4	38.7	23.0	25.7
	2012	7.1	12.5	23.5	29.6	34.4	16.5	19.4
Ecuador [d]	1990	5.5	17.2	25.4	27.0	30.4	11.4	12.3
	1999	5.6	14.1	22.8	26.5	36.6	17.2	18.5
	2002	6.7	15.4	24.3	26.0	34.3	15.6	16.8
	2011	7.4	18.5	26.6	28.4	26.5	9.7	10.7
	2012	7.9	18.1	27.1	26.9	27.9	10.0	10.9
El Salvador	1995	6.2	15.4	24.8	26.9	32.9	14.1	16.9
	1999	6.6	13.8	25.0	29.1	32.1	15.2	19.6
	2001	6.7	13.4	24.6	28.7	33.3	16.2	20.2
	2010	5.6	17.8	26.4	27.7	28.1	10.3	11.4
	2012	5.6	19.2	26.7	26.9	27.2	9.7	10.3
Guatemala	1989	6.0	11.8	20.9	26.8	40.5	23.6	27.3
	1998	7.1	14.3	21.6	25.0	39.1	20.4	19.7
	2002	6.8	14.1	22.3	27.2	36.4	18.6	19.3
	2006	7.6	12.8	21.7	25.7	39.8	22.0	23.9
Honduras	1990	4.3	10.1	19.7	27.0	43.2	27.3	30.9
	1999	3.9	11.8	22.9	28.9	36.4	22.3	26.5
	2002	4.3	11.3	21.7	27.6	39.4	23.6	26.3
	2010	5.1	11.4	22.6	29.2	36.8	20.6	25.2

Table I.A.2 (concluded)

Country	Year	Average income [b]	Share of total income (percentages)				Ratio of average per capita income (times) [c]	
			40% poorest	Next 30%	20% below the richest 10%	Richest 10%	D10 / D(1 a 4)	Q5 / Q1
México	1989	8.6	15.8	22.5	25.1	36.6	17.2	16.9
	1998	7.7	15.1	22.7	25.6	36.6	18.4	18.5
	2002	8.2	15.7	23.8	27.3	33.2	15.1	15.5
	2010	7.4	17.7	25.4	27.2	29.7	12.8	13.3
	2012	7.1	17.4	24.9	26.3	31.4	14.2	14.0
Nicaragua	1993	5.2	10.4	22.8	28.4	38.4	26.5	37.2
	1998	5.6	10.4	22.1	27.1	40.4	25.4	34.6
	2001	5.8	12.0	21.6	25.6	40.8	23.8	27.3
	2009	5.7	16.5	25.5	28.1	29.9	12.9	14.5
Panamá	1991 [d]	11.1	14.1	23.8	29.4	32.7	16.8	20.2
	1999 [d]	12.9	15.6	25.2	27.8	31.4	13.9	15.9
	2002	9.8	12.1	23.6	28.0	36.3	20.1	25.8
	2010	10.2	15.1	26.0	27.0	31.9	14.4	17.7
	2011	10.4	14.4	25.8	26.4	33.4	16.3	20.3
Paraguay	1990 [i]	7.7	18.6	25.7	26.8	28.9	10.2	10.6
	1999	6.3	13.3	23.4	27.6	35.7	19.1	23.2
	2001	6.3	13.5	23.6	26.2	36.7	19.5	23.2
	2010	5.8	13.8	24.2	26.2	35.8	17.1	20.0
	2011	6.5	12.5	22.7	26.8	38.0	17.4	21.3
Perú	1997	7.5	13.4	24.6	28.7	33.3	17.9	20.8
	1999	7.5	13.4	23.1	27.1	36.4	19.5	21.6
	2001	6.4	13.4	24.6	28.5	33.5	17.4	19.3
	2011	8.7	16.1	27.2	28.3	28.4	11.2	12.8
	2012	8.8	15.9	27.3	28.6	28.2	10.9	12.7
Uruguay [d]	1990	9.9	18.9	23.3	22.5	35.3	11.0	10.5
	1999	11.9	21.6	25.5	25.8	27.1	8.8	9.5
	2002	9.4	21.7	25.4	25.6	27.3	9.5	10.2
	2011	10.4	23.2	27.2	26.3	23.3	7.5	8.0
	2012	10.7	24.7	28.4	26.4	20.5	6.7	7.3
Venezuela (Bolivarian Republic of)	1990	8.9	16.7	25.7	28.9	28.7	12.1	13.4
	1999	7.2	14.5	25.1	29.0	31.4	15.0	18.0
	2002	7.1	14.3	24.9	29.5	31.3	14.5	18.1
	2011	7.7	20.1	28.7	28.3	22.9	7.7	9.1
	2012	8.8	19.8	28.6	28.0	23.6	8.0	9.4

Source: Economic Commission for Latin America and the Caribbean (ECLAC) on the basis of special tabulations of data from household surveys conducted in the respective countries.
[a] Households of the whole of the country ranked according to their per capita income.
[b] Average monthly income of households in multiples of the poverty line on a per capita basis.
[c] D(1 a 4) represents the 40% of lowest income households, while D10 refers to the 10% of households with the highest income. A similar notation is used in the case of quintiles (Q), which represent 20% of households.
[d] Urban total.
[e] Greater Buenos Aires.
[f] Eight main cities plus El Alto.
[g] Figures not comparable with those of previous years owing to a change in the criteria for construction of the income aggregate.
[h] Figures not comparable with those of previous years, owing to a change in the survey used.
[i] Asunción metropolitan area.

Table I.A.3
Latin America (18 countries): indicators of income concentration, 1990-2012 [a]

Country	Year	Concentration indices				
		Gini [b]	Theil	Atkinson		
				(ε=0.5)	(ε=1.0)	(ε=1.5)
Argentina [c]	1990 [d]	0.501	0.555	0.216	0.360	0.473
	1999	0.539	0.667	0.250	0.410	0.530
	2002	0.578	0.724	0.282	0.464	0.593
	2011	0.492	0.511	0.204	0.351	0.473
	2012	0.475	0.457	0.189	0.332	0.454
Bolivia (Plurinational State of)	1989 [e]	0.537	0.573	0.242	0.426	0.587
	1999	0.586	0.657	0.293	0.537	0.736
	2002	0.614	0.775	0.322	0.553	0.732
	2009	0.508	0.511	0.223	0.413	0.594
	2011	0.472	0.398	0.187	0.359	0.527
Brazil	1990	0.627	0.816	0.324	0.528	0.663
	1999	0.640	0.914	0.341	0.537	0.662
	2001	0.639	0.914	0.340	0.536	0.665
	2011	0.559	0.666	0.261	0.435	0.567
	2012	0.567	0.797	0.277	0.443	0.568
Chile	1990	0.554	0.644	0.255	0.422	0.546
	1998	0.560	0.654	0.261	0.430	0.553
	2003	0.552	0.674	0.257	0.418	0.535
	2009	0.524	0.585	0.231	0.384	0.501
	2011	0.516	0.541	0.221	0.371	0.485
Colombia	1994	0.601	0.794	0.308	0.517	0.684
	1999	0.572	0.734	0.275	0.450	0.589
	2002	0.567	0.672	0.268	0.447	0.579
	2011 [f]	0.545	0.599	0.247	0.419	0.551
	2012 [f]	0.536	0.568	0.238	0.410	0.546
Costa Rica	1990	0.438	0.328	0.152	0.286	0.412
	1999	0.473	0.395	0.179	0.328	0.457
	2002	0.488	0.440	0.193	0.349	0.491
	2011 [g]	0.503	0.481	0.207	0.367	0.501
	2012 [g]	0.504	0.481	0.209	0.372	0.511
Dominican Republic	2002	0.537	0.569	0.236	0.404	0.536
	2011	0.558	0.632	0.258	0.437	0.575
	2012	0.517	0.499	0.218	0.387	0.530
Ecuador [c]	1990	0.461	0.403	0.173	0.306	0.422
	1999	0.526	0.567	0.228	0.381	0.498
	2002	0.513	0.563	0.222	0.370	0.484
	2011	0.434	0.353	0.154	0.277	0.382
	2012	0.444	0.387	0.164	0.290	0.397
El Salvador	1995	0.507	0.502	0.213	0.376	0.520
	1999	0.518	0.495	0.224	0.414	0.590
	2001	0.525	0.527	0.232	0.423	0.599
	2010	0.454	0.372	0.168	0.304	0.418
	2012	0.437	0.368	0.159	0.284	0.389
Guatemala	1989	0.582	0.735	0.282	0.459	0.587
	1998	0.56	0.760	0.273	0.428	0.534
	2002	0.542	0.583	0.239	0.401	0.515
	2006	0.585	0.773	0.291	0.467	0.590
Honduras	1990	0.615	0.816	0.317	0.515	0.647
	1999	0.564	0.636	0.263	0.451	0.603
	2002	0.588	0.719	0.288	0.476	0.608
	2010	0.567	0.625	0.265	0.458	0.601

Table I.A.3 (concluded)

Country	Year	Concentration indices				
		Gini [b]	Theil	Atkinson		
				(ε=0.5)	(ε=1.0)	(ε=1.5)
Mexico	1989	0.536	0.680	0.248	0.400	0.509
	1998	0.539	0.634	0.245	0.403	0.515
	2002	0.514	0.521	0.218	0.372	0.485
	2010	0.481	0.458	0.192	0.335	0.448
	2012	0.492	0.503	0.203	0.344	0.451
Nicaragua	1993	0.582	0.670	0.269	0.454	0.600
	1998	0.583	0.730	0.284	0.479	0.644
	2001	0.579	0.782	0.288	0.469	0.615
	2005	0.532	0.614	0.241	0.402	0.526
	2009	0.478	0.437	0.189	0.337	0.462
Panama	1991 [c]	0.530	0.543	0.228	0.398	0.534
	1999 [c]	0.499	0.459	0.202	0.361	0.490
	2002	0.567	0.616	0.266	0.465	0.616
	2010	0.519	0.529	0.226	0.401	0.543
	2011	0.531	0.561	0.237	0.415	0.559
Paraguay	1990 [h]	0.447	0.365	0.161	0.287	0.386
	1999	0.558	0.659	0.264	0.452	0.601
	2001	0.558	0.673	0.265	0.450	0.606
	2010	0.533	0.666	0.248	0.416	0.557
	2011	0.546	0.630	0.253	0.432	0.583
Peru	1997	0.532	0.567	0.238	0.414	0.553
	1999	0.545	0.599	0.249	0.424	0.560
	2001	0.525	0.556	0.231	0.397	0.526
	2011	0.452	0.382	0.170	0.309	0.429
	2012	0.449	0.370	0.167	0.307	0.429
Uruguay [c]	1990	0.492	0.699	0.227	0.349	0.441
	1999	0.440	0.354	0.158	0.286	0.393
	2002	0.455	0.385	0.169	0.300	0.406
	2011	0.402	0.291	0.132	0.241	0.334
	2012	0.380	0.246	0.116	0.219	0.310
Venezuela (Bolivarian Republic of)	1990	0.471	0.416	0.183	0.327	0.446
	1999	0.498	0.464	0.202	0.363	0.507
	2002	0.500	0.456	0.201	0.361	0.501
	2011	0.397	0.275	0.127	0.239	0.345
	2012	0.405	0.289	0.133	0.249	0.357

Source: Economic Commission for Latin America and the Caribbean (ECLAC), on the basis of special tabulations of data from household surveys conducted in the respective countries.
[a] Based on per capita income distribution across the country.
[b] Includes persons with zero income.
[c] Urban total.
[d] Greater Buenos Aires.
[e] Eight main cities plus El Alto.
[f] Figures not comparable with those of previous years, owing to a change in the criterion for constructing the income aggregate.
[g] Figures not comparable with those of previous years, owing to a change in the survey used.
[h] Asunción metropolitan area.

Chapter II

Child poverty in Latin America and the Caribbean

A. Rights-based approach and child[1] poverty

In the 1990s, studies began to reflect concerns about the "infantilization" of poverty in Latin America. The United Nations General Assembly defines children living in poverty as deprived of nutrition, water, access to basic health-care services, shelter, education, participation and protection. Child poverty means that children and adolescents are unable to enjoy their rights, which limits their ability to achieve their goals and play an active role in society. A multidimensional measurement perspective is required to understand the nature of child poverty. In recent years, the Economic Commission for Latin America and the Caribbean (ECLAC) and the United Nations Children's Fund (UNICEF) have been using this multidimensional perspective with a focus on rights and multiple deprivations, adapting to the region the methodology used in a global study conducted by UNICEF in 2003 jointly with researchers from the University of Bristol and the London School of Economics.

1. Introduction

In this second decade of the twenty-first century, poverty still poses a huge challenge for Latin America and the Caribbean. A very worrying aspect of the trend in monetary poverty is that its impact is heaviest on households with a high dependency ratio, which is particularly detrimental to children and adolescents.

Studies conducted more than 20 years ago, in the 1990s, began to reflect the overrepresentation of children and adolescents in income-poor households in Latin America, showing, in turn the close link existing between monetary poverty and the presence of children in households (ECLAC, 1994, 1997, 1998). While economic achievements in the first half of the 1990s decreased the number of poor by the year 2000, the benefits were not shared equally, with a much lower reduction in the poverty rate among households with children and adolescents (ECLAC, 2000).

This triggered a debate in the region concerning the "infantilization" of poverty, a concept still relevant today, which recognizes the overrepresentation of children and adolescents among the poor compared with other age groups, and the greater likelihood that children and adolescents will live in poor households (a likelihood that increases the younger the children are). Evidence showed that not only was poverty among children and adolescents more rigid during business cycle upswings, it was also more elastic during downswings. Most striking was that children and adolescents proved to be worst hit by crises, despite representing a shrinking share of the total population as a result of the deep-seated demographic changes occurring in the region. In short, child poverty decreased less than poverty in the total population and much less than that of older adults (Rossel, 2013; ECLAC, 2010), indicating that children and adolescents are seeing fewer benefits from the overall reduction in monetary poverty as has occurred recently.

A large proportion of children and adolescent face deprivations that harm them directly at this stage of their lives, continue to have a negative impact on the rest of their lives and are passed on to future generations. Children are often trapped in situations of household income poverty that deny them such rights as survival, shelter, education, health and nutrition. In other words, they are deprived of assets and opportunities to which all human beings are entitled. Moreover, poverty is closely linked with other social phenomena, such as exclusion and inequality, which are created and perpetuated to a large extent by unfair and inequitable resource distribution.

---

[1] This study uses the definition of a child —every human being below the age of eighteen years— set forth in article 1 of the Convention on the Rights of the Child. As in other studies by ECLAC and UNICEF, therefore, childhood is understood to refer to the population aged 0 to 17 years.

Addressing and understanding the specific kind of poverty children face requires a multidimensional method of measurement that identifies the deprivations associated with the provision and quality of public goods and services affecting children directly, as well as the income shortfall as regards the needs of all household members. The particular concern for children and adolescents comes in response not only to their overrepresentation among the poor but also to their greater dependency and lack of autonomy within families and to their particular vulnerability to the consequences of poverty and inequality. Any measurement of poverty among children should recognize their specific characteristics and adopt households and individuals as the unit of analysis.

While there is no single approach to defining and measuring child poverty, most of the studies and organizations dealing with this issue consider it to be a multidimensional phenomenon. According to *The State of the World's Children 2005*, "children living in poverty experience deprivation of the material, spiritual and emotional resources needed to survive, develop and thrive, leaving them unable to enjoy their rights, achieve their full potential or participate as full and equal members of society" (UNICEF, 2005, p. 18).

2. Rights-based approach and multidimensional measurement of child poverty

A view of child poverty that goes beyond the strictly monetary perspective should consider such factors as access to services and the psychosocial development of children and adolescents (e.g. discrimination and exclusion). It should also underscore the explicit link between these factors and the violation of human rights as universally accepted principles enshrined in the Convention on the Rights of the Child, the Universal Declaration of Human Rights, the Millennium Declaration and other international instruments. In this framework, the United Nations General Assembly defines children living in poverty as deprived of nutrition, water, access to basic health-care services, shelter, education, participation and protection (UNICEF, 2007). When children and adolescents are denied these rights, it limits their ability to achieve their goals, play an active role in society and enjoy opportunities.

The choice of conceptual approach influences the definition of indicators for poverty measurement and the identification of poor children and adolescents and their needs. UNICEF (2004) states that the concept of child poverty, together with estimates of its scope, can be built on the principle of access to a specific number of economic and social rights enshrined in article 27 of the Convention on the Rights of the Child, affirming that "States Parties recognize the right of every child to a standard of living adequate for the child's physical, mental, spiritual, moral and social development." This and other articles on specific areas of deprivation have led to the application of a rights-based approach regarded as a framework for analysis and action for overcoming poverty (Abramovich, 2006), with a view to combating this scourge and achieving greater equality.

Much has been written in recent years on multidimensional poverty measurement. The measures proposed by Bourguignon and Chakravarty (2003) and Alkire and Foster (2009) have resulted in diverse applications for different countries. Despite criticism of the methodology for aggregating the different dimensions (see Ravallion, 2011), there is growing consensus that poverty is a multidimensional phenomenon. The use of this multidimensional approach to poverty analysis has become consolidated in a number of spheres. Since 2011, the indicators in the *Human Development Report* of the United Nations Development Programme (UNDP) have included the multidimensional poverty index (MPI) based on a proposal by Alkire and Santos (2010), which combines 10 indicators to reflect deprivations in the three traditional dimensions of human development (health, education and quality of life) in 104 countries (see box I.3 in chapter I).

In 2003, UNICEF, jointly with researchers from the University of Bristol and the London School of Economics, launched a major large-scale initiative to measure child poverty with a focus on rights and multiple deprivations. This is considered the first scientific estimate of child poverty in the developing world (Expert Group on Poverty Statistics (Rio Group), 2007). The Bristol study lists a basket of goods and services considered essential for child well-being and defines different thresholds of deprivation (Gordon and others, 2003). This set of indicators is based on the principle of child rights with regard to adequate nutrition, clean water, acceptable sanitation facilities, health, housing, education and information (Minujin, Delamónica and Davidziuk, 2006). The study conceptualizes deprivation as a continuum extending from no deprivation to extreme deprivation at the end of the scale, and provides operational definitions for each level. It argues that children's needs differ in degree and nature from those of adults and that the unit of analysis should be the child and not the household, even though the needs of adults and children may overlap in certain dimensions, making it difficult at times to separate children's conditions and experiences from those of adults in the same family or household. The analysis was designed to highlight policy measures needed to generate a specific impact.

3. Measurement of child poverty in Latin America and the Caribbean

The joint study on poverty measurement by ECLAC and the UNICEF Regional Office for Latin America and the Caribbean, designed to estimate child poverty, conceives it as the deprivation of the rights of children and adolescents in certain dimensions widely acknowledged as constituting poverty: education, nutrition, housing, water, sanitation and information (ECLAC/UNICEF, 2012a).

These dimensions are an integral part of the indicators and methodology for estimating child poverty directly, using a human-rights-based approach developed jointly by UNICEF, the University of Bristol and the London School of Economics. The dimensions were replicated and adapted to the reality of Latin America and the Caribbean and the availability of information for the region (ECLAC/UNICEF, 2010; Espíndola and Rico, 2010). Following the global initiative, a study on child poverty was conducted in Latin America and the Caribbean (ECLAC/UNICEF, 2010), which measured child poverty using two major traditional methodologies: (a) direct methods, the best-known in the region being the measurement of unmet basic needs (these methods, based on a proposal by University of Bristol (Gordon and others, 2003), were adapted to measure various levels of multiple deprivation in children); and (b) indirect methods, represented by the measurement of absolute poverty according to per capita household income. The study showed that, around 2008, approximately 45% of children under the age of 18 were living in poverty in 18 countries in the region, meaning that nearly 81 million children and adolescents were suffering deprivation because some of their rights were not being fulfilled.

The 2003 Bristol study was based on data from Demographic and Health Surveys (DHS) and Multiple Indicator Cluster Surveys (MICS). Although new surveys have recently become available, coverage in Latin America is low and patchy. For this reason and in order to incorporate income measures at the same time, the current study was based on household surveys, which are available for all countries in the region and include satisfactory data for implementing both methodologies. To make these estimates, the indicators were adapted to the data available in household surveys. Not only did this meet the data availability criterion, it also recognized the necessary sociocultural relevance of the exercise of rights, especially to determine the thresholds for identifying when a child or adolescent was experiencing extreme child poverty or total child poverty.[2] The deprivation thresholds established in the 2003 global measurement based on the Bristol indicators had been confined to the severest situations of child deprivation. For Latin America, it was decided to follow the above criterion but to also define thresholds to identify situations of moderate deprivation, as they too reflect needs that, when unmet, affect children's well-being and development. Table II.1 describes the dimensions reflecting the basic needs that must be met for children to develop, the relevant indicators available in the aforementioned instruments and thresholds for identifying moderate and severe deprivation.

The characteristics of the rights-based approach determined the choice of methodology. For example, the universal nature of rights calls for each right (or deprivation of that right) and its levels to be assessed in the same way for all groups of children and adolescents. This led to the construction of national thresholds without the usual differentiation between urban and rural areas and making no allowances for the fact that the deprivation or violation of a right might stem from the high investment costs involved in providing access to basic services in rural areas, as rights should apply in all circumstances. Accordingly, the standard threshold was set in accordance with the traditional metrics of deprivation in rural areas, while taking care to avoid distorting the degree of rights enforceability (overly strict).

---

[2] The Demographic and Health Surveys (DHS) and the Multiple Indicator Cluster Surveys (MICS) were used as a reference for estimating child undernutrition levels by means of logistic models to estimate the probability of undernutrition, applicable to household surveys, and so incorporate this essential dimension into estimated child poverty levels in the region.

Table II.1
Definition of indicators and thresholds for moderate and severe child deprivation[a]

Dimension and indicators of deprivation	Level of deprivation		Unit of analysis to which the indicator applies	Article in the Convention on the Rights of the Child infringed "States Parties ..."
	Moderate	Severe		
Nutrition[b] Weight/age ratio Height/age ratio	(General and chronic undernutrition) Moderate-severe underweight or moderate-severe low height for age: less than -2 standard deviations from the reference standard	Severe underweight or severe stunting: less than -3 standard deviations from the reference standard	Individual. Children aged 0 to 4 years	24 (1)... recognize the right of the child to the enjoyment of the highest attainable standard of health... 24 (2c) ...shall take appropriate measures to... combat disease and malnutrition...
Sanitation (1) Access to drinking water by: - Source - Supply - Access time	(a) Water from a well or water wheel (b) Supply of water outside the dwelling and off-premises (public standpipe, tanker truck or other means)	(a) Unsafe water source: natural water source (river, stream) (b) Access time to water source: 15 minutes or more (if such indicator data are available)	Dwelling. Children and adolescents aged 0 to 17 years	24 (1)... recognize the right of the child to the enjoyment of the highest attainable standard of health... 24 (2c)... shall take appropriate measures to combat disease and malnutrition... through the provision of adequate nutritious foods and clean drinking water...
Sanitation (2) Sewer connection (waste disposal)	No connection to sewer system (e.g. cesspit) or access outside the dwelling or property	No waste disposal system (e.g. directly into the river)	Dwelling. Children and adolescents aged 0 to 17 years	24 (1)... recognize the right of the child to the enjoyment of the highest attainable standard of health... 24 (2e) shall take appropriate measures... to ensure... hygiene and environmental sanitation...
Housing Ratio of persons per room Flooring material Wall materials Roofing material	Overcrowding: three or more people per room (excluding bathroom and kitchen), mud flooring, unsafe construction materials (mud walls or ceilings or similar)[c]	Overcrowding: five or more people per room, temporary housing (tents, etc.), or with walls or ceilings made from waste materials	Dwelling. Children and adolescents aged 0 to 17 years	27 (1)... recognize the right of every child to a standard of living adequate for the child's [...] development. 27 (3) shall... provide material assistance and support programmes, particularly with regard to nutrition, clothing and housing.
Education School attendance and number of years of completed schooling	Children who, having attended school, dropped out before completing secondary education	Children and adolescents who have never attended school	Individual. Children from 7 or 8 years of age up to 17 years	28 (1)... recognize the right of the child to education... 28 (1a)... shall make primary education compulsory and available free to all; 28(1b)... shall encourage the development of different forms of secondary education, including general and vocational education
Information Access to electricity Radio, television or telephone ownership	No access in the home to electricity, telephone (landline or mobile), radio/television (at least two components are unavailable)	No access in the home to electricity, telephone (landline or mobile) or radio/television (simultaneously)	Household. Children and adolescents aged 0 to 17 years	13 (1) The child shall have the right to freedom of expression; this right shall include freedom to seek, receive and impart information... 17... shall ensure that the child has access to information and material from a diversity of national and international sources...

Source: Economic Commission for Latin America and the Caribbean (ECLAC)/United Nations Children's Fund (UNICEF), on the basis of David Gordon and others, *Child Poverty in the Developing World*, Bristol, The Policy Press, 2003.

[a] As the situations defined are those of deprivation, the deprivation thresholds are implicitly defined as better well-being than that described in the each cell.

[b] These indicators were obtained from the Demographic and Health Surveys (DHS) and the Multiple Indicator Cluster Surveys (MICS), and were developed into a set of models to estimate the probability of malnourishment with binary logical regressions, which was then applied to household surveys.

[c] Unlike in the Bristol study, which considered mud flooring as severe deprivation, in this measurement mud flooring was defined as moderate deprivation.

Similarly, based on the child-rights approach and the indivisibility and interdependence of human rights, rights were considered to be absolutely equivalent, with the result that no rights were prioritized either substantively or technically, as no single right carries greater weight than any other. This means that each deprivation is regarded as an indicator of poverty because it violates or infringes at least one right. As a corollary, children or adolescents are considered to be experiencing poverty if they are either moderately or severely deprived in at least one of the dimensions considered, even if it is only that one.[3] Despite the fact that children and adolescents can be affected by their parent's decisions, community discrimination or problems not directly associated with insufficient resources or access to basic social services, such deprivations constitute an infringement of their rights irrespective of the cause. By ratifying the Convention on the Rights of the Child, States undertake to devote the maximum available resources to comply with all child rights —which includes defraying health-care and other costs that households find difficult to pay— and to ensure that no discrimination exists.

As with the multiple deprivation method, three situations were defined according to the potential ability of households with children to meet their basic needs through market mechanisms. This was done by comparing per capita income with poverty and extreme poverty lines, in order to identify households with inadequate levels of well-being: indigent households, poor (but not indigent) households and non-poor households. In the late 1980s, several attempts were made in Latin America to integrate monetary and non-monetary methodologies (ECLAC/DGEC, 1988). A point of note is that, rather than considering insufficient income as a separate dimension alongside material deprivations, such integrative approaches regard income as a potential factor for meeting needs (input factor) and material deprivations as a result of insufficient or inequitably distributed household income (for example, see Townsend, 1979), or the State's failure to provide public goods and services (see box I.4 in chapter I).

Measurement of well-being and poverty by the income method alone is not enough to account for all the deprivations that might undermine children's development. However, income measurement provides valuable data for characterizing the situation of children, as well as for public policy decision-making. Despite the high correlation, at aggregate level, between income poverty and child poverty according to deprivation —with an even greater correlation in the case of total poverty than extreme poverty— the correlation is less clear at the level of individuals (and households). This makes it necessary to examine the situation of children using the two methodologies.

B. Child poverty in Latin America and the Caribbean

Around 2011, a total of 40.5% of children and adolescents in Latin America were living in poverty. Total child poverty affected 70.5 million children under 18, with 16.3% of children and adolescents living in extreme poverty (28.3 million). Between 2000 and 2011, all the Latin American countries studied saw a decrease in the percentage of poor children under age 18. The reduction in total poverty was just over 14 percentage points, while that of extreme poverty was 10.5 percentage points. The intensity of poverty also diminished, in particular extreme child poverty (in 2011, one in four children suffered more than one severe deprivation). In five Caribbean countries, child poverty ranged from 31% to 71%, and extreme poverty, from 10% to 38%.

Child poverty in a country in a given year refers to children under the age of 18 with at least moderate deprivation of one or more of the rights constituting child poverty: sanitation, access to drinking water, quality housing, enrolment in the education system, access to information or good nutrition. If they experience at least one severe deprivation, children are considered to be living in extreme child poverty. It is important to bear in mind that the following estimates of total child poverty also include children living in extreme poverty.

---

[3] Under the general unmet basic needs method, this decision is called "co-realization criterion": if the indicators were considered perfect substitutes, households or individuals with at least one deprivation are poor (Expert Group on Poverty Statistics (Rio Group), 2007).

Around 2011, a total of 40.5% of children and adolescents in 17 Latin American countries were living in either moderate or extreme poverty. Total child poverty in the region affected 70.5 million children under 18 and 16.3% of children and adolescents were living in extreme poverty. This means that one in six children is extremely poor and the scourge of poverty affects more than 28.3 million children and adolescents (see figure II.1 and table II.2). These children experience one or more severe deprivations in terms of dwellings with unsafe construction materials and overcrowding, lack of access to drinking water or sanitation facilities in the home, general and/or chronic undernutrition, lack of access to the education system (children who have never attended school) or lack of access to communication and information systems (including lack of electricity in the home).

Figure II.1

Latin America (17 countries): incidence of extreme poverty and total child poverty, and children in indigent and poor households (by the income method), circa 2011[a]

(Percentages)

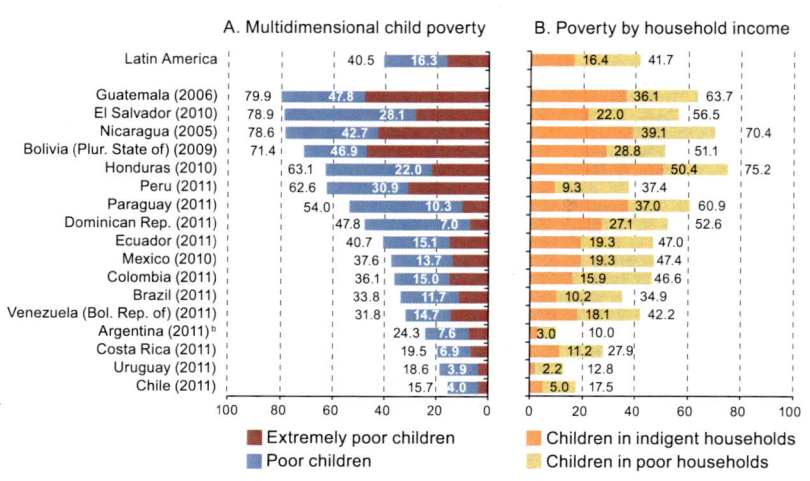

Source: Economic Commission for Latin America and the Caribbean (ECLAC), on the basis of special tabulations of household surveys conducted in the respective countries.
[a] The figures for total child poverty include extreme child poverty and those for income poverty include children in indigent households.
[b] Urban areas.

However, diverse realities lead to marked differences from one country to another. An average 72% of children in countries with the highest total child poverty levels (El Salvador, Guatemala, Honduras, Nicaragua, Peru and the Plurinational State of Bolivia) were extremely poor (20.2 million in these six countries). Among the countries with the lowest total child poverty levels (Argentina, Chile, Costa Rica, Ecuador and Uruguay), a simple average of 19.5% of children were extremely poor (2.8 million).

It is also important to consider the simultaneous presence of deprivations, as they lead to an exponential loss of the exercise of rights, which policymakers should consider and evaluate, especially as deprivation in one dimension often impacts on the opportunity and ability to exercise a right in one or more other dimensions (Gordon and others, 2003; Minujin Delamónica and Davidziuk, 2007; Kaztman, 2011). For this reason, it is important to ascertain not only the percentage of deprived children but also how poor they are. Even though the family of indices used in multidimensional child poverty calculation includes the depth index of poverty —based on calculating the gaps between levels of deprivation in each dimension and the respective thresholds— in this chapter the depth of poverty among the poor is represented by counting the number of deprivations. Although this method of presenting information does not reflect the magnitude of the gaps (because it does not differentiate between poor children with severe and moderate deprivations), it readily illustrates the distribution of poverty by intensity, expressed by counting children with a different number of deprivations and averaging them (Minujin, Delamónica and Davidziuk, 2007; Alkire and Foster, 2009).[4]

---

[4]   See for example the poverty intensity index represented as A in the Alkire and Foster equation in box II.1.

Table II.2

Latin America (17 countries): incidence of extreme poverty and total child poverty, circa 2000 and 2011[a]

(Percentages and number of children and adolescents)

Country		Incidence of extreme poverty	Population	Incidence of total poverty	Population
Argentina (urban)	1999	11.5	835 422	29.0	2 106 785
	2011	7.6	552 241	24.3	1 761 562
Bolivia (Plurinational State of)	1999	56.1	2 046 219	92.2	3 360 480
	2009	46.8	1 986 117	71.4	3 027 071
Brazil	1999	21.2	12 202 634	48.3	27 822 232
	2011	11.7	6 550 679	33.8	18 936 842
Chile	2000	10.0	494 199	28.2	1 392 969
	2011	3.9	174 561	15.7	692 813
Colombia	1999	22.1	3 322 547	47.2	7 105 547
	2011	14.9	2 290 653	36.1	5 530 277
Costa Rica	2002	9.0	132 520	28.0	410 630
	2011	6.8	91 655	19.5	261 418
Dominican Republic	2002	28.2	1 004 543	59.2	2 111 148
	2011	7.0	243 165	47.8	1 664 290
Ecuador (urban)	2002	14.8	479 607	65.2	2 114 159
	2011	4.4	134 979	24.4	751 793
Ecuador	2011	15.1	731 718	40.7	1 968 577
El Salvador	1999	45.0	1 171 944	88.1	2 297 503
	2010	28.1	658 879	78.9	1 849 518
Guatemala	1998	56.2	3 027 604	86.2	4 640 585
	2006	47.8	3 017 179	79.9	5 039 541
Honduras	1999	50.1	1 510 947	75.4	2 272 040
	2010	22.0	757 167	63.1	2 171 965
Mexico	2000	26.1	10 211 623	52.8	20 670 820
	2010	13.7	5 438 549	37.6	14 871 241
Nicaragua	2001	52.2	1 280 974	85.6	2 098 579
	2005	42.7	946 117	78.6	1 742 032
Paraguay	2000	29.7	719 950	67.3	1 629 875
	2011	10.3	247 293	54.0	1 290 885
Peru	1999	48.3	5 297 033	87.4	9 577 983
	2011	30.9	3 142 842	62.6	6 374 238
Uruguay (urban)	1999	7.1	55 571	26.1	204 378
	2011	3.6	30 375	17.4	146 748
Uruguay	2011	3.9	35 883	18.6	170 932
Venezuela (Bolivarian Republic of)	1999	17.1	1 651 583	42.8	4 125 838
	2011	14.7	1 473 226	31.8	3 197 520
Latin America (14 countries) [b]	**2000**	**27.2**	**44 074 047**	**55.3**	**89 516 062**
	2011	**16.7**	**27 017 999**	**41.2**	**66 418 973**
Latin America (17 countries) [c]	**2011**	**16.3**	**28 337 797**	**40.5**	**70 550 504**

Source: Economic Commission for Latin America and the Caribbean (ECLAC), on the basis of special tabulations of household surveys conducted in the respective countries.
[a] Children aged 0 to 17.
[b] Excludes Argentina, Ecuador and Uruguay because at least one of the two measures in these countries is for urban areas only.
[c] Includes urban areas of Argentina.

The depth of extreme poverty tends to be greater precisely when the percentage of extremely poor children is higher.[5] Not only are high levels of extreme child poverty associated with fairly widespread deprivation in one of the dimensions of children's rights, in many cases they are also linked to the existence of multiple extreme deprivations, which are manifested simultaneously in a significant percentage of children. While the existence of even one extreme deprivation is already damaging to a child's development, the presence of a "syndrome" of multiple deprivation is a sure sign of lost opportunities for children to tap their full potential and ultimately perpetuates the intergenerational transmission of poverty. One in four extremely poor children is severely deprived of more than one fundamental right and two in three poor children are deprived of one (see table II.4).

According to data for 17 countries around 2011, a total of 27.4% of the more than 28 million extremely poor children suffer more than one severe deprivation and just over 7% suffer three or more severe deprivations (see table II.3). With regard to total child poverty, 58.8% of the more than 70 million children affected suffer a single

---

[5] These results are consistent with those in chapter I.

moderate or severe deprivation (just over 41 million children) and only one in six poor children are deprived in three or more dimensions of well-being (see table II.4). Notwithstanding the above, the diversity and varying intensity of child poverty situations among countries of the region should be borne in mind, as should their differing capacity to finance large-scale pro-child policies. Indeed, countries with the highest levels of child poverty (total and extreme) tend to have the largest concentration of children with multiple deprivations but also the fewest resources to tackle the problem.

Table II.3
Latin America (17 countries): distribution of extremely poor children aged 0 to 17 years, by number of severe deprivations, around 2000 and 2011
(Percentages)

Country		Total	One deprivation	Two deprivations	Three deprivations	Four deprivations	Five deprivations
Argentina (urban)	1999	100	79.9	17.6	2.5	0.0	0.0
	2011	100	90.0	9.3	0.7	0.0	0.0
Bolivia (Plurinational State of)	1999	100	38.4	34.7	22.8	4.0	0.1
	2009	100	55.8	33.2	10.2	0.8	0.0
Brazil	1999	100	64.7	27.7	6.7	0.9	0.0
	2011	100	78.9	16.7	4.2	0.3	0.0
Chile	2000	100	78.5	20.1	.1.3	0.1	0.0
	2011	100	93.9	5.3	0.5	0.3	0.0
Colombia	1999	100	62.2	23.4	11.7	2.6	0.1
	2011	100	71.4	22.1	5.3	1.1	0.2
Costa Rica	2002	100	81.8	14.2	3.4	0.6	0.0
	2011	100	93.3	6.1	0.6	0.0	0.0
Dominican Republic	2002	100	77.2	19.3	3.1	0.4	0.0
	2011	100	79.4	16.0	4.3	0.3	0.0
Ecuador (urban)	2002	100	86.4	10.0	3.0	0.6	0.0
	2011	100	92.5	6.8	0.7	0.0	0.0
Ecuador	2011	100	76.6	16.0	5.0	2.0	0.4
El Salvador	1999	100	57.7	26.5	11.9	3.6	0.4
	2010	100	74.0	19.3	5.8	0.9	0.1
Guatemala	1998	100	54.0	28.6	13.2	3.8	0.3
	2006	100	55.9	26.1	12.4	5.0	0.7
Honduras	1999	100	50.0	28.7	15.5	4.6	1.2
	2010	100	76.0	20.0	3.6	0.3	0.0
Mexico	2000	100	63.9	26.4	8.6	1.2	0.0
	2010	100	83.6	13.3	2.5	0.6	0.0
Nicaragua	2001	100	57.5	23.9	13.5	4.5	0.5
	2005	100	59.7	27.4	9.4	3.0	0.5
Paraguay	2000	100	77.9	17.5	3.6	0.8	0.2
	2011	100	84.8	11.8	3.4	0.0	0.0
Peru	1999	100	36.2	32.8	23.7	7.1	0.2
	2011	100	64.0	24.8	8.6	2.3	0.2
Uruguay (urban)	1999	100	82.3	15.3	2.3	0.1	0.0
	2011	100	90.3	9.7	0.0	0.0	0.0
Uruguay	2011	100	90.5	9.5	0.0	0.0	0.0
Venezuela (Bolivarian Republic of)	1999	100	67.6	24.1	7.4	0.8	0.1
	2011	100	70.6	25.3	3.9	0.1	0.0
Latin America (14 countries) [a]	**2000**	**100**	**58.8**	**27.3**	**11.2**	**2.5**	**0.1**
	2011	**100**	**72.1**	**20.5**	**6.0**	**1.3**	**0.1**
Latin America (17 countries) [b]	**2011**	**100**	**72.6**	**20.2**	**5.8**	**1.3**	**0.1**

Source: Economic Commission for Latin America and the Caribbean (ECLAC), on the basis of special tabulations of household surveys conducted in the respective countries.
[a] Excludes Argentina, Ecuador and Uruguay because at least one of the two measures in these countries is for urban areas only.
[b] Includes urban areas of Argentina.

Table II.4
Latin America (17 countries): distribution of poor children aged 0 to 17 years,
by number of deprivations, around 2000 and 2011
(Percentages)

Country		Total	One deprivation	Two deprivations	Three deprivations	Four deprivations	Five deprivations
Argentina (urban)	1999	100	73.8	18.4	6.8	1.0	0.0
	2011	100	85.6	11.2	2.8	0.4	0.0
Bolivia (Plurinational State of)	1999	100	22.6	22.4	19.3	25.0	10.8
	2009	100	31.7	28.6	23.5	14.2	2.0
Brazil	1999	100	56.9	23.1	14.0	5.2	0.8
	2011	100	73.9	19.3	5.0	1.6	0.1
Chile	2000	100	50.8	23.6	17.3	7.5	0.8
	2011	100	77.2	17.7	4.3	0.8	0.0
Colombia	1999	100	45.9	23.3	16.9	11.0	3.0
	2011	100	57.1	23.7	12.3	5.3	1.6
Costa Rica	2002	100	63.8	19.2	10.2	5.4	1.4
	2011	100	74.5	18.2	5.4	1.6	0.3
Dominican Republic	2002	100	37.0	36.5	17.8	7.2	1.6
	2011	100	48.9	33.9	12.4	4.1	0.6
Ecuador (urban)	2002	100	42.2	28.2	17.5	10.0	2.0
	2011	100	70.6	21.6	6.7	1.0	0.0
Ecuador	2011	100	50.6	26.3	15.2	6.3	1.6
El Salvador	1999	100	43.0	22.3	19.7	11.9	3.2
	2010	100	60.2	23.3	10.8	4.8	0.9
Guatemala	1998	100	18.1	19.5	29.6	25.6	7.2
	2006	100	28.4	29.7	25.1	13.5	3.4
Honduras	1999	100	28.5	25.5	22.9	16.8	6.3
	2010	100	50.2	25.4	14.8	7.7	1.9
Mexico	2000	100	40.6	26.0	19.8	10.9	2.6
	2010	100	63.1	24.4	9.0	3.0	0.4
Nicaragua	2001	100	27.6	27.5	24.1	15.8	5.1
	2005	100	28.3	29.4	21.8	16.0	4.5
Paraguay	2000	100	24.3	22.8	28.8	18.4	5.7
	2011	100	46.2	28.0	18.5	6.2	1.0
Peru	1999	100	20.7	23.8	20.6	25.4	9.5
	2011	100	44.5	26.7	18.6	8.0	2.2
Uruguay (urban)	1999	100	65.1	25.2	8.2	1.5	0.0
	2011	100	84.3	12.7	3.1	0.0	0.0
Uruguay	2011	100	81.5	14.2	4.0	0.3	0.0
Venezuela (Bolivarian Republic of)	1999	100	58.7	24.8	11.7	4.3	0.5
	2011	100	70.6	20.7	7.2	1.4	0.2
Latin America (14 countries) [a]	2000	100	42.3	24.2	18.2	11.9	3.4
	2011	100	58.3	23.9	11.6	5.1	1.1
Latin America (17 countries) [b]	2011	100	58.8	23.6	11.5	5.0	1.1

Source: Economic Commission for Latin America and the Caribbean (ECLAC), on the basis of special tabulations of household surveys conducted in the respective countries.
[a] Excludes Argentina, Ecuador and Uruguay because at least one of the two measures in these countries is for urban areas only.
[b] Includes urban areas of Argentina.

Box II.1
Multidimensional measurement of child poverty: identification and aggregation

In order to construct child poverty rates under the multidimensional approach adopted by the Economic Commission for Latin America and the Caribbean (ECLAC) and the UNICEF Regional Office for Latin America and the Caribbean, the dimensions described in table II.1 (nutrition, drinking water, sanitation, housing, education and information) were established on the basis of data available in national household surveys, which have the usual advantage of being representative of the entire country (or urban areas) and of including household income measures and hence monetary measures of poverty.

The use of national household surveys as the main source for measuring child poverty has one major limitation: lack of information on children's nutritional status. To remedy this, logistic models were constructed to estimate the probability of undernutrition (underweight and moderate-severe and severe stunting) based on Demographic and Health Surveys (DHS) and Multiple Indicator Cluster surveys (MICS). These models used predictor variables (and corresponding levels of measurement) capable of being replicated in household surveys. They were subsequently rebuilt in the household surveys in order to make an individual assessment of the probability of undernutrition (for details of the models and predictor variables used, see ECLAC/UNICEF, 2010).

After establishing the dimensions, the thresholds determining levels of deprivation were defined (see table II.1), with three situations for each dimension: severe deprivation; moderate deprivation; and no deprivation. These thresholds were based on the "continuum of deprivation" concept put forward by Gordon (2006), which served as the basis for the global study on child poverty (UNICEF, 2005).

Children and adolescents living in extreme poverty and total poverty were identified using the union approach: a child is extremely poor if he or she is severely deprived in at least one dimension; a child is poor if he or she has at least one moderate deprivation (see table II.1 for a definition of the thresholds). This means that the process of identifying poor and extremely poor children is independent of the weight that may be assigned to the dimensions.

ECLAC and the United Nations Children's Fund (UNICEF) assigned the weight of each dimension on the basis of how widespread each deprivation was among children: the less widespread a deprivation was in each country, the more importance it was given (weighting) in preventing the exercise of the corresponding child right. Therefore the weight of each dimension was defined operationally as the complement of the proportion of deprived children (divided by the sum of all the complements). The same procedure was used for severe deprivations and for moderate or severe deprivations. As the weight of the dimensions is irrelevant to the identification process, owing to use of the union approach, its relevance is confined to the aggregation process, reflecting greater intensity, depth and severity of poverty when a deprivation affects a small group of children.

Two of the possible mathematical options used to aggregate poverty and extreme child poverty are the Bourguignon and Chakravarty (2003) or Alkire and Foster (2009) equations (see box I.5 in chapter I). Although the Alkire and Foster equation allows multidimensional poverty to be identified and aggregated for more than one dimension and the Bourguignon and Chakravarty equation allows only for the union approach, the main indicators of both are equivalent if the foregoing methodology is used.

Usual formulations for multidimensional indices of aggregation allowing for the union approach

Bourguignon and Chakravarty (2003)

$$P_\alpha^\theta(X;z)=\frac{1}{n}\sum_{i\in S_i}\left(\sum_{j=1}^{m}a_j\cdot MAX\left(1-\frac{x_j}{z_j};0\right)^\theta\right)^{\alpha/\theta}$$

Where $\alpha=0$ gives rise to the headcount index (poverty or extreme poverty rate: H or P0), $\alpha=1$ to the depth index (P1) and $\alpha=2$ to the severity index of poverty (P2).

Alkire and Foster (2009)

$$M_\alpha=\mu\big(g^\alpha(k)\big)=\frac{\sum_{i=1}^{n}\sum_{j=1}^{d}w_i\cdot g_{ij}^0(k)\left(1-\frac{x_{ij}}{z_i}\right)^\alpha}{nd}$$

Where $\alpha=0$ gives rise to the adjusted headcount index (M0), $\alpha=1$ to the adjusted depth index (M1) and $\alpha=2$ to the adjusted severity index (M2) (not the original name given by the authors). The usual headcount index (H) is obtained by breaking down M0. K is the number of dimensions whose simultaneous deprivation identifies the poor.

Similarities and differences between the two equations in calculating total child poverty

Equation	Index	Example of index equivalence in ...				
		Chile 2011	Colombia 2011	Ecuador 2011	Mexico 2010	Peru 2011
Bourguignon and Chakravarty (2003)	Headcount index (H=P0)	0.15661	0.36082	0.40662	0.37563	0.62609
	Depth index (P1)	0.01329	0.04313	0.04974	0.03922	0.07721
	Gap ratio (depth calculated only among the poor)	0.08487	0.11953	0.12232	0.10441	0.12332
	Severity index (P2)	0.00152	0.00807	0.00918	0.00598	0.01525
Alkire and Foster (2009)	Headcount index (H)	0.15661	0.36082	0.40662	0.37563	0.62609
	(Weighted) average of deprivations among the poor (A)	0.21075	0.26783	0.28775	0.24232	0.26563
	Adjusted headcount index (M0 = H*A)	0.03301	0.09664	0.11701	0.09102	0.16631
	Average poverty gap (only dimensions with deprivation) (G)	0.40272	0.44629	0.42509	0.43088	0.46426
	Adjusted depth index (M1 = H*A*G)	0.01329	0.04313	0.04974	0.03922	0.07721
	Gap ratio (among the poor) (A*G)	0.08487	0.11953	0.12232	0.10441	0.12332
	Adjusted severity index (only dimensions with deprivation) (S)	0.18050	0.22407	0.20287	0.20866	0.24203
	Adjusted severity index (M2 = H*A*S)	0.00596	0.02165	0.02374	0.01899	0.04025

Source: Commission for Latin America and the Caribbean (ECLAC), on the basis of special tabulations of household surveys conducted in the respective countries; F. Bourguignon and S.R. Chakravarty, "The measurement of multidimensional poverty", *Journal of Economic Inequality*, vol. 1, No. 1, April 2003; S. Alkire and J. Foster, "Counting and multidimensional poverty measurement", *Working Paper*, No. 32, Oxford Poverty and Human Development Initiative (OPHI), December 2009; ECLAC/UNICEF, "Guía para estimar la pobreza infantil", 2012 [online] http://dds.cepal.org/infancia/guia-para-estimar-la-poverty-infantil/.

Box II.1 (concluded)

As the comparative table shows, the two headcount indices agree, as do the depth indices (P_1 and M_1) and gap ratios between the poor. Note that only indices P_1, P_2, M_1 y M_2 comply with the axiomatic principles of poverty measures (focal axiom, monotonicity axion, transfer axiom, subgroup monotonicity, and so forth). The main difference between the indices calculated in the previous examples (using the methodological options mentioned) lies in the method of calculating the severity of poverty: while the Bourguignon and Chakravarty index squares the sum of the distances between deprivations and thresholds, the Alkire and Foster index determines each distance before adding them together.

The 2010 study on child poverty in Latin America and the Caribbean (ECLAC/UNICEF, 2010) opted explicitly for the Bourguignon and Chakravarty equation because it is similar to the extended aggregate measure of monetary poverty known as the Foster-Greer-Thorbecke (FGT) index (1984) and is easiest to disseminate in-country through technical assistance activities and short training workshops. ECLAC/UNICEF (2010) and (2012a) provide more details on the various steps in identifying and aggregating child poverty and the meaning and calculation of the various components of the Bourguignon and Chakravarty and Alkire and Foster equations, together with their similarities and differences.

Lastly, a complex methodological decision is required to define two deprivation thresholds by dimension: if two children have a deprivation (and are therefore poor) but the first child is experiencing moderate deprivation and the second is experiencing severe deprivation, they should have a different gap ratio in that dimension (distance from the threshold). This means that, when calculating total poverty, different distances must be captured for moderate and severe deprivation. This was done by assigning a score of 1 for severe deprivation, 2 for moderate deprivation and 3 for no deprivation (the value 0 was reserved for the situation of extreme deprivation, which is not amenable to measurement by conventional surveys). However, the distances represented by these scores are metric, whereas the three situations (severe, moderate and no deprivation) relate to an ordinal system (where the actual distances cannot be established). So, even though it is possible to differentiate between groups of poor children using depth and severity indices of total poverty, they should be considered merely illustrative of the severity of poverty in these groups.

Source: Sabina Alkire and James Foster, "Counting and multidimensional poverty measurement", *Working Paper*, No. 32, Oxford Poverty and Human Development Initiative (OPHI), December 2009; F. Bourguignon and S.R. Chakravarty, "The measurement of multidimensional poverty", *Journal of Economic Inequality*, vol. 1, No. 1, April 2003; Economic Commission for Latin America and the Caribbean (ECLAC)/United Nations Children's Fund (UNICEF), "Pobreza infantil en América Latina y el Caribe" (LC/R.2168), Santiago, Chile, 2010; ECLAC/UNICEF, "Guía para estimar la pobreza infantil", 2012 [online] http://dds.cepal.org/infancia/guia-para-estimar-la-pobreza-infantil/; E. Espíndola and M.N. Rico, "Child poverty in Latin America: multiple deprivation and monetary measures combined", *Global Child Poverty and Well-being. Measurement, concepts, policy and action*, Alberto Minujin and Sailen Nandy, Bristol, The Policy Press, 2012; D. Gordon, "Cómo monitorear el derecho a la salud", *Exclusión y derecho a la salud. La función de los profesionales de la salud*, Lima, Educación en Derechos Humanos con Aplicación en Salud (EDHUCASALUD)/Federación Internacional de Organizaciones de Derechos Humanos y Salud (IFHHRO), 2007; United Nations Children's Fund (UNICEF), *The State of the World's Children, 2005*, New York, 2005.

1. Changes in child poverty in the period 2000-2011

Although several countries in the region have made great strides in recent years in analysing child poverty, together with its determinants and the different approaches for measuring it (Tuñón, 2012; CONEVAL/UNICEF, 2013), so far there has been little study of changes over time. However, a temporal perspective is essential for assessing the progressive realization of rights and countries' current efforts in that direction. This has been facilitated by changes to countries' data gathering instruments —particularly household surveys, the main source for estimating child poverty— and poses a dual challenge: to make comparisons over time to provide information for assessing changes in the various dimensions of child poverty and to promote better surveys. This is crucial, for example, for survey questions on information access by households and individuals, in a world where access to information and communication technologies is so important.

During the period under consideration, the household surveys closest to the stipulated years (2000-2011) are encouraging insofar as they show a drop in the percentage of children under 18 deprived of any basic right (total poverty) in all the Latin American countries studied. In the region (14 countries comparable nationally over time), the decrease in total child poverty was a little over 14 percentage points over the period, falling from 55.3% of children around 2000 to 41.2% around 2011. The biggest decrease occurred in Peru, where the percentage of children living in poverty fell by nearly 25 percentage points between 1999 and 2011. In spite of this, 62.6% of children under 18 in Peru were poor in 2011. The smallest decline in total child poverty occurred in Argentina (urban areas), where it amounted to a little under 5 percentage points between 1999 and 2011, although only 24.3% of the country's children had a deprivation.[6] Around 2011, Guatemala (2006) was the country with the highest percentage of children and adolescents with moderate or severe deprivations, at nearly 80%, although a decrease was observed here, too. Also suffering severe deprivations were children in: El Salvador, with a poverty rate of nearly 79% in 2010; Nicaragua (2005), with 78.6%; and the Plurinational

---

[6] The fact that no information indicators are available for Argentina leads not only to lower child poverty levels but also to less significant progress in reducing it.

State of Bolivia (2009), with 71.4%.[7] In contrast, countries with the lowest percentage of children and adolescents living in total poverty in 2011 were Chile, with 15.7%, and Uruguay, with 17.4% (see table II.2).

Figure II.2 illustrates the distribution of the number of moderate or severe deprivations and severe deprivations across the region and changes over time (see tables II.3 and II.4 for a breakdown by country). Table II.4 shows that, in 14 countries, the percentage of poor children with a single deprivation increased from 42.3% to 58.3%, while the proportion of poor children with multiple deprivations (two or more) declined significantly (from nearly 58% to 42%). Furthermore, the percentage of poor children with several deprivations (three or more) fell from 33.5% to 17.8% and the percentage of children and adolescents with many deprivations (five) fell from 3.4% to 1.1%. This attests not only to progress in reducing the percentage of children experiencing a deprivation but also to a decrease in the intensity of poverty among poor children.

Figure II.2
Latin America (14 countries): changes in the cumulative distribution of the number of severe deprivations and the total number of deprivations, 2000 and 2011[a]
(Percentages)

A. Cumulative distribution of the number of severe deprivations among extremely poor children

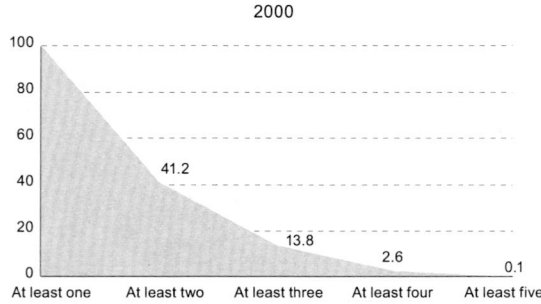
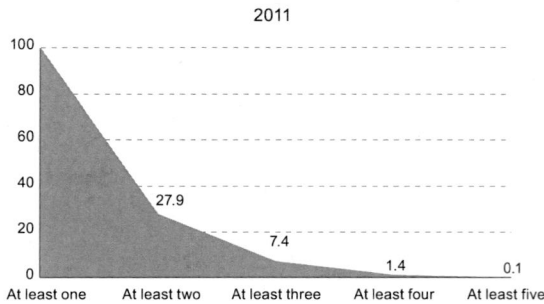

B. Cumulative distribution of the total number of deprivations among poor children[b]

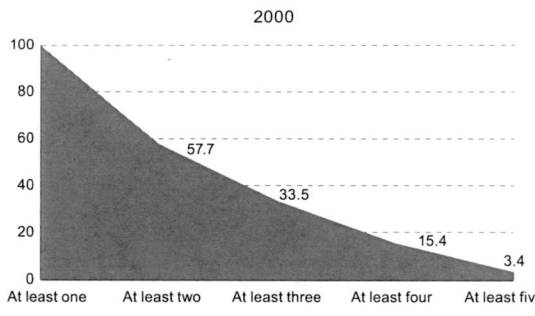
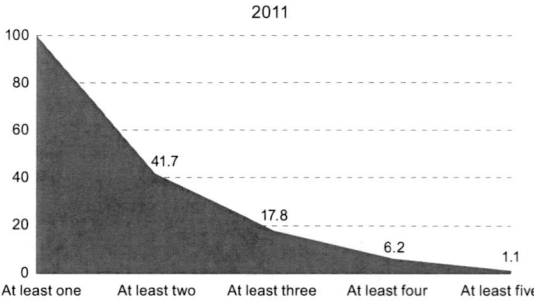

Source: Economic Commission for Latin America and the Caribbean (ECLAC), on the basis of special tabulations of household surveys conducted in the respective countries.
[a] The figures present cumulative deprivations. For example, the percentage of children with at least three deprivations includes those with four or five deprivations. The baseline values equal 100% (children with at least one deprivation) because the universe for calculating distributions was poor or extremely poor children, as appropriate.
[b] Includes extremely poor children and adolescents.

Table II.2 shows that extreme child poverty fell from 27.2% to 16.7% across the region (14 countries) and that all countries saw a decrease in the percentage of children under 18 severely deprived of some of these rights. Like total child poverty, extreme poverty fell more than 10 percentage points in the space of a decade. Proportionally, the decline in extreme poverty was even greater, representing a reduction of nearly 40% compared with a 25% decrease in total child poverty.

---

[7] Several countries in the region are developing multidimensional measures of poverty, in particular child poverty. Unlike national measures, which are more closely geared to States' specific conditions and public policy objectives, international measures seek to make comparisons among countries over time, which is why they may diverge from national measures.

The biggest decrease in the number of children experiencing extreme child poverty was observed in Honduras, where it fell by 28 percentage points between 1999 and 2010 to 22% of children under 18. Next was the Dominican Republic, with a reduction of 21 percentage points (7% in 2011), and El Salvador, with 28.1% of children extremely poor in 2010. The smallest decreases occurred in Costa Rica (2.2%), Bolivarian Republic of Venezuela (2.4%), Uruguay (3.5%) and Argentina (3.9%), in that order, partly because they already had low levels of extreme child poverty in 2000 (see table II.2).

The intensity of both extreme and total child poverty has also eased significantly. Whereas in the first decade of the 2000s, 41.2% of all extremely poor children and adolescents had more than one severe deprivation in one basic right and 13.8% had deprivations in three or more rights, by around 2011 the situation had improved markedly. This reflected not only a sharp reduction in extreme child poverty levels, but also a decrease in the proportion of extremely poor children with more than one severe deprivation (in 2011, only 27.9% of extremely poor children had two or more severe deprivations) (see figure II.2.A). The intensity of total child poverty also fell sharply across the region during the period in question. The biggest decreases were observed among children and adolescents with at least two deprivations and at least three deprivations in 2000 (more than a 15-percentage-point drop in both cases). While the decline is much smaller among children with at least five deprivations (from 3.4% in 2000 to 1.1% in 2011 in total child poverty) who, by definition, suffer an appalling violation of their rights (see figure II.4.B), it does point to positive outcomes in tackling multidimensional child poverty over the decade: not only did its incidence decrease, but the percentage of children and adolescents with the largest number of deprivations also decreased. This also has policy implications insofar as interventions need to focus on a smaller number of dimensions.

2. Evolution of deprivation in Latin America

As the composition of multidimensional child poverty was seen to change between 2000 and 2011, with the levels of poverty and extreme poverty falling and their intensity (measured in number of deprivations) easing, it is important to consider the evolution of each dimension in order to analyse how gaps in the realization of each of the rights constituting child poverty have been closing.

(a) Deprivation in housing quality

When measuring child poverty, children under 18 are considered to suffer severe housing deprivation if they live in dwellings with no roof or a straw roof, dwellings built from waste material, or houses with five or more people per room. Children with moderate deprivations are those living in dwellings with walls of straw or palm, or mud flooring, or where three or more people are living per room. In 2011, of all the dimensions constituting child poverty, housing showed the highest percentage of children and adolescents suffering moderate or severe deprivations in most of the countries studied, with the exception of Brazil, Costa Rica and the Dominican Republic, where the highest percentage of deprivations was in sanitation.[8]

In 5 of the 16 countries with national data for 2011 (El Salvador, Guatemala, Nicaragua, Peru and the Plurinational State of Bolivia), over 10% of children and adolescents were severely deprived of this right to quality housing. Brazil, Chile, Costa Rica, Dominican Republic and Uruguay had less than 3% of children experiencing severe deprivations in this dimension in 2011 (see table II.5).

All countries show a decline in the percentage of children and adolescents with moderate or severe housing deprivation. The greatest reductions —over 10 percentage points— were in Ecuador (urban areas), El Salvador, Mexico, Nicaragua, Paraguay and the Plurinational State of Bolivia. Honduras also saw a significant decrease in moderate or severe housing deprivation. A point of note is that the housing deprivation level at the start of the new millennium was 30% or more in all these countries, and in most, it exceeded 50% (see table II.6).

Countries with consistently high levels of moderate or severe deprivation in the housing dimension are concentrated in Central America: El Salvador, Guatemala and Nicaragua (all with a current incidence of 60%). They are followed by the Plurinational State of Bolivia and Peru (with 51% and 53%, respectively).

Most countries have achieved a decline in the number of children under 18 with severe housing deprivation, except Argentina (urban areas), the Bolivarian Republic of Venezuela and Chile, which show a slight (but not statistically significant) increase. The largest decreases were recorded in El Salvador and Nicaragua (more than 13 percentage points), followed by Mexico (more than 11 percentage points).

---

[8]   Because the National Household Survey of Brazil (PNAD) does not record the flooring material of dwellings, Brazil's child poverty may be underestimated in this regional comparison.

(b) Deprivation in sanitation

Children under 18 required to defecate in the open because they have no access to sanitation in the dwelling or property where they live are considered to suffer severe deprivation with regard to sanitation. Moderate deprivation in this area consists of access to a latrine or cesspit unconnected to the sewer system. In 12 of the 16 countries with national data for 2011, more than 10% of children and adolescents had some level of deprivation in sanitation (see figure II.3). Between 2000 and 2011, all countries showed a decline in the total number of sanitation-deprived children and adolescents (see table II.6). Indeed, several countries have achieved large decreases in this area: a reduction of 10 percentage points or more occurred in Brazil, Chile, the Dominican Republic, Guatemala, Honduras, Mexico, Paraguay, Peru and the Plurinational State of Bolivia. The smallest decrease was in Nicaragua (only 2.9 percentage points between 2001 and 2005, to just over 50% of children with deprivation in sanitation). While other countries experienced small percentage reductions, they are nevertheless significant because these countries had started with much lower levels of deprivation (e.g. Costa Rica).

Table II.5
**Latin America (17 countries): severe deprivation in the different dimensions of extreme child poverty,
around 2000 and 2011**
(Percentages)

Country		Access to drinking water	Access to sanitation	Housing quality	Access to education	Access to information
Argentina (urban)	1999	2.0	5.6	5.7	0.2	...
	2011	0.9	1.2	5.8	0.1	...
Bolivia (Plurinational State of)	1999	38.4	38.2	17.6	1.1	12.0
	2009	31.4	23.0	13.9	0.2	3.4
Brazil	1999	7.0	17.0	2.8	1.2	2.2
	2011	2.9	9.1	1.5	0.6	0.5
Chile	2000	6.7	3.3	0.2	0.2	1.8
	2011	2.9	0.5	0.4	0.2	0.2
Colombia	1999	7.2	10.6	7.3	1.8	6.8
	2011	6.1	7.8	4.0	0.6	1.6
Costa Rica	2002	4.8	1.6	2.7	0.8	1.2
	2011	5.0	0.6	1.0	0.3	0.3
Dominican Republic	2002	25.5	3.5	2.6	1.2	2.7
	2011	1.1	3.6	1.5	1.2	1.4
Ecuador (urban)	2002	0.7	2.8	11.5	0.7	0.7
	2011	0.5	0.7	2.5	0.2	0.1
Ecuador	2011	7.8	5.3	4.5	0.3	1.5
El Salvador	1999	12.2	12.9	33.9	3.0	10.0
	2010	7.7	4.9	20.8	1.1	2.6
Guatemala	1998	14.2	16.4	42.0	7.5	11.0
	2006	9.7	11.3	36.0	4.4	16.5
Honduras	1999	13.5	18.8	14.8	4.3	36.9
	2010	6.5	10.6	7.3	1.3	2.0
Mexico	2000	8.3	11.0	15.0	1.2	2.1
	2010	6.7	4.4	3.8	0.7	0.7
Nicaragua	2001	12.9	17.2	37.6	5.9	12.3
	2005	15.4	13.3	24.1	4.6	8.6
Paraguay	2000	3.4	6.8	18.5	1.5	7.2
	2011	2.1	2.1	6.9	0.3	0.3
Peru	1999	23.0	26.4	12.7	0.6	34.4
	2011	18.6	12.6	12.5	0.2	1.8
Uruguay (urban)	1999	0.7	1.0	5.5	0.3	0.5
	2011	0.0	1.4	1.7	0.1	0.2
Uruguay	2011	0.2	1.6	1.7	0.1	0.2
Venezuela (Bolivarian Republic of)	1999	5.2	8.6	8.4	1.2	0.8
	2011	3.7	6.8	8.5	0.6	0.04
Latin America (14 countries) [a]	**2000**	**9.9**	**14.5**	**10.2**	**1.6**	**6.2**
	2011	**6.5**	**7.8**	**5.8**	**0.8**	**1.6**
Latin America (17 countries) [b]	**2011**	**6.2**	**7.5**	**5.8**	**0.8**	**1.5**

Source: Economic Commission for Latin America and the Caribbean (ECLAC), on the basis of special tabulations of household surveys conducted in the respective countries.
[a] Excludes Argentina, Ecuador and Uruguay because at least one of the two measures in these countries is for urban areas only.
[b] Includes urban areas of Argentina.

Table II.6
**Latin America (17 countries): moderate or severe deprivations in the different dimensions
of child poverty, around 2000 and 2011**
(Percentages)

Country		Access to drinking water	Access to sanitation	Housing quality	Access to education	Access to information
Argentina (urban)	1999	2.0	8.0	22.9	3.5	...
	2011	1.3	2.1	20.7	2.6	...
Bolivia (Plurinational State of)	1999	38.5	65.2	77.6	31.7	34.9
	2009	34.1	52.9	51.3	3.7	12.3
Brazil	1999	15.2	43.6	5.4	5.4	9.5
	2011	7.6	29.4	2.8	3.2	1.4
Chile	2000	9.9	13.7	12.1	2.5	12.9
	2011	6.0	3.5	7.0	1.6	1.7
Colombia	1999	7.8	20.2	31.9	9.5	21.1
	2011	8.8	14.6	24.6	5.3	4.9
Costa Rica	2002	9.4	8.4	9.3	8.2	8.2
	2011	10.5	4.8	3.9	4.9	1.0
Dominican Republic	2002	41.6	46.2	14.0	3.7	10.0
	2011	30.2	32.8	11.0	3.4	4.4
Ecuador (urban)	2002	8.4	20.6	30.0	6.5	57.4
	2011	3.9	5.2	14.1	3.0	1.9
Ecuador	2011	11.7	20.9	23.8	4.5	7.9
El Salvador	1999	35.8	18.6	82.1	10.8	30.3
	2010	21.5	13.3	71.4	7.8	10.4
Guatemala	1998	22.0	68.7	74.3	17.5	46.7
	2006	13.6	56.3	67.6	13.1	22.7
Honduras	1999	15.8	51.1	54.0	17.1	37.5
	2010	15.7	25.0	44.4	13.5	12.9
Mexico	2000	18.2	29.2	37.6	9.5	10.2
	2010	8.3	13.2	22.4	7.8	4.1
Nicaragua	2001	17.7	53.1	73.4	13.0	44.6
	2005	18.9	50.2	62.7	12.3	38.4
Paraguay	2000	40.1	53.3	48.1	8.6	18.6
	2011	24.7	31.5	32.1	5.8	3.4
Peru	1999	36.7	47.2	63.6	6.2	82.9
	2011	26.8	26.4	53.3	2.6	9.4
Uruguay (urban)	1999	2.5	11.2	12.5	5.8	2.4
	2011	0.3	2.2	9.1	5.0	0.4
Uruguay	2011	1.4	2.6	9.2	5.4	0.8
Venezuela (Bolivarian Republic of)	1999	8.6	15.1	30.3	7.0	8.8
	2011	6.9	8.5	24.2	3.7	1.3
Latin America (14 countries) [a]	**2000**	**18.2**	**36.7**	**29.2**	**8.3**	**19.1**
	2011	**11.2**	**23.3**	**21.4**	**5.3**	**5.0**
Latin America (17 countries) [b]	**2011**	**10.8**	**22.3**	**21.4**	**5.2**	**4.9**

Source: Economic Commission for Latin America and the Caribbean (ECLAC), on the basis of special tabulations of household surveys conducted in the respective countries.
[a] Excludes Argentina, Ecuador and Uruguay because at least one of the two measures in these countries is for urban areas only.
[b] Includes urban areas of Argentina.

Figure II.3
**Latin America (17 countries): moderate or severe deprivation and severe deprivation
in the different dimensions of child poverty, around 2011**
(Percentages)

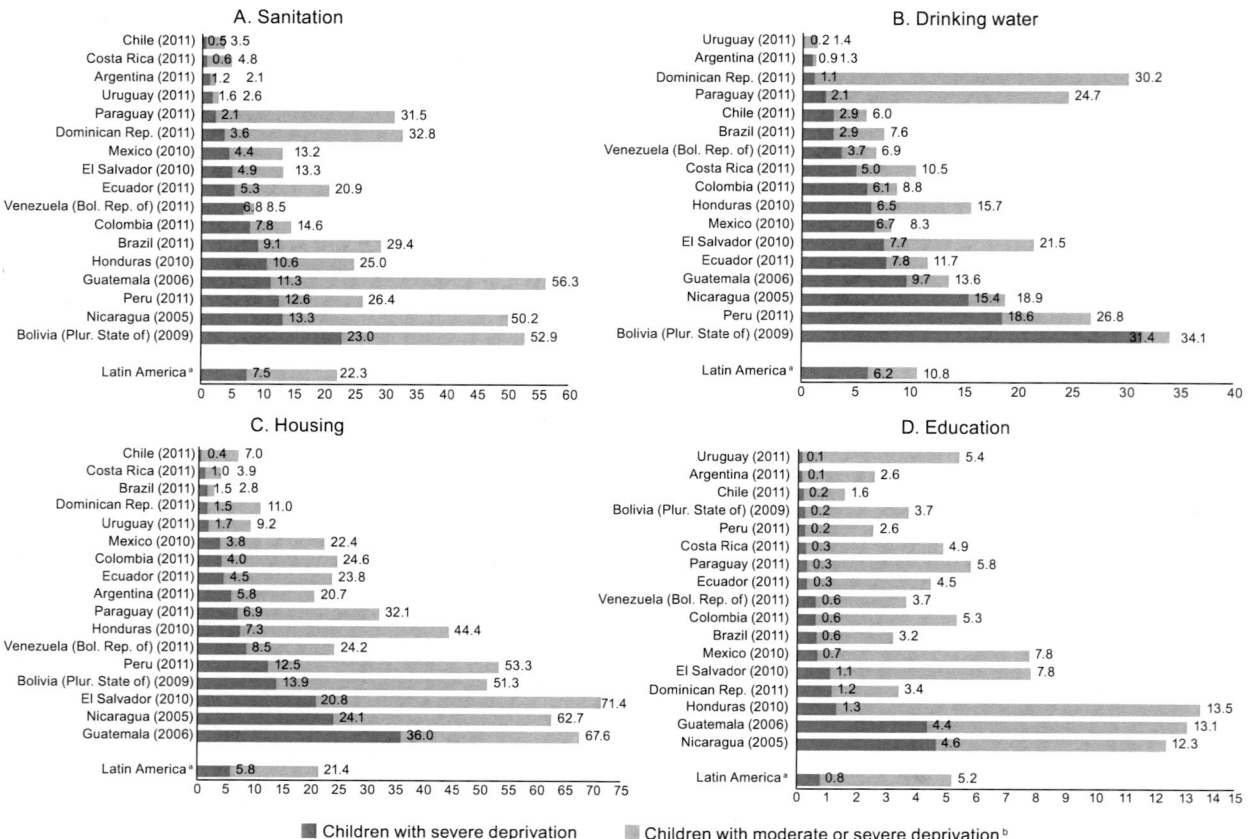

Source: Economic Commission for Latin America and the Caribbean (ECLAC), on the basis of special tabulations of household surveys conducted in the respective countries.
a Average of 17 countries (includes urban areas of Argentina).

Guatemala has the highest percentage of children and adolescents with moderate or severe deprivation in sanitation, with 56.3% of children under 18 deprived in 2006. The countries with the lowest percentage of children and adolescents with moderate or severe deprivation in sanitation nationwide are Chile (3.5%) and Uruguay (2.6%).

At the regional level, the percentage of children and adolescents with severe deprivation in sanitation was 7.8% in 2011, a sharp drop of nearly 7 percentage points from the 14.5% recorded in 2000. A major decrease was observed in all countries. The biggest reduction occurred in the Plurinational State of Bolivia (15.2 percentage points), followed by Peru (13.8%) and Honduras, El Salvador and Brazil (in that order).

(c) Deprivation in access to drinking water

Deprivation in access to drinking water is understood as deprivation of the "right of everyone to sufficient, safe, acceptable, physically accessible and affordable water for personal and domestic uses."[9] Access to drinking water is also assumed to be a prerequisite for the realization of the right to life, food, health and housing.[10] The Millennium Development Goals (MDGs) therefore emphasize this right, setting out to halve the proportion of the population without sustainable access to safe drinking water (MDG 7, target 7C).

---

[9] The right to water (articles 11 and 12 of the International Covenant on Economic, Social and Cultural Rights), General Comment, No. 15.

[10] In July 2010, the United Nations recognized the right to safe and clean drinking water and sanitation as a human right that is essential for the full enjoyment of life and all human rights (ECLAC/UNICEF, 2012b).

Children under 18 who lack access to drinking water and consume water from natural sources (stream, river, pond or rainwater), or who have to travel more than 15 minutes to a source of drinking water, are considered to suffer severe deprivation regarding access to drinking water. Access to hauled water (outside the home) is considered to represent moderate deprivation.[11]

Access to drinking water is the dimension in which the third highest percentage of children and adolescents in Latin America has moderate or severe deprivation. Around 2011, 10.8% of children across the region (17 countries) were moderately or severely deprived and 6.2% were severely deprived of access to drinking water. In 10 of the 16 countries with national data (Costa Rica, the Dominican Republic, Ecuador, El Salvador, Guatemala, Honduras, Nicaragua, Paraguay, Peru and the Plurinational State of Bolivia), over 10% of children and adolescents suffered some kind of deprivation associated with access to drinking water, and in three countries (Nicaragua, Peru and Plurinational State of Bolivia), the figure was over 10% for severe deprivation alone (see tables II.5 and II.6).

The vast majority of countries showed an improvement in the total number of children and adolescents with moderate or severe deprivations in this dimension, with the exception of Colombia, Costa Rica and Nicaragua, which registered a slight increase (around 1%). The largest reductions were observed in Paraguay, El Salvador, the Dominican Republic, Mexico and Peru, in that order (between 10 and 15 percentage points in 2000-2011).

The Plurinational State of Bolivia, Peru and Nicaragua showed the highest percentages of children with moderate or severe deprivations, with rates of over 15%. By contrast, the lowest percentages of children and adolescents with some kind of deprivation in access to drinking water were found in Uruguay and Argentina, where less than 1% of children experienced deprivation (see figure II.3).

The percentage of children under 18 with no access to drinking water (severe deprivation) fell in all the countries except Nicaragua, where it rose from 12.9% in 2001 to 15.4% in 2005. The sharpest falls were recorded in the Dominican Republic (24 percentage points) and in the Plurinational State of Bolivia and Honduras (7 percentage points). Despite the reductions recorded over the decade, levels of severe deprivation in access to drinking water are still high in a number of countries, especially in the Andean region: in the Plurinational State of Bolivia, 31.4% of children were severely deprived of access to drinking water in 2009 and, in Peru, 18.6% of children were severely deprived in 2011.

(d) Deprivation in education

School-age children under 18 who have never been in the education system are considered to be severely deprived with regard to the education dimension. Those who were not attending school at the time of measurement and had not completed secondary education but had attended school at some time are considered to be moderately deprived. Education is one of the child poverty dimensions with the lowest percentage of moderately or severely deprived children and adolescents.[12] In 2011, 5.2% of the region's under-18-year-olds suffered moderate or severe deprivation of their right to education (they had never attended school or had dropped out), although only 0.8% suffered severe deprivation. From this it may be surmised that virtually all children have access to formal basic education (see table II.6).

In only 3 of the 16 countries with national data do more than 10% of children and adolescents have moderate or severe deprivation in education: Guatemala (13.1% in 2006); Honduras (13.5% in 2010) and Nicaragua (12.3% in 2005). Only two countries (Nicaragua and Guatemala) recorded levels of severe deprivation at or above 4% when last measured (see figure II.3).

The total number of children and adolescents with moderate or severe deprivation in education has declined in all countries in the region. The biggest improvements were observed in the Plurinational State of Bolivia, where figures show education deprivation to have been slashed in a single decade from nearly 32% in 1999 to nearly 4% in 2009, mainly through a reduction in the school dropout rate. Although the decline was no more than 4 percentage points in the remaining countries, their deprivation levels were already low around 2000.

---

[11] In cases where the use of bottled water for drinking was recorded, it was considered a moderate deprivation if combined with the use of natural water sources for other purposes (WHO/UNICEF Joint Monitoring Programme for the Water and Sanitation Sector).

[12] This indicator is measured among children over the age of 6 or 7, depending on the national education system, as preschool education is still not compulsory throughout the region and access to this level of education is not usually measured.

(e) Deprivation in information

Children under 18 living in dwellings with no electricity or who have no media goods in the home (no television, radio or telephone of any sort, either landline or mobile) are considered to be severely deprived in the dimension of access to information. Those with only one media good in the home (either radio or television, or some kind of telephone) are considered to be moderately deprived. Many characteristics of this dimension vary from one country to another, and it is this dimension that has undergone the greatest changes in measurement owing to spectacular advances in communications markets and their fast-expanding coverage. In many cases, differences from one year to another stem from the addition or removal of various household information or communication goods. This is the case with Honduras and the Plurinational State of Bolivia, where the changes stem not from the scale of deprivation but from differences in the way the dimension is estimated, and Argentina, where there is no possibility of measuring this dimension.

Nevertheless, the level of information deprivation is clearly falling (see tables II.5 and II.6). At the start of the new millennium, around 19% of the region's children and adolescents suffered some sort of information deprivation. This has changed dramatically, partly owing to fairly widespread access to telecommunications and related goods (especially mobile phones), with the result that, by around 2011, only 5% of children suffered limited access to information (moderate or severe deprivation) in the 14 countries that can be compared nationally over time. Similarly, around 2000, only 6.2% children were severely deprived of their right to information (they had no access to information or communication goods or to a basic electricity supply). This had dropped to 1.6% by around 2011.

While these figures attest to an overall reduction in deprivation of the right to information, in some countries the levels were still high in 2011: El Salvador (10.4%); Guatemala (22.7%); Honduras (12.9%), Nicaragua (38.4%) and the Plurinational State of Bolivia (12.3%). Severe breach of the right to information persists in Guatemala (16.5% of children) and Nicaragua (8.6%). In Guatemala, in fact, the figure actually rose 5.5 percentage points in 1998-2006.

To sum up, both severe and moderate deprivation dropped sharply between 2000 and 2011, and the gaps with regard to sanitation, housing and access to information narrowed significantly. Deprivation decreased less in the areas of education and nutrition because it was already low among the region's children early in the last decade in these areas. An overall reduction in deprivation across all the dimensions explains the significant decline in both total and extreme child poverty, as well as in their intensity (see figure II.4).

Figure II.4
Latin America (14 countries): severe deprivation and moderate or severe deprivation in the different dimensions of child poverty, around 2000 and 2011[a]
(Percentages)

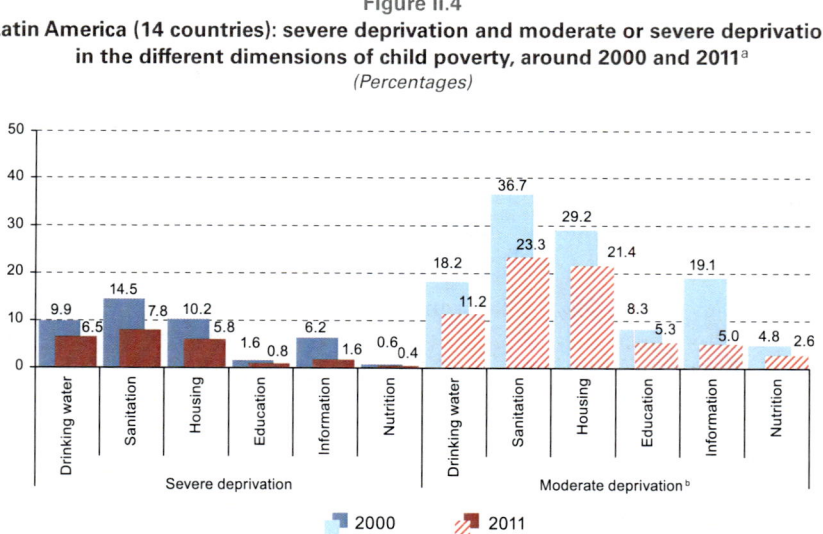

Source: Economic Commission for Latin America and the Caribbean (ECLAC), on the basis of special tabulations of household surveys conducted in the respective countries.
[a] Average of 14 countries with national data at both points in time.
[b] Includes severe deprivation.

Box II.2
Time use: helping to understand child poverty

One of the deprivations facing children and adolescents is lack of time to enjoy childhood, that is, to engage in activities that help ensure their proper development at this stage in their lives. The activities children under 18 perform and how much time they spend on them provide important information for measuring their well-being and the realization of their economic, social and cultural rights (Rico, 2013). Time-use surveys, the best statistical information tool for ascertaining this information, are designed to quantify the time spent on a range of activities throughout the day and provide a detailed picture of day-to-day life and its implications, which cannot be captured from other information sources. Thus far, time-use surveys in Latin America have not been designed or geared to measure the activities of children and adolescents; indeed most do not include interviews with children under the age of 12.

However, when the under-12 age group is included, depending on the interview method used, detailed information can be obtained about the activities in which children engage and their sequence throughout the day, whether they are performed alone or with others in the family unit or household, and the place where the activities are carried out (school, home, street or elsewhere). These activities and their context provide a full picture that can be used to identify a number of potential indicators of factors that protect —or risk— comprehensive child development in various areas, and to link the ways children spend their time with these areas. For example, a recreational or leisure activity may be linked with health and education. However, although a child may appear to spend an adequate amount of time on daily play and recreation, further investigation may reveal that this consists of watching television, playing video games or on the computer, which can make children more prone to obesity than engaging in non-sedentary recreational or sporting activities. School performance may also be affected when studying time is curtailed.

Child well-being depends on which activities are postponed or displaced by others. Children forced to work are more likely to have higher absenteeism rates, drop out from school or have less time to study. Unpaid domestic duties may also affect children's other activities. For example, when children have to stand in for adults in caring for young children, the sick or elderly, it severely limits their access to activities that promote their development. Such problems occur more frequently among children and adolescents from households experiencing monetary poverty.

International studies have illustrated the potential of using time measurements to gauge child well-being. For instance, a time-use survey in Japan identified a number of specific problems among children and their families, revealing that many families no longer eat lunch or dinner together, and that some children go to school without having eaten breakfast. Extremely low levels of participation in physical activities were also observed, as most Japanese people use free time to watch television. A study conducted in the United States (Hofferth and Sandberg, 2000) to analyse time-use differences among children of Asian, Hispanic and African descent demonstrated clear cultural influences. The study found that Asian children spent the most time studying, while those of African descent spent the most time on church activities and those of Hispanic descent spent the most time with their families eating and performing unpaid activities.

In Latin America, time-use surveys in Ecuador (2011), Mexico (2009) and Peru (2011) showed that indigenous adolescents aged 15-19 of both sexes have a longer working day than non-indigenous adolescents (i.e. they spend more time on paid work and unpaid domestic work and less on rest, recreation and socializing). This might suggest that indigenous adolescents have a poorer quality of life and a lower level of well-being than other adolescents of their age (see the figure below).

Ecuador (2011), Mexico (2009) and Peru (2011): time spent on groups of activities by the indigenous and non-indigenous population aged 15-19[a]
(Hours per week)

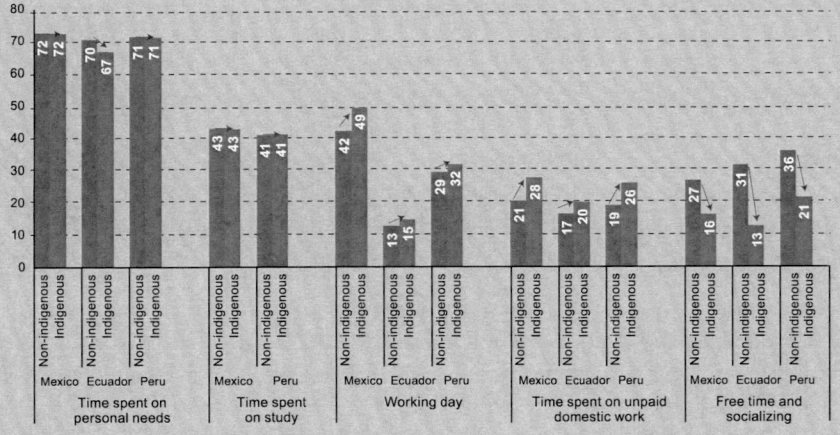

Source: Economic Commission for Latin America and the Caribbean (ECLAC), on the basis of special tabulations of time-use surveys conducted in Peru (2010), Mexico (2009) and the employment, unemployment and underemployment survey in urban and rural areas (2011) of Ecuador.
[a] In Ecuador no question was asked regarding study-related activities.

Time-use surveys have also shown how significant differences that exist between girls and boys, even at an early age, can develop into gender inequalities because of their impact on current and future well-being. Adolescent girls aged 12 to 14 spend more time than their male counterparts on unpaid domestic work and less time on recreation, revealing the presence of cultural and gender roles that disadvantage women. The behaviour and attitudes learned in childhood are carried forward into later life, where they reinforce gender roles and models with respect to adult duties and opportunities for a better quality of life (see the figure below).

Box II.2 (concluded)

Ecuador (2011), Mexico (2009) and Peru (2011): time spent on groups of activities by the population aged 12‑14, by sex [a]
(Hours per week)

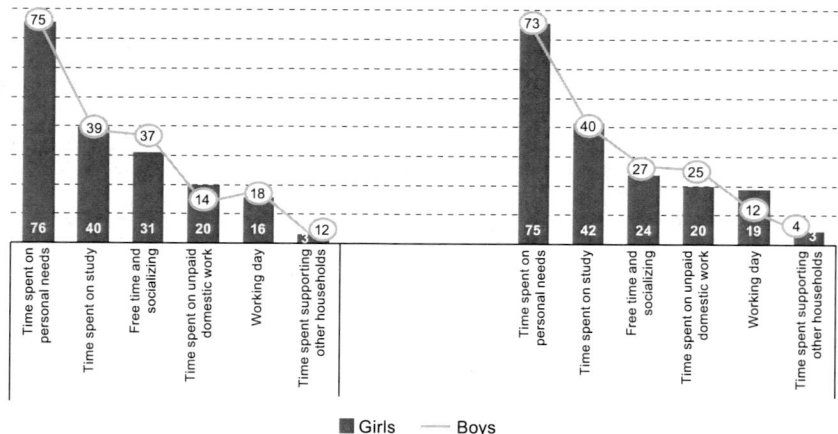

Source: Economic Commission for Latin America and the Caribbean (ECLAC), on the basis of special tabulations of time-use surveys conducted in Peru (2010), Mexico (2009) and the employment, unemployment and underemployment survey in urban and rural areas (2011) of Ecuador.
[a] In Ecuador no question was asked regarding study-related activities.

Time-use surveys provide ample opportunity to identify factors associated with variations in the time spent on certain activities. Factors such as family size, whether or not a child lives with both parents, the educational climate at home, ethnicity, geographical area, socioeconomic status, and gender, age, birth-order and other characteristics, provide a full picture of the children's situation and of generally overlooked aspects of child poverty.

Discussion of these issues also leads to further reflection on how to make the shift from the rhetoric of rights to an operating definition of dimensions, variables and indicators reflecting that will and conviction. Information is a public policy tool and opportunity. The calculation of indicators for children's economic, social and cultural rights helps to ensure full enjoyment of the rights set forth in the Convention on the Rights of the Child and other human rights instruments. The challenge is to leverage the existing information and develop new child-centred methodologies.

Source: Sandra L. Hofferth and John F. Sandberg, *How American Children Spend their Time,* University of Michigan, April 2000; Vivian Milosavljevic, "Estadísticas para la equidad de género. Magnitudes y tendencias en América Latina", *Cuadernos de la CEPAL,* No. 92 (LC/G.2321-P), Santiago, Chile, ECLAC, June 2007; Vivian Milosavljevic and Odette Tacla, "Incorporando un módulo de uso del tiempo a las encuestas de hogares: restricciones y potencialidades", *Mujer y Desarrollo series,* No. 83 (LC/L.2709-P/E), Santiago, Chile, ECLAC, July 2007; María Nieves Rico, "Derechos de la infancia. Enfoque, indicadores y perspectivas", *Seminario Internacional Indicadores de Derechos Económicos, Sociales y Culturales (DESC) y seguimiento de las políticas sociales para la superación de la pobreza y el logro de la igualdad,* Santiago, Chile, National Human Rights Institute (INDH), 2013.

3. Contribution of different deprivations to child poverty

As discussed earlier, the fall in child poverty is not only a matter of lower levels and severity of deprivation in each dimension. The drop in total and extreme child poverty levels has also been associated with a lesser intensity of poverty (understood as the number of simultaneous deprivations or violations of basic rights), albeit to differing degrees from one country to another.

As children and adolescents living in poverty gradually come to be affected by one main deprivation and the proportion of those experiencing a syndrome of multiple deprivation narrows, it becomes more important to analyse which deprivations predominate in order to determine the scale of poverty and extreme child poverty. Whereas an individual analysis of deprivations by dimension is useful for identifying which rights are most breached among children and adolescents in general, a look at those dimensions among the poor or extremely poor specifically helps identify priority areas for the action of social policy and its sectoral components.

As figure II.5 shows, the importance of the various factors (dimensions) in reducing extreme poverty and total child poverty has not changed much. The three key dimensions are still access to sanitation, quality housing and drinking water, which even retained the same order of importance between 2000 and 2011. However, as extreme poverty has declined, these three dimensions have become even more prominent, suggesting that greater strides have been made in education, information and nutrition than in sanitation, housing and drinking water. Whereas around 2000 nearly 82% of extremely poor children in the region suffered some sort of deprivation in terms of quality housing, access to drinking water or adequate sanitation (alone or in combination with others), this figure had risen to 88.4% by 2011. These three dimensions contribute heavily to total child poverty, too, and their significance has increased as total poverty among children has decreased —from 73% in 2000 to 82% in 2011.[13] Unlike in the case of extreme poverty, education has increased in importance as a contributing factor to total poverty, suggesting that little progress has actually been made in reducing education deprivation. The fact that its relative contribution to extreme poverty has diminished indicates that more than proportional progress had been made in reducing the percentage of children with no access to schooling. The fact that the same did not happen with total poverty means that progress in reducing the school dropout rate had been less significant than achievements in other areas.

Figure II.5
Latin America (14 countries): contribution to extreme poverty and total child poverty of deprivations in the different dimensions, around 2000 and 2011[a]
(Percentages)

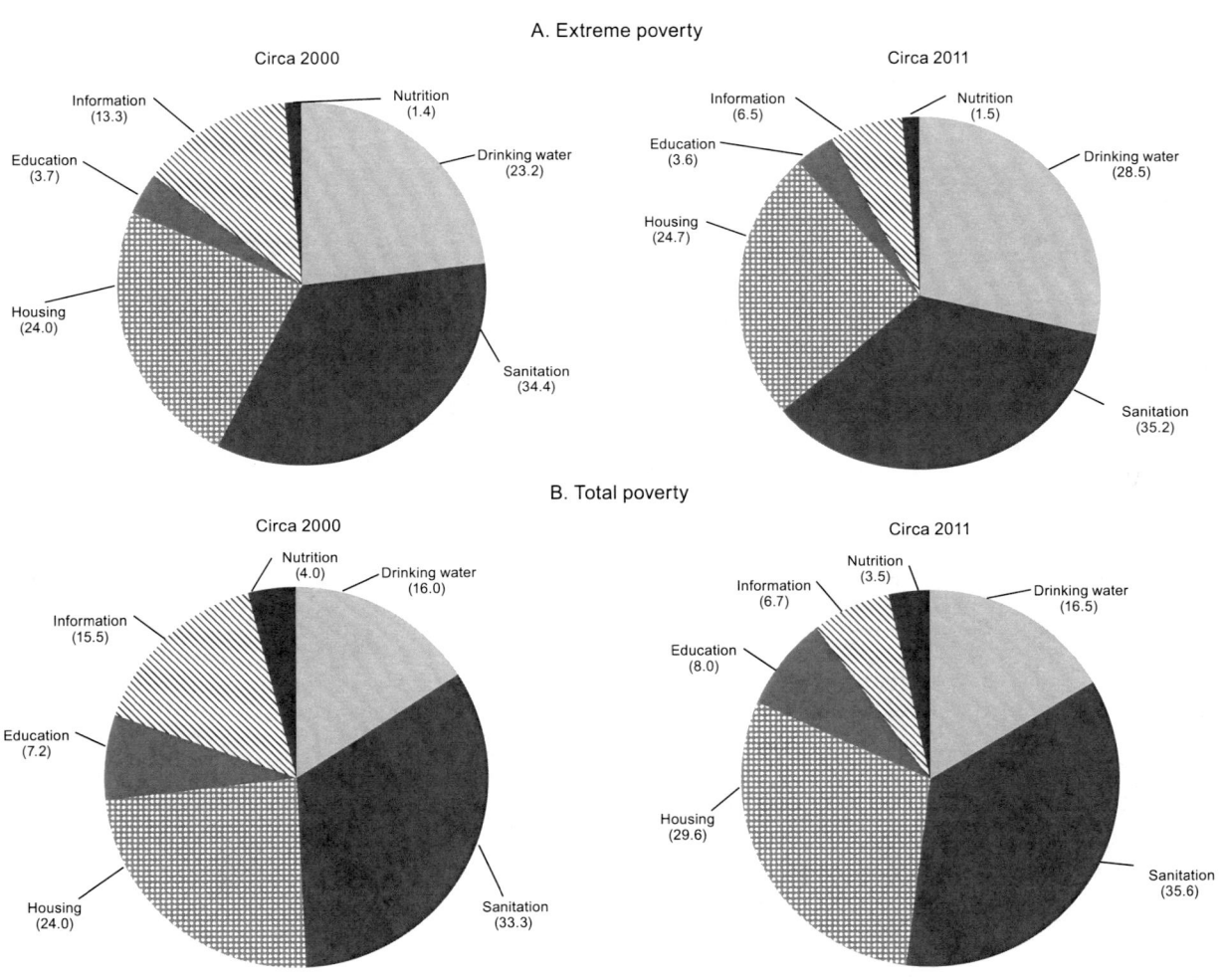

A. Extreme poverty

Circa 2000

Information (13.3)
Nutrition (1.4)
Education (3.7)
Drinking water (23.2)
Housing (24.0)
Sanitation (34.4)

Circa 2011

Information (6.5)
Nutrition (1.5)
Education (3.6)
Drinking water (28.5)
Housing (24.7)
Sanitation (35.2)

B. Total poverty

Circa 2000

Nutrition (4.0)
Drinking water (16.0)
Information (15.5)
Education (7.2)
Housing (24.0)
Sanitation (33.3)

Circa 2011

Nutrition (3.5)
Information (6.7)
Drinking water (16.5)
Education (8.0)
Housing (29.6)
Sanitation (35.6)

Source: Economic Commission for Latin America and the Caribbean (ECLAC), on the basis of special tabulations of household surveys conducted in the respective countries.
[a] Excludes Argentina, Ecuador and Uruguay because at least one of the two measures in these countries is for urban areas only.

In 11 of the 14 countries with national data (with the exception of Brazil, Costa Rica and Nicaragua), the contribution of housing deprivation to total child poverty increased. Its contribution to extreme poverty also increased in 10 countries in the region. Special cases were Peru, where the housing dimension's contribution to extreme

---

[13] An important point to bear in mind is that the indicator of the contribution of deprivations in the different dimensions does not incorporate the degree of deprivation (moderate or severe). Although this has no bearing on the contribution of the dimensions to extreme poverty, it is relevant to their contribution to total poverty.

poverty increased by 14 percentage points, and Costa Rica and Mexico where, on the contrary, it decreased by more than 10 percentage points. The overall conclusion to be drawn from these data is that States in the region have failed to fully address the issue of access to quality housing without overcrowding, much less consider it in child policies (see tables II.7 and II.8). By contrast, progress has been recorded in several countries in sanitation, another dimension that contributes heavily to poverty. In the Bolivarian Republic of Venezuela, Chile, Costa Rica, Honduras and Mexico, its importance diminished steadily during the decade under consideration, reflecting improved provision of household waste treatment methods. However, the contribution of the drinking water dimension to total child poverty was found to have increased in 11 countries. A notable case is Costa Rica, where it increased from 20.8% in 2002 to 40% in 2011 (see table II.8). In this country the drinking water dimension contributed even more to extreme poverty, rising from 42.8% in 2002 to 67.6% in 2011, as table II.7 shows.

Table II.7
Latin America (17 countries): contribution of the various dimensions of deprivation to extreme child poverty, around 2000 and 2011
(Percentages)

Country		Nutrition	Access to drinking water	Access to sanitation	Quality of housing	Access to education	Access to information
Argentina (urban)	1999	4.1	14.2	39.9	40.2	1.6	...
	2011	5.5	11.0	13.6	68.5	1.5	...
Bolivia (Plurinational State of)	1999	0.9	35.5	35.3	16.3	1.0	11.1
	2009	1.6	43.0	31.4	19.0	0.3	4.6
Brazil	1999	1.0	23.0	55.7	9.2	4.0	7.1
	2011	0.8	19.6	62.0	9.8	4.3	3.5
Chile	2000	0.8	54.5	26.7	1.6	2.0	14.3
	2011	1.0	68.7	12.9	9.3	4.1	3.9
Colombia	1999	1.5	21.1	31.1	21.3	5.2	19.9
	2011	1.5	29.6	38.3	19.7	3.1	7.9
Costa Rica	2002	1.2	42.8	14.0	24.4	7.0	10.6
	2011	2.8	67.6	8.4	13.6	3.5	4.0
Dominican Republic	2002	0.6	71.3	9.8	7.4	3.4	7.5
	2011	0.8	12.7	40.9	17.2	13.1	15.4
Ecuador (urban)	2002	6.5	3.9	15.8	66.0	3.9	3.8
	2011	15.6	11.1	14.9	51.7	5.1	1.7
Ecuador	2011	3.4	38.8	26.4	22.1	1.6	7.6
El Salvador	1999	1.5	16.7	17.6	46.4	4.1	13.7
	2010	1.6	20.3	12.9	55.3	2.9	6.9
Guatemala	1998	3.4	15.1	17.4	44.6	7.9	11.7
	2006	3.4	12.1	14.1	44.7	5.4	20.4
Honduras	1999	1.3	15.1	21.0	16.5	4.8	41.3
	2010	1.8	22.9	37.5	25.9	4.7	7.2
Mexico	2000	2.1	21.6	28.6	39.0	3.2	5.5
	2010	1.9	40.6	26.3	23.1	4.0	4.1
Nicaragua	2001	1.4	14.8	19.7	43.2	6.8	14.1
	2005	1.5	23.0	19.8	35.9	6.9	12.9
Paraguay	2000	1.8	8.8	17.9	48.7	3.9	18.9
	2011	3.9	17.3	17.3	56.4	2.5	2.7
Peru	1999	0.8	23.5	27.0	12.9	0.6	35.1
	2011	1.4	40.1	27.2	26.9	0.5	3.9
Uruguay (urban)	1999	7.0	8.4	11.1	64.3	3.4	5.8
	2011	14.8	0.0	35.9	43.4	2.2	3.7
Uruguay	2011	13.4	3.5	37.0	38.7	2.6	4.8
Venezuela (Bolivarian Republic of)	1999	0.0	21.4	35.5	34.8	4.8	3.4
	2011	0.0	18.7	34.7	43.2	3.2	0.2
Latin America (14 countries) [a]	2000	1.4	23.2	34.4	24.0	3.7	13.3
	2011	1.5	28.5	35.2	24.7	3.6	6.5
Latin America (17 countries) [b]	2011	1.7	28.4	34.6	25.5	3.5	6.4

Source: Economic Commission for Latin America and the Caribbean (ECLAC), on the basis of special tabulations of household surveys conducted in the respective countries.
[a] Excludes Argentina, Ecuador and Uruguay because at least one of the two measures in these countries is for urban areas only.
[b] Includes urban areas of Argentina.

Table II.8

Latin America (17 countries): contribution of the various dimensions of deprivation to child poverty, around 2000 and 2011

(Percentages)

Country		Nutrition	Access to drinking water	Access to sanitation	Quality of housing	Access to education	Access to information
Argentina (urban)	1999	7.1	5.1	20.5	58.4	8.9	...
	2011	7.4	4.5	7.3	71.9	8.9	...
Bolivia (Plurinational State of)	1999	3.5	15.0	25.4	30.2	12.4	13.6
	2009	4.4	21.1	32.8	31.8	2.3	7.6
Brazil	1999	3.7	18.5	53.2	6.5	6.6	11.6
	2011	2.5	16.8	64.4	6.1	7.0	3.2
Chile	2000	1.5	19.1	26.4	23.3	4.8	24.9
	2011	1.9	29.8	17.6	34.7	7.7	8.3
Colombia	1999	5.1	8.2	21.2	33.4	10.0	22.2
	2011	5.5	14.3	23.7	39.9	8.7	8.0
Costa Rica	2002	3.8	20.8	18.6	20.5	18.2	18.1
	2011	4.6	40.0	18.3	14.8	18.5	3.8
Dominican Republic	2002	2.4	35.2	39.0	11.8	3.1	8.5
	2011	1.4	36.4	39.5	13.3	4.1	5.3
Ecuador (urban)	2002	6.5	6.4	15.7	22.8	5.0	43.7
	2011	6.5	6.4	15.7	22.8	5.0	43.7
Ecuador	2011	16.6	11.7	15.4	41.9	8.8	5.7
El Salvador	1999	4.1	19.3	10.0	44.3	5.8	16.4
	2010	3.3	16.7	10.3	55.5	6.1	8.1
Guatemala	1998	6.5	9.0	28.0	30.3	7.1	19.1
	2006	7.3	7.3	30.1	36.2	7.0	12.1
Honduras	1999	5.6	8.5	27.5	29.0	9.2	20.2
	2010	5.1	13.3	21.3	37.8	11.5	11.0
Mexico	2000	5.3	16.5	26.5	34.0	8.6	9.2
	2010	3.4	14.4	22.8	38.8	13.5	7.1
Nicaragua	2001	3.1	8.5	25.5	35.2	6.2	21.4
	2005	2.9	10.1	26.7	33.3	6.6	20.4
Paraguay	2000	2.9	23.1	30.7	27.7	5.0	10.7
	2011	3.9	24.4	31.1	31.6	5.7	3.3
Peru	1999	3.1	15.0	19.3	26.1	2.5	34.0
	2011	3.7	21.8	21.4	43.3	2.1	7.7
Uruguay (urban)	1999	9.7	6.5	29.4	32.7	15.3	6.4
	2011	17.2	1.3	10.9	44.1	24.4	2.1
Uruguay	2011	15.3	6.2	11.5	40.1	23.4	3.5
Venezuela (Bolivarian Republic of)	1999	0.0	12.3	21.6	43.3	10.1	12.6
	2011	0.0	15.4	19.0	54.5	8.2	2.9
Latin America (14 countries) [a]	2000	4.0	16.0	33.3	24.0	7.2	15.5
	2011	3.5	16.5	35.6	29.6	8.0	6.7
Latin America (17 countries) [b]	2011	3.7	16.2	34.6	30.8	8.0	6.6

Source: Economic Commission for Latin America and the Caribbean (ECLAC), on the basis of special tabulations of household surveys conducted in the respective countries.
[a] Excludes Argentina, Ecuador and Uruguay because at least one of the two measures in these countries is for urban areas only.
[b] Includes urban areas of Argentina.

4. Child poverty in the Caribbean

For the first time, this edition of *Social Panorama* publishes multidimensional estimates of child poverty for seven Caribbean countries: Antigua and Barbuda, Belize, Grenada, Guyana, Saint Lucia, Suriname, and Trinidad and Tobago. In the case of Jamaica, it shows some of the deprivations for which data are available. These estimates were based on Multiple Indicator Cluster Surveys (MICS) and, in the case of Antigua and Barbuda, Grenada and Saint Lucia, on surveys of lving conditions. The surveys were conducted between 2005 and 2008. The estimates give an initial idea of the child poverty situation in the Caribbean from a multidimensional and rights-based perspective. As the surveys were prepared using the same methodology as for Latin America, they allow child poverty in the Caribbean to be compared with that in the rest of the region, something that cannot be done using monetary poverty statistics, which are constructed using different methodologies.

Table II.9
The Caribbean (7 countries): incidence of total and extreme child poverty [a]
(Percentages)

	Incidence of total child poverty	Incidence of extreme child poverty
Antigua and Barbuda (2005) [b]	10	1
Belize (2006)	71	36
Grenada (2008) [b]	32	7
Guyana (2006)	74	46
Saint Lucia (2005) [b]	25	5
Suriname (2006) [c]	41	30
Trinidad and Tobago (2006) [d]	28	10

Source: Economic Commission for Latin America and the Caribbean (ECLAC), on the basis of special tabulations of multiple indicator cluster surveys and living standards surveys conducted in the respective countries.
[a] Uses the United Nations Children's Fund (UNICEF) definition of a child, covering the population aged 0 to 17 years. The dimensions used in estimating multidimensional child poverty are: drinking water, sanitation, housing, education, information and nutrition.
[b] Does not include the nutrition dimension.
[c] Deprivations in the information dimension are underestimated because there is a high level of omission in the survey.
[d] Does not include the information dimension.

Estimates reveal that a significant proportion of children and adolescents experience poverty in these seven Caribbean countries, as in Latin America: total child poverty levels in the Caribbean range from 10% to 74% and extreme child poverty levels, from 1% to 46% (see table II.9). This variability is very similar to that observed in Latin America. In the Caribbean countries with the highest child poverty levels (Guyana and Belize), the percentages of poor children (total and extreme) are in the same range as in Latin American countries with high child poverty, such as Nicaragua and Peru. The Caribbean countries with low child poverty levels (Saint Lucia and Antigua and Barbuda) are in the same range as the Latin American countries with the lowest levels, i.e. Chile and Uruguay. Poverty levels in the other Caribbean countries range from medium-high (Suriname) to medium-low (Grenada and Trinidad and Tobago). These initial estimates suggest that the scale of child poverty in the subregion, at least in the seven countries studied, is similar to that in Latin America.

In the Caribbean, a marked difference is apparent between continental countries (Belize, Guyana and Suriname) and island countries (Antigua and Barbuda, Grenada, Saint Lucia and Trinidad and Tobago). In Belize, Guyana and Suriname, total poverty averages over 60% and extreme poverty, over 35%. By contrast, in island countries of the Caribbean, total child poverty averages 24% and extreme poverty, 6%. The difference is explained in part by high levels of rural poverty in Belize, Guyana and Suriname. Unlike in Caribbean small island States, the disparities between urban and rural areas in these three countries are very sharp.

With respect to the different dimensions of child poverty, in all eight countries (including Jamaica), there is a significant incidence of moderate or severe deprivation in access to drinking water, quality housing and information. However, the percentage of children deprived of their rights to education, nutrition and access to sanitation tends to be lower (see table II.10).

Table II.10
The Caribbean (8 countries): incidence of moderate or severe deprivation and severe deprivation among children aged 0 to 17 years
(Percentages)

	Moderate or severe deprivation						Severe deprivation					
	Nutrition	Drinking water	Sanitation	Housing	Education	Information	Nutrition	Drinking water	Sanitation	Housing	Education	Information
Antigua and Barbuda (2005)	...	7	1	3	1	0	...	0	1	0	0	0
Belize (2006)	5	24	7	44	8	34	2	21	3	15	0	6
Grenada (2008)	...	5	2	14	3	16	...	0	1	4	1	2
Guyana (2006)	6	34	3	51	6	39	3	29	2	20	0	15
Jamaica (2005)	...	21	3	...	2	...	...	15	1	...	0	...
Saint Lucia (2005)	...	3	5	9	4	11	...	0	3	1	0	3
Suriname (2006)	5	28	16	18	7	...	1	27	15	6	1	...
Trinidad and Tobago (2006)	1	18	0	8	5	...	1	9	0	2	0	...

Source: Economic Commission for Latin America and the Caribbean (ECLAC), on the basis of special tabulations of multiple indicator cluster surveys and living standards surveys conducted in the respective countries.

As regards quality housing, countries with the highest percentage of (moderately or severely) deprived children and adolescents are Guyana (51%) and Belize (44%). The lowest percentages are seen in Antigua and Barbuda (3%), followed by Trinidad and Tobago (8%). In five of the eight countries (including Jamaica), at least 18% of children are moderately or severely deprived of access to drinking water. At least 20% of children in Belize, Guyana and Suriname are severely deprived in this dimension, while the percentage in the other countries is lower: 15.2% in Jamaica; 8.6% in Trinidad and Tobago; and close to 0% in Antigua and Barbuda, Grenada and Saint Lucia.

Belize, Guyana and Suriname have not only the highest poverty levels, but also the largest percentage of children and adolescents suffering moderate or severe deprivation in two or more dimensions. In these three countries, the percentage of children with multiple deprivations ranges from 21% to 42%, compared with 1% to 6% in the other countries (see figure II.6). Between 9% and 16% of children are severely deprived in two or more dimensions in the continental countries (Belize, Guyana and Suriname), but very few children are in this situation in the other countries.

Figure II.6
The Caribbean (7 countries): poor and extremely poor children aged 0 to 17 years,
by number of deprivations
(Percentages)

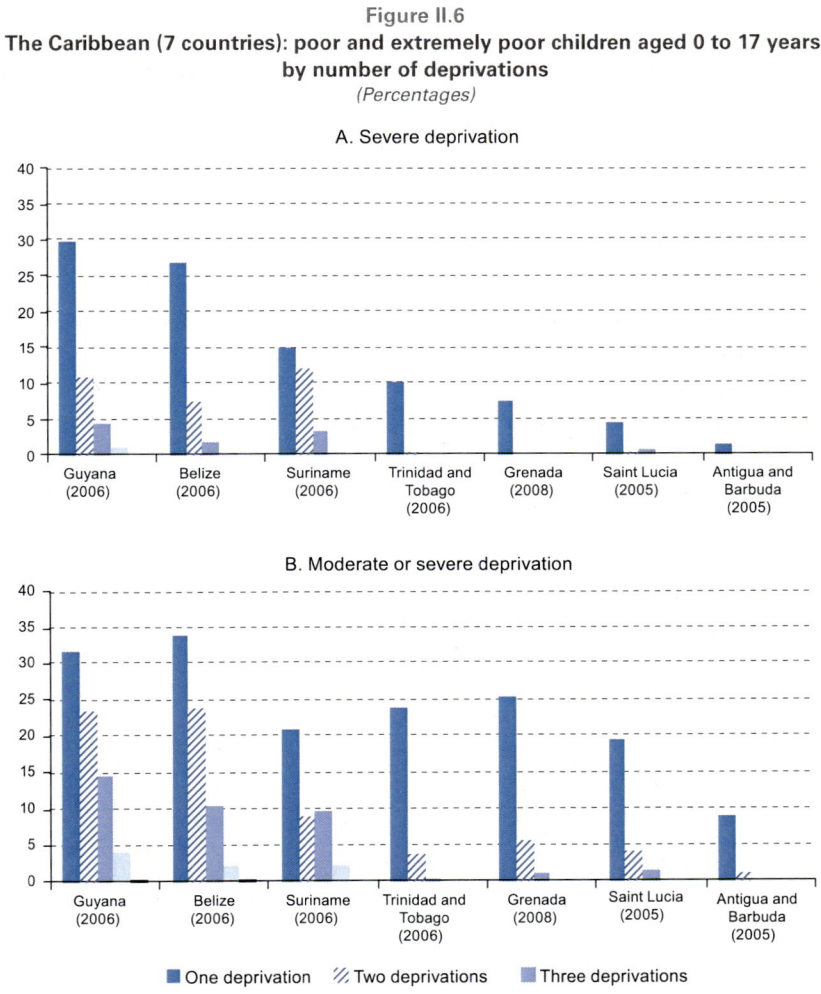

Source: Economic Commission for Latin America and the Caribbean (ECLAC), on the basis of special tabulations of multiple indicator cluster surveys and living standards surveys conducted in the respective countries.

In general, child poverty is greatest in low-income countries and in countries with the highest monetary poverty. Of the seven countries for which child poverty can be estimated, the World Bank classes Guyana as lower-middle income, Belize, Grenada, Jamaica, Saint Lucia and Suriname as upper-middle income, and Antigua and Barbuda and Trinidad and Tobago as high income. Belize, Grenada, Guyana and Suriname are the countries with the highest levels of monetary poverty (between 36% and 51% of the total population), followed by Saint Lucia (29%) and by Antigua and Barbuda, Jamaica, and Trinidad and Tobago (between 17% and 18%). However, neither national income nor monetary poverty fully explains the variability in child poverty levels. For example, although Trinidad and Tobago has the highest per capita gross domestic product in the Caribbean, it does not have the lowest level of child poverty. Unlike other indicators, estimates of multidimensional child poverty provide a unique and detailed picture of the situation of children and adolescents moderately or severely deprived of their rights. They serve as a benchmark for focusing government efforts to reduce this scourge and provide a basis for measuring progress in poverty eradication in the coming years.

5. Child poverty and children in households with income below the monetary poverty line

A multidimensional methodology was adopted in this chapter to identify poor children, because the method of multiple deprivations, associated with the violation of a measurable set of child rights, was considered more appropriate to the specific characteristics and well-being gaps of children and adolescents. As noted earlier, the multiple deprivation approach differs from monetary poverty measurement in both its conceptualization and empirical method. The well-being gaps revealed by the indirect (monetary) method are usually correlated with directly observable deprivations that may be measured as child poverty. However, the correlation is not exact. It is useful to study child and adolescent well-being from both approaches, because this allows for the combination of different issues and the analysis of various public policy measures for childhood, and the adoption of a holistic policy perspective.

Poverty among children and adolescents, measured by household income, has declined sharply over the past two decades, albeit with ups and downs. Between 1990 and 2010, poverty and extreme poverty diminished by around 20% among children aged 0 to 5. However, in both cases, by midway through the period (2000) the levels were still nearly the same as in 1990 and most of the reduction occurred after 2005 (Rossel, 2013). The reduction has also varied from one country to another.

Although both sets of figures evolved similarly, not all poor children live in income-poor households, nor do all children in income-poor households have their basic rights breached. This makes it necessary to examine the combined evolution of child poverty and household monetary poverty (as measured in children).

While 39.3% of children in the region (a total of 63.6 million) experienced both child poverty and monetary poverty around 2000, the percentage had fallen to 25.1% (40.6 million children) by around 2011 (see table II.12). This means that the number of children experiencing simultaneous child and monetary poverty had dropped by more than 20 million. The question is whether the remaining 40 million children form a hard core of multidimensional poverty (including monetary poverty) as a result of geographical isolation, social exclusion or discrimination, or whether their living standards could be improved fairly rapidly, as has happened with the 23 million children who have escaped simultaneous child and monetary poverty.

At the same time, in the early 2000s, 16% of children (25.8 million) experienced child poverty but were not income-poor. This category remained almost constant and the value was the same by around 2011, suggesting that the reduction in the number of poor (by both methods) stemmed, in part, from higher household income that had not necessarily improved objective living standards for children. Similarly, the percentage of non-poor children experiencing household monetary poverty increased from 15.8% (25.7 million) to 18.0% (29 million). This suggests that the reductions in child and monetary poverty recorded in the region were largely unconnected, that is to say, public policy action did not link up the two approaches to poverty. Accordingly, more coordinated action is needed in tackling child poverty (see table II.12 and figure II.7).

Figure II.7
**Latin America (14 countries): distribution of children aged 0 to 17 years, by combinations
of child poverty and income poverty categories, around 2011**
(Percentages)

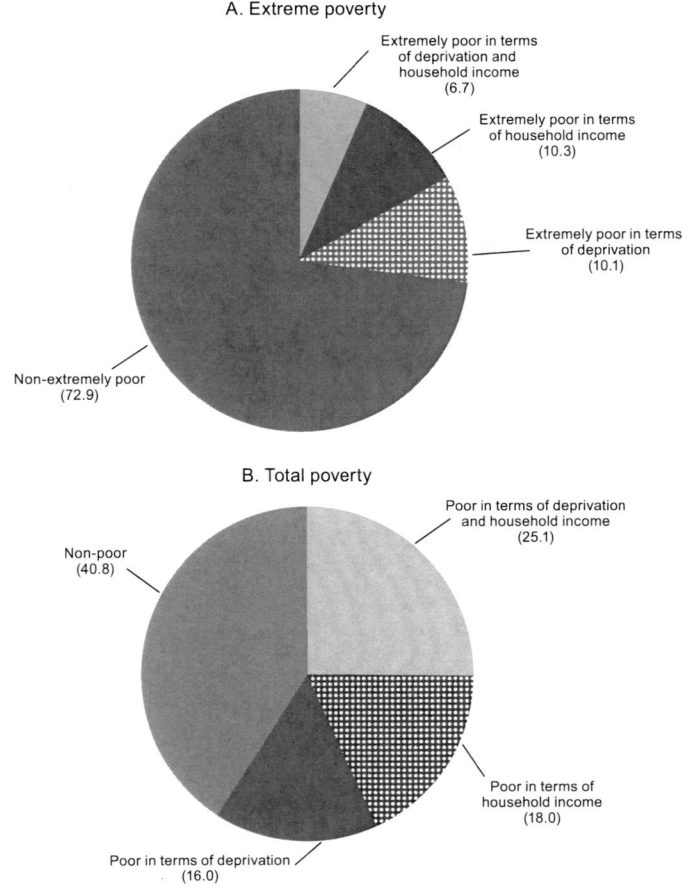

A. Extreme poverty

Extremely poor in terms
of deprivation and
household income
(6.7)

Extremely poor in terms
of household income
(10.3)

Extremely poor in terms
of deprivation
(10.1)

Non-extremely poor
(72.9)

B. Total poverty

Poor in terms of deprivation
and household income
(25.1)

Non-poor
(40.8)

Poor in terms of
household income
(18.0)

Poor in terms of deprivation
(16.0)

Source: Economic Commission for Latin America and the Caribbean (ECLAC), on the basis of special tabulations of household surveys conducted in the respective countries.

Table II.11
**Latin America (14 countries): distribution of children aged 0 to 17 years, by combinations of extreme
child poverty and indigence categories, around 2000 and 2011**
(Percentages and number of children)

	Extremely poor in terms of deprivation and household income	Extremely poor in terms of household income	Extremely poor in terms of deprivation	Non-extremely poor	Total	Extremely poor in terms of deprivation and household income	Extremely poor in terms of household income	Extremely poor in terms of deprivation	Non-extremely poor	Total
	(percentages)					*(number of children)*				
2000	13.7	11.6	13.5	61.1	100	22 194 566	18 855 969	21 879 481	98 979 888	161 909 904
2011	6.7	10.3	10.1	72.9	100	10 745 578	16 651 778	16 272 420	117 697 274	161 367 051

Source: Economic Commission for Latin America and the Caribbean (ECLAC), on the basis of special tabulations of household surveys conducted in the respective countries.

Table II.12

Latin America (14 countries): distribution of children aged 0 to 17 years, by combinations of total child poverty and income poverty categories, around 2000 and 2011

(Percentages and number of children)

	Poor in terms of deprivation and household income	Poor in terms of household income	Poor in terms of deprivation	Non-poor	Total	Poor in terms of deprivation and household income	Poor in terms of household income	Poor in terms of deprivation	Non-poor	Total
	(percentages)					*(number of children)*				
2000	39.3	15.8	16.0	28.9	100	63 660 168	25 658 509	25 855 894	46 735 333	161 909 904
2011	25.1	18.0	16.0	40.8	100	40 575 921	29 039 281	25 843 052	65 908 797	161 367 051

Source: Economic Commission for Latin America and the Caribbean (ECLAC), on the basis of special tabulations of household surveys conducted in the respective countries.

Table II.13

Latin America (17 countries): distribution of children aged 0 to 17 years, by extreme child poverty and household indigence categories, around 2000 and 2011

(Percentages)

Country	Year	Extremely poor in indigent households	Non-extremely poor in indigent households	Extremely poor in non-indigent households	Subtotal of extremely poor	Subtotal children in indigent households	Non-extremely poor in non-indigent households
Argentina (urban)	1999	4.0	7.6	7.5	11.5	11.5	80.9
	2011	0.6	2.4	7.0	7.6	7.6	90.0
Bolivia (Plurinational State of)	1999	33.0	9.0	23.1	56.1	56.1	34.9
	2009	21.6	7.2	25.3	46.8	46.8	46.0
Brazil	1999	9.8	10.2	11.4	21.2	21.2	68.6
	2011	3.4	6.8	8.3	11.7	11.7	81.5
Chile	2000	1.8	6.5	8.2	10.0	10.0	83.5
	2011	0.5	4.5	3.5	3.9	3.9	91.6
Colombia	1999	11.8	22.8	10.3	22.1	22.1	55.2
	2011	5.8	10.1	9.1	14.9	14.9	75.0
Costa Rica	2002	2.4	8.5	6.6	9.0	9.0	82.5
	2011	1.8	9.3	5.0	6.8	6.8	83.9
Dominican Republic	2002	10.7	15.1	17.5	28.2	28.2	56.8
	2011	3.2	23.9	3.8	7.0	7.0	69.1
Ecuador (urban)	2002	7.2	18.3	7.6	14.8	14.8	66.9
	2011	1.6	12.8	2.7	4.4	4.4	82.8
Ecuador	2011	6.0	13.4	9.2	15.1	15.1	71.5
El Salvador	1999	19.9	7.7	25.0	45.0	45.0	47.3
	2010	11.6	10.5	16.5	28.1	28.1	61.4
Guatemala	1998	28.2	9.1	28.0	56.2	56.2	34.6
	2006	26.6	9.5	21.2	47.8	47.8	42.6
Honduras	1999	40.1	23.6	10.0	50.1	50.1	26.3
	2010	16.6	33.7	5.4	22.0	22.0	44.3
Mexico	2000	13.1	8.7	12.9	26.1	26.1	65.2
	2010	6.2	13.2	7.6	13.7	13.7	73.1
Nicaragua	2001	33.8	15.9	18.4	52.2	52.2	31.9
	2005	24.3	14.8	18.4	42.7	42.7	42.5
Paraguay	2000	19.2	18.8	10.5	29.7	29.7	51.5
	2011	6.5	30.5	3.8	10.3	10.3	59.2
Peru	1999	23.5	6.0	24.9	48.3	48.3	45.7
	2011	6.6	2.7	24.3	30.9	30.9	66.5
Uruguay (urban)	1999	1.7	2.1	5.4	7.1	7.1	90.8
	2011	0.4	1.8	3.2	3.6	3.6	94.6
Uruguay	2011	0.4	1.8	3.5	3.9	3.9	94.3
Venezuela (Bolivarian Republic of)	1999	8.5	19.8	8.6	17.1	17.1	63.1
	2011	5.6	12.5	9.1	14.7	14.7	72.9
Latin America [a]	2000	13.7	11.6	13.5	27.2	27.2	61.1
	2011	6.7	10.3	10.1	16.7	16.7	72.9

Source: Economic Commission for Latin America and the Caribbean (ECLAC), on the basis of special tabulations of household surveys conducted in the respective countries.
[a] Excludes Argentina, Ecuador and Uruguay because at least one of the two measures in these countries is for urban areas only.

Table II.14

Latin America (17 countries): distribution of children aged 0 to 17 years, by child poverty and household income poverty categories, around 2000 and 2011

(Percentages)

Country	Year	Poor in terms of deprivation or income			Subtotal of poor in terms of deprivation	Subtotal of income-poor	Non-poor in terms of deprivation or income
		Poor in terms of deprivation and income	Non-poor in terms of deprivation but income-poor	Poor in terms of deprivation but not income-poor			
Argentina (urban)	1999	19.3	18.5	9.7	29.0	37.8	52.5
	2011	5.1	4.9	19.2	24.3	10.0	70.8
Bolivia (Plurinational State of)	1999	66.3	2.5	25.9	92.2	68.8	5.3
	2009	43.2	8.0	28.2	71.4	51.1	20.7
Brazil	1999	34.2	17.4	14.1	48.3	51.6	34.3
	2011	17.6	17.3	16.2	33.8	34.9	48.9
Chile	2000	13.3	15.1	15.0	28.2	28.4	56.7
	2011	4.1	13.3	11.5	15.7	17.5	71.0
Colombia	1999	37.1	28.4	10.1	47.2	65.5	24.4
	2011	24.1	22.5	12.0	36.1	46.6	41.4
Costa Rica	2002	11.3	15.1	16.7	28.0	26.4	56.9
	2011	7.9	20.0	11.6	19.5	27.9	60.5
Dominican Republic	2002	38.3	15.5	20.9	59.2	53.7	25.3
	2011	30.8	21.7	17.0	47.8	52.6	30.4
Ecuador (urban)	2002	47.6	11.3	17.6	65.2	58.8	23.5
	2011	16.4	27.6	8.0	24.4	44.0	48.0
Ecuador	2011	25.1	21.8	15.5	40.7	47.0	37.5
El Salvador	1999	54.5	4.3	33.6	88.1	58.8	7.5
	2010	47.6	8.9	31.3	78.9	56.5	12.2
Guatemala	1998	64.4	4.1	21.8	86.2	68.4	9.7
	2006	58.2	5.4	21.6	79.9	63.7	14.7
Honduras	1999	68.9	15.7	6.4	75.4	84.7	8.9
	2010	52.2	23.1	11.0	63.1	75.2	13.8
Mexico	2000	37.0	14.2	15.8	52.8	51.2	33.0
	2010	24.5	22.9	13.1	37.6	47.4	39.5
Nicaragua	2001	69.9	6.7	15.7	85.6	76.6	7.7
	2005	61.2	9.2	17.4	78.6	70.4	12.2
Paraguay	2000	55.9	12.7	11.4	67.3	68.6	20.0
	2011	39.7	21.3	14.3	54.0	60.9	24.8
Peru	1999	56.7	2.0	30.8	87.4	58.6	10.6
	2011	32.8	4.6	29.8	62.6	37.4	32.8
Uruguay (urban)	1999	11.3	7.1	14.8	26.1	18.4	66.8
	2011	5.4	7.8	12.0	17.4	13.2	74.8
Uruguay	2011	5.4	7.4	13.3	18.6	12.8	73.9
Venezuela (Bolivarian Republic of)	1999	31.7	28.0	11.1	42.8	59.7	29.2
	2011	18.8	23.4	13.0	31.8	42.2	44.8
Latin America [a]	2000	39.3	15.8	16.0	55.3	55.2	28.9
	2011	25.1	18.0	16.0	41.2	43.1	40.8

Source: Economic Commission for Latin America and the Caribbean (ECLAC), on the basis of special tabulations of household surveys conducted in the respective countries.
[a] Excludes Argentina, Ecuador and Uruguay because at least one of the two measures in these countries is for urban areas only.

6. Territorial distribution of deprivation

As discussed earlier, deprivation of the right to housing, education, information, health and nutrition is an integral part of child and adolescent poverty. The under-18 age group is not only more vulnerable than other age groups in some dimensions, but is also exposed to poverty to differing extents, as structural factors make some more likely than others to be denied the exercise of rights fundamental to their development and well-being. Contextual factors can also increase the incidence of child poverty, including the way poverty is distributed in a country. The child poverty situation in the region calls for a study of inequalities broken down to lower geographical levels within countries, in order to target public policies and sectoral projects for improving the living standards of children and adolescents in different areas defined on a geopolitical or territorial basis. As child poverty is unevenly distributed within countries, the aim is to deepen the information and analysis, which thus far has been confined chiefly to regional and national levels, and to break it down by urban and rural areas or political and administrative divisions.

When child poverty is analysed using a multidimensional approach that includes its territorial distribution, the reference unit is the municipality —one of the spaces or scenarios where child poverty is most apparent— while also recognizing local communities and authorities as crucial in triggering change and breaking the cycle of poverty and inequality affecting children and adolescents.

As part of the policy decentralization process, it is important to lower the geographical level of analysis to a subnational level —like the municipality— because, for one thing, spatial analysis of a specific poverty indicator facilitates the determination of clusters of municipalities. This allows priority clusters to be identified for public policy implementation, as they have high concentrations of children and adolescents suffering deprivation and can even cross national and geographical boundaries, attesting to a reality that affects several subregions in Latin America and the Caribbean.

Such subnational measurements use geographical information systems (GIS) as a platform to map the spatial distribution of the social deprivation in which many children and adolescents live. Geographic information systems are specialized computer programs for analysing spatial patterns in information. Used by local governments and assuming the right information is accessed, they can be very useful tools for planning development schemes, public policies and social projects to optimize conditions in housing, education and basic and social services for the population at large and children and adolescents in particular. Geographic information systems can show the spatial distribution of different socioeconomic and demographic variables through a simple analysis of digital mapping or spatial autocorrelation. This helps, in turn, to identify subregions with identical incidences, as well as the spatial distribution of socioeconomic and demographic variables (child poverty measured from the perspective of deprivation in the dimensions of drinking water, sanitation, adequate housing and education).[14] After ascertaining the spatial distribution of phenomena and studying similarities and differences between areas on the basis of spatial autocorrelation, the concentration of deprivations can be determined from the distribution of municipalities with the highest incidence, so providing decision makers with more information for developing proposals.

To implement this methodology, a further source of information is required to supplement household and demographic and health surveys, as these do not capture data representing smaller geographical areas. This study used national population and housing censuses, which, because of their universality, provide information on every individual, household and dwelling in a country. Nationwide censuses are conducted by national statistical offices approximately every 10 years and capture information on a number of characteristics, including education, migration, labour, demography, ethnicity, housing quality, availability of basic services, overcrowding and access to information and communication goods. The census data can then be represented for smaller geographical areas (e.g. municipalities, districts or blocks).

In their adaptation of the University of Bristol's child poverty measurement method, ECLAC and UNICEF (2010 and 2012a) used population censuses to calculate deprivation indicators and their thresholds for the dimensions of housing, sanitation, drinking water, education and access to information, each for smaller geographical areas. These deprivation indicators can be mapped to identify municipalities with a higher percentage of children and adolescents living in poverty.

There follows a description of two countries in which poverty measurement has been broken down into indicators of sanitation and drinking-water deprivation, on the basis of information from the 2010 round of population censuses. The selected deprivation indicators and countries are the percentage of children under 18 experiencing housing deprivation in Costa Rica and the percentage of children under 18 experiencing drinking-water-related deprivation in the Bolivarian Republic of Venezuela. Databases available in REDATAM (Retrieval of data for small areas by microcomputer) format were used because of their versatility for data processing.[15]

---

[14] See ECLAC/UNICEF (2010), chapter VI, for an example of exploratory data analysis and spatial autocorrelation to identify specific areas defined by key zones, such as municipalities, where there is a high proportion of the deprivation indicator.

[15] The REDATAM format was developed by the Latin American and Caribbean Demographic Centre (CELADE)-Population Division of ECLAC (www.cepal.org/redatam).

(a) Costa Rica: housing deprivation

Although, as noted earlier, Costa Rica's rates of total and extreme child poverty are the lowest in Central America, they are still worrisome. At the same time, when only national data are available, it is very difficult to target policies for reducing existing social inequities because social programmes struggle to generate a positive impact on extremely poor children in localized areas. The measurement of housing deprivation is presented for Costa Rica, based on a threshold of overcrowding (three or more people per room, excluding the bathroom and kitchen), mud flooring or unsafe construction materials, such as ceilings or exterior walls made from mud, waste materials or similar.

The burgundy-coloured cantons in map II.1 are those housing the highest concentration of children and adolescents experiencing housing deprivation. Table II.15 lists the cantons in which over 25% of children are housing-deprived: Los Chiles, Talamanca, Garabito, La Cruz, Upala, Carrillo and Buenos Aires. These cantons are located on the borders with either Nicaragua or Panama, apart from Garabito (with 30% housing-deprived children), which is located on the Pacific Ocean. Costa Rica shares a 312-kilometre border with Nicaragua. This border area not only hosts a large mobile and migrant population, mainly from Nicaragua, but is also an international transit area for the movement of people and goods between northern and southern Central America. The most salient feature of the border dynamic between Costa Rica and Nicaragua is migration. In recent years, Costa Rica has been a net recipient of immigrants (7.8% of the country's inhabitants were international migrants in 2000 and 97% of that group were Nicaraguans). Nicaragua has experienced major population outflows to two main destinations: Costa Rica and the United States (Morales, Acuña and Wing-Ching, 2010).

Map II.1
Costa Rica: children and adolescents aged under 18 years experiencing housing deprivation, by canton, 2011
(Percentages)

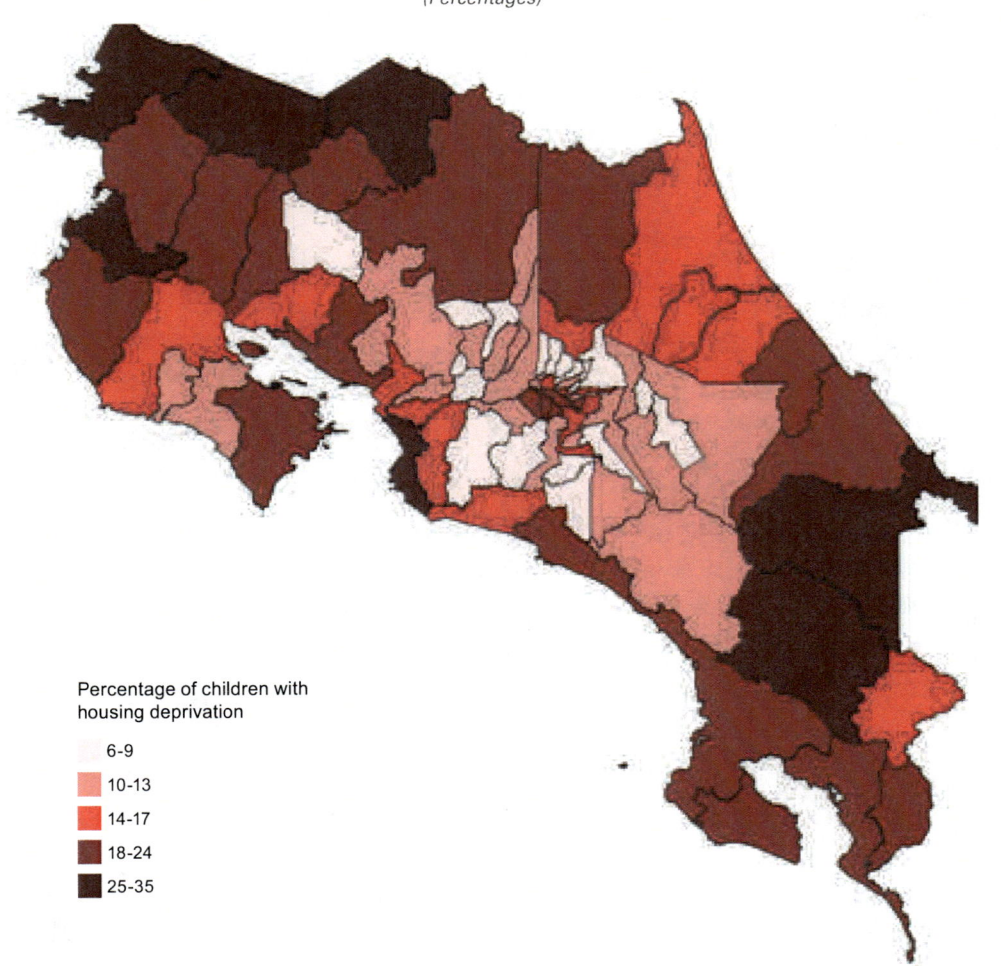

Percentage of children with housing deprivation

- 6-9
- 10-13
- 14-17
- 18-24
- 25-35

Source: Latin American and Caribbean Demographic Centre (CELADE) - Population Division of ECLAC, on the basis of census cartography for the 2010s provided by the National Institute of Statistics and Census of Costa Rica (INEC).

Table II.15
Costa Rica: cantons with the most children and adolescents under 18 experiencing housing deprivation
(Percentages and number of children)

Canton	Percentage	Housing-deprived children aged 0 to 17 years
Los Chiles	34.84	3 232
Talamanca	32.09	4 138
Garabito	30.79	1 810
La Cruz	29.29	2 181
Upala	26.83	4 527
Carrillo	25.37	3 065
Buenos Aires	25.03	4 472

Source: Economic Commission for Latin America and the Caribbean (ECLAC), on the basis of 2011 census data processed using the REDATAM software.

(b) Bolivarian Republic of Venezuela: drinking-water-related deprivation

In the Bolivarian Republic of Venezuela, the spatial distribution of drinking water deprivation was analysed using a threshold defined as households whose water needs were met not from a connection to the water supply network or other piped supply but from a well, water wheel, tanker truck, public standpipe or pond, river, rainwater or other, and a water supply located outside the dwelling, plot or yard where the dwelling is situated. Map II.2 and table II.16 show this deprivation to be concentrated in urban areas, as well as rural areas with large indigenous populations, such as the Amazon region (home to the Yanomami, Ye'kuana and Warakeno tribes); the State of Apure (home to the Guahibo, Yaruro, Inga and Kumba); and the State of Delta Amacuro (home to the Inga and Warao). The resulting information is useful for policies on drinking water supply, as well as child policies targeted at indigenous peoples and poverty reduction policies.

Map II.2
Bolivarian Republic of Venezuela: children and adolescents aged under 18 years experiencing drinking water deprivation, by smaller administrative divisions, 2011
(Percentages)

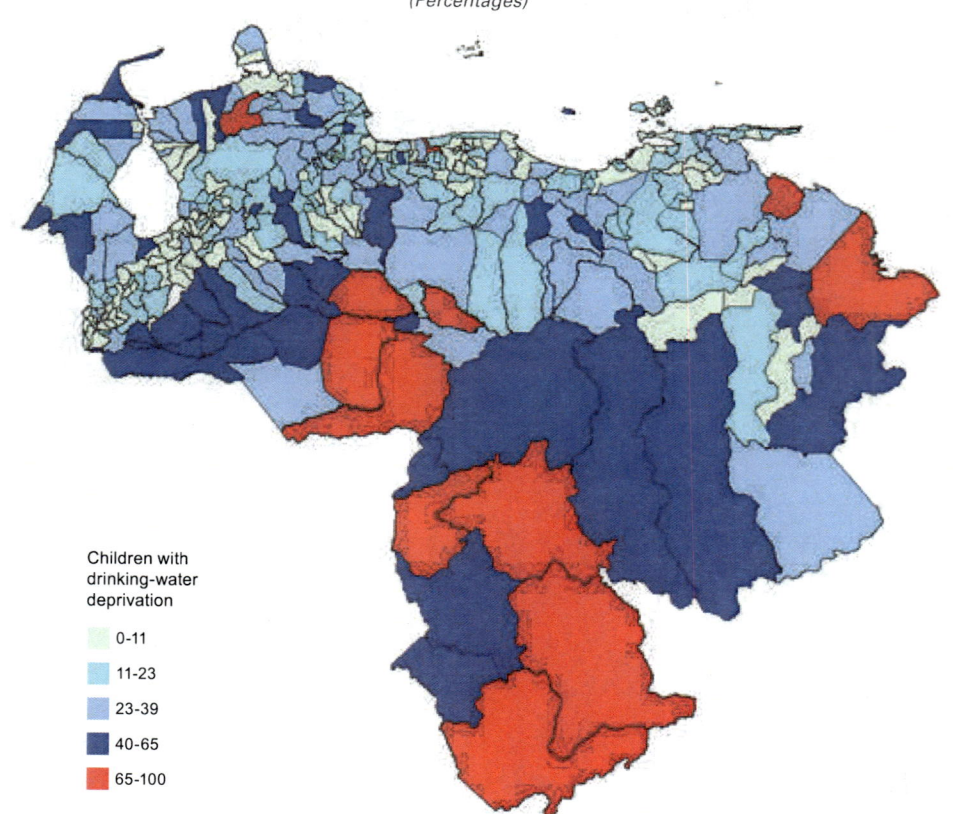

Children with drinking-water deprivation

- 0-11
- 11-23
- 23-39
- 40-65
- 65-100

Source: Latin American and Caribbean Demographic Centre (CELADE) - Population Division of ECLAC, on the basis of census cartography for the 2010s provided by the National Institute of Statistics and Census of Costa Rica (INEC).

Table II.16

Bolivarian Republic of Venezuela: municipalities in which over 65% of children and adolescents aged under 18 years experience drinking water deprivation

(Percentages and number of children)

Municipality	Percentage	Children aged 0 to 17 years with drinking water deprivation
Autónomo Alto Orinoco	97,23	6 280
Democracia	95,14	3 131
Autónomo Río Negro	94,97	1 039
Antonio Díaz	92,30	11 933
Autónomo Manapiare	88,63	3 548
Pedernales	83,57	2 625
Pedro Camejo	77,58	9 593
Autónomo Autana	74,13	3 097
Achaguas	73,54	17 815
San Gerónimo de Guayabal	65,63	5 407

Source: Economic Commission for Latin America and the Caribbean (ECLAC), on the basis of 2011 census data processed using the REDATAM software.

Although the methodology establishes no causality regarding the concentration of specific deprivations in specific municipalities, it can be used to link deprivations with certain determinants, such as indigenous ethnicity, residence in an urban or rural area or proximity to a border with another country. The two deprivation indicators analysed by smaller geographical areas are consistent with previous studies, inasmuch as that deprivations in both countries tend to be concentrated in and around border areas and areas historically settled by indigenous peoples.

C. Concluding remarks

Child poverty is widespread in Latin America and the Caribbean and represents a priority challenge for governments and society at large. However, major differences are observed from one country to another. The multiple facets of poverty among children and adolescents (deprivation in the areas of nutrition, housing, access to drinking water and sanitation, education, information and household income) cause permanent adverse effects that mark them throughout the rest of their lives. To a large extent, these effects also lead to the intergenerational transmission of poverty and, in some cases, serve to deepen inequality.

Although child poverty by multiple deprivations has diminished over the past decade, the pace has been slow considering it was a period of economic growth in the region when income poverty decreased sharply. At an average 10-percentage-point reduction per decade, it would take a further half a century to eradicate child poverty from the region.

While there was also a reduction in combined child poverty and monetary poverty among children in income-poor households, structurally the "mix" of the two measures of poverty has remained more or less the same. As this reduction has not resolved the problem of the infantilization of poverty, the question is whether the remaining child poverty will become more entrenched and demand more drastic measures to eradicate.

The evidence set forth speaks to an improvement in living standards among children and adolescents. However, current measurements of child poverty are confined to specific gaps quantifiable by household surveys. To tap the full potential of the multidimensional and rights-based approach, the analysis should be complemented by studies of deprivations in other dimensions of well-being, such as time, as discussed in box II.2.

The measures being taken in specific areas to address the various deprivations should be coordinated under a comprehensive approach to tackling poverty. In this regard, many of the steps taken to improve children's quality of life will also improve that of other family members. Furthermore, although measures in one area may ease deprivation in one dimension of child poverty, they do not necessarily ensure that other fundamental children's rights are realized. In a culture of poverty, rights which are not envisaged in poverty reduction measures per se tend to be infringed too, leading to such abuses as child exploitation or physical or psychological violence against children. A comprehensive approach to combating child poverty takes not only coordinated action by the State across different sectoral policies and programmes, but also measures addressing psychosocial aspects, in particular to develop a culture of recognition and respect for child rights within the family.

Given the scale and seriousness of the problem, various areas of public policy, especially policy on poverty reduction, urgently need to be rethought. To break the cycle of poverty and inequality reproduction, decisive and well-planned actions must be designed for target populations to produce a real, positive impact. Accordingly, public policies should not only tackle existing poverty but also build advocacy and social protection systems to offset the effects of poverty (such as poor health, education and self-esteem, informal work and low income) and so mitigate the impact of factors contributing to the transmission or resurgence of poverty.

The human-rights approach in development policies, and principally in poverty reduction programmes, implicitly recognizes that child poverty violates human rights in two ways: it prevents the current exercise of human rights and limits opportunities and capacity-building for exercising them in the future. The rights of most poor children and adolescents are violated, ignored or part or in full on a daily basis and their families are powerless to protect them because they are unable to enjoy their own rights.

Government policies and programmes targeting children and adolescents are part of the comprehensive child development framework. As ECLAC has noted, perhaps the main shift needed to promote children's rights is to cease relegating the conditions of access to and exercise of rights to the private sphere: households and families or the market. The private sphere contributes to generating child well-being, but should not be the sole guarantor and architect of child rights. This role falls primarily to the State and public policy.

If rights are to be genuinely comprehensive, they must be reflected in governance through coherent systems of cross-sector tools under which the institutions involved assume specific responsibilities, direct resource investment towards achieving goals and use results-based monitoring and control mechanisms. A necessary first step in any policy for comprehensive child development and child rights protection is to overcome child poverty. The combat of child poverty is a moral and political imperative, because its dire consequences affect not only children and adolescents but society as a whole, undermining the foundations of sustainable, long-term economic and social development. Thus there is international recognition that the post-2015 development agenda and Latin American and Caribbean countries must strive to protect the rights of children and adolescents, broaden poverty reduction programmes and translate the political will to prioritize children and equality into action.

Box II.3
Multidimensional poverty indicators as public policy tools

The impact of the debate on multidimensional methods of poverty measurement and their application in different countries has moved beyond academia and international organizations into the public policy sphere. Colombia and Mexico have already adopted multidimensional poverty indices as official measures. The ability of these multidimensional poverty measures to break down each dimension's contribution to poverty and to disaggregate poverty by population groups, including children and adolescents, makes them very useful tools for monitoring and evaluating public policy. This comes with some caveats, however, because setting poverty reduction targets on the basis of a particular (multidimensional or income) indicator may have major implications. First, the size of the population identified by the multidimensional method may (and indeed often does) differ significantly from that identified using the income method. This should be taken into account when such measures are used to define public policy goals. Similarly, setting

poverty reduction targets based on a particular indicator involves redirecting public measures towards different policies. Ideally, official poverty indicators should cover both multidimensional and income aspects, bearing in mind that they are support measures designed to illustrate the population's situation.

The potential of multidimensional poverty measurement as a tool for targeting public policies has also been discussed. Cash transfer programmes, which feature in the social protection systems of most countries in the region, typically ascertain eligibility using statistical or econometric targeting methods. Most of these programmes use substitutes for means testing (usually based on discriminant analysis or probit models), in which households are scored by their characteristics (observed during a field visit or declared). Households are then screened in or out for benefits depending on their ranking in relation to a cut-off point, which is defined in terms of a certain target population or by fiscal

Box II.3 (concluded)

constraints. Although one of the most prized aspects of cash transfer programmes has been their relatively good targeting, the use of multidimensional poverty measures as identification and selection tools should reduce targeting errors and increase policy effectiveness.

The main argument in favour of using multidimensional deprivation indicators as targeting tools is that, although means testing alternatives include different dimensions, they are not truly multidimensional because they fail to capture deprivation in each of these dimensions. Their aim is still to assess family income levels, albeit using multiple indicators to do so. Another argument is that the targeting mechanisms they use have focused on income shortfall rather than on human-capital-related deprivations, despite the fact that tackling these deprivations, particularly among children and adolescents, is an explicit objective of poverty reduction policies.

Azevedo and Robles (2013) illustrate the potential of multidimensional poverty measures as a targeting instrument by means of an exercise involving Mexico's *Oportunidades* programme. The authors analyse the ability of targeting via multidimensional measurement to capture low-income households, as well as households where children do not attend school or engage in child labour, and compare it with alternative mechanisms (including the one the programme actually uses). The authors found the multidimensional targeting method to be better at identifying households suffering deprivation in these three dimensions. A similar exercise on Uruguay's Family Allowances programme (Lavalleja, Mathieu and Messina, 2013), which considers both household characteristics and children's individual attributes, stresses the advantage of using a flexible indicator to focus efforts on, for example, children deprived in a certain dimension, giving that dimension greater weight.

Source: S. Alkire and J. Foster, "Counting and multidimensional poverty measurement", *Working Paper*, No. 32, Oxford Poverty and Human Development Initiative (OPHI), December 2009; S. Alkire and M.E. Santos, "Acute multidimensional poverty: a new index for developing countries", *Human Development Reports Research Paper*, July 2010; R. Angulo, B. Díaz and R. Pardo, "Multidimensional poverty in Colombia, 1997-2010", *ISER Working Paper Series*, No. 2013-03, January 2013; V. Azevedo and M. Robles, "Multidimensional targeting: Identifying beneficiaries of conditional cash transfer programs", *Social Indicators Research*, vol. 112, No. 2, 2013; F. Bourguignon and S.R. Chakravarty, "The measurement of multidimensional poverty", *Journal of Economic Inequality*, No. 1, 2003; M. Lavalleja, G. Mathieu and P. Messina, "Evaluación de los mecanismos de selección de beneficiarios de asignaciones familiares" research paper, Facultad de Ciencias Económicas y de Administración, Universidad de la República, 2013; M. Ravallion, "On multidimensional indices of poverty", *Journal of Economic Inequality*, vol. 9, No. 2, 2011.

Bibliography

Abramovich, Víctor (2006), "La articulación de acciones legales y políticas en la demanda de derechos sociales", *Los Derechos Económicos, Sociales y Culturales en América Latina. Del invento a la herramienta*, Alicia Yamin (ed.), Plaza y Valdés/ International Development Research Centre (IDRC).

Alkire, Sabina and Maria Emma Santos (2010), "Acute multidimensional poverty: a new index for developing countries", *Human Development Reports Research Paper*, July.

Alkire, Sabina and James Foster (2009), "Counting and multidimensional poverty measurement", *Working Paper*, No. 32, Oxford Poverty and Human Development Initiative (OPHI), December.

Azevedo, V. and M. Robles (2013), "Multidimensional targeting: Identifying beneficiaries of conditional cash transfer programs", *Social Indicators Research*, vol. 112, No. 2.

Bourguignon, François and Satya R. Chakravarty (2003), "The measurement of multidimensional poverty", *Journal of Economic Inequality*, vol. 1, No. 1, April.

CELADE (Latin American and Caribbean Demographic Centre -Population Division of ECLAC), "Definición de viviendas en situación de hacinamiento" [online] http://celade.cepal.org/redatam/PRYESP/SISPPI/Webhelp/viviendas_en_situacion_de_hacinamiento.htm [date of reference: 20 January 2011].

CONEVAL/UNICEF (National Council for the Evaluation of Social Development Policy/United Nations Children's Fund) (2013), *Pobreza y derechos sociales de niñas, niños y adolescentes en México, 2008-2010*, Mexico City, UNICEF office in Mexico.

ECLAC (Economic Commission for Latin America and the Caribbean) (2010), *Social Panorama of Latin America 2009* (LC/G.2423-P), Santiago, Chile.

___(2000), *Social Panorama of Latin America 1999-2000* (LC/G.2068-P), Santiago, Chile.

___(1998), *Social Panorama of Latin America 1998* (LC/G.2050-P), Santiago, Chile.

___(1997), *Social Panorama of Latin America 1997* (LC/G.1982-P/E), Santiago, Chile.

___(1994), *Social Panorama of Latin America 1994* (LC/G.1844-P/E), Santiago, Chile.

ECLAC/UNICEF (Economic Commission for Latin America and the Caribbean/United Nations Children's Fund) (2012a), "Guía para estimar la pobreza infantil. Información para avanzar en el ejercicio de los derechos de los niños, niñas y adolescentes" (LC/M2)" [online] http://dds.cepal.org/infancia/guia-para-estimar-la-pobreza-infantil/.

___(2012b), "Pobreza infantil en pueblos indígenas y afrodescendientes de América Latina", *Project Documents*, No. 477 (LC/W.477), Santiago, Chile, Economic Commission for Latin America and the Caribbean (ECLAC).

___(2010), "Pobreza infantil en América Latina y el Caribe" (LC/R.2168), Santiago, Chile, Economic Commission for Latin America and the Caribbean (ECLAC).

___(2009), "Child abuse: a painful reality behind closes doors", *Challenges Bulletin*, No. 9, Santiago, Chile, Economic Commission for Latin America and the Caribbean (ECLAC), July.

ECLAC/DGEC (Economic Commission for Latin America and the Caribbean/Department of Statistics and Censuses) (1988), *La heterogeneidad de la pobreza: una aproximación bidimensional* (LC/MVD/R.12/Rev.1), Montevideo, ECLAC office in Montevideo.

Espíndola, Ernesto and María Nieves Rico (2012), "Child poverty in Latin America: multiple deprivation and monetary measures combined", *Global Child Poverty and Well-Being. Measurement, concepts, policy and action,* Alberto Minujín and Sailen Nandy, Bristol, The Policy Press.

___(2010), "Child poverty: a priority challenges", *Challenges Bulletin,* No. 10, Santiago, Chile, Economic Commission for Latin America and the Caribbean (ECLAC)/United Nations Children's Fund (UNICEF).

Expert Group on Poverty Statistics (2007), *Compendium of Best Practices in Poverty Measurement* [online] http://www.ibge.gov.br/poverty/pdf/rio_group_compendium.pdf.

Foster, James, Joel Greer and Erik Thorbecke (1984), "A class of decomposable poverty measures", *Econométrica*, vol. 52, No. 3, May.

Gordon, David (2006), "Cómo monitorear el derecho a la salud", Conferencia Educación en Derechos Humanos con Aplicación en Salud (EDHUCASALUD)/International Federation of Health Records Organizations (IFHHRO).

___(ed.) (2003), "Final draft: The distribution of child poverty in the developing world", Report to UNICEF, Bristol, Centre of International Poverty Research, University of Bristol [online] http://www.ibge.gov.br/poverty/pdf/Social%20 Exclusion/REFERENCE%20CHILD%20POVERTY%20REPORT.pdf] [date of reference: 12 July 2013].

Gordon, David and others (2003), *Child Poverty in the Developing World*, Bristol, The Policy Press.

Hofferth, L. Sandra and John F. Sandberg (2000), *How American Children Spend their Time*, Michigan, University of Michigan, April.

Kaztman, Rubén (2011), "Infancia en América Latina: privaciones habitacionales y desarrollo de capital humano", *Project Documents*, No. 431 (LC/W.431), Santiago, Chile, Economic Commission for Latin America and the CaribbeanEconomic Commission for Latin America and the Caribbean (ECLAC)/United Nations Children's Fund (UNICEF).

Lavalleja M., G. Mathieu and P. Messina (2013), "Evaluación de los mecanismos de selección de beneficiarios de asingaciones familiares", research paper, Faculty of Economic Sciences, Universidad de la República.

Minujin, Alberto, Enrique Delamónica and Alejandra Davidziuk (2006), "Pobreza infantil. Conceptos, medición y recomendaciones de políticas públicas", *Cuaderno de Ciencias Sociales*, No. 140, San José, Latin American Faculty of Social Sciences (FLACSO).

Morales, Abelardo, Guillermo Acuña and Karina Wing-Ching (2010), "Migración y salud en zonas fronterizas: Nicaragua y Costa Rica", *Población y Desarrollo series*, No. 94 (LC/L.3249-P), Santiago, Chile, Economic Commission for Latin America and the Caribbean (ECLAC). United Nations publication, Sales No. S.10.II.G.54.

___(2000), Millennium Development Goals [online] http://www.un.org/english/millenniumgoals [date of reference: 20 January 2011].

Ravallion, Martin (2011), "On multidimensional indices of poverty", *Policy Research Working Paper*, Washington, D.C., World Bank.

Rico, María Nieves (2013), "Derechos de la infancia. Enfoque, indicadores y perspectivas", *Seminario Internacional Indicadores de Derechos Económicos, Sociales y Culturales (DESC) y seguimiento de las políticas sociales para la superación de la pobreza y el logro de la igualdad*, Santiago, Chile, National Human Rights Institute (INDH).

Rossel, Cecilia (2013), "Desbalance etario del bienestar. El lugar de la infancia en la protección social en América Latina", *Políticas Sociales series*, No.176 (LC/L.3574), Santiago, Chile, Economic Commission for Latin America and the Caribbean (ECLAC).

Towsend, P. (1979), *Poverty in the United Kingdom*, London, Allen Lane and Penguin.

Tuñón, Ianina (2012), *La infancia argentina sujeto de derecho. Progresos, desigualdades y desafíos pendientes en el efectivo cumplimiento de los derechos de niños, niñas y adolescentes,* Buenos Aires, Observatorio de la Deuda Social Argentina, Universidad Católica Argentina.

UNICEF (United Nations Children's Fund) (2007), "UN General Assembly adopts powerful definition of child poverty", New York [online] http://www.unicef.org/media/media_38003.html] [date of reference: 12 July 2013].

___(2005), *The State of the World's Children 2005*, New York.

___(2004), "PRSPs & children: child poverty, disparity and budgets", *CD PRSPs Resource Package*, New York.

Chapter III

Some overlooked dimensions of well-being in Latin America

A. Conceptual and methodological considerations

> Well-being is a wide-ranging concept that has been defined in many and varied ways. It is a positive physical, social and mental state, rather than simply the absence of pain, discomfort and incapacity. It requires that basic needs are met, that individuals have a sense of purpose, that they feel able to achieve important personal goals and participate in society. It is enhanced by conditions that include supportive personal relationships, strong and inclusive communities, good health, financial and personal security, rewarding employment, and a healthy and attractive environment (British Government, 1999).

1. Current state of the debate

The many definitions of well-being reflect its multifaceted nature and can be seen as stepping stones towards conceptual, methodological and policy proposals. In broad terms, "well-being" has been used to refer to the life situation of a given person or group in society (Gasper, 2007). The most common approaches to conceptualizing well-being encompass quality of life, living standards and human development as well as notions such as social well-being, usefulness, satisfaction with life, prosperity, satisfaction of needs, fulfilling potential and happiness. Although some of these terms have specific meanings, there are significant overlaps between them, and they are sometimes used interchangeably (McGillivray, 2005).

For much of the post-war period, development theory equated well-being with economic progress, expressed as the total of what a society could produce, in the belief that the spread of economic growth would bring about universal well-being. It was as an expression of this view that gross domestic product (GDP) was established as an indicator of the economic development and progress of societies. In both political theory and policy planning, GDP has been used as a proxy for well-being (Boarini, Johansson and D'Ercole, 2006).

Many different critics subsequently highlighted the limitations of GDP as a barometer of the well-being of a society. From the 1970s onwards, proposals were put forward with a view to establishing an adjusted indicator able to take account of both the creation of wealth and well-being on a society and the production of goods and services that are not for sale on the market. These initiatives sought to adjust conventional economic indicators (such as GDP) to reflect social and environmental costs and benefits that would not normally be covered in national accounts.[1]

Approaching the issue from another perspective, other efforts have concentrated on building composite indices in an attempt to gain a better grasp of the multifaceted nature of well-being. One such attempt is the Human Development Index (HDI), which is based on three indicators (income, life expectancy and educational attainment) and whose theory is underpinned by Amartya Sen's capability approach. The HDI represents a departure from the view that well-being should be understood purely in terms of income and other material dimensions. In essence it posits that progress and development take place, and poverty is reduced, when people are afforded greater freedom (or capabilities). "Development can be seen ... as a process of expanding the real freedoms that people enjoy" (Sen, 2000). It therefore follows that a "good life" is, in part, a life in which people are genuinely free to choose what they do, rather than being obliged to seek new life experiences. The intrinsic value of freedom is thus linked to empowering people so they can themselves act as the protagonists, or creative agents, of their own development.

---

[1] Notable such efforts include: Nordhaus and Tobin's Measure of Economic Welfare of 1972, Daly and Cobb's Index of Sustainable Economic Welfare (ISEW) of 1989, Cobb, Halstead and Rowe's Genuine Progress Indicator of 1995 and the New Economics Foundation's Measure of Domestic Progress.

Another approach entails introducing subjective aspects to assess well-being.[2] A key aspect is the interplay between the economic (or material) development of society and subjective well-being, namely how people rate their well-being or quality of life. The central idea is that when societies reach a given level of economic and material development, the law of diminishing returns begins to apply in terms of the relationship between economic growth and well-being. In economics literature this is known as the "Easterlin Paradox", namely that although people with higher incomes are happier than those with lower incomes, once individuals reach a certain level of prosperity, no further increases in income will cause levels of happiness to rise (Easterlin, 1974).

Despite the major contribution they have made to understanding of the phenomenon of well-being, these indicators have been much criticized. Firstly, the weightings assigned to the various elements measured have proved highly controversial (Conceição and Bandura, 2008). Secondly, criticism of the chosen methodology has focused on whether there is a collinear relationship between indicators, and therefore on the robustness of the variables used. Thirdly, indicators based on a purely subjective vision of well-being betray significant methodological weaknesses that make it difficult to take account of the multifaceted nature of well-being.

Despite this criticism and the variety of methodological and conceptual problems that remain to be resolved, new debates have gone beyond academic spheres and come to the attention of various governments.

A crucial milestone was the establishment of the Stiglitz, Sen and Fitoussi Commission at the behest of the then President of France, Nicolas Sarkozy, with the support of the European Commission, to take stock of progress and well-being in the twenty-first century. The Commission's findings stressed that well-being was to be understood as a multidimensional phenomenon. Although these findings drew on previous efforts, including discussions on happiness, in the selection and construction of indicators, they surpassed them in that they laid down —or at least began discussions with a view to laying down— a set of indicators that were comparable across countries.

Stiglitz, Sen and Fitoussi (2008) took an examination of the limits of GDP as the basis on which to make a series of recommendations for improving the indicators currently used to measure progress and well-being. In economic terms, they proposed favouring net indicators over gross indicators, analysing the quality and quantity of services and changes and flows in them, improving the measurement of services provided by governments, and paying more attention to the consumption of households than total consumption within the economy. The intention was, firstly, to measure income, wealth and consumption as a whole and not separately, and to quantify services provided and consumption generated in the home and any related inequalities. Secondly, the commission sought to analyse the quality of life using both subjective well-being indicators and indicators accounting for people's opportunities and conditions in terms of health, education, security, political representation, environmental conditions and other considerations. Thirdly, it stressed the need to consider sustainable development, an issue around which there is little consensus, and to analyse economic and environmental dimensions separately, while paying special attention to rises and falls in reserves of key resources for human life.

2. Ongoing initiatives

Building on the work of this commission, in 2010 the Organisation for Economic Co-operation and Development (OECD) established a partnership between a number of international organizations to measure progress in societies.[3] The partnership has thus far focused on defining indicators for periodic and future examination in isolation with a view to creating a composite index of well-being. These indicators are built on three variables: economic resources, quality

---

[2] Approaches introducing subjective dimensions of well-being have given rise to several indices to measure happiness. One such indicator is Bhutan's Gross National Happiness Index, which is based on the view that genuine human development takes place when material and spiritual development are combined. It consists of four pillars: sustainable and equitable socioeconomic development, environmental conservation and the promotion of culture and good governance (see [online] http://www.grossnationalhappiness. com/wp-content/uploads/2012/04/Short-GNH-Index-edited.pdf). The World Happiness Report (2013) of Helliwell Layard and Sachs is another such recent initiative.

[3] In addition to OECD sponsorship, this initiative, the Global Project on Measuring the Progress of Societies, receives support from the World Bank, the United Nations Development Programme (UNDP), the United Nations Children's Fund (UNICEF), the Inter-American Development Bank (IDB), the African Development Bank (AfDB), the United Nations Economic and Social Commission for Western Asia (UN-ESCWA), the United Nations Economic and Social Commission for Asia and the Pacific (ESCAP) and the International Organization of Supreme Audit Institutions (INTOSAI) (see [online] http://www.midiendoelprogreso.org/english/partners.html).

of life and sustainability. Proposals have also been made to analyse human environments in relation to ecosystems and to distinguish between individual and social well-being when examining links between indicators (Quiroga, 2007).

In a similar vein, *Wellbeing and Poverty Pathways* (2011), a partnership between various educational institutions in the United Kingdom, India and Zambia, has established a set of internationally comparable indicators to define well-being and quality of life in relation to the following eight dimensions: physical and mental health, economic resources, characteristics of the local environment, agency and participation, social connections, close relationships, competence and self-worth, and values and meaning.[4] These dimensions are, in turn, framed by the wider context of the physical environment, infrastructure, the economic and political system, social institutions, the dynamics of peace and conflict, the available services and the policy regime. The need is also stressed to consider supplementary qualitative indicators to contextualize analysis of the various variables and for culture to play a key role in definitions of well-being, among other factors.

As the New Economics Foundation (NEF) has shown, successive governments have paid much attention to these discussions, and their impact has grown over time (NEF, 2008). The United Kingdom has been a pioneer in this area, and in 1994 launched, as part of the Agenda 21 action plan, a sustainable development strategy entitled *Sustainable Development: the UK Strategy* (Government of the United Kingdom, 1994). In 1997, the British Government announced that it would be drawing up a new strategy and therefore issued a consultation document —*Opportunities for Change*— as well as a series of publications on various aspects of sustainable development. The new strategy took the achievements of the 1994 strategy as its basis, but followed a new approach that stressed the social dimension of sustainable development together with economic and environmental considerations. In 1999 the government published the document *A Better Quality of Life* (1999), which set out a system of around 150 indicators providing a detailed overview of progress made and challenges to face in terms of sustainable development. The system included a subset of headline indicators, of which three concern the economy (growth, investment and employment), five relate to social affairs (poverty, education, health, housing and crime) and seven refer to the environment (climate change, air quality, traffic, water quality in rivers, wildlife, land use and waste).

Several countries other than the UK have also launched similar initiatives. These include long-established projects run by the Governments of Australia (*Measures of Australia's Progress* (MAP)),[5] Denmark (*Structural Monitoring. International Benchmarking of Denmark*),[6] Ireland (*Measuring Ireland's Progress*)[7] and New Zealand (*Monitoring Progress Towards a Sustainable New Zealand*).[8]

Similar initiatives are also being introduced in Latin America with a view to defining indicators to measure well-being in a multidimensional manner. Two such initiatives are of particular importance, firstly the Mexican project launched in late 2009 for the multidimensional measurement of poverty. This initiative is the first to take account of the different forms that household poverty can take, by considering both social factors (health, housing, education and access to food) and income at national, federal-state and municipal levels. This multidimensional method of measuring poverty can be summed up as follows: (a) the dimensions chosen by Mexico's Congress for measurement are based on social entitlements; (b) the cut-off thresholds are based primarily on the Mexican Constitution and the most important applicable social standards (to bring measurements of poverty in line with the Mexican legal system); (c) the chosen methodology highlights the link between poverty and social programmes and public-policy strategies, and (d) poverty indices are estimated every two years at national and federal-state level and every five years at the municipal level.[9] In its presentation of the methodology used, Mexico's National Council for the Evaluation of Social Development Policy (CONEVAL) defines the concept of the multidimensionality of poverty and sets out the dimensions and components it consists of, the thresholds for each indicator and the criteria used. Under this new definition, a person suffers from multidimensional poverty if their income is insufficient to provide for the goods and services they require to meet their needs and if they suffer from one or more of the following factors of discomfort:

---

4   See [online] http://www.wellbeingpathways.org/.
5   See [online] http://www.abs.gov.au/ausstats/abs@.nsf/mf/1370.0.55.001.
6   See [online] http://uk.fm.dk/publications/2000/structural-monitoring-_-international-benchmarking-of-denmark/.
7   See [online] http://www.cso.ie/en/releasesandpublications/measuringirelandsprogress/.
8   See [online] http://www.stats.govt.nz/browse_for_stats/environment/sustainable_development/monitoring-progress-towards-sustainable-nz.aspx.
9   See [online] http://www.coneval.gob.mx/Paginas/principal_EN.aspx.

educational gaps, insufficient access to health care, insufficient social-security coverage, poor-quality housing and living spaces, lack of basic housing services and insufficient access to food.[10]

The other major initiative is the Latin American Conference on Measuring Well-Being and Fostering the Progress of Societies, whose participants included agencies from the region and beyond such as IDB, the Economic Commission for Latin America and the Caribbean (ECLAC), the United Nations Educational, Scientific and Cultural Organization (UNESCO) and UNDP. The event was held in Mexico City in May 2011 by Mexico's National Institute of Statistics and Geography (INEGI) and its Scientific and Technological Consultative Forum (FCCyT), with the support of OECD and its Development Centre, and formed part of a series of regional conferences organized as part of the project *Measuring the Progress of Societies*, in the run-up to the fourth OECD Global Forum, held in New Delhi in October 2012.[11] The conference followed on from the previous OECD global forums held in Palermo (2004), Istanbul (2007) and Bhutan (2009). Major influences on its conceptual framework included the report *the Measurement of Economic Performance and Social Progress Revisited. Reflections and Overview* (Stiglitz, Sen and Fitoussi, 2008). The main conclusions of the conference were as follows:

(a) Understanding of people's well-being and of its determinants is crucial, since it shapes the direction in which society should move in order to achieve progress and influences policy-makers.

(b) Commonly used indicators only partially grasp the complexity of this phenomenon. As stated above, such is the problem with GDP, which focuses exclusively on the economic production of goods and services to the detriment of issues such as income distribution, justice, freedoms, people's capacity to achieve a meaningful life, their life satisfaction and the sustainability of economic progress. A proper measure of progress should take a multidimensional approach.

(c) The measurement of well-being goes beyond GDP and money, requiring the consideration of both objective and subjective dimensions and a focus on individuals and households.

(d) The key dimensions of well-being should include factors affecting health, education, working conditions, housing, economic situation, interpersonal relationships, the availability of free time, access to social protection, effective citizenship, the rule of law, gender equality and ethnic identity.

(e) There is a close relationship between well-being, equity and social cohesion. In spite of significant economic growth, Latin America remains the most unequal region in the world. Inequalities are manifest not only in income but also in education, health, access to quality services, security, the availability of free time and the exercise of citizenship. In analysing well-being, emphasis should be placed on ethnic and gender gaps, and other vulnerable groups, and on intergenerational social mobility.

(f) In respect of measuring well-being, the goal is not to build a synthetic well-being index, but to produce a limited number of indicators that are relevant and can inform policy design and decision-making. There is a consensus on the need to improve official information sources and to establish other sources that capture aspects of well-being that have not yet been measured (Rojas, 2011).

In sum, a consensus has therefore emerged around the world, including in Latin America, on the need to rethink what constitutes progress in societies. Narratives maintaining that economic growth is the only way to achieve well-being are, to say the least, inadequate. Rethinking traditional ways of measuring well-being is also required, incorporating issues such as the environment —and the current and intergenerational costs of harming it— as well as subjective aspects of people's lives.

3. Well-being, inequality and social malaise

Rethinking what well-being is and the way in which it is measured is of singular importance in Latin America, a context marked by three distinct factors: (a) major progress towards meeting overall development goals, (b) persistent inequality, and (c) the emergence of increasingly visible signs of social malaise.

---

[10] For further information on the methodology used for the multidimensional measurement of poverty in Mexico, as well as welfare lines, maps and reports on the state of poverty in Mexico and its regions, see [online] http://www.coneval.gob.mx/InformesPublicaciones/Paginas/Publicaciones-sobre-Medicion-de-la-pobreza-en.aspx.

[11] See [online] http://www.midiendoelprogreso.org/english/index.html.

As a recent report has shown (Alarcón, 2013), the countries of Latin America and the Caribbean have made great strides towards meeting the Millennium Development Goals. There remain, however, very serious obstacles to overcome. Deforestation is a serious threat to environmental sustainability, and the greatest loss of forest areas has occurred in South America. More widespread access to reproductive health services is essential to prevent maternal mortality and to reduce the rate of adolescent pregnancies. Urbanization continues to advance more quickly than slum upgrading, so the major challenge lies in how to improve housing and domestic water systems (Alarcón, 2013).

This does not, however, detract from the substantial progress that has been made in reducing poverty, but there remain very serious inequalities in income distribution that have only been slightly alleviated. "The distributional improvements in the early part of the last decade were encouraging, the evidence points to four key aspects that will constrain future progress towards equality: income distribution, the distribution of education and knowledge, the highly unequal capacity to take advantage of that education and knowledge in the labour market, and the intergenerational transmission of inequality" (ECLAC, 2010a). This is compounded by two factors that exacerbate inequality gaps. "On the one hand, access to health care and systems of insurance against risk and vulnerability remains deeply segmented, including highly unequal access to health and social security benefits. On the other hand, the fastest growth in social expenditure has been on those instruments that do the least for redistribution, such as social security. Accordingly, the structure of the social safety net needs to be adjusted to move towards greater equality" (ECLAC, 2010a).

Quite aside from the aforementioned elements, the conviction that rethinking what constitutes well-being is necessary has emerged at a time of crisis and increasingly visible social unrest. For several years now in Chile, and more recently in Brazil —to name but two countries that have made significant progress towards meeting the Millennium Development Goals— there has been a wide-ranging malaise that has become evident through large-scale protest movements. At the root of it is dissatisfaction with issues such as education, public transport and environmental conflicts that has channelled wider feelings of frustration present in every society. Young people have been the first group in society to react, both by demonstrating in the street and by voicing their displeasure using the many means at their disposal associated with the new technologies that form part of their cultural universe.

These movements may have formed in response to diverse issues (such as education, public transport or the contamination of food with agrochemicals or the poisoning of the environment with toxic chemicals), but are symptoms of a social unrest that threatens to define our age. What defines these movements is that they lack a clear, unified set of demands and that are resistant to input from political parties for fear of losing the independence that they feel safeguards their ability to stand for what people really want.

It is thus paradoxical that interest in well-being has peaked at a time in which the countries of the region have made significant progress towards meeting the Millennium Development Goals, while a general malaise has become visible via the symptoms of very diverse protest movements. Meanwhile, traditional indicators do not appear to take account of issues that are essential to the well-being of the protagonists of the development process.

4. Proposal for analysis on the basis of some key dimensions of well-being

ECLAC has not proposed setting up a new synthetic well-being index. There are at least four reasons for this. Firstly, a synthetic index would entail simplifying a very complex phenomenon, since the very fact of selecting the dimensions to be considered in the index is, by definition, arbitrary. In addition, some of the dimensions selected, such as literacy and undernutrition, can see themselves downgraded in importance over time. The weightings assigned to each factor or indicator can also prove controversial: why should certain factors or indicators be seen as more important than others when the very countries or people being analysed value them differently still? Although synthetic indices, such as the Human Development Index, are useful in drawing up rankings of countries, they are also difficult to interpret because thresholds (or cut-off lines) need to be drawn to ascertain which elements lie below expected levels for well-being. It should also be noted that the requisite conditions for building an index are not yet in place, as some of the most significant factors remain insufficiently documented in the official statistics of the countries in question: there are significant areas where information is scarce or practically non-existent, so official sources therefore need to be developed and refined. Efforts also need to be made to standardize (or harmonize) information produced by countries with a view to making it comparable. Ultimately, a solution to both the problems associated with selecting indicators and other technical and methodological difficulties needs to be found before the creation of a multivariate measurement system can be considered, if that were the objective.

Nor can the objective be to move towards a comprehensive system of indicators, which would be a tempting choice as it has the advantage of not simplifying the complicated phenomenon of well-being, which is the problem with synthetic indices. However, it is the all-encompassing nature of the information that makes it difficult to use for the purposes of analysing progress in well-being in countries, as part of an integrated and, ideally, comparative overview. A case in point is the system developed in 1999 by the British Government, which involved some 150 indicators. It was conceived as the culmination of a public consultation process as part of a strategy stressing the social dimension of sustainable development, alongside economic and environmental considerations (*A Better Quality of Life*, 1999, *Quality of Life Counts*, 2004). This system did indeed provide a comprehensive overview of the progress and challenges on the road to achieving sustainable development, but proved so complex that a subset of headline indicators had to be defined to provide a more concise account of progress made and challenges encountered in achieving sustainable development policy objectives in the United Kingdom. This was clearly a very useful exercise in terms of local and central government policy-making in that country but would be difficult to replicate in Latin America, given that many of the countries have no official statistics on many key issues to be addressed in the multidimensional measurement of well-being.

This proposal aims to find a middle way, like the aforementioned headline indicators, but has substituted indicators for a small selection of key dimensions. It is a modest proposal that considers three dimensions that have been overlooked in discussions on well-being in Latin America but which can be seen as necessary preconditions for well-being: space, time and coexistence. These dimensions go beyond basic "first-generation" needs, which are essential for human life and refer to areas such as health, education, working conditions, housing, or economic situation. They can also be seen as "windows" which provide a comprehensive, multidimensional view of issues which have been discussed above in a cursory and fragmented manner.

The space in which we live is undoubtedly a fundamental dimension of well-being. The central element is the quality of this space and, particularly, of the environment. A healthy environment is fundamental for people's well-being, but pollution, toxic substances and noise undermine this well-being. The OECD has stated that environmental factors play a role in more than 80% of the major diseases, and around a quarter of diseases and overall deaths worldwide are due to poor environmental conditions. Environmental factors of a more extreme nature, such as natural disasters (earthquakes, cyclones, floods, drought, volcanic eruptions and epidemic outbreaks) may also cause deaths, injury and disease in significant proportions. Preserving environmental and natural resources is also one of the most important challenges for ensuring the sustainability of well-being over time (OECD, 2011, p. 212).

The ability to strike the right balance in allocating time for various activities —work, family life, relationships, or leisure time— is a second key dimension of well-being. When people are unable to juggle these activities adequately, this balance is upset, which means insufficient time for family life, interpersonal relationships, leisure and other activities. People's ability to maintain this balance is challenged by two hugely time-consuming activities: (a) time in paid employment – working hours have historically been overly long, thus minimizing people's time for other activities (policies to promote a better work-life balance came to the fore in the 1990s to reconcile these two aspects of life) and (b) time spent on unpaid household work. The total time people spend in paid and unpaid work is known as their overall workload, which determines the amount of leisure at their disposal and eats into their well-being.

Harmonious coexistence is the third key dimension of well-being. The concept of coexistence encompasses the many ways in which people live side-by-side in the various spheres of everyday life: within the family, at work, and in public spaces. Harmonious coexistence requires moral values such as respect for diversity, tolerance and the ability to place trust in others, as well as acceptance of (and compliance with) the rules governing social interaction. People's well-being suffers when their relations with others turn sour as a result of intolerance, mistrust and lack of acceptance of diversity. It also suffers when the rules governing social interaction lack legitimacy (ECLAC, 2007). From the perspective of this document, the various forms of violence present in different social spheres, both public and private, show both a breakdown in harmonious coexistence and are thus factors that greatly reduce well-being.

A final important point is that this proposal includes no subjective aspects of well-being. This does not, however, mean that it affords little importance to them, but rather supports the view that a broader approach to understanding well-being is needed, one that goes beyond measuring objective variables, and incorporates aspects of well-being that cannot be "bought" by income. "In this context, an emerging issue in the Latin American debate is the need to include subjective factors, such as people's perceptions and attitudes concerning their living conditions and social relations, in assessments of their well-being" (Villatoro, 2012).

ECLAC has made use of subjective indicators to assess well-being in previous studies, (ECLAC, 2007, 2010a and 2012), but it is precisely because subjective factors are not a separate dimension of well-being, but are rather cross-cutting factors affecting numerous sectors, that they require more thorough analysis. In view of the dimensions encompassed by the proposal, this analysis should consider, among other things, how people view environmental pollution and the effect it has on their well-being, how satisfied they are with their amount of free time and the time they spend in paid and unpaid work as well as their concerns at issues of safety and violence.

B. Space

Space is a fundamental material dimension of human life. It encompasses the environment we inhabit, including water, earth, air, objects, living beings, relationships between men and women and intangible factors such as cultural values. A healthy space (or environment) to live in is a prerequisite for a decent standard of well-being.

In the past few decades, the environment in Latin America has been affected in various ways, and in varying degrees of severity, by the model of development. Current environmental debate focuses on many of the ways in which this has happened, via such problems as deforestation, due to logging and the burning of forest areas, a reduction in biodiversity and damage to ecological systems, which are of key importance for food chains; overfishing, which threatens a great many species of wildlife, soil erosion, which reduces productivity and water quality and causes land degradation, contamination of rivers and seas with sewage, waste, agricultural runoff and industrial waste, air pollution, from the emission of toxic substances into the atmosphere, and global warming, which in turn leads to floods, heat waves, drought, rises in sea levels and the melting of glaciers and ice sheets.

These changes to the environment — the space we live in— all have an impact on human well-being. To illustrate this, one of the aforementioned factors, the deterioration of air quality, particularly, urban air pollution, will now be examined.[12]

1. Air pollution in Latin American cities

The world Health Organization (WHO) defines air pollution as contamination of the indoor or outdoor environment by any chemical, physical or biological agent that modifies the natural characteristics of the atmosphere. Household combustion devices, motor vehicles, industrial facilities and forest fires are common sources of air pollution. Pollutants of major public health concern include particulate matter (PM), carbon monoxide, ozone, nitrogen dioxide and sulphur dioxide.[13]

Air pollution is a problem experienced chiefly in urban areas and has reached critical levels in Latin America. In the past three decades, Latin America's urban population has grown by 240% —while its rural population has increased by just 6.1%— and has risen from 70.6% of the total population of the region in 1990 to 79.5% in 2010, making it one of the most urbanized areas of the planet. Countries such as Argentina, the Bolivarian Republic of Venezuela,

---

[12] This section will refer specifically to outdoor spaces in urban areas. As space is limited in this chapter, air pollution within the home will not be considered, despite the fact that it is a major problem within the region.

[13] See [online] http://www.who.int/phe/health_topics/outdoorair/en/index.html.

Chile and Uruguay have even higher urbanization rates, exceeding 86%.[14] Furthermore, as far back as 1990, three of the world's 10 largest "megacities" were located in Latin America: Buenos Aires, Mexico City and São Paulo.

It has been said that at least 100 million people in Latin America and the Caribbean are exposed to air pollution at levels above those recommended by WHO (Cifuentes and others, 2005). The groups most vulnerable to the effects of air pollution are children, the elderly, people with certain pre-existing health conditions and those in poverty.

Particulate matter is a major air pollutant,[15] alongside ozone (O_3), nitrogen dioxide (NO_2) and sulphur dioxide (SO_2). Figure III.1 shows the annual average PM_{10} levels in 27 selected cities in Latin America and the Caribbean. In 2007-2008, all these cities (located in 15 countries in the region) exceeded WHO maximum recommended PM_{10} levels, set (in the 2005 edition of the WHO *Air Quality Guidelines*) at 20 micrograms per cubic metre ($\mu g/m^3$) on average over an entire year and 50 $\mu g/m^3$ on average over a period of 24 hours (WHO, 2006).

Thirteen of the cities referred to in figure III.1 are capitals: Bogota, Buenos Aires, Caracas, Guatemala City, Kingston, Lima, Mexico City, Montevideo, Panama, Quito, San José, San Salvador and Santiago. In 2008-2009, the capitals in the region with the highest levels of PM10 were Lima, Bogota and Santiago, whose annual averages were over three times the minimum recommended by WHO. Great strides have been made in Mexico City in reducing the historically high levels of air pollution and reducing the amount of lead and particulate matter emitted into the atmosphere by means of a raft of measures, including eliminating leaded petrol and implementing the *"Hoy no circula"* ("No-drive days") programme to limit vehicle use. The city remains, however, above minimum air-quality levels.[16]

Figure III.1

Latin America and the Caribbean (27 selected cities): annual average PM_{10} pollution, around 2008-2009 [a]

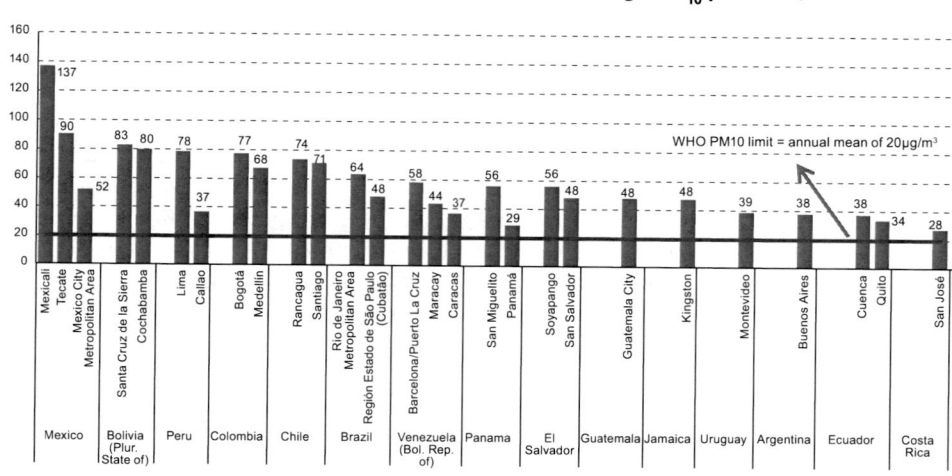

Source: Economic Commission for Latin America and the Caribbean (ECLAC), on the basis of information from the World Health Organization (WHO), "Outdoor air pollution in cities" [online] http://www.who.int/phe/health_topics/outdoorair/databases/en/.
[a] For further details on how data in the WHO database are estimated, go to [online] http://www.who.int/phe/health_topics/outdoorair/databases/en/#.

Aside from capital cities, the level of PM_{10} pollution in medium-sized cities is also a cause for alarm. One such case is Mexicali in Mexico, a city with one of the highest levels of urban air pollution in the world.[17] Other such cities include Santa Cruz de la Sierra and Cochabamba in the Plurinational State of Bolivia, which have pollution levels four times the WHO-recommended maximum, and Medellin in Colombia and Rancagua in Chile whose air pollution is only marginally better.

---

[14]   See [online] http://www.eclac.org/celade/proyecciones/basedatos_BD.htm.
[15]   Particulate matter is the sum of all solid and liquid particles in the air we breathe. PM10 is particulate matter with a diameter of up to and including 10 micrometres (a micrometre is a one-thousandth of a millimetre). Some PM10 is small enough to enter the human respiratory system, and the smaller particles are the more hazardous they tend to be.
[16]   For further information see SEMARNAT (2011).
[17]   Mexicali has an annual average of 137 $\mu g/m^3$. The city with the worst annual average air pollution in the world is Ulaanbaatar in Mongolia with 279 $\mu g/m^3$ (2008 data).

2. Exposure to air pollution as a cause of death

Exposure to urban air pollution, especially PM_{10}, poses a serious risk to human health and leads to higher rates of mortality and morbidity. As WHO has stated "urban outdoor air pollution increases the risk of acute (e.g. pneumonia) and chronic (e.g. lung cancer) respiratory disease as well as cardiovascular disease. Different groups of individuals are affected by air pollution in different ways. The most severe health impacts are seen among those people who are already ill. In addition, more vulnerable populations like children, the elderly and those households with lower incomes and limited access to health care are more susceptible to the adverse effects from exposure to air pollution" (WHO, 2011).

The WHO Global Health Observatory provides access to databases on priority health issues such as mortality and global burden of disease.[18] Figure III.2 shows the number of deaths attributable to air pollution in Latin America and the Caribbean in 2004 and 2008. The countries with the most deaths attributable to this problem in 2008 were Cuba (26), Argentina (24), Chile (19) and Uruguay (19), the Dominican Republic (16), Mexico (13), Peru (13), Brazil (12) and Saint Kitts and Nevis (12).

WHO estimates that 400,000 people die each year in Latin America and the Caribbean as a result of exposure to particulate matter, a high proportion of them owing to exposure indoors to fumes from the burning of biomass or other matter (quoted in Korc, 2000, p. 17). The Clean Air Institute has stated, in its study Air Quality in Latin America: An Overview, that high concentrations of air pollutants are impacting citizens and causing premature death and illness (Clean Air Institute, 2012). The OECD has warned that "air pollution is set to become the world's top environmental cause of premature mortality, overtaking dirty water and lack of sanitation" with "the number of premature deaths from exposure to particulate matter projected to more than double worldwide, from just over 1 million today to nearly 3.6 million per year in 2050". (OCDE, 2012, quoted by the Clean Air Institute, 2012).

Figure III.2 shows that, in a period of around four years (2004-2008), less than a third of the countries considered (7 of 24) saw a reduction in deaths from causes related to air pollution. This is despite the clear and urgent need for action in response to deaths that could have been avoided if preventive public health measures had been taken. Indeed, as WHO has stressed, a reduction in PM_{10} from 70 to 20 micrograms per cubic metre would reduce deaths related to air quality by approximately 15%. Over this period, it can also be seen that, in ten countries (including Brazil, Chile and Peru), no change has been registered in the number of deaths attributed to air pollution, so at least it can be said that these countries have put a brake on this alarming trend. Conversely, the remaining seven countries have seen an increase in the number of such deaths, which is unsatisfactory to say the very least.

Figure III.2

Latin America and the Caribbean (24 countries): deaths attributable to outdoor air pollution, around 2004 and 2008

(Per 100 000 inhabitants)

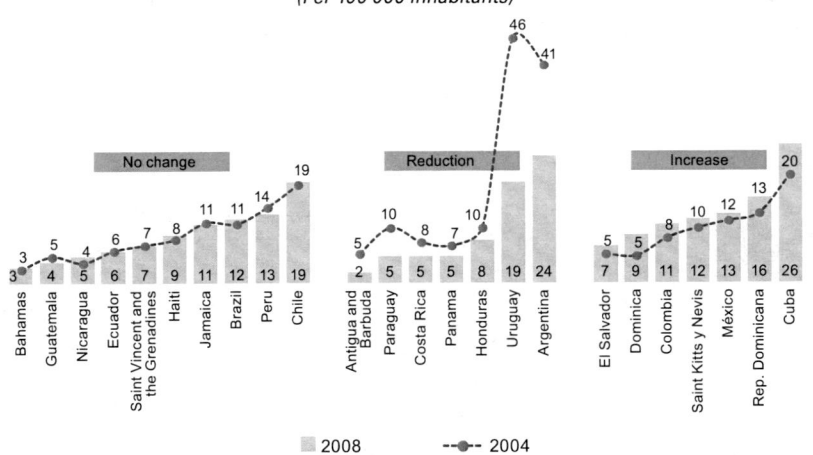

Source: Economic Commission for Latin America and the Caribbean (ECLAC), on the basis of information from the WHO Global Health Observatory Data Repository [online] http://apps.who.int/gho/data/node.main.688.

---

[18] WHO has defined the disease burden as the impact of a health problem on a given area, as measured by mortality and morbidity. It is often quantified in terms of disability-adjusted life years (DALYs), which estimate the number of years lost due to disease. The overall disease burden can be thought of as a measure of the gap between current health status and the ideal health status, where the individual lives to old age free from disease and disability. These measures allow for comparison of the disease burden in different regions, nations or localities and have also been used to forecast the possible impacts of health interventions.

The Global Health Observatory (GHO) of the WHO also provides data on other causes of mortality. Comparisons between the death rate attributable to air pollution and other causes of death, such as suicides, traffic accidents and homicides, clearly show the magnitude of the problem and the need for urgent action to address its underlying causes. GHO data show that in Argentina, Chile and Uruguay the death rate attributable to air pollution is higher than that relating to suicides, traffic accident deaths and homicides. In Mexico, Peru and the Dominican Republic, air pollution is the second most common cause of fatalities after traffic accidents, and in Brazil and Colombia it is the third most common cause, after murders and traffic accidents.[19] There can therefore be no doubt that exposure to air pollution, as a major cause of mortality, must be addressed by means of effective public-policy action.

3. Increase of the motor vehicle fleet and its impact on air pollution

Are there sufficient safeguards to guarantee the right of the people of the region to breathe clean air? Over the last two decades, considerable efforts have been made to curb air pollution in several Latin American urban areas. Actions implemented in Bogota, Mexico City, Sao Paulo, and Santiago, to name some of the most active and successful examples, have been extensively documented. However, air pollution remains an issue in Latin America's established urban centres and is becoming an issue in the region's emerging cities (Clean Air Institute, 2012).

Since the late 1990s, air-quality management programmes have been implemented in Bogota (10-year Bogota air decontamination plan), Kingston (Jamaica Air Quality Management Programme), Lima (Comprehensive Lima-Callao Clean-Air plan), Montevideo (Air-quality Monitoring Network) and San Jose (Costa Rica Greater Metropolitan Area Air-Quality Improvement Programme), to name but a few. All these cities have rules on air quality, and some have emission limits for moving and stationary facilities, as well as vehicle-inspection and -maintenance programmes (roadworthiness tests). However, despite this progress, several countries in the region have still to create the right conditions for their cities to grow in a sustainable manner with a view to safeguarding the present and future well-being of their inhabitants.

One of the principal causes of the rising levels of air pollution in large urban areas is the increasing number of motor vehicles. "Motor vehicle use, in large part private, is one of the main sources of urban pollution. The high rate of vehicle ownership would not necessarily cause serious pollution if cars were not used daily by their owners to travel to work along very congested roads. Such behaviour is encouraged by deficient public transport and by the huge size and functional segregation of the cities. These factors contribute to vehicle emissions, and thereby directly affect levels of air pollution" (Simioni, 2003).

It has been noted that in cities such as Santiago, the transport sector is responsible for approximately 50% of the fine particles in the air; Santiago can therefore serve as a benchmark for other Latin American cities with air pollution problems (Bull 2003, p. 164). Other main sources of air pollution include industry, power stations and the use of fuel by households for heating, cooking and refrigeration. Curbing the effects of the rising number of motor vehicles is thus an issue of critical importance in ensuring the sustainability of cities, both in respect of air pollution and traffic congestion.

Figure III.3 shows that the motor vehicle fleet has risen significantly in virtually all countries of the region in recent years. The fastest growth was registered in Mexico, which has moved from 200 cars per 1,000 inhabitants in 2004 to 275 cars per 1,000 in 2009. It is followed by Brazil (from 164 to 209 cars per 1,000 people), Chile (from 135 to 184 cars), Costa Rica (from 152 to 177), Panama (from 118 to 132) and the Dominican Republic (from 105 to 128). In other countries, such as Colombia, Honduras and Peru, upward trends have also been seen in vehicle ownership, but the number of vehicles remains comparatively small.

Studies of the auto market in Latin America have stressed that demand for vehicles is conditioned by several factors: price reductions, expectations of improved economic growth and poor-quality public transport, particularly due to insufficient infrastructure for railways and other forms of transport. Such studies have also spoken of the "large number of households whose rising incomes have lifted them into the middle classes, thus giving them greater access to credit and a family purchasing power that enables them to buy their first car" (BBVA, 2010). What is broadly being referred to here are young families who are the first generation to have access to this type of consumer goods.

---

[19] See [online] http://www.who.int/gho/en/index.html.

Figure III.3 also illustrates that Argentina is the Latin American country with the highest number of vehicles per 1,000 inhabitants (314 in 2008). This remains, however, substantially below rates of vehicle ownership in developed countries. For example, in 2008 the United States had the highest rate of automobile ownership in the world, with 815 vehicles per 1 000 inhabitants (approaching a rate of one vehicle per person), while countries such as Japan (592), France (598) and Sweden (521) are closer to a ratio one vehicle for every two people. The Latin American average in 2008 was 182 vehicles per 1,000 people, which is still some way from the situation in developed countries.

Figure III.3
Latin America and the Caribbean (18 countries): growth of the motor vehicle fleet in around five years [a]
(Per 1,000 inhabitants)

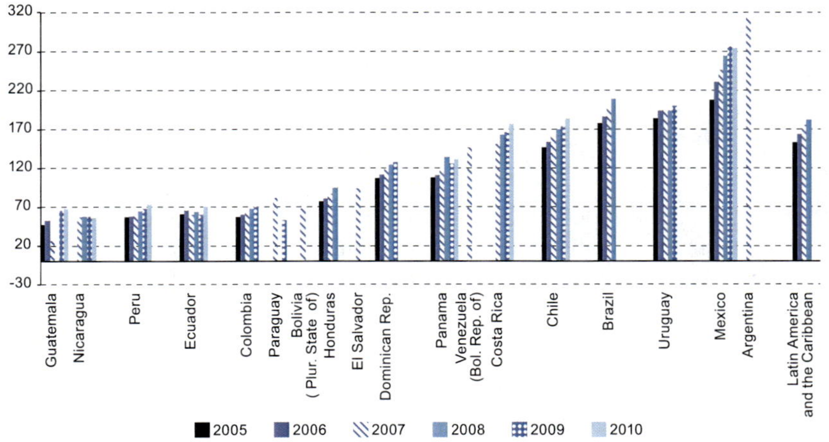

Legend: ■ 2005 ■ 2006 ⧄ 2007 ■ 2008 ⊞ 2009 ▨ 2010

Source: Economic Commission for Latin America and the Caribbean (ECLAC), on the basis of information from the World Bank, International Road Federation (IRF), World Road Statistics.
[a] Figures for vehicles include cars, buses and goods vehicles, but not two-wheeled vehicles.

Despite the increase in the motor vehicle fleet over recent years, Latin America's automotive sector still has significant growth potential, as the stock of vehicles in several countries remains both small and old. Vehicles are also highly concentrated in urban areas, especially in large and medium-sized cities as in the case in Lima (where two thirds of Peru's vehicles are based), Argentina (50% of vehicles are in the province of Buenos Aires) or Caracas (38% of vehicles) (BBVA, 2010).

In purely mercantile terms, this could be seen as an opportunity, but in respect of sustainable urban development and the well-being of local inhabitants, there is clearly a need for a set of regulations to reconcile growth in the automotive sector with improvements in air quality. This is a major challenge which necessitates action above and beyond the measures included in several of the region's air-quality-management programmes (such as setting emissions limits for mobile sources, banning vehicles from driving on certain days and running roadworthiness-testing and vehicle-maintenance programmes). In addition to more stringent checks on vehicles already in circulation, sustainable urban transport programmes need to be drawn up and implemented, taking account of such schemes as Bogotá's TransMilenio mass-transit bus system and Mexico City's Metrobús network.

Another key factor for the sustainable development of cities is public awareness. As ECLAC stated some years ago, "citizen awareness is a key factor in environmental management geared to reducing air pollution. It is written in the conviction that the systematic progress made to date can only be maintained if all citizens are committed to the cause. This means, on the one hand, that the State should consider citizen participation as a central factor in policy-making. On the other, it means that citizens should take charge of the problem since responsibility for it, in the end, is shared" (Simioni, 2003). The problem is that "none of these cities has attained a degree of citizens' awareness that goes beyond the most basic level, and that a proactive approach to environmental protection is still a very distant goal" (Simioni, 2003, p. 12). Now, several years since this was written, it must be acknowledged that little has been done to raise the awareness of citizens with a view to increasing their involvement in air quality policy-making.

C. Time

Time is another fundamental dimension of human life. Our well-being at a given moment is greatly dependent on what we do and what we are able to do and, therefore, on the time that we can devote to our various activities. The importance of time-use lies in the fact that people's well-being is contingent not only on what they earn or consume but also on their substantive freedom to use their time (Gammage, 2009, p. 7). In other words, the availability of free time is an indicator of the well-being of an individual or social group.

However, in their daily lives, people are subject to numerous restrictions that curtail this freedom. Time has been described as a rare, and therefore valuable, commodity. There is no endless supply of time; preparing for the future and setting goals and deciding on the means by which to achieve them are always subject to time pressure (Lechner, 1990, p. 66). Similarly it has also been suggested that time is a scarce resource that is consumed, spent and used up (Lash and Urry, 1998, p. 315).

Time is a resource that is limited throughout a person's life. The more time an individual dedicates to paid and unpaid work, the less time is available for other activities, including rest and recreation. A person who lacks adequate time to sleep and rest may be considered to live and work in a state of time poverty. (Gammage, 2009, p. 7). Individuals in such a state cannot be said to enjoy much well-being.

This section will examine how the social organization of time affects people's well-being. To that end, it will first consider recent trends in working hours, and then analyse the allocation of time to paid and unpaid work (what is known as the overall workload) and to free time, on the basis of information from time-use surveys conducted in four countries in the region.

1. The working day

Time spent in paid employment, whose purpose is to generate monetary resources to provide for a wide range of needs, is an essential part of most people's lives. The more time people spend at work, the less they have for other activities, such as family responsibilities, leisure and rest. For this reason, reductions in working hours were one of the most commonly made demands from workers' movements for much of the twentieth century.

Campaigns by workers' movements to reduce working hours were part of efforts to make the world of work a less harsh and more human environment. Their goals included preserving the health of male and female workers (including their mental health) and ensuring adequate time for rest and family life. The duration of the working day is currently seen as a key element of the quality of employment and is, therefore, an indicator of decent work, in the words of the International Labour Organization (ILO).

In the early days of industrialization, the working day lasted between 14 and 16 hours, but was gradually reduced to 12, 11 and then 10 hours. On the eve of the First World War, a 10-hour working day was fairly widespread in Europe. By the end of the war, pressure from workers' organizations precipitated progress towards the eight-hour working day (Valticos and von Potobsky, 1995), a process that culminated just before the Second World War, when a working week of between 40 and 45 hours became standard in the United States, most of European countries and in much of Latin America.

Continual efforts were made to safeguard the 8-hour day over the final decades of the twentieth century, and a global shift took place towards a weekly limit of 40 hours, despite significant regional differences and disparities in the manner in which working hours were limited by law (Lee, McCann and Messenger, 2007). Figure III.4 shows that, while in Europe the average working week is 37 hours, in Latin America it is 42 hours. In 2011, only four Latin American countries (Argentina, the Bolivarian Republic of Venezuela, Honduras and Peru) had average working weeks of 40 hours, which was in sharp contrast with the situation in Europe, where most countries showed an average of between 35 and 39 hours per week. Alarmingly, in two countries in the region (Colombia and Mexico), average weekly working hours even exceeded 45 hours per week.

Figure III.4

Latin America and the Caribbean (18 countries): working hours of the economically active population of 15 years and over, around 2002 and 2011

(Hours per week)

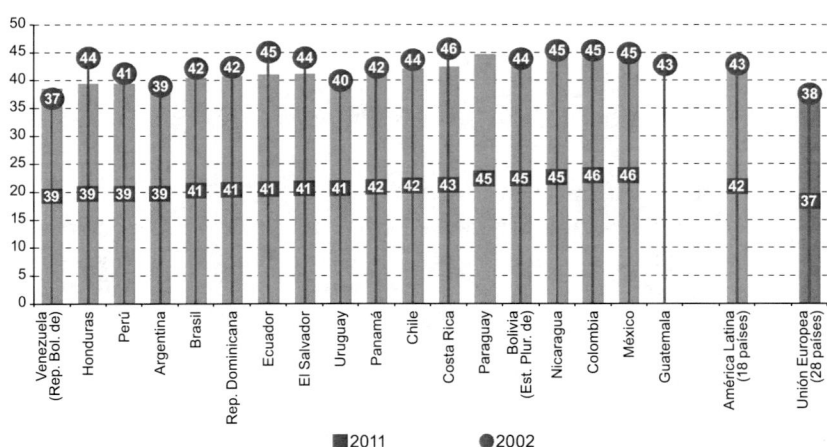

■ 2011   ● 2002

Source: Economic Commission for Latin America and the Caribbean (ECLAC), on the basis of special tabulations of household surveys conducted in the respective countries.

Average figures fail to take account of the way in which working time is distributed between different occupational categories and types of work. It should be noted that men work longer hours than women in Latin America and the Caribbean. This difference in working time ranges from two hours per week (in El Salvador) to ten hours per week in Argentina and Mexico (see figure III.5), and is between five and seven hours in most countries. This is evidence of a clear gender gap in working hours in paid employment. For women living in couples, especially those with young children, this is a reflection of the fact that the time at their disposal for paid work is curtailed by the work and responsibilities they have within the home.

Figure III.5

Latin America and the Caribbean (17 countries): working hours of the employed population of 15 years and over, broken down by gender, around 2011

(Hours per week)

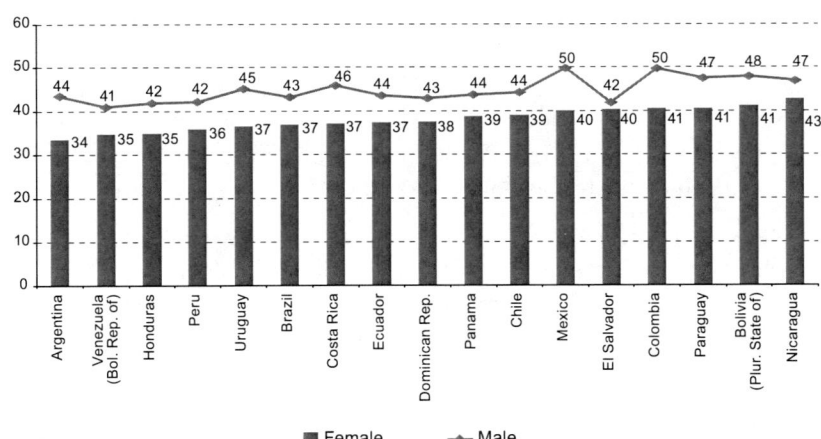

■ Female   ─◆─ Male

Source: Economic Commission for Latin America and the Caribbean (ECLAC), on the basis of special tabulations of household surveys conducted in the respective countries.

Informal work, which accounts for a significant proportion of labour markets in Latin America, is another very important element that helps shape people's working hours. The ILO has stated (2011) that "according to available information for 16 countries, 93 million people (half of the employed population) worked in informal employment at the end of the first decade of this century. Of this total, 60 million worked in the informal sector, 23 million were employed in the formal sector but had no social protection and 10 million had informal employment in domestic service. Moreover, 6 of every 10 employed youth could only find informal employment". ILO studies on job creation in the informal sector have shown that such work is very seriously deficient in areas such as wages, contracts, working hours, social protection and employee-employer negotiations. To illustrate differences between formal and informal labour, for example, a study by Infante Martinez and Tokman (1999) estimated that informal workers work on average 6% longer hours than their counterparts in large and medium-sized businesses in the formal economy. In Latin America and the Caribbean, low-paid, unskilled workers in the informal sector are also very likely to be obliged to work long hours, since they must struggle hard to get enough work to earn a decent living.

In sum, although there are significant differences in working hours according to occupational category and type of employment, the average working week in Latin America, unlike in most European countries, remains overly long: well over the weekly limit of 40 hours.

2. Time in paid and unpaid work and free time

As noted earlier, time spent in paid employment forms a major part of most people's lives at present. The previous section spoke of the gender gap in terms of hours spent in paid work, but this should be viewed in conjunction with one of the most important social changes to have taken place in the region in recent decades: the incorporation of women into the labour force. "From 1990 to 2007, labour market participation rates among women in the economically active age range (typically, 25 to 54 years) rose by nearly 20 percentage points, while employment rates increased more than 15 percentage points. [...] This increase in women's participation rates is the result of a range of factors, including long-term processes of individuation and autonomy, combined with declining fertility and delayed childbearing. The rise in educational credentials among women has also played a role. In addition, a decline in wages, employability and job stability among men has created pressure for women to join the labour force, as a result of which women in many households have either become the main wage-earners or are earning as much as their male partners. Changing family structures, rising divorce rates and growing prevalence of single-parent households headed by women are also prompting more women to enter the labour market and, increasingly, turning them into the sole income-earners in their households" (ECLAC, 2010c, p. 162).

This unprecedented rise in their participation in the world of work has enabled women to earn a living in their own right and become more personally and economically autonomous. They have not, however, seen a comparable improvement in the quality of the work they carry out. A gender-focused study on the quality of work in the countries of MERCOSUR and Chile (Valenzuela and Reinecke, 2001) has shown that, in the five countries of the Southern Cone, women of all age groups and levels of educational attainment earn less than men across virtually all sectors, types of work and occupational categories. It also states that, although both men and women have been affected by the decline in stable employment, namely jobs on permanent contracts and protected by labour laws, women are more vulnerable to this phenomenon.

This chapter has thus far examined time spent in paid employment. However, not all of the value generated by productive work has a price attached to it. Indeed, a large proportion of what societies produce has no monetary value and no price. Domestic work —such as cooking, cleaning and caring for others— is chiefly done by women without pay or any contract that sets a price for the services rendered or establishes the responsibilities and benefits associated with the work. However, domestic work does create value, particularly for the individuals who benefit from it but also for society at large. Moreover, time spent performing domestic and care work cannot be devoted to other activities such as self-care, leisure, political participation or paid work (ECLAC, 2010c, p.175; and ECLAC, 2012). Feminist literature has made important contributions to the study of unpaid work, stressing gender issues and highlighting the fact that, despite its invisibility, unpaid work plays a key role in both social reproduction and the functioning of the economy.

Time-use surveys can be used to analyse the relationship between statistics on paid and unpaid work. Figure III.6 provides an overview of information from three time-use surveys —from Mexico (2009), Peru (2010) and Panama (2011)— that are relatively comparable in terms of their structure and the activities they cover. The social organization of time encompasses three principal, broad-based categories: working time (including time spent commuting), unpaid domestic work (including, among a great many other duties, cooking, cleaning and caring for others) and free time (including rest, leisure activities and time spent with family members and friends)[20].

Figure III.6
Latin America and the Caribbean (4 countries): time spent by the employed population in paid and unpaid work and their free time
(Hours per week)

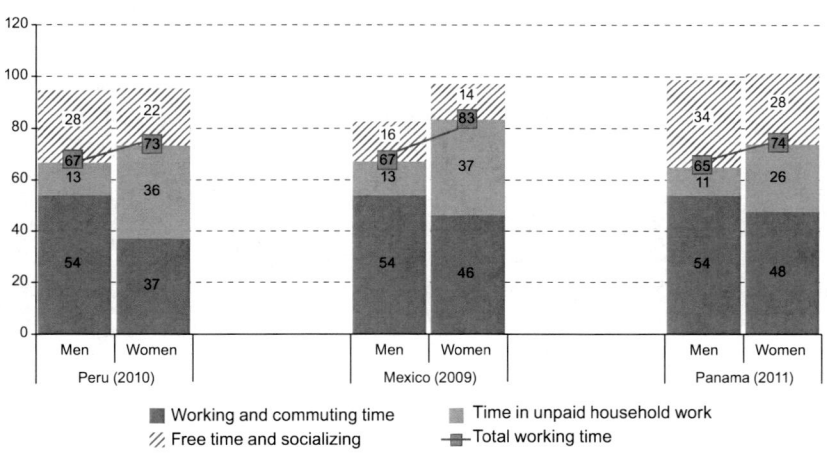

Source: Economic Commission for Latin America and the Caribbean (ECLAC), on the basis of time-use surveys from the respective countries: Panama (2011), Mexico (2009) and Peru (2010).

Information from these time-use surveys shows, firstly, that men work longer hours than women. In all three countries, men's working hours exceed 45 hours per week, and in two countries (Mexico and Panama) both men and women work more than 45 hours. This overly long working week may be explained by the fact that commuting time is included in working hours and this pushes up the figures, particularly for workers in large cities, who spend a great deal of time travelling to and from work (as result of the long distances involved and traffic congestion). Commuting time also eats away at time for other activities such as rest or leisure pursuits.[21]

Secondly, the surveys indicate that women spend many more hours a day than men in unpaid domestic work. The increasing incorporation of women into the labour force has therefore not been offset by any greater involvement by men in household work. Thus, in Latin America the sexual division of labour has only changed in a partial and uneven manner.[22]

The overall workload is the sum of hours spent in both paid employment (working hours) and unpaid household work, including caring for children and elderly and sick relatives. Time-use surveys show that women in employment shoulder a greater overall workload than men (see figure III.6). Indeed, their average overall weekly workload of between 73 and 83 hours per week is a sign that working women are very seriously overworked, to the detriment of their well-being. Research has shown that the excessive burden of their workload is directly linked to women's greater likelihood to succumb to medical conditions such as depression, stress and anxiety (Artázcoz, L. and others, 2001).

Here again the averages conceal differences. The working hours of employed women vary according to their marital status. Women who live with a partner are more overworked and can suffer exhaustion as a result of having to juggle paid and unpaid work and caring for pre-school-age children (Milosavljevic, 2007). Women who are heads of households also face a high workload.

---

[20] The other activities measured in the time-use surveys but which fall outside the categories appearing in figure III.6 groupings are: personal activities (activities that cannot be delegated to anyone else, such as eating, drinking, sleeping and exercising), studying and volunteering.

[21] There is insufficient space to analyse commuting times in large cities, which are particularly long for low-income workers, who tend to live far away from their places of work.

[22] The sexual division of labour is the way in which work is assigned according to gender; in most societies, the bulk of the responsibility for paid work (productive work) falls on men, while the responsibility for unpaid work in the home and the community (reproductive work) falls on women.

While the average weekly workload of working women is excessive, working men have a lighter burden, ranging from 65 to 67 hours per week. This difference is due in large part to the fact that the rising numbers of women in paid employment have not generally been offset by a greater involvement of men in household work. Ensuring a more equal distribution of unpaid household work is thus an ongoing challenge that requires legislation and deep-rooted cultural change.

Leisure time is the free time people have after completing their mandatory duties —principally paid work and unpaid domestic work— to spend on the activities of their choice for purposes of pleasure, relaxation or personal fulfilment. Everyday leisure activities include rest, recreation or creative pursuits. Leisure activities may also be active or passive in nature, depending on whether they entail being a participant or spectator.

The leisure activities measured in time-use surveys include socializing (family life and celebrations), attending (cultural, artistic or sporting) events, cultural and media content (TV, books, music and cinema) and sport. These kinds of pastime are important for personal development, improving health and relieving stress.

An adequate amount of leisure time is thus a contributing factor towards well-being. Time-use surveys show that women tend to have insufficient leisure time, and live in a state of "time poverty" which curtails their well-being. Men, on the other hand, (especially in Panama and Peru) have more leisure time. However, there is no definitive yardstick to determine how much leisure time is needed to have a decent level of well-being.

D. Coexistence

Coexistence, like space and time, is a fundamental dimension of human life and entails social interaction in groups and institutions. It is an ongoing constructive process in which, among other things, transactions are made, meaning is negotiated and solutions are found (Brunner, 1990). The manner in which people interact gives rise to historically-constructed concepts that make certain ways of behaving feel natural and predictable, and familiarize people with "the way things are" and with "the way we do things". These patterns of behaviour go on to form part of the group identity of that community of individuals. Thus, certain groups coexisting in the same space become imbued with a shared group identity, which is expressed in specific ways of relating with one another, a given logic underlying what they do and what they mean, and particular in-built values and beliefs. A culture can be seen as such a historically-constructed concept of common meaning (Geertz, 1994). The way in which we live is both a cultural and a human construct, but it feels so natural and predictable to people that it imparts a sensation of inevitability and security. This does not, however, mean that there is uniformity of experience; differences and conflicts can and do emerge between people in the same social space.

People's well-being is contingent on their participation in a process in which different people forge a sense of belonging to a shared existence. What is therefore needed is a model for positive, democratic and peaceful social coexistence, in which everyone can feel part of society, in an atmosphere of tolerance, trust and mutual respect, with values and rules to encourage fairness and social integration, as well as mechanisms to resolve conflicts of interest that arise within society (ECLAC, 2006).

However, the rapid processes of modernization and urbanization that Latin America has gone through in the past two decades have given rise to numerous problems involving coexistence. This section will examine how violence, one of the most serious social problems in Latin America today, affects people's well-being. To this end, it will analyse two of the most serious forms of violence in the region: homicide, an act of extreme violence that instils a deep-seated sense of insecurity among citizens, and domestic violence against women and children.[23]

1. Violence

The currently accepted definition of violence in the specialized literature is "the use or threat of use of physical force, with the intention of causing harm" (Buvinic, Morrison and Shifter, 1999). This definition encompasses both the use and the threat of use of force, which plays a key role in perceptions of violence and safety in a given context. The intentional nature of this behaviour excludes accidents from this definition but includes the use of aggression to resolve conflicts. It also includes suicide and other self-destructive actions. It should be noted that violence can be either physical or psychological in nature, and the use of force with the intention of harming includes sexual abuse. Violence as defined here can occur between strangers or acquaintances, including among members of the same family (domestic or intra-familial violence).

Violence and crime —defined as any action deemed illegal under the judicial system— are closely related but not equivalent. The definition of violence stresses the use or threat of use of force with the intent to harm, while the definition of crime is more concerned with the description and classification of cases of illegal behaviour. This difference is illustrated by the existence of both non-violent crime (fraud, theft and prostitution without coercion) and non-criminal violence (certain cases of State-perpetrated violence and the fact that certain countries have not criminalized domestic violence) (Buvinic, Morrison and Shifter, 1999; Buvinic and Morrison 2000.).

Violence is a complex, multidimensional phenomenon which arises as a result of multiple factors (of a psychological, biological, economic, social and cultural nature). Phenomena caused by violent behaviour frequently cross over boundaries between the individual, family, the community and society, with knock-on effects in various individual, social, family, and community spheres. The multifaceted nature of violence means that it manifests itself in many different ways (Buvinic, Morrison and Shifter, 1999).

According to the Global Study on Homicide conducted by the United Nations Office on Drugs and Crime (UNODC), 31% of the world's homicides in 2010 were committed in the Americas (including Canada and the United States), second only to Africa (36%). Asia was third on the list with 27%, followed by Europe and Oceania, which together accounted for barely 6% (UNODC, 2012). The average global homicide rate in 2010 was 6.9 persons per 100.000, but rates varied greatly from region to region. The homicide rate in the Americas was 15.6 persons per 100,000, more than twice the global average. Africa had the highest rate in the world: 17.4 per 100,000 (UNODC, 2012).

Latin America's high average homicide rate masks considerable differences from country to country (see figure III.7). Honduras, El Salvador and Nicaragua have the highest homicide rates in the region, and indeed are among the highest rates in the entire world. Jamaica and Colombia have the next highest homicide rates, an upper-intermediate level in global terms. They are followed by the Dominican Republic, Argentina and Ecuador, which can be said to have a lower intermediate level, and, finally, by Uruguay and Chile, which have relatively low homicide rates (fewer than 10 persons per 100,000).

Markedly different trends have been observed in the homicide rate in the region over recent years (see figure III.7). Certain countries, such as El Salvador, Honduras, Peru and Mexico, have seen a marked increase, but rates in Colombia, Jamaica and Nicaragua have decreased, a major victory for the public security policies of these countries. The fall in homicides in Colombia is noteworthy in view of its historically extremely high homicide rate. Certain countries have seen little change in their murder rates. This is good news in countries such as Chile and Uruguay, which have the lowest levels in the region, but less so in the Dominican Republic, which has seen no change to its relatively high homicide rate.

---

[23] Violence is a highly complex issue, and there is insufficient space in this short section to cover other forms of violence (such as rape, kidnapping and, armed robbery) which may also have an impact on people's well-being.

Figure III.7
Latin America and the Caribbean (15 countries): gross homicide rate, 2008-2011 [a]
(Per 100,000 persons)

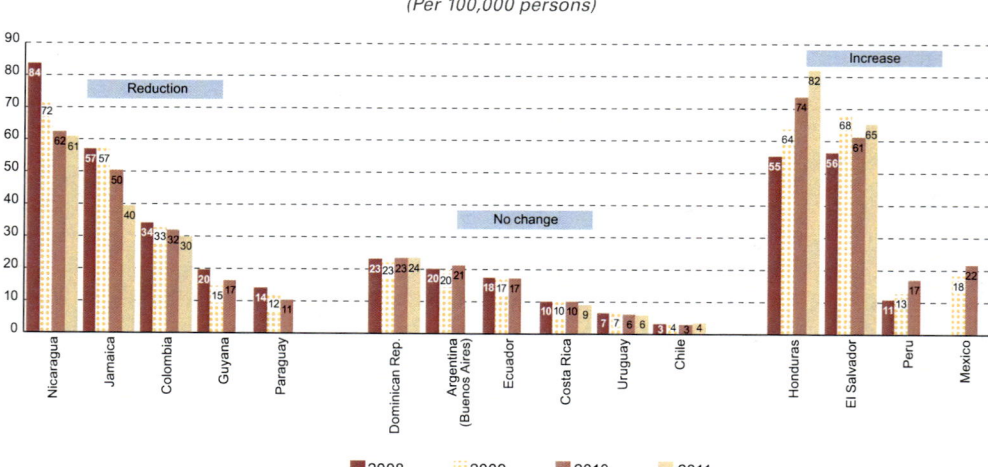

Source: Inter-American Development Bank (IDB) Regional system of standardized indicators in peaceful coexistence and citizen security [online] http://www. seguridadyregion.com/images/Indicadores/muertes%20por_homicidio.pdf.

[a] The regional system of standardized indicators in peaceful coexistence and citizen security defines homicide as "Intentional injuries caused by a person to another causing death" (deaths caused by traffic accidents or other non-intentional injuries are not included). The figures include all cases of homicide known to the authorities occurring anywhere in the country, as well as femicides. There is no information on Brazil as it is in the process of joining the RIC.

The Hemispheric Citizen Security Observatory of the Organization of American States (OAS) has released statistics on subregional trends over 2000-2010. The average homicide rate in the Americas (34 countries) remained relatively stable over this decade: moving from 16.4 persons per 100,000 in 2000 to 15.6 per 100,000 in 2010. The homicide rate in North America (three countries) barely changed over the decade (7.3 per 100,000 in 2000 to 7.8 per 100,000 in 2010) and is the lowest in the four subregions. In South America (12 countries) the rate fell significantly, from 26.1 persons per 100,000 in 2000 to 21.1 in 2010. Central America, however, saw an alarming increase, with the rate almost doubling from 26.6 to 43.3 persons per 100,000. The Caribbean also saw its rate rise, but not quite as steeply as in Central America (from 16.4 per 100,000 in 2000 to 21.9 per 100,000 in 2010) (OAS, 2012).

Lastly, a United Nations report has stated that, in 2010, 42% of homicides world-wide were committed with firearms (UNODC, 2012), but this rate was much higher in the Americas: 75% on average (OAS, 2012), and was greater still in certain countries: 88% in Brazil, for example, 84% in Guatemala, 83% in Honduras and 79% in Colombia. These figures can also be used as an indicator of the ease with which people can acquire firearms in these countries.

Although homicide is only one of many causes of the phenomenon, it should be noted that many of the people of Latin America, especially in urban areas, live in a constant state of fear of crime. These feelings are captured by public opinion polls such as Latinobarometer, where crime is ranked as one of the most serious problems affecting the countries of the region, alongside unemployment, inflation, poverty and corruption (Latinobarometer, 2004). These fears have grown over the years as people have come to feel increasingly vulnerable to, and endangered by, high rates of crime or persecution.

Violent crime has a more serious effect on public opinion because violence is an attack not only on what the victims possess, but also a violation of their most fundamental rights to privacy and sovereignty over their body. Violence may leave the victim or their loved ones suffering from post-traumatic stress, and cause them to be greatly afraid in certain situations. It can also have a far more noticeable effect on third parties, a phenomenon known as vicarious traumatisation that occurs when people transfer trauma affecting others on to themselves (Lagos and Dammert, 2012).

In a survey on fear of violent crime, 76.7% of respondents stated they were worried "all the time", "most of the time" or "sometimes". Violent crime is therefore a daily concern for the public, even those who have never been victims of it, despite the fact that the actual likelihood of them being attacked is small (their perceived fears grow as they are exposed to more and more images of violent crime). Fear of violent crime is endemic in Latin America, and is felt by over 80% of the population in Brazil, the Bolivarian Republic of Venezuela, Costa Rica, Ecuador and El Salvador.

Table III.1
Latin America (18 countries): concern about falling victim to violent crime [a]
(Percentage of the population)

	2009	2010	2011
Argentina	69.2	66.9	74.5
Bolivia (Plurinational State of)	77.4	75.5	77.2
Brazil	76.6	77.5	87.3
Colombia	61.5	64.2	71.8
Costa Rica	71.6	70.6	82.9
Chile	66.7	64.8	68.8
Ecuador	70.8	74.9	84.0
El Salvador	72.1	75.7	81.2
Guatemala	75.8	59.9	76.8
Honduras	58.8	70.9	74.1
Mexico	64.1	71.2	78.1
Nicaragua	82.2	53.7	73.7
Panama	65.5	61.8	69.7
Paraguay	69.7	70.6	77.8
Peru	71.7	69.7	77.3
Uruguay	58.7	58.9	65.4
Venezuela (Bolivarian Republic of)	80.2	79.1	85.8
Dominican Republic	71.1	65.7	74.3
Average	70.2	68.4	76.7

Source: Economic Commission for Latin America and the Caribbean (ECLAC), on the basis of information from Latinobarometer.
[a] Percentage of respondents stating they were worried "all the time", "most of the time" and "sometimes".

In conclusion, not only has Latin America become one of the most violent regions in the world, but fear of violent crime is widespread among the people of the various countries in the region. Feelings of insecurity are prevalent both in countries with a high homicide rate, such as El Salvador, Guatemala or Honduras, and in countries where there are relatively few homicides, such as Chile or Uruguay. Such feelings are the result of a great many factors, including, as research has shown, distrust of the police, the perception of government neglect, increasing crime rates and a lack of social cohesion (Lagos and Dammert, 2012).

2. Domestic violence

Another prevalent form of violence is violence within a family or a household. Domestic violence against a woman by her partner is sometimes used as a ploy to gain control of household income or to exert dominance over her. In either case there is often an emotional component —the wish to cause emotional distress— that aggravates the vicious circle of violence if it is successful. There are also deep-seated causal links between manifestations of violence. There is both theoretical (behavioural learning models) and empirical evidence that children who suffer or observe domestic violence have a greater propensity to develop violent tendencies as adults (Berkowitz, 1996, quoted in Buvinic and Morrison (2000).

In respect of violence against women, account needs to be taken of the Declaration on the Elimination of Violence against Women (United Nations, 1993) and the Inter-American Convention on the Prevention, Punishment and Eradication of Violence against Women (OAS, 1994). Firstly, the Declaration on the Elimination of Violence against Women defines violence against women as "any act of gender-based violence that results in, or is likely to result in, physical, sexual or psychological harm or suffering to women, including threats of such acts, coercion or arbitrary deprivation of liberty, whether occurring in public or in private life." It encompasses "physical, sexual and psychological violence occurring in the family, including battering, sexual abuse of female children in the household, dowry-related violence, marital rape, female genital mutilation and other traditional practices harmful to women, non-spousal violence and violence related to exploitation; physical, sexual and psychological violence occurring within the general community, including rape, sexual abuse, sexual harassment and intimidation at work, in educational institutions and elsewhere, trafficking in women and forced prostitution; physical, sexual and psychological violence perpetrated or condoned by the State, wherever it occurs".

The Inter-American Convention on the Prevention, Punishment and Eradication of Violence against Women (Convention of Belém do Pará) states that "violence against women constitutes a violation of their human rights and fundamental freedoms, and impairs or nullifies the observance, enjoyment and exercise of such rights and freedoms". It further states that "violence against women shall be understood as any act or conduct, based on gender, which causes death or physical, sexual or psychological harm or suffering to women, whether in the public or the private sphere [...] Violence against women shall be understood to include physical, sexual and psychological violence that occurs within the family or domestic unit or within any other interpersonal relationship, whether or not the perpetrator shares or has shared the same residence with the woman, including, among others, rape, battery and sexual abuse; that occurs in the community and is perpetrated by any person, including, among others, rape, sexual abuse, torture, trafficking in persons, forced prostitution, kidnapping and sexual harassment in the workplace, as well as in educational institutions, health facilities or any other place; and that is perpetrated or condoned by the state or its agents regardless of where it occurs."[24]

From a methodological point of view, it is important to note that cases of physical, psychological and sexual violence against women by their spouse or partner are often either under-reported or not reflected in the statistics, as few women report such crimes or make use of the assistance facilities available to them. Only a fraction of cases of violence against women therefore actually show up in statistics, since they are based on records provided by the police, the judiciary, health services and NGOs, among others, thus obscuring the true magnitude of the problem of violence against women (Milosavljevic, 2007).

It is difficult to quantify the prevalence of violence by means of surveys, mainly owing to the fact that it is such a sensitive and emotive issue for abused women and the need to ensure that interviews take place in an appropriate, confidential setting. Procedures for collecting information concerning this issue should follow special protocols and be overseen by highly qualified staff who have received specific training (WHO, 2001).

In Latin America, few studies have taken representative surveys as a basis to assess adequately the situations and contexts in which domestic violence or intimate partner violence occurs. The studies most commonly used to gauge the magnitude of this phenomenon are surveys of population and health, designed primarily to assess the health of women of childbearing age (15-49 years), since they entail interviewing women in confidential, secure conditions in which the issue of violence can be broached alongside other confidential topics such as reproductive health.

Figure III.8 provides statistics on the proportion of women who suffer or have ever suffered physical violence at the hands of a partner in seven countries of the region.[25] Physical violence is defined as the intentional use of physical force that may cause death, incapacitation or harm; it includes, among other things, scratching, pushing, biting, throwing objects, hair pulling, slapping, hitting, burning, the use of firearms or sharp implements and attacks using the aggressor's body. The percentage of women aged between 15 and 49 years who suffer or have ever suffered physical violence at the hands of a partner ranges from 33% in Colombia to 14% in Haiti. The statistics thus show that a high proportion of women in the region have been physically attacked by their partner.

Lastly, it is important to highlight the phenomenon of domestic violence against children in Latin America and the Caribbean, a hugely pervasive, everyday reality that is commonly overlooked (ECLAC/UNICEF, 2009). Frequent forms of abuse against children can take the form of direct attacks, but can also come as a result of their witnessing violence between their parents or simply because they live in an environment in which violent relationships and abuses of power are frequent. Children growing up in such settings see this culture of violence become part and parcel of their personal and emotional relationships. They can be said to internalize a negative model of interpersonal relationships that harms their development if they witness the ill-treatment of their mother or have a parent that mistreats, rather than protects them (Orjuela, undated).

---

[24] For a more in-depth examination of the issue, see Almeras and others (2002).

[25] As space is limited, only physical violence against women will be considered (and not sexual abuse or psychological or economic violence).

Figure III.8

Latin America (7 countries): women aged between 15 and 49 years, who are or have been in a couple and have suffered physical violence at the hands of their partner

(Percentages)

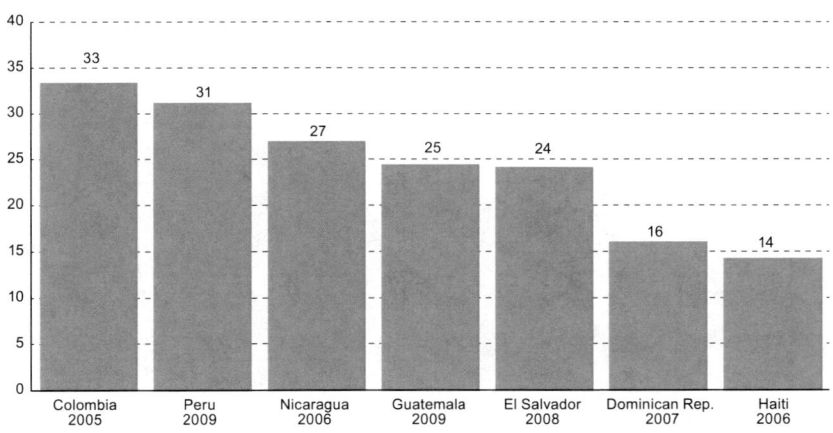

Source: Economic Commission for Latin America and the Caribbean (ECLAC), on the basis of household, demographic and health surveys conducted in the respective countries: Colombia, 2005; Dominican Republic, 2007; Guatemala, 2008-2009; Haiti, 2005-2006; Peru, 2009; El Salvador, 2008; Nicaragua, 2006.

A particularly severe form of violence against children is child abuse, a violation of the fundamental rights of children and adolescents that are enshrined in the Universal Declaration of Human Rights, which stresses children's right to physical and psychological integrity and to protection from all forms of violence. Article 19 of the Convention on the Rights of the Child, adopted by the United Nations in 1989, calls on all States to "take all appropriate legislative, administrative, social and educational measures to protect the child from all forms of physical or mental violence, injury or abuse, neglect or negligent treatment, maltreatment or exploitation, including sexual abuse, while in the care of parent(s), legal guardian(s) or any other person who has the care of the child". Similarly, the United Nations International Committee on the Rights of the Child has emphasized the importance of member countries' prohibiting all forms of physical punishment and degrading treatment of children.

The United Nations Children's Fund (UNICEF) defines the victims of child abuse as children or adolescents of up to 18 years who suffer occasionally or habitually from physical, sexual or emotional violence within a family environment or in institutions within society. Child abuse may constitute ignoring or violating the individual or collective rights of children and includes partial or total abandonment (UNICEF, 2006).

Figure III.9 presents statistics on the ways in which parents punish their children. Data from Colombia and Peru come from national demographic and health surveys in which the respondents were mothers. The punishments most commonly used in Colombia and Peru by both parents are verbal reprimands. However, the very high proportion of children receiving corporal punishment, including smacking, shows that physical violence against children is an everyday reality in the region. This is worrying as violence towards children represents a serious violation of their rights.

In the surveys in Chile and Paraguay it was the children themselves who were interviewed. In Chile, 71% of children stated that they suffered some form of violence from their mother, their father or both, with 51.5% suffering physical violence, of whom 25.9% suffered acute physical violence.[26] In Paraguay, 60.5% suffered some form of violence from their mother, their father or both, with 47.7% suffering some form of physical violence, of whom 12.8% suffered psychological violence. Child abuse is, without any doubt, "a painful reality behind closed doors" that has profound effects on the lives of children and adolescents, seriously harms their development and growth, causes their relationship with the parents to break down, affects their school performance, harms their mental health and causes problems with their classmates, among other problems (UNICEF, 2012).

---

[26] The definitions used were as follows: acute physical violence includes kicks, bites, punches, burning (with a cigarette or scalding with hot water) hitting or attempting to hit with objects, beatings and threatening with a knife or weapon. Mild physical violence includes throwing objects, pulling hair or ears, pushing, shaking, slapping and spanking. Psychological violence includes yelling, telling the child it is not loved, using insults or swearwords, ridicule in front of a third party, ignoring the child for long periods, threatening to hit or throw objects and locking the child up.

Figure III.9
Latin America (selected countries): domestic violence against children
(Percentages)

A. Frequency of different forms of punishment by parents

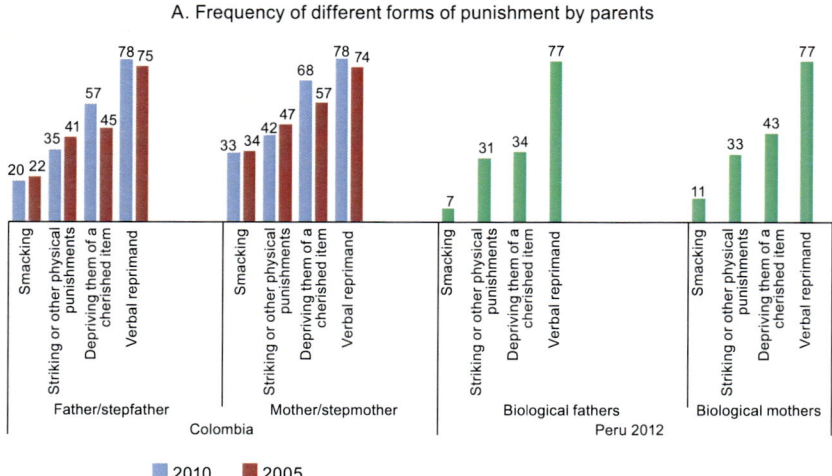

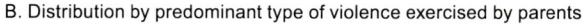

B. Distribution by predominant type of violence exercised by parents

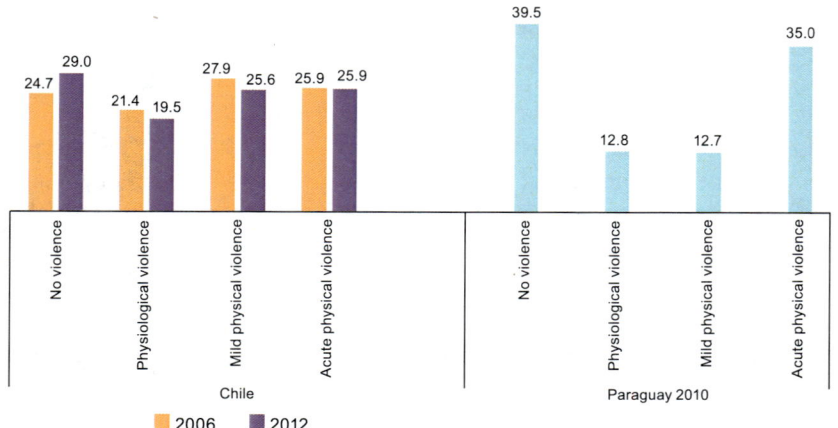

Source: Economic Commission for Latin America and the Caribbean (ECLAC), on the basis of household, demographic and health surveys conducted in the respective countries: Chile, 2012; Colombia, 2010; Paraguay, 2010; Peru, 2012.

In sum, parents often use physical, verbal and psychological violence to attempt to impose their will on their children. It is paradoxical that the home, where children and adolescents should be the most secure, can become the scene of different forms of violation of their rights (physical or psychological abuse or neglect and abandonment) at the very hands of those who ought to give them the care and attention they need to thrive.

E. Final remarks

Some interesting conclusions may be drawn from analysis of commonly overlooked aspects of well-being in Latin America. Rethinking what is meant by progress in our societies means going beyond traditional ways of measuring well-being, since commonly used indicators only partially grasp the complexity of the phenomenon. As stated above, considerable progress has been made in setting up information sources on environmental issues and the effect they have on health (the establishment of the WHO World Health Observatory is a significant development). Great strides have also been made in the analysis of violence, particularly elements relating to public security. The regional system of standardized indicators in peaceful coexistence and citizen security, a project in which 15 countries are working to establish 12 common indicators, is another initiative that deserves to be highlighted. Although they remain at an embryonic stage, efforts are under way in Latin America to develop sources of information on violence against women using specialized protocols (demographic and health surveys are of particular use in this regard). There remain, however, large information gaps concerning violence against children. Time-use surveys in the countries of the region, meanwhile, despite their lack of a common, comparable methodological and technical basis, have clearly demonstrated the importance of time in people's lives and shown how it conditions their well-being. In short, progress has been made but much remains to be done to improve sources of information on key aspects of well-being and on why certain sectors of the region's population are so lacking in well-being.

Public goods are defined as goods which are both non-excludable and non-rivalrous. A good is non-excludable when its use cannot be monopolized, i.e. once it has been provided, on a public or private basis, it is available to all, and thus no longer subject to the laws of the market as it can no longer be priced, bought or sold. A good is said to be non-rivalrous when it can be consumed by many people, without one person's use reducing the amount available to others. These commonly overlooked dimensions of well-being should be considered to be public goods, and policies should be enacted to ensure that they can be enjoyed by all in perpetuity.

The air we breathe is a public good. It is non-excludable since it is not subject to the laws of the market and no price can be put on it, and is non-rivalrous in that one person's breathing does not prevent others from doing likewise. This is why the State intervenes to ensure the quality of the air we breathe. Not all people enjoy the same quality of air and, although everyone theoretically has access to air as a good, the reality is that the quality differs greatly depending on where people live. Certain studies have shown a greater prevalence of respiratory problems among people living in highly polluted areas, particularly children, older persons and low-income families, than among those less exposed to environmental pollution.

Public security —understood as the set of measures, governed by the principles of democracy and the law of a country, put in place to ensure peaceful coexistence and the security of citizens and their property— is also a public good. Public security is not subject to the laws of the market (non-excludable) and is non-rivalrous (the fact of one person enjoying security does not impinge on anyone else's security). As a public good, ensuring security is primarily the responsibility of the State, but it also falls within the remit of local authorities and civil society. At present, the main challenge lies in making the various policies implemented by States to ensure citizen security compatible with human rights. For example, the Organization of American States (OAS) argues that when the State is unable to respond effectively to violence and crime, sometimes policies that have proved to be ineffective are blindly stepped up, thus making matters worse and laying the groundwork for the emergence of paramilitary or vigilante movements (OAS, 2009).

The right balance between time spent in paid employment, in unpaid domestic work and at leisure (free time) is another necessary precondition of well-being. Free time should also be seen as a public good. The amount of free time people have tended to be regulated by law, particularly labour legislation; in workers' campaigns throughout the twentieth century rest time was seen as a right, and this right is enshrined in all current labour regulations. Average working hours in the region remain overly long when compared with most European Union countries, for example. Furthermore, the increasing incorporation of women into the labour force has not been offset by a greater involvement of men in household work, and women, having little free time, suffer from what is known as time poverty. Legal recognition of unpaid domestic work and of the right to rest should be put near the top of the public policy agenda (including by drawing up robust care policies).

Finally, the interlinked nature of the dimensions making up well-being needs to be stressed. By way of example, the growth in numbers of motor cars in recent years in all countries of the region, together with the highly inadequate public transport infrastructure, has seriously aggravated urban air pollution and grievously harmed human health. The related traffic congestion has greatly increased journey times within cities, which become "dead time" for travellers that eats into their time for leisure and socializing and is a source of discomfort and stress. This is but one example of how these dimensions are linked.

Bibliography

Alarcón, D. (2013), "Informe sobre los ODM 2013. Grandes avances hacia más metas alcanzables", New York, United Nations Department of Economic and Social Affairs.

Alméras, Diane and others (2002), "Violence against women in couples: Latin America and the Caribbean. A proposal for measuring its incidence and trends", *Mujer y desarrollo* series, N° 40 (LC/L.1744-P), Santiago, Chile, Economic Commission for Latin America and the Caribbean (ECLAC), June. United Nations publication, Sales No: S.02.II.G.56.

Artázcoz, L. and others (2001) "Trabajo doméstico, género y salud en la población ocupada", *Gaceta Sanitaria*, vol.15, N° 2, March [online] http://zl.elsevier.es/es/revista/gaceta-sanitaria-138/trabajo-domestico-genero-salud-poblacion-ocupada-13021118-originales-breves-2001.

BBVA Research LATAM (2010), "Latinoamérica. Situación automotriz. Análisis económico" [online] serviciodeestudios.bbva.com/KETD/fbin/mult/ESTAULT_14122010_tcm346-239499.pdf?ts=16102013.

BECA/UNICEF (Base Educativa y Comunitaria de Apoyo/United Nations Children's Fund) (2010), *Estudio sobre maltrato infantil en el ámbito familiar: Paraguay*, Asunción, Ade Comunicaciones.

Boarini, R., A. Johansson and M. d'Ercole (2006), "Alternative measures of well-being", *Statistics Brief*, N° 11, Paris, Organisation for Economic Co-operation and Development (OECD).

Brunner, J. (1990), "La autobiografía del yo", *Actos de significado,* Madrid, Alianza Editorial.

Bull, A. (coord.) (2003), "Traffic congestion: the problem and how to tackle it", *Cuadernos de la CEPAL* series, N° 87 (LC/G.2199-P), Santiago, Chile, Economic Commission for Latin America and the Caribbean (ECLAC) / German Agency for Technical Cooperation (GTZ). United Nations publication, Sales No. S.03.II.G.88.

Buvinic, M. and A. Morrison (2000), "Living in a more violent world", *Foreign Policy*, N° 118, Washington, D.C.

Buvinic, M., A. Morrison and M. Shifter (1999), *Violence in Latin America and the Caribbean: A Framework for Action*, Washington, D.C., Inter-American Development Bank (IDB).

Cifuentes, L. and others (2005), *Urban Air Quality and Human Health in Latin America and the Caribbean*, Washington, D.C., Pan American Health Organization (PAHO)

Clean Air Institute (2012), *Air Quality in Latin America – An Overview* [online] http://www.cleanairinstitute.org/calidaddelaireamericalatina/index.php?id_sitio=1&p_idioma=ING&idp=60

Cobb, C., T. Halstead and J. Rowe (1995), *The Genuine Progress Indicator: Summary of Data and Methodology (Redefining Progress)*, San Francisco.

Conceição, P. and R. Bandura (2008), *Measuring Subjective Wellbeing: A Summary Review of the Literature*, New York, United Nations Program for Development (UNDP).

Daly, H.E. and J.B. Cobb (1989), *For the Common Good*, Boston, Beacon Press.

Easterlin, R. (1974), "Does economic growth improve the human lot? Some empirical evidence", *Nations and Households in Economic Growth: Essays in Honor of Moses Abramovitz*, Paul A. David and Melvin W. Reder (eds.), New York, Academic Press.

ECLAC (Economic Commission for Latin America and the Caribbean) (2012), *Social Panorama of Latin America, 2012* (LC/G.2557-P), Santiago, Chile. United Nations publication, Sales No: S.13.II.G.6.

___ (2010a), *Time for equality: closing gaps, opening trails* (LC/G.2432(SES.33/3)), Santiago, Chile.

___ (2010b), *Latin America in the Mirror: Objective and Subjective Dimensions of Social Inequity and Well-Being in the Region* (LC/G.2419), Santiago, Chile, April.

___ (2010c), *Social Panorama of Latin America, 2009* (LC/G.2423-P/E), Santiago, Chile. United Nations publication, Sales No: S.09.II.G.135.

___ (2007), *Social Cohesion. Inclusion and a sense of belonging in Latin America and the Caribbean* (LC/G.2335), Santiago, Chile.

ECLAC/UNICEF (Economic Commission for Latin America and the Caribbean / United Nations Children's Fund) (2009), "Maltrato infantil: una dolorosa realidad puertas adentro", *Boletín Desafíos*, N° 9, Santiago, Chile.

Gammage, S. (2009), *Género, pobreza de tiempo y capacidades en Guatemala: Un análisis multifactorial desde una perspectiva económica* (LC/MEX/L.955), Mexico City, ECLAC subregional Headquarters in Mexico.

Gasper, D. (2007), "Human well-being: concepts and conceptualizations", *Human Well-Being. Concept and Measurement*, M. McGillivary (ed.), United Nations University.

Geertz, C. (1994), *Conocimiento local: ensayo sobre la interpretación de las culturas,* Buenos Aires, Editorial Paidós.

Helliwell, John F., Richard Layard y Jeffrey Sachs (eds.) (2013), *World Happiness Report 2013*, New York, UN Sustainable Development Solutions Network.

ILO (International Labour Organization) (2011), *2011 Labour Overview. Latin America and the Caribbean*, Lima, Regional Office for Latin America and the Caribbean.

Infante, Ricardo, Daniel Martínez and Víctor Tokman (1999), "América Latina: calidad de los nuevos empleos en los noventa", *La calidad del empleo: la experiencia de los países latinoamericanos y de los Estados Unidos*, Ricardo Infante (ed.), Santiago, Chile, International Labour Organization (ILO).

Korc, M. (2000), *Situación de los Programas de Gestión de Calidad del Aire Urbano en América Latina y el Caribe* (OPS/CEPIS/99.15(AIRE)), Organización Panamericana de la Salud (OPS), January [online] http://www.ambiente. gov.ar/archivos/web/salud_ambiente/File/Gestion_Calidad_UrbanoAmerica_2000.pdf.

Lagos, M. and L. Dammert (2012), *La seguridad ciudadana. El problema principal de América Latina*, Santiago, Chile [online] www.latinobarometro.org.

Lash, S. and J. Urry (1998), *Economías de signos y espacios*, Buenos Aires, Amorrortu Editores.

Latinobarómetro (2004), "Una década de mediciones, una década de evolución. Informe resumen Encuesta 2004" [online] http://www.dw.de/aumenta-percepción-de-inseguridad-en-latinoamérica/a-15945006.

Lechner, N. (1990), *Los patios interiores de la democracia*, Santiago, Chile, Facultad Latinoamericana de Ciencias Sociales (FLACSO)/Fondo de Cultura Económica.

Lee, S., D. McCann and J.C. Messenger (2007), *Working Time Around the World: Trends in working hours, laws, and policies in a global comparative perspective,* Geneva, International Labour Organization (ILO).

McGillivary, M. (2005), "Measuring non-economic well-being achievement", *Review of Income and Wealth*, vol. 51, N° 2.

Milosavljevic, V. (2011), "El tiempo. Otra expresión de la pobreza femenina", Santiago, Chile, Economic Commission for Latin America and the Caribbean (ECLAC), unpublished.

___ (2007), "Estadísticas para la equidad de género. Magnitudes y tendencias en América Latina", *Cuadernos de la CEPAL*, N° 92 (LC/G.2321-P/E), Santiago, Chile, Economic Commission for Latin America and the Caribbean (ECLAC). United Nations publication, Sales No: S.06.II.G.132.

NEF (New Economics Foundation) (2008), *Measuring Well Being in Policy* [online] http://www.neweconomics.org/ publications/entry/measuring-well-being-in-policy.

Nordhaus, W. D. and J. Tobin (1972), "Is growth obsolete?", *Economic Growth, National Bureau of Economic Research, General Series*, N° 96, New York.

OAS (Organization of American States) (2012) Report on Citizen Security in the Americas 2012, Washington, DC, Secretariat for Multidimensional Security.

___ (2009) *Report on Citizen Security and Human Rights* [online] http://www.cidh.org

___ (1994), *Convention on the Prevention, Punishment, and Eradication of Violence against Women (Convention of Belém do Pará)*.

OECD (Organisation for Economic Co-operation and Development) (2012), *Environmental Outlook to 2050: The Consequences of Inaction*, Paris, OECD Publishing.

___ (2011), *How's Life? Measuring well-being*, Paris, OECD Publishing [online] http://dx.doi.org/10.1787/9789264121164-en.

Orjuela, L. (undated), *Manual de atención para los niños y niñas víctimas de violencia de género en el ámbito familiar*, Save de Children [online] http://www.ocse.org.mx/pdf/159_Orjuela.pdf.

Quiroga, R. (2007), "Indicadores ambientales y de desarrollo sostenible: avances y perspectivas para América Latina y el Caribe", *serie Manuales*, N° 55 (LC/L.2771-P), Santiago, Chile, Economic Commission for Latin America and the Caribbean (ECLAC).

Rojas, Mariano (coord.) (2011), *Apuntes de la Conferencia latinoamericana para la medición del bienestar y la promoción del progreso de las sociedades*, México, D.F., Foro Consultivo Científico y Tecnológico/Instituto Nacional de Estadística y Geografía (INEGI) [online] http://www.midiendoelprogreso.org/publicaciones.html.

SEMARNAT (Secretaría de Medio Ambiente y Recursos Naturales de México) (2011) *Programa para mejorar la calidad el aire de la Zona Metropolitana del Valle de México 2011-2020*, Mexico City Government of Mexico, Secretaría de Salud.

Sen, Amartya (2000), *Desarrollo y libertad*, Editorial Planeta.

___ (1999), *Development as Freedom*, New York, Anchor.

Simioni, D. (comp.), "Contaminación atmosférica y conciencia ciudadana", *Libros de la CEPAL*, N° 73 (LC/G.2201-P), Santiago, Chile, Economic Commission for Latin America and the Caribbean (CEPAL). United Nations publication, Sales No: S.03.II.G.59.

Stiglitz, J., A. Sen y J.P. Fitoussi (2008), *The Measurement of Economic Performance and Social Progress Revisited. Reflections and Overview* [online] http://stiglitz-sen-fitoussi.fr/documents/overview-eng.pdf.

UNICEF United Nations Children's Fund) (2012), *4° Estudio de Maltrato Infantil*, Santiago, Chile, Regional Office for Latin America and the Caribbean.

___ (2006), *Violence against Children in the Caribbean Region. Regional assessment. UN Secretary General's Study on Violence Against Children*, Panama City.

United Nations (1993), *Declaration on the Elimination of Violence against Women*, New York.

___ (1989) *Convention on the Rights of the Child*, New York.

UNODC (United Nations Office on Drugs and Crime), (2012), *Global Study on Homicide 2011. Context, Trends, Data*, Vienna.

United Kingdom Government (2004), *Quality of Life Counts. Indicators for a Strategy for Sustainable Development for the United Kingdom. 2004 update*, London, Department for Environment, Food and Rural Affair (DEFRA).

___ (1999), *A Better Quality of Life. Strategy for Sustainable Development for the United Kingdom - 1999*, London, Department for Environment, Food and Rural Affair (DEFRA).

___ (1994), *Sustainable Development: the UK strategy*, London, Department for Environment, Food and Rural Affair (DEFRA).

___ Valenzuela, María Elena and Gerhard Reinecke (eds.) (2001), *More and Better Jobs for Women. The Experience of Mercosur countries and Chile*, ILO, Regional Office for Latin America and the Caribbean.

Valticos, N. and G. von Potobsky (1995), *International Labour Law*, revised second edition, Boston, Kluwer.

Villatoro, P. (2012), "La medición del bienestar a través de indicadores subjetivos: una revisión", *serie Estudios Estadísticos y Prospectivos*, N° 79 (LC/L.3515), Santiago, Chile, Economic Commission for Latin America and the Caribbean (ECLAC).

WHO (World Health Organization) (2011), "*Air quality and health*", *Fact sheet* N°313 [online] http://www.who.int/mediacentre/factsheets/fs313/en/index.html

___ (2006), *WHO Air quality guidelines*, Washington, D.C.

___ (2001), *Putting women first: ethical and safety recommendations for research on domestic violence against women* - (WHO/FCH/GWH/01.1), Geneva.

Landmarks in the discourse on social protection in Latin America and overview of health and pension system coverage: a synopsis

The welfare state can be viewed as an insurance contract entered voluntarily by risk-averse individuals behind John Rawls's veil of ignorance…From this viewpoint, not only social insurance, narrowly defined, but also "universal" benefits and social assistance are a form of insurance.

Nicholas Barr (2001)

The present and future well-being of all individuals is subject to risks such as illness, the multiple restrictions involved in meeting the care needs of children and the frail or those with disabilities, periods of unemployment and underemployment, and the radical decline in (or loss of) income during old age, whose impact varies in both duration and intensity. Although asymmetrical socioeconomic circumstances are a crucial determining factor, they are, to differing degrees, beyond individuals' control.

Insurance makes it possible to address what has been dubbed the "welfare economics of uncertainty". This is a reference to uncertainties surrounding access to the necessary protection, the length of time protection will be required, the costs involved, and the degree to which personal well-being and income will be affected. By its nature, therefore, this is a demand for services that is often irregular and unpredictable. Pricing systems have a limited application, since they are unable to deal properly with certain risks, with the result that market insurance is restricted in both coverage and amount. For example, the limitations of private health insurance mean that large medical expenses —the very ones it would be most desirable to insure— go uncovered (Arrow, 1963 and Arrow, 2000).

Solidarity-based insurance enables individuals to diversify risk and narrow the gap between actual incomes and desired levels of protection, by reducing individual aggregate risk. Such is the central objective of this insurance, regardless of the kind of resources that are used to fund it (tax revenues or contributions). While this distinction may be relevant in a national or political context, it does not in and of itself constrain policy options, as it does not affect the way services are offered and purchased, risk diversification or benefit specification (Kutzin, 2008).

Insurance is also analogous with saving, which narrows the gap between income and consumption levels at different points in time (Ehrlich and Becker, 2000). Many of the benefits people receive have been paid for by them at another time in their lives (Brittan, 2001). This is known as redistribution across the life cycle (Falkingham and Hills, 2001), whereby the welfare State acts as a "savings bank".

From a social equity point of view, in a region as unequal as Latin America and the Caribbean, individual ability to use informal or market instruments to manage risk should not be overestimated.[1] Private insurance markets may not exist or may not be fully developed; in countries where income is particularly concentrated, the price/income ratio leads to underconsumption of insurance. Without adequate risk diversification, exclusions and inequalities are magnified.

The principle of solidarity thus applies to several dimensions.[2] A crucial part of evaluating social protection policies is to determine how they respond to the dynamics and social distribution of risk. Social cohesion is undermined when there is the perception of a "first class" and a "second class" of citizenship in risk protection, and the situation takes on the character of a fixed social divide when this hierarchy is perpetuated across generations. Conversely, when the State and society create insurance mechanisms to reduce the impact of events on individual well-being, the sense of belonging to society is heightened (ECLAC, 2007).

---

[1] This is demonstrated by a broad economic literature dating back to Arrow, who fifty years ago carried out a fruitful microeconomic analysis of the health-care market (Arrow, 1963), postulating that it is fraught with failures since the risks are not fully insurable, and because of information asymmetries. Health-care providers are described as adaptations to market inefficiencies, but they in turn lead to inefficiencies owing to limited competition in these markets. A select but extensive bibliography of the economic theory of welfare and the welfare State (100 articles) was compiled in three volumes by Barr (2001), covering theoretical and empirical discussions on pensions, health, education and poverty reduction.

[2] International experience demonstrates that, even in the case of individual pension accounts, risk can be diversified, which is one of the main goals of social security. For example, in variants of a notional defined contribution system, pension system shares and their earnings are not held in accounts attributed to individual workers; each worker's contributions accumulate according to a rate set by law, which reflects the benefits the system can pay. This way, the system's assets are managed centrally, they fund the system as a whole and they are not attributed to individual accounts (Barr and Diamond, 2010). But this has not occurred in Latin America, where risk diversification within individual account systems does not exist. On international experiences of notional accounts, see Holzmann, Palmer and Uthoff (2008).

Solidarity-based funding has redistributive objectives, since it allows for cross-subsidies among income, age and risk strata, and can take account of the following points that are not properly dealt with by pricing systems: individuals should not have to meet all the costs associated with their current risk structure; protection is needed against risks related to assets (such as sound health) for which there is no market substitute; market prices do not reflect the social opportunity costs or externalities of private consumption and the public good aspects that this consumption may have; and there is a need to address the underconsumption associated with low incomes or high individual risk, when there is no access to insurance even where there is a market. It also corrects externalities, since the benefit from the insurance accrues not only to the person insured but also to society through externalities such as a healthy population and fewer social upheavals (Sojo, 2003).

Taking these considerations as the interpretative framework, this chapter is divided into two parts. First, it looks at a number of discursive landmarks regarding the concept of social protection. Second, with a view to reporting on progress, constraints and emerging inequalities, two dimensions of social protection coverage in the region are analysed: health care and pensions.

A. Landmarks, mutations, shifts and discursive iterations on social protection relevant to the region: from reductionism to heterodoxy?

According to "discursive institutionalism", discourse not only embodies the substantive content of ideas, it also represents interactive processes of coordination and communication in an institutional context. When social and labour policies are developed and redesigned to address social risks, the ideas that prevail do not depend solely on their content, or on whether they are the product of consensus, are effective or can be defended regardless of their viability in terms of group interest, identity or solidarity. It also has to do with power —both the coercive capacity of the parties influencing policy and their discursive powers— that is, their ability to convince the other participants in the debate to make concessions, or even to change the way they perceive their interests or what is appropriate for their values (Schmidt, 2013).

Regarding welfare policies elsewhere in the world, the interpretive patterns that have been proposed and debated have changed significantly in recent decades. Policy themes, preferences, values, and symbols all affect the way policies are shaped and the solutions that are found (Bonoli and Natali, 2012). This shift has also been important in Latin America and the Caribbean; it would therefore be useful to look at some of the landmarks in the way social protection has been conceptualized and discussed and which have been used to influence public policy.

1. Reductionism in social policy

The targeted approach that emerged in the 1980s had such an impact on public policy during the so-called "lost decade" and in the 1990s that it is useful to review the thinking behind it. These proposals called into question and negatively evaluated the principle of universality in social policy and assumed —although this was not supported by research or hard data— that concentrating public social spending on the most vulnerable population groups and limiting the State's action in social policy matters was efficient, effective and generally valid. As a corollary, they proposed a relative and variable dismantling of universalist policies and advocated the privatization of social services. They ignored the problems associated with the private provision of services arising from market failures, such as risk selection (Sojo, 1990 and 2007).

This approach to social policy began to lose ground the mid-1990s because of its negative impact and as it was challenged by alternative, more successful ones. Very different conceptual considerations have also led to more nuanced insights on universality; these concern, for example, the health sector, with recognition of the positive impact of universal policies when the inequalities inherent to financing systems are removed (Sojo, 1990 and 2007).

The social risk management approach was put forward at the start of the new millennium. In retrospect, it was the main conceptual remainder of reductionism, but given its relative impenetrability, was less influential than reductionist targeting. Along with certain definitions of risk and insurance, its global approach to social policy was based on a functional public-private combination that confined the social welfare responsibilities of the State to the fight against poverty, viewed risk insurance as an individual responsibility and essentially ruled out solidarity in risk diversification. In these terms, individual market insurance, the use of safety nets to provide services to the poor and targeting as opposed to universality all go to make up a social policy strategy that assigns a minimal role to the public sector in social protection, places the financing and provision of the remaining social-welfare-related services in private hands and once again departs from the solidarity principle in financing. These approaches and the associated policies were vigorously promoted by the World Bank (Sojo, 2003).

2. Universality as a set of benefits, and the controversy surrounding dichotomous views of contributory funding

At the Inter-American Development Bank (IDB), the Inter-American Institute for Social Development (INDES) advocated some years ago the idea of basic universalism (Filgueira and others, 2006). It criticized "false universalism" on the grounds that it concealed the segmented nature of supply of and access to goods that differed in quality and were of the greatest benefit to those who could best afford them. It also criticized "ineffective universalism" that provided poor quality services with little concern as to their impact.

Basic universalism proposes measures of universal coverage and selected deliveries, which should constitute true protection floors that must be gradually strengthened. The idea is to provide universal coverage for a limited set of essential services for defined population groups based on certain attributes, or a limited set of basic benefits that vary according to each country's possibilities and definitions (Filgueira and others, 2006).

Specific failures of the insurance markets are not considered; it is merely stated that the market lacks the necessary strength (and sometimes the regulatory frameworks and instruments) to provide large sectors of the population with access to the goods and services they need for full social integration. Labour markets receive greater attention because they stratify corporate labour based systems. The State is assigned the role of guaranteeing access to and enjoyment of goods, rents and services of homogeneous quality (Filgueira and others, 2006).

A close look at references to the feasibility of establishing various benefits shows that they essentially refer to the use of non-contributory fiscal resources, and the term "non-contributory basic universalism" is even used (Rezk, 2006). In response, warnings were sounded of a likely contraction in fiscal resources earmarked for such purposes and of the need to reframe social protection by improving the design of contributory systems, to ensure greater convergence among its different subsystems and to prevent any further intensification of existing segmentation (Tokman, 2006).

Another restrictive approach that takes issue with contributory financing has recently emerged in the region from a source close to the IDB. Devised this time for Mexico, it places much of the blame for informality on contributory financing, in that informality is caused by distortions in the tax and social security regime (Levy, 2012). Among other things, it proposes replacing payroll taxes with VAT increases, which represents a shift in social security terms from a tax on work to a tax on consumption (Levy, 2012).[3] Certain employee benefits would still be funded using payroll taxes. Compensation, channelled through the Opportunities programme, would be provided to mitigate the impact of consumer taxes (which benefit the system) on poorer families.

The Mexican social protection system is still one of the most stratified in Latin America. In that context, the "universal social security" approach seeks the convergence of benefits for all workers, along with other benefits specifically for wage earners. The current coverage offered by the Mexican Social Security Institute (IMSS) would form an important part of this set of benefits (Levy, 2012).

As will later be seen, levels of pension and health-care system affiliation (which are indicators of labour-market informality) do not appear to depend on the way systems are funded: there are contributory schemes with broad coverage and others where it is very restricted, depending on the specific path taken by the country.

Diametrically opposed to this line of thought is the argument that in order to develop labour markets and increase formality, insurance quality must be the focus, rather than the contributory or fiscal nature of its funding. When wages are flexible, the cost of employer-provided benefits is partially transferred to the worker in the form of lower wages; if workers do not value these benefits as much as foregone earnings, they may, in the formal sector, agree with their employer to avoid contributions (or may be pressured to do so) or may seek work in the informal sector, where remuneration is wholly monetary. This can occur when the provision of pensions or medical benefits is very inefficient or the link between benefits and contributions is very weak, or if some member of the family who is already working in the formal sector provides coverage for the whole family. Good-quality, efficient social security systems are therefore essential. Insufficient pension benefits and precarious health-care benefits are negative externalities that do not create an adequate incentive for deeper labour markets (Sojo, 2003).

The equity of funding derived from general taxation hinges on the overall equity of a country's tax system, while the equity of a contributory system depends largely on the design of the system and the basis upon which the compulsory contribution is levied. In evaluating financing reforms, the objectives of the system should not be forgotten: how reforms affect service quality, risk pooling and administrative costs (Gutiérrez, Acosta and Alfonso, 2012).

With regard to funding social investment with consumption taxes, the situation in Chile irrefutably demonstrates that progressive social spending is not enough to modify an unequal income structure: progressive taxation is key (Rivera, 2013). Resorting to indirect taxation to fund social protection makes the tax structure more regressive; funding it out of net indirect tax revenue instead of employer contributions can lead to further declines in the business sector's contribution to public and social spending. Moreover, equity is not only an issue when it comes to sources of financing; it also plays a role in the way in which resources from different sources are combined, collection methods, central transfers to subnational entities that are adjusted for levels of social development, and sourcing of services from different public-private permutations. None of these aspects are adequately accounted for in a dichotomous view of financing.

Meanwhile, an important process is under way as part of the comprehensive health-care reform that is currently being negotiated on a political level in Colombia. In 2013 the employer's share of contributions was revised, but through progressive taxation: the tax reform embodied in Act 1607 modified the structure of the sector's financing by introducing an "income tax for equity" (CREE) to boost fiscal resources. The goal is that, from 2014, over 60% of health-care funds will come from taxation. Changing the balance between tax and contributory-based financing has also created a need for a body that will concentrate the sources. The reform proposed by the executive branch includes substantial changes to the responsibilities of health-care providers and insurers, handing over to a single public financial entity (Salud-Mía) the duties of signing up participants and collecting, managing and transferring the funds to pay for health services (Ministry of Health of Colombia, 2013).

In terms of the dichotomy between types of financing, new studies carried out within the World Bank itself have warned of the complexity of and the problems involved in moving away from contributory financing in the region towards basic benefit packages funded by general or specific taxation, in conjunction with complementary and voluntary plans managed by the public or the private sector. They stress that there are few cases of funding based solely

---

[3]   In a country that tends to resort to indirect taxation, the specific context of this approach should be considered: if revenue from levies on hydrocarbon production is classified as non-tax, Mexico currently has one of the lowest tax burdens of Latin America and has recently come to rank even lower. If these revenues are counted, the burden is slightly smaller than the regional average and has increased moderately since the 1980s. In that instance, the bias towards indirect taxation, compared with the rest of the subregion, would be very marked in this country (Gomez-Sabaini and Morán, 2013).

on these sources and describe the fiscal, legal and administrative constraints that would be faced in Latin America. Other drawbacks include low levels of tax receipts in many countries. On the other hand, the existence of strong social security institutions in several countries that already offer health benefits, pensions, and, sometimes, unemployment benefits —that are sometimes even greater than these basic packages (Ribe, Robalino and Walker, 2012).

The position that the central goal should be to give all citizens or residents access to the same social insurance system, under the same rules and conditions, regardless of where they work (Ribe, Robalino and Walker, 2010) represents a fundamental shift in the thinking associated with the World Bank. Contributory schemes in the formal sector may be insufficient, but parallel contributory and non-contributory systems are also inefficient, and therefore integrated systems are needed (Ribe, Robalino and Walker, 2012).

Concerns are also raised regarding the adequacy of the region's non-contributory programmes, since the benefits are very small in many cases, especially in the health sector, and they are poorly integrated with contributory programmes. Moreover, it is felt that social insurance suffers from institutional fragmentation, characterized by multiple, poorly coordinated plans, which is detrimental to labour mobility, creates horizontal inequality among workers and drives up administrative costs. According to the long-term vision of social protection and labour-market policies, the same contributory social insurance should be available to everyone, regardless of where they work. This would entail maintaining mandatory insurance in the formal sector and establishing financial and institutional incentives to promote the inclusion of informal workers (Rashid, 2012; Ribe, Robalino and Walker, 2010).

With a view to making progress on universal pension coverage, the Inter-American Development Bank has recently suggested that citizens should have pension insurance, meaning a universal pension for older persons that is sustainable in fiscal and institutional terms, and has highlighted an urgent need to strengthen contributory systems in order to guarantee pension levels in the long term. It has also proposed the gradual incorporation of non-wage-earners, who have traditionally been excluded from social security, with the same costs and benefits as wage earners, and based on a mode of implementation that allows for more flexibility in making payments and offers new ways to compel saving among groups that are disconnected from social security, but without creating parallel systems or creating incentives for employers to reassign workers to small, unproductive production units. To encourage the growth of formal employment, social security contributions would be subsidized, which would reduce the cost of formality and boost present and future contribution density for all workers, regardless of their job category. Suggestions for financing the increase in coverage include cutting back on the multiple taxes on formal employment or, at least, not adding new ones, since this has a negative effect on labour formality, and exploring alternative forms of financing, such as consumption taxes and public revenues from commodities (Bosch, Melguizo and Pagés, 2013). On using consumption taxes as a source of funding, see the problems described above in relation to another proposal that reflects IDB thinking on this issue.

There is a growing recognition in the region that contributory funding need not be solely associated with employment status, and that the poor can contribute through family schemes and at differential rates according to their income level. Studies on various countries in the region have demonstrated that informal workers and even non-wage-earners who receive remittances are able to contribute through subsidized schemes (Gutiérrez, Acosta and Alfonso, 2012; Carrera, Castro and Sojo, 2010). In countries with poorly developed schemes, it is crucial to expand coverage, improve the quality of insurance in the labour market and boost redistributive impact. To that end, in addition to using tax revenues, contributory ceilings must be removed (Carrera, Castro and Sojo, 2010).

The health economics literature also warns of a clash of opposing views on contribution- or tax-based financing. An interesting warning has been sounded in that regard: it is increasingly recognized that the source of the funds does not determine the organizational structure of the sector, the mechanisms through which these resources are allocated, or the precision with which benefits are specified. Labels such as taxpayer-funded system or social security system do not adequately describe the current systems. The traditional way of thinking about social security places unnecessary restrictions on the range of policy options available to countries (Kutzin, 2012).

In Latin America, discussions on social protection funding sometimes use technical arguments that conceal the strictly political determinants of the social protection architecture. The vast contemporary literature on the welfare State, which looks at its history and the changes over time around the world, provides in-depth information on the historical and political factors underpinning the financing options.[4]

---

[4]   See Schmidt and Thatcher (2013); Palier (2010); Barr and Diamond (2008); Hemerijck (2013); Bonoli and Natali (2012); and Porter (1999).

Fragmentation and segmentation are ingrained within social protection systems and in their political and discursive action; that is, they are not exogenous (they do not result purely from labour-market dynamics, for example). Therefore, any strategy for universalizing social protection in the region cannot focus exclusively on boosting resources; it must also act on the morphology of social protection and place institutional change at the heart of innovation efforts (Sojo, 2013).

3. The evolution of the "social protection floor" approach and of proposals on universal health-care coverage

The concept of the social protection floor, developed by the International Labour Organization (ILO) in collaboration with the World Health Organization (WHO), is another important landmark in the social protection debate. The concept has been revised considerably over time.

Initially, the idea of a basic benefits package prevailed. The basic social protection floor was first put forward by the World Commission on the Social Dimension of Globalization (WCSDG) in 2002. It was defined as a basic and modest set of social security guarantees, to be implemented through cash transfers and benefits (ILO, 2008).

Described as a set of guarantees of access to basic transfers, rather than a set of benefits, it had more in common with social assistance than social security, given the amounts in question (which corresponded to income security for children, and older and disabled persons, to prevent them falling below the poverty line, and some targeted support for the poor and unemployed of working age). Social security benefits, in contrast, are the result of rights acquired on the basis of payment of contributions or taxes, and usually represent a high level of income replacement (ILO, 2008).

It was later recast as the interplay between basic guarantees, plus a second level with guaranteed benefits as an entitlement, and an upper floor consisting of regulated voluntary insurance (Cichon, Behrendt and Wodsak, 2011).

The concept evolved over time thanks to these and subsequent modifications (Sojo, 2012). Owing to trade union pressure in the tripartite discussions within ILO, the word "basic" was removed. The "social protection floor" is distinct from a "safety net", which was considered as residual to social policies and aimed to cushion the effects of structural adjustment through measures that were temporary, fragmented and targeted to the poor and the vulnerable, according to certain criteria (Social Protection Floor Advisory Group, 2011). The floor should not be viewed as an alternative, but as a complement to existing social security institutions; that is, it is a component of a pluralistic and comprehensive social protection system (Social Protection Floor Advisory Group, 2011). In countries with segmented but comprehensive social protection systems, the floor fills gaps in coverage and promotes consistent social policies (Social Protection Floor Advisory Group, 2011).

Within the framework of the Advisory Group chaired by Michelle Bachelet, former Executive Director of the United Nations Entity for Gender Equality and the Empowerment of Women (UN-Women), the universality of social protection is described as a progressive search in the framework of institutional plurality, within a two-dimensional strategy comprising a horizontal dimension (basic set of guarantees for all) and a vertical dimension (gradual implementation of higher standards) (Social Protection Floor Advisory Group, 2011). The horizontal dimension concerns basic, fundable services in health, education, sanitation, food security, housing, basic income security or basic (or very basic) measures established at the national level whose scope depends on the available fiscal and financial space (Ibid).

The recommendations on the subject made by the General Conference of the International Labour Organization in 2012 reflect what may be described as "inherent institutional pluralism", inasmuch as they state that making the floor a reality may include universal benefits, social insurance, social assistance, tax and employment schemes. Given the considerable challenge of ensuring that the interdependent horizontal and vertical steps do not result in further fragmentation of the existing social protection (Sojo, 2012 and 2013), the need to develop the two dimensions simultaneously is currently under discussion at ILO (Schwarzer, 2013).

The World Health Report 2010 (WHO, 2010) highlights certain trade-offs that are needed when benefits are designed in order to make headway on universal health care. Three dimensions are considered: who benefits from resources, the services to which people have access, and how much they cost. Progress towards universal coverage and its mechanisms is represented by a cube to be filled, depicting the population, the costs and the services. Along the horizontal axis, starting with the poor and vulnerable, the idea is to try to extend coverage to the uninsured. Services should be of good quality and based on distribution of the disease burden, prioritizing the needs of the most vulnerable and advancing towards the inclusion of other services. Along the vertical axis, the aim is to reduce out-of-pocket health expenditure, considering the specific needs of the most disadvantaged groups and reducing co-payments and fees.

In conclusion, it is clear that the international debate on social protection has evolved towards more pluralistic approaches to expanding social protection. These approaches are heterodox and are likely to have an impact in the region. Progress towards these kinds of interpretations of social security is reflected in assertions that there is no single international model for providing social protection in health, or single pathway to greater coverage, given the differences between countries in terms of their governance structures, financing mechanisms and sources of funding, risk diversification, resource allocation and benefits. Social protection is evolving —in the framework of financing systems that either cover separately or overlap to cover very diverse population groups— thanks, among other things, to economic development, cultural values, institutional factors and political commitment and leadership (Scheil-Adlung, 2013).

4. ECLAC and social protection as a citizens' right

As proposed by ECLAC (2006), a social protection system is more than an institutional structure; it is a political agreement that enables society to lay the foundations for building and regulating coexistence. This agreement is under permanent review, and it determines which rights apply to all, how they are protected and how they are rendered viable. A certain level of cohesion is required to build consensus in this matter, which is reflected in institutions, standards, programmes and resources. Social cohesion is also needed to make the transition from a set of social policies to a comprehensive social protection system. This has to be promoted and involves addressing conflicts between rights, resources, distribution patterns and institutional designs. For a rights-based, cohesion-oriented social protection model, a stance must be taken on four key elements: the levels and sources of contributory and non-contributory financing; the extent of solidarity in financing; the development of social institutions for efficient management of the benefits policy; and the identification of explicit, guaranteed and enforceable rights in terms of access to social benefits (ECLAC, 2007).

So as to address the reductionist view of social policy analytically, ECLAC has formulated principles of social policy, and thus of social protection, from a rights-based perspective. The principle of universality dictates that all citizens, as members of society, are entitled to certain types of protection or benefits, which must have certain characteristics in terms of quantity and quality, and which are necessary for their full participation in society. It seeks to ensure that all members of society are guaranteed a certain level of well-being, which must be the maximum permitted by economic development at any given time. This does not mean that any benefit can be made universal, but rather that society sets, on the basis of agreements, standards for quality and coverage that must be guaranteed for all its members (ECLAC, 2000 and 2007).

The principle of universality is closely tied to the principle of solidarity, which holds that everyone should participate in funding social policy in accordance with their means. Thus solidarity helps ensure universality and equity of access to social security benefits, taking into account asymmetrical economic conditions and risk exposure, particularly with regard to health and employment. This principle also assumes that, given the externalities of individual well-being, there is a close interrelationship between individual well-being and social well-being. Individual lives and society's development are accordingly both affected by the quality and extent of social services and protection (ECLAC, 2000 and 2006).

The greatest obstacles to universal social policies and benefits are limited resources, a lack of social agreements that make universality a priority, and implementation difficulties. Universality does not preclude the use of selectivity criteria when resources are scarce, to ensure that social services reach the poorest. In order to address the multidimensional and heterogeneous nature of poverty, there must be a beneficial interaction between universal and comprehensive policies and selective and differentiated policies. As barriers mainly affect the poorest, selectivity represents a tool or set of tools to be used for guiding action and in particular for allocating subsidies, so that the poor can access social services and guarantees. Targeting is thus intended is to make the universalization of social policies more effective (ECLAC, 2000 and 2006).

For equity to be substantive, public resources must be used efficiently. Efficiency in the use of public resources for social policy is also an intrinsic element of equity since it enhances, rather than counteracts, the principles of universality and solidarity. This principle should not be understood solely in terms of its macro and microeconomic impact; ultimately, it concerns the ability to achieve the social objectives set with scarce resources (ECLAC, 2000 and 2006). In addition, reforms that introduce subsystems in an integrated social protection system must also regulate the market and private options, establishing rules that ensure an appropriate mix of public and private so as to achieve the socially and publicly desired goals (ECLAC, 2007).

The labour market has not demonstrated sufficient capacity for inclusiveness either through the creation of good-quality jobs or in terms of contributory coverage. It cannot therefore be expected to serve as the only mechanism for protecting the bulk of the population against the risks associated with a possible loss of income, health problems and aging, among other factors. Social protection cannot be restricted to mechanisms offered by the world of work: the big challenge is thus to reformulate social protection within a framework of integral solidarity that combines contributory and non-contributory mechanisms (ECLAC, 2006).

To improve the coverage and quality of social protection in the subregion, action must be taken on various labour-market matters that have been put off and remain unaddressed, and the playing field must be levelled in the productive sphere, as this has exacerbated the considerable heterogeneity of the production structure for decades. Unless these disparities are (at least partially) corrected, it will be difficult for social policies to contribute to building a more inclusive social model. The underlying labour-market dynamics must be rethought, since historically the development of social protection has been associated with labour legislation, regulations governing working conditions and dismissals, collective bargaining, and training and education policies, and the capacity to monitor compliance with the regulations (ECLAC, 2010).

These discursive landmarks have characterized the social protection debate in recent decades, a period during which many reforms have also been carried out. This chapter will now outline, in quantitative terms, recent trends in social protection in health care and pensions, which illustrate the magnitude and specificity of inequality, as well as the outstanding challenges.

B. Mapping health and pension coverage in Latin America during and after working life

As stated at the beginning of this chapter, the range of risks against which people should be protected is very wide. These risks change as societies evolve, and public policy is still severely myopic in certain areas. *Social Panorama of Latin America 2012* thus delved into the need to make care another pillar of social protection and a source of rights. It analysed employment in this sector and private spending on care, described existing policies and programmes, and made policy proposals (ECLAC, 2012).

Health care and pensions (for which institutional coordination varies considerably across the region) have traditionally been allocated the lion's share of the contributory and non-contributory resources available for social protection. And not without justification, since these two spheres are crucial to the well-being of present and future generations and they have been central to the demands for social protection made all over the world since the nineteenth century. The relative and absolute magnitude of the resources dedicated to these two spheres of social protection calls for a close study of their trajectories. On this occasion, *Social Panorama* is presenting an overview of coverage in these two areas and reporting on the region's heterogeneity and the asymmetries that emerge at the country level.

It is important to note the limitations of the information provided by the household surveys drawn on for this chapter. Given that the surveys only record affiliation or contributory status, they tell us nothing about the quality or the range of health services to which people have access. It may also be the case that workers report being affiliated when in fact their employers are not making the contributions on their behalf despite deducting the relevant amounts from their wages. Furthermore, participation in a pension scheme does not per se mean that the participants are actually making contributions; if they are not, they will be generating contribution gaps that, depending on their size, could seriously compromise their future pensions. Wage-earner participation in pension schemes only indicates that they expect to receive a pension at the age prescribed by law; it does not show how much it will be. Surveys are, however, able to measure pensioners' income, which provides clues as to their employment histories and the pension systems in their countries.

1. A regional overview

Although to differing degrees and from very different starting points, wage-earner health care and pension coverage[5] has expanded; in just one country was a slight contraction observed. In affiliation terms, this reflects positive labour market trends, in particular considering that it occurred during the most severe global financial and economic crisis since the Great Depression, which affected the region in a number of domains.[6] Nevertheless, it is very worrying that wage-earner coverage is so limited in five countries, where less than half are affiliated, since the superior labour-market position of this population group makes them more likely to be covered. What is more, although significant progress has been made in two of these countries, in three there has been virtually no improvement. The most notable increases have occurred in countries where population coverage may be described as intermediate, while they are more modest in countries with extensive population coverage (see table IV.1). In some countries, health-care and pension coverage have both expanded. In others, the trends differ, which could indicate that greater emphasis is placed on one area, or it may mean that one form of social protection (individual versus solidarity-based) is more effective than the other.[7]

Except in Honduras, wage earners are more likely to participate in health systems than in pension funds. However, given that the two forms of coverage are highly correlated, countries reporting low levels of coverage in one area tend to do so in the other, as well. Countries with the highest levels of pension scheme participation (on average, 76%) record health-care affiliation of around 90%, and in several cases their health systems are making progress towards universal provision through contributory and non-contributory mechanisms. In countries with intermediate pension coverage, levels of health-care affiliation vary widely: although the average is nearly 65%, it ranges from 49% to 75%. The great exception in this group is Colombia, where health coverage expanded from 53% to 92% over 11 years, while pension coverage underwent a significant but lesser increase (16 percentage points).

In terms of gender, coverage was more extensive among female than male wage earners at both points in time (2002 and 2011) on average in 16 countries in the region, and they have gained more, proportionally speaking, where access has expanded for both indicators. However, some countries buck this trend: in Argentina, Brazil, Chile, Costa Rica, the Dominican Republic, Peru and Uruguay —a group that includes some of the countries with the broadest coverage— levels of affiliation to pension schemes (but not health care, apart from in the Dominican Republic) are lower among female wage earners. Men, meanwhile, gained more in proportional terms from improvements in the two indicators in Chile, Colombia, Guatemala and Honduras (see table IV.1).

There are disparities in access to both pension and health systems based on income quintile. Education level is also a source of significant gaps (see table IV.3), but these are narrowing, especially with regard to health. Between the two extremes (wage workers with a university education versus those who did not complete primary

---

[5]   With respect to wage earners, at a certain level of abstraction a joint reference to health care and pensions is valid. With only a few exceptions, levels of affiliation to health systems among wage earners are highly correlated with pension scheme affiliation (r = 0.89), largely because in many countries social security associated with wage employment involves simultaneous compulsory contributions to both systems, or because they form a joint system.

[6]   In the area of social protection, for example, financial volatility has had a direct, negative impact on saving levels in individual pension accounts, heightened by limited financial risk diversification and the deficiencies of, or liberalizing guidelines concerning, regulation of these funds' investments.

[7]   For example, in Colombia the health system reform encompassed different solidarity-based components, while the pension reform led to pensions based on individual funding. Affiliation has followed a very different course in each sphere.

education), the difference in affiliation to pension and health systems is 55 percentage points and 40 percentage points, respectively. In terms of trends by age group, although affiliation to both pension and health-care systems increased in all age groups, access for both indicators can be described as an inverted U-curve, because affiliation levels are lower both at the beginning and at the end of people's working lives. This is problematic because it means that young people are deferring saving for their pensions, and older persons do not have access to the full range of health services (see figure IV.1).

Table IV.1
Latin America (18 countries): affiliation to pension and health-care systems among wage earners aged 15 years and over, by sex
(Percentages)

Country	Year	Both sexes		Men		Women	
		Pensions	Health care	Pensions	Health care	Pensions	Health care
Argentina (urban areas)	2004	54.7	65.1	59.3	66.4	49.0	63.5
	2011	68.7	77.7	71.7	77.5	64.8	77.9
Bolivia (Plurinacional State of)	2002	26.3	29.8	25.6	27.5	27.6	34.1
	2009	32.4	44.4	30.7	40.5	35.4	51.2
Brazil [a]	2001	65.0	...	65.6	...	64.2	...
	2011	75.9	...	76.9	...	74.6	...
Chile	2000	77.0	92.4	79.1	91.5	73.6	93.8
	2011	81.7	96.7	84.3	96.1	78.2	97.7
Colombia	1999	40.9	53.2	36.5	48.5	47.7	60.4
	2011	57.2	91.9	57.6	90.7	56.6	93.6
Costa Rica [b]	2002	...	83.7	...	81.7	...	87.2
	2011	74.6	86.9	77.3	84.7	70.4	90.3
Dominican Republic	2005	42.5	51.1	42.6	52.6	42.4	49.0
	2011	63.3	75.4	66.7	76.2	59.4	74.4
Ecuador (urban areas)	2002	42.0	45.0	40.8	43.6	44.2	47.5
	2011	64.7	66.2	61.6	62.7	69.7	72.1
El Salvador	1999	48.6	50.0	45.0	45.6	54.6	57.5
	2010	46.6	48.9	43.2	44.5	52.2	56.4
Guatemala	2002	35.8	38.5	33.7	36.4	40.8	43.4
	2006	38.5	44.5	36.4	42.5	42.8	48.9
Honduras	2006	38.0	36.0	30.8	30.2	51.8	47.1
	2010	38.8	37.2	32.4	31.8	51.2	47.7
Mexico	2002	41.0	53.8	39.5	52.0	44.0	57.0
	2010	41.3	71.8	40.0	69.3	43.6	76.3
Nicaragua	2001	33.2	28.8	28.6	24.9	42.4	36.5
	2005	34.0	36.3	28.0	30.2	45.7	48.3
Panama [b]	2002	...	73.2	...	71.6	...	75.6
	2011	...	80.1	...	77.8	...	83.4
Paraguay	2000	28.1	33.2	27.2	30.9	29.6	36.9
	2011	35.1	40.1	33.8	36.6	37.0	45.3
Peru	2001	27.1	39.3	27.1	38.9	26.9	40.0
	2011	50.4	65.0	53.3	63.7	46.3	67.0
Uruguay (urban areas)	2002	76.8	98.2	79.7	97.8	73.4	98.7
	2011	84.7	98.6	85.7	98.3	83.5	99.0
Venezuela (Bolivarian Republic of) [a]	2002	60.9	...	57.5	...	66.4	...
	2011	72.8	...	69.4	...	77.6	...
Latin America [c]	2002	46.1	54.4	44.9	52.5	48.7	58.0
	2011	55.4	66.4	54.5	63.9	57.4	70.6

Source: Economic Commission for Latin America (ECLAC), on the basis of special tabulations of data from household surveys conducted in the respective countries.
[a] Health-care system affiliation could not be determined from the surveys used.
[b] Pension-system affiliation could not be determined from the surveys used.
[c] Simple average for 16 countries. Excludes countries on which no data are available for the two points in time taken as a reference.

Figure IV.1

Latin America: [a] affiliation to pension and health-care systems among wage earners aged 15 years and over, by sex, per capita income quintile, education level and age group, around 2002 and 2011

(Percentages)

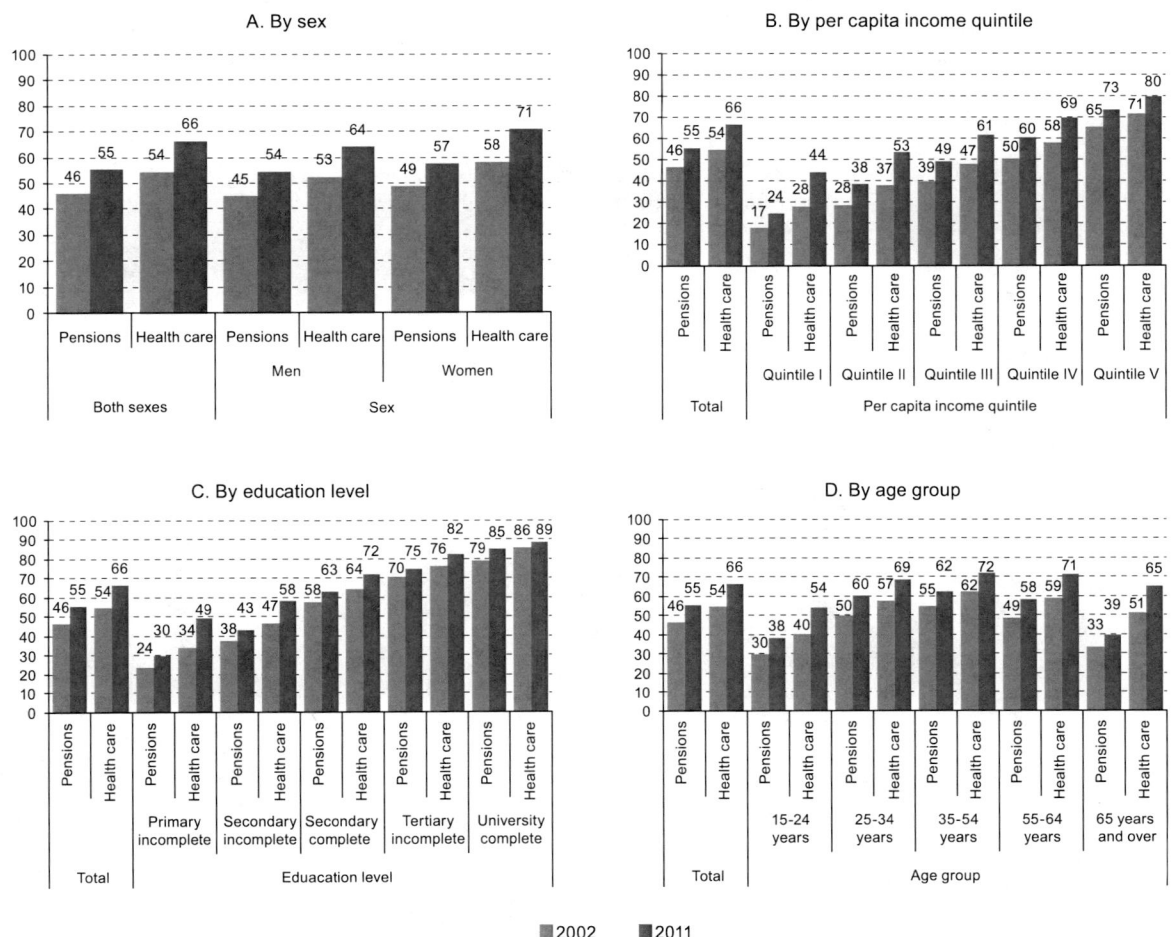

■ 2002 ■ 2011

Source: Economic Commission for Latin America (ECLAC), on the basis of special tabulations of data from household surveys conducted in the respective countries.
[a] Simple average for 16 countries: Argentina (urban areas), Bolivarian Republic of Venezuela (only in the case of pensions), Brazil (only in the case of pensions), Chile, Colombia, Costa Rica (only in the case of health care), Dominican Republic, Ecuador (urban areas), Guatemala, Honduras, Mexico, Nicaragua, Panama (only in the base of health care), Paraguay, Peru, Plurinational State of Bolivia and Uruguay (urban areas).

The concept of solidarity in financing social protection clearly has an altruistic basis in that it seeks to meet the needs of others as well as one's own needs. However, it also serves a purpose across time: the idea is to save while healthy and in secure employment, as insurance against the times when one is sick or has less job security, and for the future when one will need a pension. The magnitude of the risks and their unpredictable nature means that everyone must share the risk, even high earners, by signing up to protection across various stages of the life cycle. This is crucial if people are to be willing to pay taxes or make contributions to fund social protection, and cannot be emphasized enough. As will be seen, the distribution of the lack of coverage in the region constitutes grounds for strengthening universal policies with supportive financing since, although clearly to a differing degree and depth, social sectors across the income spectrum lack social protection. This goes back to a point that was made in the first part of this chapter: there is a need to safeguard the efficiency and quality of social security systems and forge proper links between benefits and contributions, in the case of contributory systems, so as to make the benefits more attractive and therefore more highly valued.

2. Aspects of health-care affiliation at the country level

On average, affiliation to health-care systems increased by around 12 percentage points between 2002 and 2011. The exceptions are El Salvador, which registered a minor setback, and Uruguay, where affiliation was already very high in 2002 (over 98%) and only marginal improvement was recorded. The most significant progress was made in Colombia, the Dominican Republic, Ecuador (urban areas) and Peru, where affiliation increased by between 24 percentage points and 39 percentage points.

Table IV.2
Latin America (18 countries): variation in affiliation to pension and health-care systems among wage earners aged 15 years and over, by sex
(Percentage points)

Country	Year	Both sexes		Men		Women	
		Pensions	Health care	Pensions	Health care	Pensions	Health care
Argentina (urban areas)	2004-2011	14.0	12.6	12.3	11.1	15.8	14.4
Bolivia (Plurinacional State of)	2002-2009	6.1	14.6	5.1	13.0	7.8	17.1
Brazil	2001-2011	10.9	...	11.4	...	10.4	...
Chile	2000-2011	4.7	4.4	5.1	4.6	4.6	3.8
Colombia	1999-2011	16.3	38.7	21.1	42.2	8.9	33.1
Costa Rica	2002-2011	...	3.3	...	3.1	...	3.1
Dominican Republic	2005-2011	20.8	24.3	24.2	23.6	17.0	25.4
Ecuador (urban areas)	2002-2011	22.7	21.2	20.8	19.0	25.5	24.5
El Salvador	1999-2010	-2.0	-1.1	-1.8	-1.0	-2.4	-1.1
Guatemala	2002-2006	2.7	6.1	2.8	6.1	2.1	5.6
Honduras	2007-2010	0.8	1.2	1.6	1.6	-0.6	0.6
Mexico	2002-2010	0.3	18.1	0.5	17.3	-0.4	19.2
Nicaragua	2001-2005	0.8	7.6	-0.6	5.3	3.2	11.9
Panama	2002-2011	...	7.0	...	6.2	...	7.8
Paraguay	2000-2011	6.9	6.8	6.6	5.7	7.4	8.4
Peru	2001-2011	23.4	25.7	26.2	24.8	19.3	27.0
Uruguay (urban areas)	2002-2011	7.8	0.4	6.0	0.4	10.0	0.3
Venezuela (Bolivarian Republic of)	2002-2011	11.9	...	11.9	...	11.2	...
Latin America [a]	**2002-2011**	**9.2**	**11.9**	**9.6**	**11.4**	**8.7**	**12.6**

Source: Economic Commission for Latin America (ECLAC), on the basis of special tabulations of data from household surveys conducted in the respective countries.
[a] Variation based on the simple average for 16 countries for which data are available.

Health-care coverage was most extensive at both points in time in Argentina, Chile, Costa Rica, Panama and Uruguay. Over a 12-year period, Colombia made substantial progress, and its health-care affiliation rates are now among the region's highest. Considerable efforts were made to extend coverage in the Dominican Republic, Ecuador, Mexico and Peru, where affiliation is at an intermediate level compared with the rest of the countries in the group. There were major increases in Argentina and the Plurinational State of Bolivia, and more moderate rises in the other countries. Affiliation was trending downwards in El Salvador prior to the health-care reform that is now under way, and has remained low and virtually unchanged in Honduras. Levels of health-care affiliation in Brazil could not be detected from the surveys consulted, as the country has a universal system.

Wage-earner affiliation in the countries may be classified as high, average or low. The lower the overall affiliation of these workers, the worse the relative position of those working in microenterprises or in domestic service.

By employment sector, affiliation is higher in the public sector than in the private sector, owing to evasion problems and a lack of labour-market oversight, among other factors. The number of new health-system participants among professionals and technicians in microenterprises declined (as did pension scheme affiliation) in four of the countries with the lowest levels of affiliation. More domestic workers signed up to health care than pension schemes but affiliation rates remain poor; they did, however, rise significantly in Colombia, Ecuador, Mexico and Peru, and more modestly in five other countries (see table IV.4).

Table IV.3

Latin America (18 countries): affiliation to pension and health-care systems among wage earners aged 15 years and over, by per capita income quintile

(Percentages)

| Country | Year | Total | | Per capita income quintile | | | | | | | | | |
| | | | | Quintile I | | Quintile II | | Quintile III | | Quintile IV | | Quintile V | |
		Pensions	Health care	Pensions	Health care	Pensions	Health care	Pensions	Health care	Pensions	Health care	Pensions	Health care
Argentina (urban areas)	2004	54.7	65.1	13.9	20.3	36.5	45.1	52.0	63.0	64.5	77.2	79.9	90.8
	2011	68.7	77.7	32.7	40.3	55.8	65.5	65.1	76.0	76.5	86.0	87.5	95.0
Bolivia (Plurinacional State of)	2002	26.3	29.8	9.8	9.0	6.9	9.8	15.5	18.5	20.4	26.1	43.1	45.3
	2009	32.4	44.4	13.3	27.8	17.6	28.1	23.6	37.1	33.0	46.4	44.3	54.4
Brazil [a]	2001	65.0	...	31.4	...	50.3	...	62.2	...	73.6	...	81.9	...
	2011	75.9	...	44.3	...	64.8	...	74.7	...	82.8	...	88.6	...
Chile	2000	77.0	92.4	54.3	89.4	69.8	91.0	77.6	91.6	82.9	93.0	87.4	95.0
	2011	81.7	96.7	67.3	97.4	77.8	96.9	82.5	96.6	82.4	95.9	89.2	97.3
Colombia	1999	40.9	53.2	10.5	17.4	21.9	33.4	27.8	41.9	39.7	53.6	62.3	73.4
	2011	57.2	91.9	6.8	83.2	25.9	87.3	44.4	90.2	61.8	92.0	79.9	95.7
Costa Rica [b]	2002	...	83.7	...	63.2	...	73.6	...	80.5	...	86.5	...	92.0
	2011	74.6	86.9	45.0	68.0	60.8	78.2	73.0	85.7	77.8	89.5	88.8	95.7
Dominican Republic	2005	42.5	51.1	26.8	34.8	35.1	43.0	41.3	48.8	44.6	52.7	53.7	64.6
	2011	63.3	75.4	44.8	58.1	53.3	69.9	59.0	72.7	71.3	81.2	76.0	84.4
Ecuador (urban areas)	2002	42.0	45.0	17.6	18.1	24.9	26.9	34.3	36.3	45.3	48.3	64.9	70.3
	2011	64.7	66.2	30.1	33.2	44.6	47.7	58.1	59.7	70.3	71.6	86.3	86.7
El Salvador	1999	48.6	50.0	6.6	7.1	17.8	18.0	36.4	37.7	52.7	54.7	76.0	77.7
	2010	46.6	48.9	8.3	8.8	21.8	22.6	36.2	38.3	49.7	52.9	72.6	75.8
Guatemala	2002	35.8	38.5	9.5	10.2	16.9	17.5	29.7	32.6	42.8	44.7	58.7	64.0
	2006	38.5	44.5	5.1	9.1	17.3	21.0	30.9	36.0	43.3	49.6	60.8	69.2
Honduras	2006	38.0	36.0	0.6	0.6	5.5	5.6	21.5	21.0	41.7	40.2	61.2	57.1
	2010	38.8	37.2	1.2	1.2	7.2	8.5	21.4	22.0	42.0	41.4	64.1	59.5
Mexico	2002	41.0	53.8	7.6	16.6	23.3	35.0	38.1	53.0	49.8	63.5	66.6	79.1
	2010	41.3	71.8	9.9	58.9	24.5	65.2	36.9	70.8	48.1	74.0	64.0	80.9
Nicaragua	2001	33.2	28.8	9.4	7.1	16.2	13.9	26.1	21.2	34.0	30.8	50.9	44.1
	2005	34.0	36.3	9.4	9.4	14.7	15.9	25.4	28.0	38.7	40.4	53.3	57.3
Panama [b]	2002	...	73.2	...	39.1	...	62.0	...	71.0	...	76.3	...	78.4
	2011	...	80.1	...	41.3	...	67.5	...	75.9	...	86.8	...	90.0
Paraguay	2000	28.1	33.2	2.0	2.6	8.1	9.9	16.3	19.1	32.0	33.5	43.0	54.0
	2011	35.1	40.1	3.9	5.5	17.2	18.8	29.7	32.4	36.1	41.3	50.8	59.3
Peru	2001	27.1	39.3	2.5	11.5	5.9	15.2	15.2	25.6	28.9	41.8	43.3	57.5
	2011	50.4	65.0	12.3	64.7	27.4	59.5	41.6	58.2	54.9	63.6	69.6	73.3
Uruguay (urban areas)	2002	76.8	98.2	41.1	98.1	65.0	97.4	76.9	97.8	85.3	98.1	91.6	99.3
	2011	84.7	98.6	56.4	97.3	76.9	97.9	85.2	98.3	90.8	99.0	95.5	99.5
Venezuela (Bolivarian Republic of) [a]	2002	60.9	...	33.6	...	49.4	...	57.2	...	66.1	...	76.6	...
	2011	72.8	...	45.1	...	60.4	...	69.3	...	75.9	...	85.8	...
Latin America [c]	**2002**	**46.1**	**54.4**	**17.3**	**27.8**	**28.3**	**37.3**	**39.2**	**47.5**	**50.3**	**57.6**	**65.1**	**71.4**
	2011	**55.4**	**66.4**	**24.4**	**44.0**	**37.9**	**53.2**	**49.0**	**61.1**	**59.8**	**69.5**	**73.0**	**79.6**

Source: Economic Commission for Latin America (ECLAC), on the basis of special tabulations of data from household surveys conducted in the respective countries.
[a] Health-care system affiliation could not be determined from the surveys used.
[b] Pension-system affiliation could not be determined from the surveys used.
[c] Simple average for 16 countries. Excludes countries on which no data are available for the two points in time taken as a reference.

Table IV.4

Latin America (18 countries): affiliation to pension and health-care systems among wage earners aged 15 years and over, by labour-market position

(Percentages)

Country	Year	Public sector employees		Private sector employees in a firm with 5 or more workers		Professionals and technicians in microenterprises		Wage earners in microenterprises		Domestic service		Total	
		Pensions	Health care	Pensions	Health care	Pensions	Health care	Pensions	Health care	Pensions	Health care	Pensions	Health care
Argentina (urban areas)	2004	70.0	74.8	67.5	75.5	42.6	71.7	24.9	40.4	6.6	32.2	54.7	65.1
	2011	92.6	95.2	77.2	83.4	53.9	80.4	34.5	50.8	19.5	45.6	68.7	77.7
Bolivia (Plurinacional State of)	2002	68.0	68.2	24.4	29.3	17.7	24.6	2.8	6.1	0.1	5.6	26.3	29.8
	2009	74.6	83.4	32.5	44.1	7.1	23.3	2.8	17.4	1.1	15.5	32.4	44.4
Brazil [a]	2001	87.6	...	72.9	...	33.5	...	58.8	...	29.3	...	65.0	...
	2011	93.6	...	84.0	...	48.0	...	63.0	...	37.1	...	75.9	...
Chile	2000	91.8	97.0	81.5	92.8	64.8	84.5	54.3	85.5	46.8	90.7	77.0	92.4
	2011	86.0	97.1	86.5	96.9	72.7	97.0	60.0	93.9	50.0	97.2	81.7	96.7
Colombia	1999 [b]	84.6	94.9	33.5	46.4	69.3	79.5	...	...	13.0	25.2	40.9	53.2
	2011	97.2	100.0	77.2	95.6	38.3	86.3	14.0	82.3	13.8	88.3	57.2	91.9
Costa Rica [c]	2002	...	99.3	...	88.9	...	84.4	...	58.4	...	68.8	...	83.7
	2011	98.2	99.7	85.3	90.9	67.9	80.2	43.1	66.6	27.5	76.5	74.6	86.9
Dominican Republic	2005	67.4	77.4	47.1	58.1	14.0	27.6	8.7	9.4	...	...	42.5	51.1
	2011	93.7	96.2	73.0	81.7	34.2	75.0	8.4	32.6	...	36.7	63.3	75.4
Ecuador (urban areas)	2002	83.7	88.0	44.4	48.2	32.8	38.6	11.5	12.1	9.6	10.9	42.0	45.0
	2011	95.7	95.9	73.9	74.9	47.6	47.6	21.3	24.0	38.7	46.8	64.7	66.2
El Salvador	1999	91.1	90.3	62.1	62.5	42.2	48.6	8.0	11.2	...	6.3	48.6	50.0
	2010	94.4	94.9	63.6	65.9	40.8	43.2	5.9	8.7	2.8	7.4	46.6	48.9
Guatemala	2002	74.3	82.6	50.9	53.6	21.0	22.7	5.1	6.5	2.1	3.3	35.8	38.5
	2006	81.0	86.2	54.0	60.0	26.5	42.9	3.6	9.7	2.9	8.3	38.5	44.5
Honduras	2006	79.4	62.8	40.4	41.2	55.6	57.1	30.9	31.0	1.7	2.0	38.0	36.0
	2010	81.6	66.0	60.1	61.5	22.3	22.3	1.6	1.7	3.1	3.1	38.8	37.2
Mexico	2002	69.2	85.4	56.6	71.5	26.0	49.2	10.1	17.8	2.0	10.4	41.0	53.8
	2010	...	...	59.3	82.0	36.2	64.1	9.9	52.7	1.5	62.1	41.3	71.8
Nicaragua	2001	70.5	60.6	41.4	36.8	35.2	24.9	6.8	4.8	1.2	2.5	33.2	28.8
	2005	73.4	79.6	45.6	47.6	14.0	14.8	2.3	3.1	0.2	2.3	34.0	36.3
Panama [c]	2002	...	96.6	...	83.0	...	51.7	...	29.5	...	29.5	...	73.2
	2011	...	97.0	...	88.2	...	71.2	...	32.0	...	47.6	...	80.1
Paraguay	2000	81.5	75.3	36.1	44.8	12.4	41.3	4.6	9.1	0.7	7.3	28.1	33.2
	2011	79.9	75.1	42.3	47.9	32.2	54.6	9.1	14.1	0.1	15.0	35.1	40.1
Peru	2001	63.0	82.1	27.1	37.6	46.1	59.6	2.8	12.5	3.0	13.2	27.1	39.3
	2011	83.3	89.0	59.5	68.5	41.9	44.6	14.5	41.9	9.0	51.1	50.4	65.0
Uruguay (urban areas)	2002	99.0	98.9	86.0	98.7	57.3	98.3	42.7	95.5	44.3	98.4	76.8	98.2
	2011	100.0	99.9	91.5	99.1	67.6	96.4	45.2	95.1	62.4	98.0	84.7	98.6
Venezuela (Bolivarian Republic of) [a]	2002	88.1	...	68.3	...	40.5	...	18.2	...	22.2	...	60.9	...
	2011	90.4	...	79.6	...	46.8	...	19.5	...	18.7	...	72.8	...
Latin America [d]	**2002**	80.0	83.2	53.8	61.5	38.2	54.0	18.1	26.9	13.0	27.1	46.1	54.4
	2011	87.8	90.4	65.5	72.8	39.4	59.0	19.7	39.2	18.4	44.3	55.4	66.4

Source: Economic Commission for Latin America (ECLAC), on the basis of special tabulations of data from household surveys conducted in the respective countries.
[a] Health-care system affiliation could not be determined from the surveys used.
[b] Pension-system affiliation could not be determined from the surveys used.
[c] No information on company size was available for 1999. Wage earners in private microenterprises are therefore combined with wage earners in companies employing five or more workers. The "Professionals and technicians in microenterprises" category includes all professionals and technicians employed in the private sector.
[d] Simple average for 15 countries. Excludes countries on which no data are available for the two points in time taken as a reference.

In the 15 countries in which health-care system affiliation among non-wage-earners could be analysed, it is clear that this group lags far behind wage earners. The gap is smallest in Chile, Colombia, Costa Rica and Uruguay. But even though there is an obvious gap in general terms, and with the exception of the countries that are furthest behind, non-wage-earner affiliation has risen in recent years, in particular in Colombia and Peru. For women, the gap in health-care system participation is smaller than for pension systems. A closer look at the socioeconomic distribution of affiliation highlights social protection inequality among non-wage-earners. There are huge differences between the first income quintile and the fifth income quintile in terms of affiliation to both pension and health systems (see table IV.5).

Table IV.5
**Latin America (15 countries): affiliation to pension and health-care systems among wage earners
aged 15 years and over, by sex, around 2002 and 2011**
(Percentages)

Country	Year	Both sexes		Men		Women	
		Pensions	Health care	Pensions	Health care	Pensions	Health care
Argentina (urban areas)	2004	...	46.9	...	42.5	...	55.3
	2011	...	56.1	...	51.6	...	65.0
Bolivia (Plurinacional State of)	2002	1.5	7.9	2.1	6.8	0.8	9.2
	2009	2.1	16.5	3.4	14.3	0.9	18.6
Brazil [a]	2001	17.3	...	20.1	...	12.7	...
	2011	24.3	...	26.1	...	21.2	...
Chile	2000	23.7	75.8	25.4	72.2	19.9	83.7
	2011	26.3	91.4	29.1	89.4	21.6	94.7
Colombia	1999	6.5	13.3	6.9	13.9	5.8	12.2
	2011	10.5	87.1	10.8	84.7	10.0	90.7
Costa Rica [b]	2002	...	64.9	...	60.6	...	73.8
	2011	43.7	78.4	53.3	75.5	24.8	84.0
Dominican Republic	2011	...	37.8	...	34.4	...	47.5
Ecuador (urban areas)	2002	11.1	13.7	12.6	15.4	9.1	11.3
	2011	15.4	20.6	17.1	19.9	13.4	21.5
El Salvador	1999	3.5	11.2	4.6	7.6	2.3	15.2
	2010	2.7	10.3	3.3	6.8	2.1	14.1
Honduras	2006	0.8	0.9	0.8	0.9	0.6	0.8
	2010	0.7	0.9	0.6	0.9	0.8	0.9
Nicaragua	2001	1.9	2.8	1.9	2.3	1.9	3.5
	2005	0.5	2.7	0.5	2.1	0.4	3.7
Panama [b]	2002	...	20.7	...	17.0	...	31.5
	2011	...	22.5	...	19.0	...	30.5
Paraguay	2000	0.3	10.0	0.3	7.4	0.2	14.0
	2011	1.0	14.3	1.1	11.3	1.0	18.4
Peru	2001	2.9	14.2	4.5	13.3	1.2	15.2
	2011	14.0	56.0	21.0	49.8	6.9	62.3
Uruguay (urban areas)	2002	32.3	94.2	32.4	93.0	32.2	96.6
	2011	39.4	94.1	40.8	92.3	37.5	96.5
Latin America [c]	2002	9.2	29.0	10.1	27.2	7.9	32.5
	2011	12.4	42.4	14.0	39.8	10.5	46.2

Source: Economic Commission for Latin America (ECLAC), on the basis of special tabulations of data from household surveys conducted in the respective countries.
[a] Health-care system affiliation could not be determined from the surveys used.
[b] Pension-system affiliation could not be determined from the surveys used.
[c] Simple average for 11 countries (pensions) and 13 countries (health). Excludes countries on which no data are available for the two points in time taken as a reference.

But even among wage earners, whenever affiliation is lower, it is more concentrated by income level (see table IV.3). Gaps by income level are smaller for health-care system affiliation than for pension scheme participation and are, in general, narrowing. In 2011 the access gap between the fifth quintile and the first quintile was a little under 36 percentage points; in 2002 it had been almost 44 percentage points.

Although the proportion of non-affiliation declines as incomes rise, even the top income quintile contains a segment of the population that is not affiliated to any health system. This occurs to a somewhat lesser degree than in the case of pensions and varies considerably between countries. It may be due to certain types of employment contracts or could reflect self-selection among those who decide not to join because —at least at the moment— they are privately insured or because they make out-of-pocket payments. If the social security system has no barriers to entry and acts as private market reinsurance, some people may try to transfer over when they require essential health treatment that is not covered by their insurance policies or their out-of-pocket expenses become too high.

The rate of health-care affiliation among pensioners is high in the 14 countries that were compared, even where total population coverage is lower. With just one exception, health-care system affiliation among pensioners also rose during the period under review.

3. Aspects of pension-system affiliation in the countries

Based on current levels of wage-earner affiliation to pension systems, the countries may be divided into three groups. The first group, in which coverage is the most extensive, comprises Argentina, the Bolivarian Republic of Venezuela, Brazil, Chile, Costa Rica and Uruguay (urban areas), where affiliation ranges from 68% to 85%. In the second group, comprising Colombia, the Dominican Republic, Ecuador (urban areas), El Salvador, Mexico and Peru, between 41% and 65% of wage earners are covered. The lowest levels of coverage are seen in Guatemala, Honduras, Nicaragua, Paraguay and the Plurinational State of Bolivia, where affiliation ranges from 30% to 40% (see table IV.1).

There was a relatively moderate increase of a little over 10 percentage points in wage-earner access to pension systems, to stand at 56.5% of all wage earners (simple average for 16 countries). Increases were especially significant in urban areas of Argentina, in Colombia, in the Dominican Republic, in urban areas of Ecuador and in Peru, ranging from between 14 percentage points and 23 percentage points. El Salvador was the only country to record a decline (two percentage points); the variations were not statistically significant in Honduras, Mexico or Nicaragua.

The marked variation in affiliation levels depending on the labour-market position of wage earners reflects differences in employment quality. Affiliation is widespread among public-sector employees. It averages almost 88% for pension systems and a little over 90% for health systems, and these figures are relatively similar to those recorded in the early 2000s (albeit seven percentage points higher in both cases). Among wage earners employed in the private sector by small, medium-sized or large enterprises, affiliation falls to 66% in the case of pension systems and 73% in the case of health systems, although with some improvement between 2002 and 2011. Even lower levels were recorded among wage earners employed by microenterprises (20% and 39%, respectively), with no significant improvement seen. The gap widens further for domestic workers, most of whom are women. In contrast to health-care coverage, no significant progress has been made in pension scheme affiliation in the least secure employment categories (see table IV.4).

In the group of countries in which the situation of non-wage-earners could be measured, there is clear evidence that women suffer exclusion and are in a worse position. But there is a trend toward broader coverage. The highest levels of affiliation within this segment of the population were found in Brazil, Chile, Costa Rica and Uruguay. Male affiliation rates in Peru increased substantially (see table IV.5).

As may be expected, there are glaring disparities in access to both pension and health systems based on per capita income quintile. In 2011, the gap in wage-earner pension affiliation between the fifth and first income quintiles, as an average for the Latin American countries, was almost 49 percentage points, having widened slightly since 2002 (see table IV.3).

However, the changes reveal that the socioeconomic distribution of pension scheme affiliation has become a little less regressive in several countries, including El Salvador and Mexico. Costa Rica, with Uruguay some way behind, reports the highest percentage of low-income workers affiliated to a pension system. Other countries have also experienced a significant relative expansion in coverage within low-income sectors; this is true of Argentina, Brazil, Chile, the Dominican Republic, Ecuador and Peru. In Ecuador, the increases have been spread more evenly across the quintiles, while in the Plurinational State of Bolivia, the first quintile's share also increased relative to that of the wealthiest quintile. Nevertheless, inequality rose in six countries.

Albeit with wide variations among countries, the top quintile contains individuals not affiliated with any pension system. There is also something of a protection gap in the second, third and fourth quintiles, but it varies considerably by socioeconomic status and in no case is it comparable to the one in the first income quintile.

Pension system affiliation has become less regressive in Argentina, Chile, Colombia, the Dominican Republic, El Salvador, Mexico, Peru and the Plurinational State of Bolivia. In Costa Rica and Ecuador it has risen fairly evenly across the income quintiles, as it has in the Dominican Republic, where the top and bottom quintiles show most progression. In Colombia, Ecuador, Paraguay, Peru and the Plurinational State of Bolivia there have been significant increases in access for the intermediate sectors. Guatemala and Uruguay saw a drop in participation in the bottom income quintile.

Table IV.6
Latin America (15 countries): affiliation to pension and health-care systems among wage earners aged 15 years and over, by per capita income quintile
(Percentages)

| Country | Year | Total | | Per capita income quintile | | | | | | | | | |
| | | | | Quintile I | | Quintile II | | Quintile III | | Quintile IV | | Quintile V | |
		Pensions	Health care	Pensions	Health care	Pensions	Health care	Pensions	Health care	Pensions	Health care	Pensions	Health care
Argentina (urban areas)	2004	...	46.9	...	15.5	...	20.7	...	28.8	...	42.5	...	69.5
	2011	...	56.1	...	21.9	...	30.5	...	41.6	...	55.0	...	75.6
Bolivia (Plurinacional State of)	2002	1.5	7.9	0.2	1.6	0.6	4.0	0.9	7.7	0.8	11.8	6.0	20.1
	2009	2.1	16.5	0.1	7.7	0.3	14.5	1.6	18.4	2.0	22.4	7.9	24.9
Brazil [a]	2001	17.3	...	1.7	...	4.8	...	9.0	...	18.3	...	44.1	...
	2011	24.3	...	5.2	...	10.3	...	18.4	...	27.3	...	49.2	...
Chile	2000	23.7	75.8	4.9	84.7	9.5	78.0	15.2	75.7	23.1	71.8	39.7	75.2
	2011	26.3	91.4	8.6	95.5	14.4	94.6	15.8	93.3	25.5	90.5	39.4	89.1
Colombia	1999	6.5	13.3	1.4	5.0	2.1	6.4	4.0	9.1	6.4	14.4	18.1	31.1
	2011	10.5	87.1	1.0	86.9	2.9	86.4	5.7	86.2	11.6	86.3	30.5	89.8
Costa Rica [b]	2002	...	64.9	...	56.2	...	63.1	...	67.0	...	66.1	...	71.2
	2011	43.7	78.4	36.7	72.5	35.5	74.8	39.1	78.3	44.9	80.1	57.3	84.0
Dominican Republic	2011	...	37.8	...	38.4	...	40.9	...	34.1	...	36.3	...	39.8
Ecuador (urban areas)	2002	11.1	13.7	4.1	4.1	5.8	6.2	8.1	9.1	9.4	10.5	22.6	30.5
	2011	15.4	20.6	6.4	16.4	7.1	14.2	11.9	16.1	13.9	17.4	33.8	36.1
El Salvador	1999	3.5	11.2	0.9	1.4	0.5	3.4	1.5	8.3	2.2	13.3	11.5	27.7
	2010	2.7	10.3	0.0	0.4	0.3	3.4	0.7	6.7	1.6	11.9	9.3	25.3
Honduras	2006	0.8	0.9	0.1	...	0.2	0.2	0.4	0.3	0.5	0.6	3.2	3.7
	2010	0.7	0.9	0.1	0.2	0.2	0.2	0.3	0.3	0.4	0.4	2.9	3.8
Nicaragua	2001	1.9	2.8	1.1	0.5	1.1	1.1	1.8	1.8	1.6	2.6	3.6	6.7
	2005	0.5	2.7	...	0.4	0.3	0.7	0.1	2.1	0.4	3.1	1.6	6.8
Panama [b]	2002	...	20.7	...	6.4	...	15.8	...	25.3	...	29.5	...	41.8
	2011	...	22.5	...	8.5	...	19.2	...	25.9	...	28.2	...	34.6
Paraguay	2000	0.3	10.0	...	1.5	...	2.0	...	4.6	0.1	12.3	1.3	30.4
	2011	1.0	14.3	...	3.7	0.1	6.2	0.3	10.7	0.7	16.0	4.0	35.2
Peru	2001	2.9	14.2	0.3	4.7	0.7	7.1	2.2	13.1	3.6	21.4	10.3	32.6
	2011	14.0	56.0	3.7	74.1	9.9	58.1	14.1	47.8	20.8	45.3	28.2	45.3
Uruguay (urban areas)	2002	32.3	94.2	3.5	94.7	11.0	92.4	21.3	92.6	43.9	92.6	68.2	97.8
	2011	39.4	94.1	5.2	92.3	17.3	92.2	32.8	92.5	50.9	94.2	75.6	97.7
Latin America [c]	2002	9.2	27.5	1.9	23.7	3.6	23.3	6.4	26.2	10.0	28.9	20.8	39.1
	2011	12.4	41.2	3.4	41.7	6.3	38.7	10.1	39.9	14.1	41.3	25.7	47.7

Source: Economic Commission for Latin America (ECLAC), on the basis of special tabulations of data from household surveys conducted in the respective countries.
[a] Health-care system affiliation could not be determined from the surveys used.
[b] Pension-system affiliation could not be determined from the surveys used.
[c] Simple average for 11 countries (pensions) and 13 countries (health). Excludes countries on which no data are available for the two points in time taken as a reference.

4. Access to pensions and pension levels

Persons aged 65 years and over may remain active in the labour market for a number of reasons, such as a need to supplement their income or a quest for self-fulfilment. Not all pensioners, therefore, are economically inactive.

This section discusses pension access within this age bracket and the amounts received. Instead of looking at affiliation within the labour market at the two points in time, this analysis sheds light on the outcomes of this group's prior affiliation. This in turn provides clues as to the inclusive or exclusive nature of the pension systems that have been in place, the employment histories of this group as reflected in the income received during their working lives, whether contributions are compulsory or voluntary (where this option exists) and contribution density.

The disparities across the region are striking. In most of the 16 countries analysed, the proportion of people aged 65 years and older who receive a pension is relatively small, although it varies considerably from country to country. Honduras is at the lower end of the spectrum, whereas this population enjoys the most protection in Argentina, Brazil, Chile, Costa Rica and Uruguay. Panama is in the middle. Distribution is also unequal by income quintile, and this is much sharper in the countries where pensioners are least likely to be covered. At more advanced ages, the percentage of pensioners covered usually rises.

Pension levels reflect factors such as income received during one's working life, primary income concentration, a differing ability to save for a pension, the architecture of the system (how contributory and non-contributory components are combined) and the presence or absence of risk pooling (see tables IV.7 and IV.8).[8] As for the pension received, measured in 2005 dollars, in the poorest quintile this rose most significantly in Brazil, the Dominican Republic, Ecuador and Uruguay but fell in six other countries. The declines seen in the wealthiest quintile in Chile and the Dominican Republic were particularly striking and were perhaps attributable to the exposure to financial risk of individually-funded schemes. Pensions in Chile were also adversely impacted in the second, third and fourth quintiles, a systematic trend not observed in any other country.

5. Determinants of employee pension affiliation: a multivariate analysis

Both as a subject for research and as a reference for public policy, it is useful to identify the determinants of pension system affiliation. This section outlines the impact of a range of explanatory variables, considered together, on the affiliation of workers aged between 15 and 64 years. As will be seen, there are both common patterns and disparities among the countries.[9]

The determinants of worker affiliation were analysed using probit model estimations. The dependent variable indicates whether the worker is affiliated to the pension system or not. Pension fund affiliation is identified[10] in the same way as elsewhere in this chapter. It was established which countries and which years around 2002 and 2011 could be included. In Argentina, the Bolivarian Republic of Venezuela, the Dominican Republic, Guatemala and Mexico, the estimations refer solely to wage earners. The explanatory variables include the worker's personal characteristics (age, sex, educational attainment and civil status), his or her household (size and head) and job (category, branch of activity, full- or part-time work, formal or informal sector and labour income quintile). Where the variables of race and place of residence (urban or rural) were available, they were included as controls. Also taken into account were interactions between educational attainment and sex and between status as head of household and sex.

---

[8] In addition, some countries, such as Chile, have only recently recognized care work in the home as a source of pension entitlement.

[9] This type of analysis has previously been carried out for the region (ECLAC, 2006; Auberbach, Genoni and Pagés, 2007; Da Costa and others, 2011). The estimates herein include more countries, which are analysed separately, and the most recent information is used. The full results of the regression analyses, which are only illustrated here in the figures, are available from ECLAC on request.

[10] The dependent variable is based on questions about pension-system affiliation in all countries, except for in Brazil, Chile, Costa Rica, Honduras, Mexico and Nicaragua, where the question relates to contributions rather than affiliation. Affiliation has been selected as the more generic term.

The estimations were corrected to eliminate the possibility of selection bias.[11] The selection equation included sex, schooling, age and the number of minors in the household (distinguishing between the group aged 0-4 years and the one aged 5-12 years), the interaction between the number of under-4s in the household and the presence of economically inactive household members aged between 15 and 64 years. The variables omitted are those in relation to which the coefficients are interpreted.

The main results are presented via the marginal effects[12] of each variable on the probability of affiliation. In the figures, the lightest colour bars indicate that the coefficients are not statistically significant (that is, the significance level is 99%). In table IV.9, the boxes with statistically significant values are highlighted in pale blue.

Table IV.7
Latin America (16 countries): persons aged 65 and over receiving pensions and pensioners affiliated to health-care systems, by sex, around 2002 and 2011
(Percentages)

Country	Year	Both sexes		Men		Women	
		Pensions	Health care	Pensions	Health care	Pensions	Health care
Argentina (urban areas)	2004	63.8	97.4	69.3	97.5	60.0	97.4
	2011	90.7	98.3	87.2	98.1	93.0	98.4
Bolivia (Plurinacional State of)	2002	13.2	86.1	18.4	87.9	8.9	82.8
	2009	21.3	90.0	27.4	95.2	15.8	81.8
Brazil	2001	85.5	...	89.3	...	82.5	...
	2011	84.7	...	88.0	...	82.1	...
Chile	2000	77.4	98.0	83.5	98.4	72.7	97.7
	2011	84.2	98.5	85.4	98.4	83.4	98.5
Colombia	1999	17.1	...	23.5	...	11.7	...
	2011	24.3	99.8	29.5	99.8	19.9	99.9
Costa Rica	2011	63.6	99.8	72.4	99.7	56.9	99.9
Dominican Republic	2005	14.6	...	20.2	...	9.3	...
	2011	16.0	82.7	22.2	83.5	10.4	81.2
Ecuador (urban areas)	2002	25.0	73.6	30.7	80.4	19.6	63.4
	2011	32.9	95.3	39.2	94.8	27.6	95.9
El Salvador	1999	14.4	77.0	20.0	79.6	10.0	72.9
	2010	16.9	92.5	21.0	93.4	13.7	91.4
Guatemala	2002	11.7	...	15.3	...	8.8	...
	2006	16.6	68.4	21.3	74.3	12.1	58.4
Honduras	2006	5.7	...	7.5	...	4.1	...
Mexico	2002	19.2	...	26.9	...	12.4	...
	2010	26.2	97.2	36.2	96.4	17.8	98.7
Panama	2002	43.0	95.3	50.3	95.1	35.9	95.5
	2011	45.6	99.5	51.9	99.9	40.0	99.0
Paraguay	2000	19.6	76.1	22.6	76.3	17.1	76.0
	2011	15.8	83.8	16.8	89.5	15.0	78.2
Peru	2001	25.6	98.5	33.6	99.0	18.0	97.5
	2011	25.4	97.8	33.5	97.8	18.1	97.9
Uruguay (urban areas)	2002	87.6	99.2	89.6	99.1	86.3	99.3
	2011	85.6	99.7	86.7	99.6	84.8	99.7
Latin America [a]	2002	37.0	89.0	42.4	90.4	32.4	86.9
	2011	41.9	95.0	46.2	96.3	38.1	93.4

Source: Economic Commission for Latin America (ECLAC), on the basis of special tabulations of data from household surveys conducted in the respective countries.
[a] Simple average for 14 countries (pensioners) and 9 countries (affiliated to health-care systems). Excludes countries on which no data are available for the two points taken as a reference.

---

[11] The Heckman correction for selection bias consists in estimating a second equation (called a selection equation) that measures the probability of being in the sample used to estimate the principal equation. In this instance, this concerns the likelihood that an economically active individual will be employed (or a wage earner, in countries where the question on contributions was only addressed to wage earners).

[12] Henceforth, the term "effects" will be used without further explanation, and they will be assumed to be marginal. This reflects the change in the likelihood of pension affiliation stemming from the variable examined.

Table IV.8

Latin America (16 countries): persons aged 65 and over receiving pensions, average monthly pension by sex and per capita income quintile, around 2002 and 2011

(Percentages and 2005 dollars)

| Country | Year | Both sexes | | Men | | Women | | Per capita income quintile | | | | | | | | | |
| | | Proportion of pensioners | Pension amount | Proportion of pensioners | Pension amount | Proportion of pensioners | Pension amount | Quintile I | | Quintile II | | Quintile III | | Quintile IV | | Quintile V | |
								Proportion of pensioners	Pension amount	Proportion of pensioners	Pension amount	Proportion of pensioners	Pension amount	Proportion of pensioners	Pension amount	Proportion of pensioners	Pension amount
Argentina (urban areas)	2004	63.8	202.1	69.3	238.4	60.0	173.5	22.2	93.8	54.5	121.7	70.6	136.0	75.4	187.6	70.8	351.1
	2011	90.7	391.9	87.2	420.3	93.0	374.5	75.8	233.0	93.9	259.1	94.7	322.0	92.5	423.9	85.4	628.9
Bolivia (Plurinacional State of)	2002	13.2	157.0	18.4	170.5	8.9	133.8	...	...	0.2	81.3	5.7	82.6	13.2	124.0	38.5	173.5
	2009	21.3	152.2	27.4	156.5	15.8	145.5	...	...	3.0	71.6	15.9	107.5	25.5	135.6	48.1	174.6
Brazil	2001	85.5	247.7	89.3	282.6	82.5	219.0	45.7	104.6	79.7	108.7	84.6	115.1	90.4	132.3	85.9	502.1
	2011	84.7	329.6	88.0	363.3	82.1	302.1	30.5	167.5	76.1	173.9	78.4	191.3	91.4	201.7	89.2	591.9
Chile	2000	77.4	279.4	83.5	338.2	72.7	227.9	65.3	132.0	77.7	156.3	77.4	176.7	83.5	225.7	73.4	519.8
	2011	84.2	219.3	85.4	254.5	83.4	193.0	68.2	130.5	87.0	145.4	89.1	167.5	86.8	218.8	81.5	397.4
Colombia	1999	17.1	288.1	23.5	313.3	11.7	245.6	0.1	142.7	3.7	151.7	9.6	166.1	19.2	189.4	38.8	355.8
	2011	24.3	382.0	29.5	415.9	19.9	339.8	0.6	134.2	4.3	178.9	12.9	196.4	28.1	230.6	52.1	481.9
Costa Rica	2011	63.6	291.5	72.4	321.1	56.9	262.6	41.4	117.7	64.9	127.0	65.8	158.5	67.4	255.5	73.0	596.3
Dominican Republic	2005	14.6	320.4	20.2	268.6	9.3	426.8	3.7	76.1	12.4	95.9	18.6	106.4	14.1	129.2	29.1	696.7
	2011	16.0	242.9	22.2	249.1	10.4	230.7	5.1	102.3	9.7	111.6	16.4	138.0	18.0	187.3	33.0	380.0
Ecuador (urban areas)	2002	25.0	110.9	30.7	115.2	19.6	104.3	9.6	51.3	15.8	76.6	24.6	99.1	31.3	95.4	40.4	148.9
	2011	32.9	295.9	39.2	328.6	27.6	256.9	5.3	117.0	12.0	153.3	21.0	212.8	36.2	234.0	60.6	356.3
El Salvador	1999	14.4	153.6	20.0	177.5	10.0	116.5	5.3	82.8	6.9	106.6	13.8	109.8	14.7	134.6	29.0	203.3
	2010	16.9	212.7	21.0	229.3	13.7	192.9	1.4	73.7	5.8	102.2	9.7	124.2	17.5	154.8	40.3	264.7
Guatemala	2002	11.7	104.9	15.3	120.4	8.8	83.7	2.9	92.6	3.8	52.2	19.8	52.6	9.3	63.6	16.6	182.5
	2006	16.6	129.6	21.3	142.2	12.1	108.4	1.6	35.8	8.0	44.4	9.0	49.4	17.1	82.6	33.1	176.5
Honduras	2006	5.7	218.5	7.5	202.7	4.1	245.2	1.0	203.6	1.5	73.9	3.0	85.8	5.9	117.6	15.6	290.6
Mexico	2002	19.2	276.1	26.9	298.7	12.4	232.9	3.5	133.3	11.0	135.9	20.9	156.5	23.2	209.3	30.0	439.9
	2010	26.2	314.0	36.2	337.4	17.8	273.6	4.3	144.6	12.8	140.3	22.1	160.3	30.5	193.5	45.7	473.2
Panama	2002	43.0	396.0	50.3	434.2	35.9	344.3	5.4	131.2	20.8	171.3	40.8	238.8	55.2	307.6	68.4	561.9
	2011	45.6	348.7	51.9	387.3	40.0	304.1	7.1	112.6	30.9	160.4	47.0	195.9	62.4	258.1	78.3	556.4
Paraguay	2000	19.6	272.3	22.6	335.0	17.1	203.3	0.9	75.7	3.0	126.0	10.7	142.0	25.6	179.3	39.8	350.9
	2011	15.8	244.5	16.8	335.8	15.0	154.9	1.9	69.3	3.4	120.4	7.9	119.7	19.8	154.8	42.9	318.8
Peru	2001	25.6	167.6	33.6	181.2	18.0	143.1	1.6	78.1	7.3	101.2	17.4	105.3	30.6	136.5	49.1	202.4
	2011	25.4	188.9	33.5	211.6	18.1	151.5	1.3	76.6	10.6	107.4	23.3	129.9	35.7	148.2	47.2	247.2
Uruguay (urban areas)	2002	87.6	293.1	89.6	345.2	86.3	256.5	76.4	125.7	84.9	149.4	86.2	172.8	89.5	229.8	89.0	484.0
	2011	85.6	329.8	86.7	382.6	84.8	294.2	70.6	149.4	84.0	171.4	87.6	208.3	87.6	285.1	86.0	581.9
Latin America[a]	2002	37.0	233.5	42.4	258.5	32.4	207.9	18.7	101.5	27.3	116.8	35.8	132.8	41.1	167.5	49.9	369.5
	2011	41.9	270.1	46.2	301.0	38.1	237.3	21.0	119.0	31.5	138.6	38.2	165.9	46.3	207.8	58.8	402.1

Source: Economic Commission for Latin America (ECLAC), on the basis of special tabulations of data from household surveys conducted in the respective countries.
[a] Simple average for 14 countries. Excludes countries on which no data are available for the two points in time taken as a reference.

Table IV.9
Latin America (17 countries): marginal effects of branch of activity on the probability of affiliation to pension systems, 2011 [a]

	Agriculture	Mining	Electricity	Construction	Commerce	Transport	Finance	Services
Argentina	-0.052	0.128	0.061	-0.116	-0.001	-0.044	0.036	0.022
Bolivia (Plurinacional State of)	-0.082	0.057	0.105	-0.092	-0.015	-0.025	-0.028	-0.004
Brazil	-0.095	-0.015	0.050	-0.146	-0.039	-0.033	-0.004	-0.082
Chile	0.017	-0.009	-0.041	-0.042	-0.022	0.081	0.047	-0.032
Colombia	-0.042	0.032	0.135	-0.054	-0.027	0.032	0.089	0.010
Costa Rica	-0.034	-0.054	0.166	-0.131	0.014	-0.019	0.020	-0.032
Dominican Republic	-0.055	-0.123	-0.011	-0.138	-0.070	-0.055	-0.025	-0.082
Ecuador	-0.055	0.087	0.150	-0.170	-0.018	-0.026	0.031	-0.016
El Salvador	-0.145	-0.145	0.002	-0.099	-0.041	-0.084	0.007	-0.058
Guatemala	-0.075	0.093	-0.103	-0.176	-0.083	-0.049	-0.087	-0.134
Honduras	-0.063	-0.138	-0.014	-0.111	-0.037	-0.076	-0.040	-0.082
Mexico	-0.221	0.036	-0.007	-0.196	-0.038	-0.134	-0.037	-0.092
Nicaragua	-0.138	-0.147	-0.026	-0.122	-0.066	-0.135	-0.048	-0.064
Paraguay	-0.062	0.003	-0.141	-0.035	-0.072	-0.014	-0.053	...
Peru	0.001	0.060	-0.136	0.027	-0.005	0.034	0.063	-0.021
Uruguay	0.011	0.010	0.107	-0.033	-0.018	0.056	0.019	-0.035
Venezuela (Bolivarian Republic of)	-0.153	0.020	-0.028	-0.196	-0.027	-0.134	0.010	-0.083

Source: Economic Commission for Latin America (ECLAC), on the basis of special tabulations of data from household surveys conducted in the respective countries.
[a] The variable for industry was omitted. The coefficients that were statistically significant at the 99% confidence level (p<0.01) are marked in pale blue.

In general terms, the main determinants relate to the nature of the job, rather than personal or household characteristics. The variables associated with the kind of job present a clear pattern across the region and carry greater weight than personal characteristics.

In all countries, working in the informal sector —understood to be a low-productivity sector[13]— has a negative and significant effect, which is greater in the Bolivarian Republic of Venezuela, the Dominican Republic and Guatemala (see figure IV.2). Honduras (2002) is the exception to the rule, since the effect is positive and significant, although of very small magnitude.

Figure IV.2
Latin America (17 countries): marginal effect of informal work on the probability of affiliation to pension systems, around 2002 and 2011 [a]
(Probabilities)

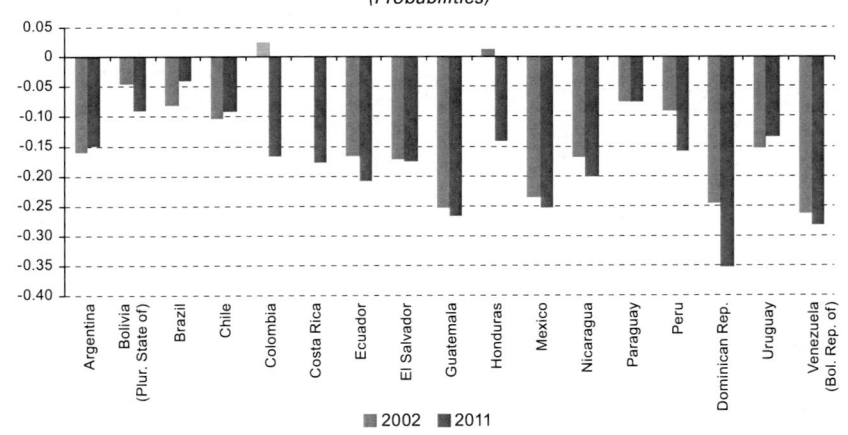

■ 2002 ■ 2011

Source: Economic Commission for Latin America (ECLAC), on the basis of special tabulations of data from household surveys conducted in the respective countries.
[a] The coefficients not statistically significant at the 99% confidence level (p≥0.01) are shown in paler colours.

---

[13] In an effort to make it a proxy for the low-productivity sector, the informal sector in this instance includes domestic service, wage earners working in private microenterprises (who are neither professionals nor technicians, by job category), and non-professional own-account agricultural, industrial and construction workers.

A clear pattern also emerges with respect to working hours: in most countries, someone who works part time (defined as less than 30 hours a week) is less likely to be affiliated (see figure IV.3).

Figure IV.3
**Latin America (17 countries): marginal effect of part-time work on the probability
of affiliation to pension systems, around 2002 and 2011** [a]
(Probabilities)

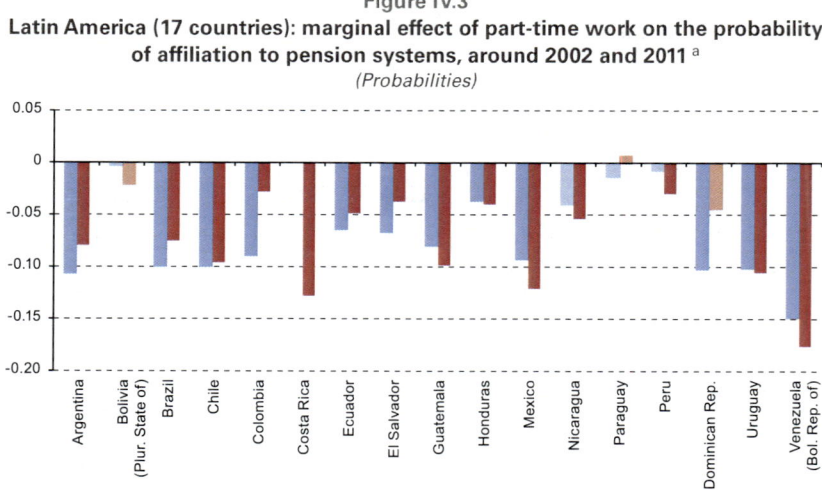

Source: Economic Commission for Latin America (ECLAC), on the basis of special tabulations of data from household surveys conducted in the respective countries.
[a] The coefficients not statistically significant at the 99% confidence level (p≥0.01) are shown in paler colours.

There are common patterns, too, relating to job category (see figure IV.4). In every country, with the exception of Chile, public sector wage earners are more likely to be affiliated than private sector wage earners (the omitted category). Being an employer, and above all an own-account worker, has negative effects, with particularly high coefficients in Chile and Brazil. The effect of domestic service is significant and negative in most countries, apart from in the Bolivarian Republic of Venezuela and Uruguay.[14]

Figure IV.4
**Latin America (17 countries): marginal effect of job category on the probability
of affiliation to pension systems, 2011**
(Probabilities)

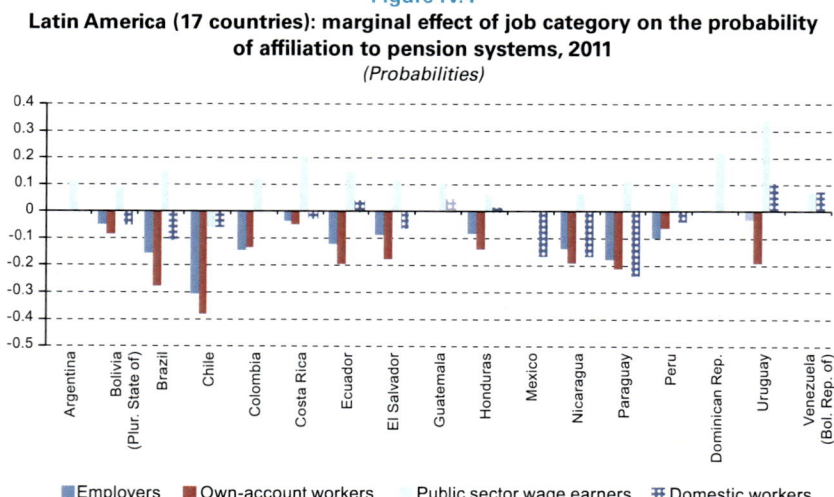

Source: Economic Commission for Latin America (ECLAC), on the basis of special tabulations of data from household surveys conducted in the respective countries.

---

[14] The negative effect of public sector wage employment in Chile is probably attributable to the fact that workers hired by the public sector who do not make contributions owing to special contracts (*contratos por honorarios*) are included in this category in the household survey. In Uruguay, following the enactment of specific regulations (Act 18065 of November 2006 and a regulatory decree of June 2007), domestic workers are entitled to all basic social security benefits. This represents significant progress, historically speaking, for the country, and it is also noteworthy at the regional level (Amarante and Espino, 2008).

As was to be expected, as wages rise, so does the probability of affiliation. The first quintile was used as the omitted category (see figure IV.5). With the exception of the Plurinational State of Bolivia, income is significant in the intermediate income bands in El Salvador, in the upper income bands in Honduras and in the lower bands in Paraguay and Peru. In Colombia, El Salvador and Honduras, the probability of affiliation is lower in the second income quintile. The largest and most significant gaps between the highest and lowest income quintiles in terms of the probability of affiliation are found in Argentina, the Bolivarian Republic of Venezuela, Brazil, Guatemala and Mexico.

Figure IV.5

Latin America (17 countries): marginal effect of labour income quintile on the probability of affiliation to pension systems, 2011 [a]

(Probabilities)

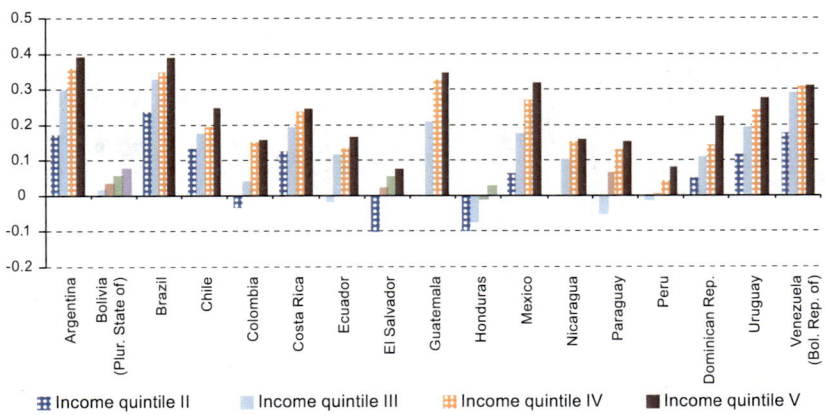

Source: Economic Commission for Latin America (ECLAC), on the basis of special tabulations of data from household surveys conducted in the respective countries.
[a] The coefficients not statistically significant at the 99% confidence level (p≥0.01) are shown in paler colours.

The effects of branch of activity are highly consistent between countries. Table IV.9 presents these marginal effects: the gray boxes indicate the significant cases (99%). The manufacturing industry was used as the omitted category. Variables corresponding to employment in the construction, commerce and agriculture sectors present significant, negative effects in most countries and their coefficients are relatively high: these workers are significantly less likely to be affiliated than industrial workers. In several Central American countries, employment in the services sector also shows negative effects. The effects of working in the transport and the financial sectors are significant in some countries, but they are sometimes negative and sometimes positive; there is no common pattern across countries.

As to the personal characteristics of workers, no clear pattern of differences between men and women was found (see figure IV.6). The probability that women would be affiliated was significant and positive in six countries in 2011 (Brazil, Chile, Costa Rica, Guatemala, Honduras and Uruguay). In Peru, meanwhile, they were significantly less likely to be affiliated.

Figure IV.6

Latin America (17 countries): marginal effect of sex on the probability of affiliation to pension systems, around 2002 and 2011 [a]

(Probabilities)

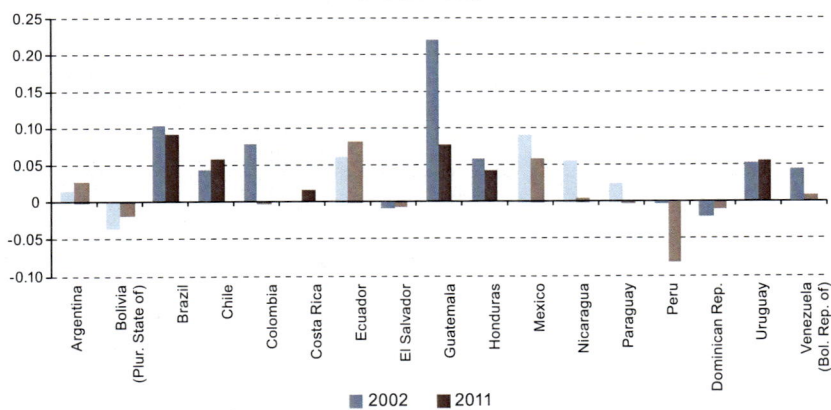

Source: Economic Commission for Latin America (ECLAC), on the basis of special tabulations of data from household surveys conducted in the respective countries.
[a] Woman=1. The coefficients not statistically significant at the 99% confidence level (p≥0.01) are shown in paler colours.

In almost all countries, the likelihood of affiliation rises with age. Figure IV.7 illustrates the effect in each age group compared with the oldest group of workers (aged 45 to 64). The exceptions are Chile, the Dominican Republic and Honduras, where age group is not significant. The likelihood of affiliation is considerably lower in the youngest age group in almost every country, but particularly so in Colombia, Ecuador and Peru. In general, middle-aged workers (aged between 30 and 44 years) are also less likely to be affiliated than older workers. This variable is not significant in the Bolivarian Republic of Venezuela, Guatemala, Mexico, Nicaragua and Paraguay, where the two oldest age groups present similar levels of affiliation.

Figure IV.7

Latin America (17 countries): marginal effect of age group on the probability of affiliation to pension systems, 2011 [a]

(Probabilities)

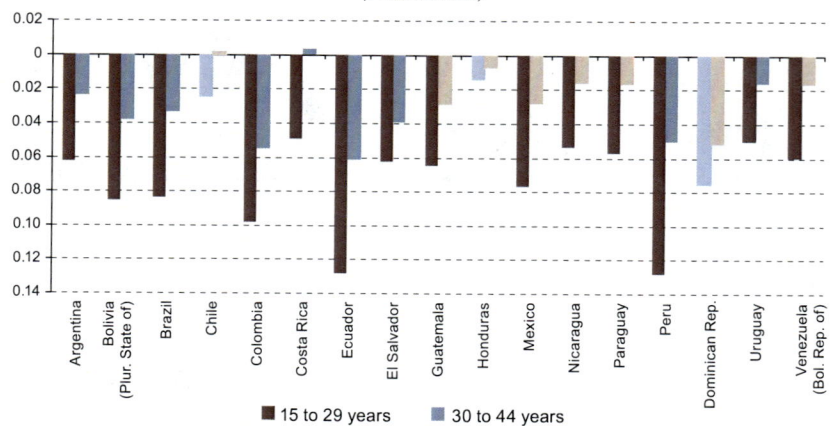

Source: Economic Commission for Latin America (ECLAC), on the basis of special tabulations of data from household surveys conducted in the respective countries.
[a] The coefficients not statistically significant at the 99% confidence level (p≥0.01) are shown in paler colours.

Education level is clearly associated with the likelihood of affiliation in all the countries. Figure IV.8 shows the negative effect for workers with the lowest levels of education (who have not completed primary school or have had no schooling at all), especially in Colombia, Costa Rica, Ecuador, Peru and Uruguay. The disparity is not so stark in Chile, the Dominican Republic, Guatemala and Paraguay. When education level is combined with the variable of sex, it has a negative and significant effect in Brazil in the three top tiers of educational attainment; that is, women at these education levels are at a disadvantage compared with men. This is not the case at the lowest level. In Colombia, Peru and Uruguay, however, the opposite is true: the interaction has a negative effect regarding women in the top tiers of educational attainment.

Figure IV.8

Latin America (17 countries): marginal effect of educational attainment on the probability of affiliation to pension systems, 2011 [a]

(Probabilities)

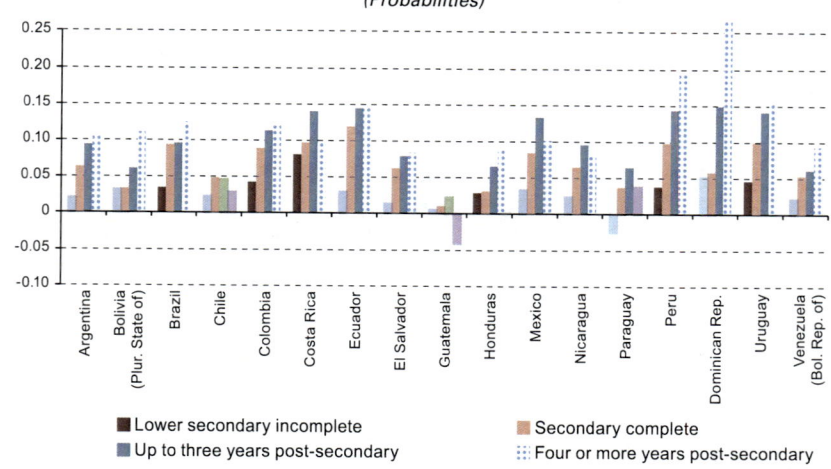

Source: Economic Commission for Latin America (ECLAC), on the basis of special tabulations of data from household surveys conducted in the respective countries.
[a] The coefficients not statistically significant at the 99% confidence level (p≥0.01) are shown in paler colours.

The variables of race and place of residence (urban or rural) were included as regressors where they were available. The effects of race, when significant, were negligible. Workers in urban areas are, generally speaking, more likely to be affiliated to the pension system. There is also a distinction between the married and the unmarried: when this variable is significant, it indicates a greater likelihood for married individuals to be affiliated. In terms of the variables relating to the household, in many cases size is negatively and significantly associated with the likelihood of affiliation to a pension system. In addition, being the head of the household corresponds, in most countries, to a greater likelihood of contribution (figure IV.9). However, the interaction of head of household status with sex tends to show a significant negative effect for women.

Figure IV.9
Latin America (17 countries): marginal effect of being head of household on probability of affiliation to pension systems, around 2002 and 2011 [a]
(Probabilities)

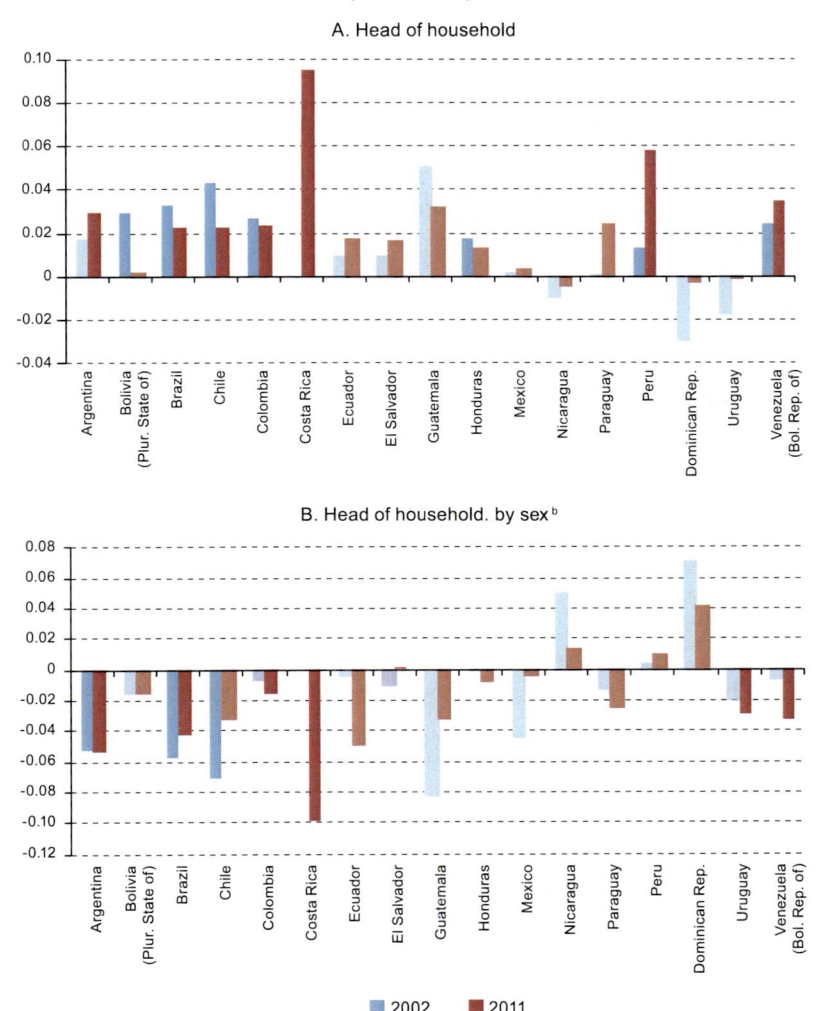

A. Head of household

B. Head of household. by sex [b]

■ 2002   ■ 2011

Source: Economic Commission for Latin America (ECLAC), on the basis of special tabulations of data from household surveys conducted in the respective countries.
[a] The coefficients not statistically significant at the 99% confidence level (p≥0.01) are shown in paler colours.
[b] Woman=1.

Bibliography

Amarante, V. and A. Espino (2008), "Situación del servicio doméstico en Uruguay", *Uruguay: ampliando las oportunidades laborales para las mujeres (60-83)*, Montevideo, National Women's Institute (INAMU)/World Bank.

Arrow, Kenneth (1963), "Uncertainty and the welfare economics of medical care", *The American Economic Review*, vol. LIII, No. 5, December.

___ (2000) "Insurance, risk and resource allocation", *Foundations of Insurance Economics. Readings in Economics and Finance*, G. Dionne and S. E. Harrington (comps.), Boston, Kluwer Academic Publishers.

Auerbach, Paula, María Eugenia Genoni and Carmen Pagés (2007), "Social security coverage and the labor market in developing countries", *IZA Discussion Papers*, Bonn, Forschungsinstitut zur Zukunft der Arbeit.

Barr, Nicholas (2001), *Economic Theory and the Welfare State. Volume 1: Theory; Volume 2: Income Transfers; Volume 3: Benefits in Kind,* Cheltenham, The International Library of Critical Writings in Economics, Edward Elgar Publishing.

Barr, Nicholas and Peter Diamond (2008), *Reforming Pensions. Principles and Policy Choices*, New York, Oxford University Press.

Bonoli, Giuliano and David Natali (2012), *The Politics of the New Welfare State*, New York, Oxford University Press.

Bosch Mariano, Ángel Melguizo and Carmen Pagés (2013), *Mejores pensiones, mejores trabajos. Hacia la cobertura universal en América Latina y el Caribe*, Washington, D.C., Inter-American Development Bank (IDB).

Brittan, Samuel (2001), "Basic income and the welfare State", *Economic Theory and the Welfare State. Volume 2: Income Transfers,* Nicholas Barr, The International Library of Critical Writings in Economics, Cheltenham, Edward Elgar Publishing.

Carrera, Fernando, María Castro and Ana Sojo (2010), "Progresar hacia la equidad: sinopsis de algunos retos del financiamiento de la salud y las pensiones en Guatemala, Honduras y Nicaragua", *Envejecimiento en América Latina. Sistemas de pensiones y protección social integral,* Antonio Prado and Ana Sojo (eds.), Libros de la CEPAL, No. 110 (LC/G.2475-P), Santiago, Chile, Economic Commission for Latin America and the Caribbean (ECLAC), November. United Nations publication, Sales No. S.10.II.G.71.

Cichon, Michael, Christina Behrendt and Verónica Wodsak (2011), "La iniciativa del piso de protección social de las Naciones Unidas. Cambiando la tendencia en la Conferencia de la OIT de 2011", *Análisis de políticas internacionales*, Friedrich Ebert Stiftung.

Da Costa, Rita and others (2011), *The Economy of the Possible: Pensions and Informality in Latin America*, Paris, Organisation for Economic Cooperation and Development (OECD), January.

ECLAC (Economic Commission for Latin America and the Caribbean) (2012), *Social Panorama of Latin America 2012* (LC/G.2557-P), Santiago, Chile. United Nations publication, Sales No. E.13.II.G.6.

___ (2010), *Time for equality: closing gaps, opening trails* (LC/G.2432(SES.33/3)), Santiago, Chile.

___ (2007), *Social Cohesion: Inclusion and a Sense of Belonging in Latin America and the Caribbean* (LC/G.2335), Santiago, Chile.

___ (2006), *Shaping the Future of Social Protection: Access, Financing and Solidarity* (LC/G.2294(SES.31/3)), Santiago, Chile.

___ (2000), *Equity, Development and Citizenship* (LC/G.2071/Rev.1-P/E), Santiago, Chile.

Ehrlich, I. and G. Becker (2000), "Market insurance, self-insurance, and self-protection", *Foundations of Insurance Economics. Readings in Economics and Finance*, G. Dionne and S.E. Harrington (comps.), Boston, Kluwer Academic Publisher.

Falkingham, Jane and John Hills (2001), "Redistribution between people or across the life cycle", *Economic Theory and the Welfare State. Volume 2: Income Transfers,* Nicholas Barr, The International Library of Critical Writings in Economics, Cheltenham, Edward Elgar Publishing.

Filgueira, Fernando and others (2006), "Universalismo básico: una nueva política social para América Latina", *Universalismo básico: una alternativa posible y necesaria para mejorar las condiciones de vida*, Carlos Gerardo Molina (ed.), Mexico City, Inter-American Development Bank (IDB)/Editorial Planeta.

General Conference of the International Labour Organization (2012), "Text of the recommendation concerning national floors of social protection" [online] http://www.ilo.org/wcmsp5/groups/public/---ed_norm/---relconf/documents/meetingdocument/wcms_183326.pdf.

Gómez Sabaini, Juan Carlos and Dalmiro Morán (2013), "Política tributaria en América Latina: agenda para una segunda generación de reformas", *Macroeconomía del Desarrollo series*, No. 133 (LC/L.3632), Santiago, Chile, Economic Commission for Latin America and the Caribbean (ECLAC).

Gutiérrez Sourdis, Catalina, Olga Lucía Acosta Navarro and Eduardo Andrés Alfonso Sierra (2012), "Financiación de la seguridad social en salud: fuentes de recursos y su administración. Problemas y alternativas", *La salud en Colombia: logros, retos y recomendaciones*, Óscar Bernal and Catalina Gutiérrez (comps.), Bogota, Universidad de los Andes, Ediciones Uniandes.

Hemerijck, Anton (2013), *Changing Welfare States*, London, Oxford University Press.

Holzmann, Robert, Edward Palmer and Andras Uthoff (2008), *Fortalecer los sistemas de pensiones latinoamericanos*, Bogota, Economic Commission for Latin America and the Caribbean (ECLAC)/Mayol.

ILO (International Labour Organization) (2008), "Can low-income countries afford basic social security?", *Social Security Policy Briefings Paper,* No. 3, Geneva.

Kutzin, Joseph (2013), "Health financing for universal coverage and health system performance: concepts and implications for policy", *Bulletin of the World Health Organization*, No. 91.

(2008), "Health financing policy: a guide for decision-makers", *Health Financing Policy Paper*, Division of Country Health Systems, WHO Regional Office for Europe.

Levy, Santiago (2012), "Seguridad social universal: un camino para México", *NEXOS en línea* [online] http://www.nexos.com.mx/?P=leerarticulo&Article=2103001 [date of reference: 24 September 2013].

Ministry of Health of Colombia (2013), "Proyecto de Ley por el cual se redefine el Sistema General de Seguridad Social en Salud y se dictan otras disposiciones", Bogota.

Palier, Bruno (ed.) (2010), *A Long Goodbye to Bismarck? The Politics of Welfare Reform in Continental Europe*, Amsterdam, Amsterdam University Press.

Porter, Dorothy (1999), *Health, Civilization and the State*, London, Routledge.

Rashid, Mansoora (2012), "La protección social y el empleo en América Latina y el Caribe", presentation at the meeting of the Joint Working Group of the Permanent Council and the Inter-American Council for Integral Development on the Draft Plan of Action of the Social Charter of the Americas, Washington D.C., Organization of American States (OAS), October.

Rezk, Ernesto (2006), "Desafíos de la viabilidad financiera", *Universalismo básico: una alternativa posible y necesaria para mejorar las condiciones de vida*, Carlos Gerardo Molina (ed.), Mexico City, Inter-American Development Bank (IDB)/Editorial Planeta.

Ribe, Helena, David A. Robalino and Ian Walker (2012), *From Right to Reality. Incentives, Labor Markets, and the Challenge of Universal Social Protection in Latin America and the Caribbean*, Latin America Development Forum Series, Washington, D.C., World Bank.

___ (2010), *Achieving Effective Social Protection for all in Latin America and the Caribbean. From Right to Reality*, Latin America Development Forum Series, Washington, D.C., World Bank.

Scheil-Adlung, Xenia (2013), "Health protection. More than financial protection", *Scaling Up Affordable Health Insurance. Staying the Course,* Alexander S. Preker and others (eds.), Washington, D.C., World Bank.

Schmidt, Vivien (2013), "Does discourse matter in the politics of building social pacts on social protection? International experiences", *Social Policy series,* No. 178 (LC/L.3649), Santiago, Chile, Economic Commission for Latin America and the Caribbean (ECLAC).

Schmidt, Vivien and Mark Thatcher (eds.) (2013), *Resilient Liberalism: European Political Economy through Boom and Bust*, Cambridge, Cambridge University Press.

Schwarzer, Helmut (2013), "El piso de protección social", presentation at the seminar "Formación e intercambio sobre la situación social, económica y de derechos de los trabajadores en la economía informal", organized by the Bureau for Workers' Activities (ACTRAV) of the International Labour International Labour Organization (ILO), Lima, August.

Social Protection Floor Advisory Group (2011), *Social Protection Floor for a Fair and Inclusive Globalization,* M. Bachelet (coord.), Geneva, International Labour Organization (ILO)/World Health Organization (WHO).

Sojo, Ana (2013), "La propuesta del piso de protección social y la extensión de la cobertura en la región, vista desde la CEPAL", presentation at the seminar "Formación e intercambio sobre la situación social, económica y de derechos de los trabajadores en la economía informal", organized by the Bureau for Workers' Activities (ACTRAV) of the International Labour International Labour Organization (ILO), Lima, August.

___ (2012), "El piso de protección social: una perspectiva sobre sus potenciales lecturas en la región", presentation at the workshop "Seguridad social para todos: el piso de protección social", organized by the International Labour Organization (ILO) and the Pan America Health Organization (PAHO), Lima, August.

___ (2007), "Evolution of the link between selective anti-poverty policies and social sectors policies", *CEPAL Review,* No. 91 (LC/G.2333-P/E), Santiago, Chile, Economic Commission for Latin America and the Caribbean (ECLAC).

___ (2003), "Social vulnerability, insurance and risk diversification in Latin America and the Caribbean", *CEPAL Review*, No. 80 (LC/G.2204-P), Santiago, Chile, Economic Commission for Latin America and the Caribbean (ECLAC), August.

___ (1990), "Nature and selectiveness of social policy", *CEPAL Review*, No. 41, Santiago, Chile, Economic Commission for Latin America and the Caribbean (ECLAC).

Tokman, Víctor (2006), "Empleo y protección: una vinculación necesaria", *Universalismo básico: una alternativa posible y necesaria para mejorar las condiciones de vida*, Carlos Gerardo Molina, (ed.), Mexico City, Inter-American Development Bank (IDB)/Editorial Planeta.

WHO (World Health Organization) (2010), *World Health Report 2010*, Geneva.

Recent trends in social spending as an element of public spending and household spending on health

The first section of this chapter looks at traditional measures of social spending that show how it ranks within total public spending in the framework of the economic cycle and the way it is distributed among the different sectors. The other sections look in greater detail at the changes in public spending on health over time, patterns in out-of-pocket household expenditure on health and projections of the health expenditure needs arising from population ageing in the region.

A. Recent and long-term trends in social public spending

Since 2010, several countries have embarked on fiscal reforms to consolidate their public finances on both the revenue and the spending side because public spending increases had triggered public account deficits in some of them. In 2010, spending continued to expand, with a greater rise in social public spending and, in several cases, a decline in non-social public spending. Since 2011, spending in the region has expanded more slowly than economic growth; the share of this increase going to non-social public spending has risen.

1. Recent trends in social spending

At the regional level the uptrend in social spending since the international financial crisis has continued. This real increase in the resources available for financing social services and transfers to households was reflected in the priority accorded to social spending at the macroeconomic level: in 1992-1993, social spending stood at 12.5% of GDP, and it rose steadily over the subsequent bienniums to reach 17.4% in 2006-2007, 18.8% in 2008-2009 and 19.2% in 2010-2011 (see figure V.1). In 2011 Latin America and the Caribbean (21 countries) allocated at least US$ 640 billion to social spending, and a further increase in those resources was estimated for 2012.

Figure V.1
Latin America and the Caribbean (21 countries): social public spending and its share in total public spending, 1992-1993 to 2010-2011 [a]
(Percentages of GDP and of total public spending)

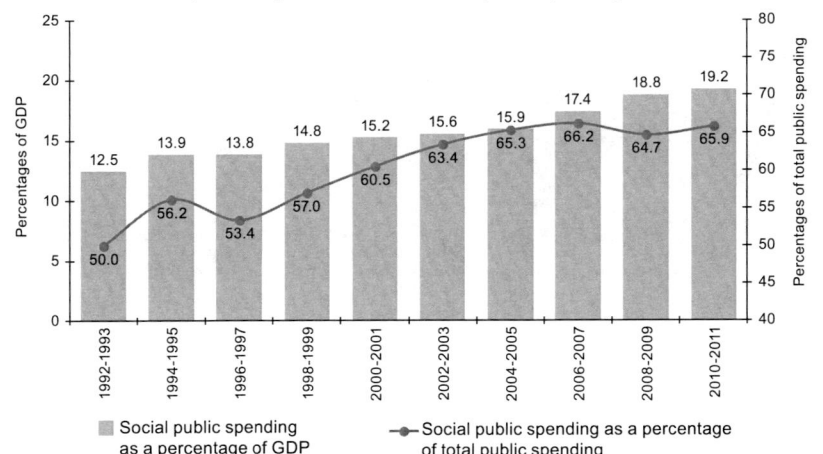

Social public spending as a percentage of GDP

Social public spending as a percentage of total public spending

Source: Economic Commission for Latin America and the Caribbean (ECLAC), social expenditure database.
[a] Weighted average for the countries.

Despite that trend, the greatest rise in social spending was in 2009 (2008 had seen a greater increase in public spending in the economic sectors). After that, it began losing relative share in GDP, which grew faster starting in 2010. Since 2011 the fiscal priority of social spending (that is, its share in total public spending) has been falling as well, while non-social spending posted larger increases.

Before the mid-2000s, public social spending tended to be highly procyclical. However, in the second half of the decade a number of countries launched systematic efforts to strengthen their social programmes, especially those designed to combat poverty. Relatively widespread efforts were also made to achieve universal primary education and to significantly expand secondary education coverage, whether public or mixed-modality. In some countries, there has also been a push for universal access to the public health-care system.

The changing pattern of social spending in the region in the second half of the decade is due also to measures implemented to cope with various external shocks: rising food and fuel prices in 2008; the surge in import and export commodity prices starting in 2003; the global financial crisis, which hit hardest towards the end of 2008 and in 2009; and, more recently, the international climate of uncertainty and the global economic slowdown owing to the slow recovery in the United States and the persistent difficulties in several European Union countries.

These three developments shaped fiscal and social policy to varying degrees. In addition to strengthening some major social programmes (to combat poverty and strengthen the social safety net, primarily its solidarity-based or non-contributory pillar), measures were adopted to redirect spending (and taxes) to offset the regressive effects of rising commodity prices, mainly in 2007 and 2008. Subsequently, once the financial crisis had started, governments adopted different measures to stabilize domestic demand, increasing non-social public spending (especially through investment in infrastructure) and, above all, social spending, which included setting up employment programmes, promoting production (loans to microenterprises) and launching housing programmes. In some countries, setbacks in drafting and enacting investment project legislation, along with implementation capacity issues, led to delays in the implementation of investments, while more rapid responses were seen in the area of social spending.

At the same time, the fiscal priority accorded to social spending, as a percentage of total public spending, has been climbing, from 50% in 1992-1993 to 60.5% in 2000-2001 and 65.9% in 2010-2011 (see figure V.1). Some increases in the fiscal priority accorded to social spending are attributable, however, to contractions in non-social public spending and, therefore, to relative reductions in total public spending, mainly between 1999 and 2004 (see figure V.2).

Figure V.2
**Latin America and the Caribbean (21 countries): total public spending
and biennial variation rates, 1992-1993 to 2010-2011** [a]
(Percentages of GDP and percentage variation)

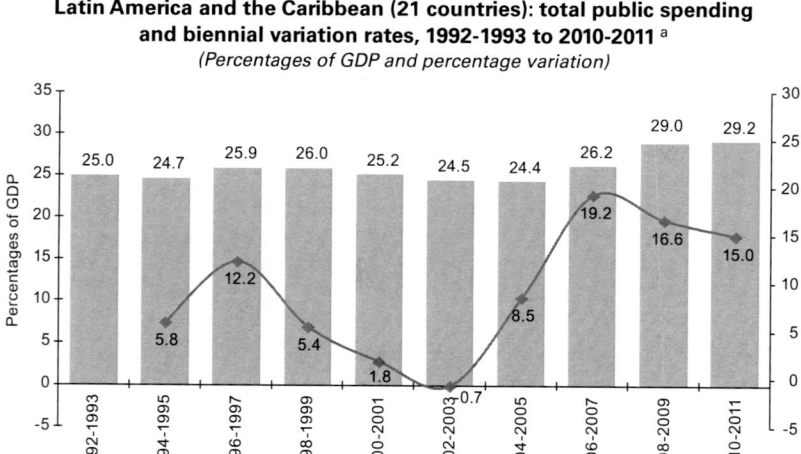

■ Total public spending as a percentage of GDP —◆— Percentage variation in public spending

Source: Economic Commission for Latin America and the Caribbean (ECLAC), social expenditure database.
[a] Weighted average for the countries. The figures for total public spending are official figures generally based on a functional classification of public spending and may not coincide with those obtained using an economic classification.

Since 2010, several countries have embarked on fiscal reforms, on both the revenue side and the spending side, to consolidate their public finances, as several years (2003-2008) of primary surpluses and falling public debt were, in some of them, followed by public account deficits triggered by higher public spending. Although the figures for 2010 show a continued countercyclical expansion of spending, this was due to faster growth of social public spending along with, in some cases, a decline in non-social public spending. Starting in 2011, spending expanded at a slower pace than the regional economy and non-social public spending accounted for much of that increase.

Already in 2011 various countries had reined in their social spending in absolute terms: Chile, Colombia, Cuba, Honduras, Peru and the Plurinational State of Bolivia (by a simple average of 5.6% compared with the level recorded in 2010). However, 2012 brought an increase in social spending in all of the countries with data available for that year: Chile, Colombia, Costa Rica, Ecuador, Guatemala, Panama, Peru and the Plurinational State of Bolivia. Only Guatemala recorded a fall in total public spending in 2012, with social public spending thus accorded a higher fiscal priority at the central government level, up from 61% to 63.5% of total public spending.

2. Long-term trends in social spending

The region's countries differ a great deal in terms of the amount of resources they can channel towards the social sectors and in terms of the macroeconomic effort represented by the social public budget.

Of course, the capacity to assign greater macroeconomic priority to social spending depends on a host of economic, political and social variables. One of the determining variables is fiscal revenue, which places a limit on the overall budget. Notwithstanding the rise in social expenditure as a percentage of GDP in the region from 12.5% in 1992-1993 to 19.2% in 2010-2011, the initial and current levels of this indicator vary considerably between the countries. In 1992-1993, countries such as Colombia, the Dominican Republic, Ecuador, El Salvador, Guatemala, Honduras, Mexico,[1] and Paraguay allocated less than 7% of GDP to the social sectors; by contrast, Argentina, Brazil, Costa Rica, Cuba, Panama and Uruguay allocated 15% or more.

Except during certain periods, all the countries have made an effort to increase the fiscal and macroeconomic priority of social expenditure, often by boosting social spending as a percentage of GDP (the regional weighted average increase was nearly 6.8 percentage points of GDP between 1992-1993 and 2010-2011). At the end of the period under review, the macroeconomic priority of social spending had increased significantly in almost all countries. In 2010-2011, social spending accounted for less than 10% of GDP in only the Dominican Republic, Ecuador and Guatemala. By contrast, Chile and the Bolivarian Republic of Venezuela joined the group of countries that had been allocating more than 15% of GDP to social spending since the early 1990s (see figure V.3).

Despite persistent differences in the macroeconomic priority of social spending, a few countries have made a notable effort to increase the percentage allocated to such spending. Measured in relation to GDP, Argentina increased the share of social spending by nearly 8 percentage points between 1992 and 2009; Costa Rica by 7.9 percentage points between 1992 and 2011; Cuba by 12 percentage points between 1997 and 2011; El Salvador by 10 percentage points between 1993 and 2009; Paraguay by 8.2 percentage points between 1990 and 2010; and the Bolivarian Republic of Venezuela by 6.2 percentage points over the same period.

It should be borne in mind that social spending expressed as a percentage of GDP masks the large variation in terms of the amount of resources actually allocated to the social sectors, which depends largely on each country's level of economic development (see figure V.4). In 1992-1993, annual per capita social spending in the region averaged US$ 518 at constant 2005 prices; almost 20 years later it had doubled to US$ 1,087 in 2010-2011. However, in Ecuador, Guatemala, Honduras, Nicaragua, Paraguay and the Plurinational State of Bolivia, annual per capita spending is still less than US$ 300, while in Argentina, Bolivarian Republic of Venezuela, Brazil, Chile, Costa Rica, Cuba, Panama, Trinidad and Tobago and Uruguay, it exceeded US$ 1,000 and in some cases was close to or more than US$ 2,000.

---

[1] Mexico is a federal country; the figures are for national (federal) government spending and do not include expenditure at the state or municipal level. This could lead to significant understatement of social expenditure.

Figure V.3

Latin America and the Caribbean (21 countries): social public spending as a proportion of GDP, 1992-1993 to 2010-2011 [a]

(Percentages)

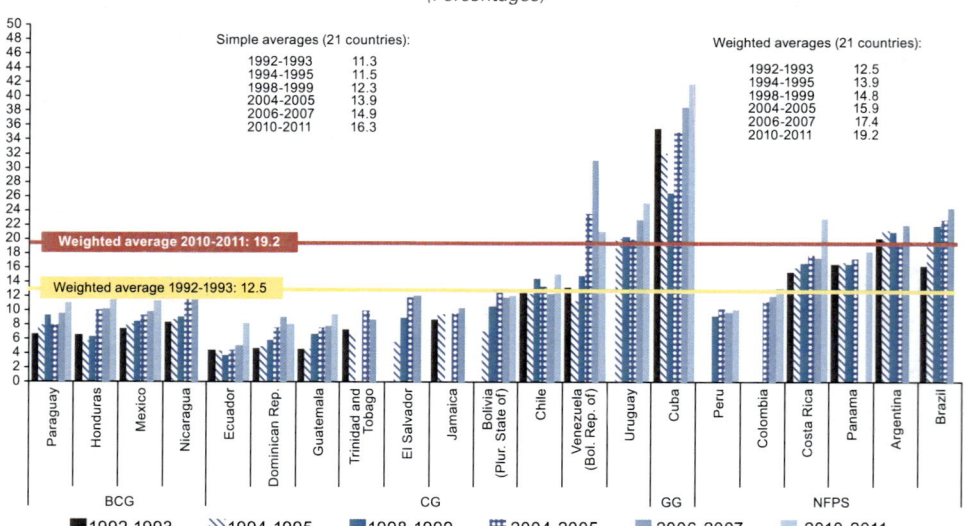

Source: Economic Commission for Latin America and the Caribbean (ECLAC), social expenditure database.

[a] The institutional coverage of countries' spending figures is as follows: BCG, budgetary central government; CG, central government (includes budgetary central government and agencies with budgetary autonomy); GG, general government (includes central government and local government); NFPS, non-financial public sector (includes general government and non-financial public enterprises).

Figure V.4

Latin America and the Caribbean (21 countries): per capita social public spending, 1992-1993 to 2010-2011 [a]

(Dollars at constant 2005 prices)

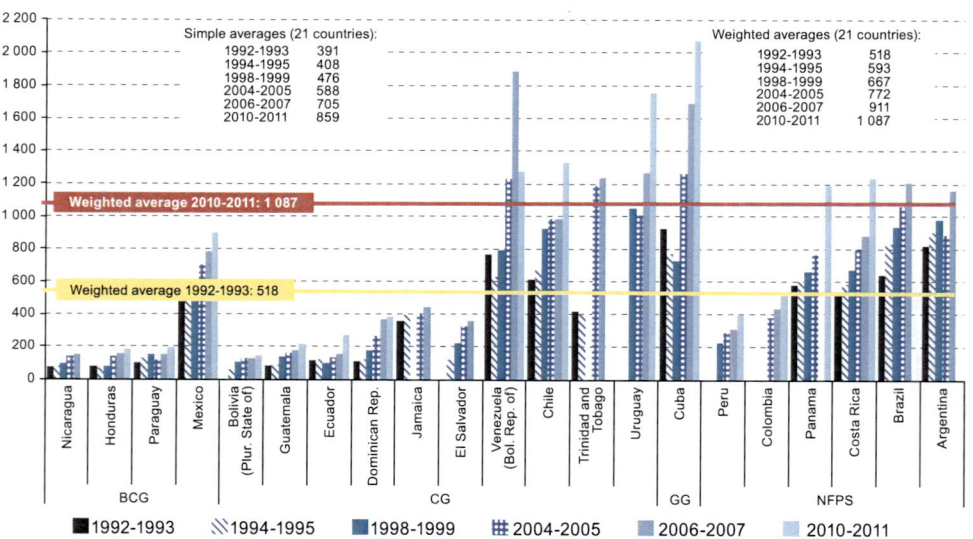

Source: Economic Commission for Latin America and the Caribbean (ECLAC), social expenditure database.

[a] The institutional coverage of countries' spending figures is as follows: BCG, budgetary central government; CG, central government (includes budgetary central government and agencies with budgetary autonomy); GG, general government (includes central government and local government); NFPS, non-financial public sector (includes general government and non-financial public enterprises).

3. Expenditure by sector

As shown above, at the regional level social spending as a percentage of GDP has risen systematically in all the periods under review. However, a look at the breakdown of expenditure by social sector (such as education, health, social security and assistance, and housing) shows that the pattern has been relatively uneven. Some social expenditure sectors have gained share, while others have seen their resources grow at a comparatively slower rate.

In order to interpret these patterns, not only should the different value attributed to sectoral social investment be taken into account, but also the fact that sectoral growth depends on the degree of institutional development and on the existing range of social services at the start of the evaluation period. Other factors include the pressures that various social groups can bring to bear on the State to boost certain types of expenditure, economic contractions that require the mobilization of welfare resources and the level of population ageing.

In general, the increase in average social spending by 6.8 percentage points of regional GDP between 1992-1993 and 2010-2011 is largely attributable to higher spending on social security and social assistance (which went up by 3.2 percentage points between the two periods). The gradual ageing of the population has meant that resources used to pay social security benefits have climbed steadily. Although a significant proportion of these resources comes from revenues based on contributory social security schemes (public or mixed), a growing number of countries have phased in solidarity mechanisms for financing social-security payments in addition to the solidarity-based redistribution mechanisms that already existed in these systems.

Although no disaggregated information is available for social security and social assistance, the data indicate that various welfare programmes were expanded, mainly in the first decade of the twenty-first century. These included anti-poverty programmes such as mechanisms for direct, conditional or non-conditional transfers to households. The implementation or significant expansion of some of the assistance programmes was linked to measures to address the effects of the international financial crisis on real economies, including higher unemployment and falling wages. Several of these were wrapped up or had their budgets cut once the crisis began to ease.

Overall, the social security and assistance sector upped its share in social public spending from 40.2% in 1992-1993 to 41.8% in 2000-2001, and again to 42.5% in 2010-2011. Over the past 20 years it accounted for almost 47% of the increase in total social spending (6.8 percentage points of GDP) (see figure V.5).

Figure V.5
Latin America and the Caribbean (21 countries): social public spending by sector, 1992-1993 to 2010-2011 [a]
(Percentages of GDP)

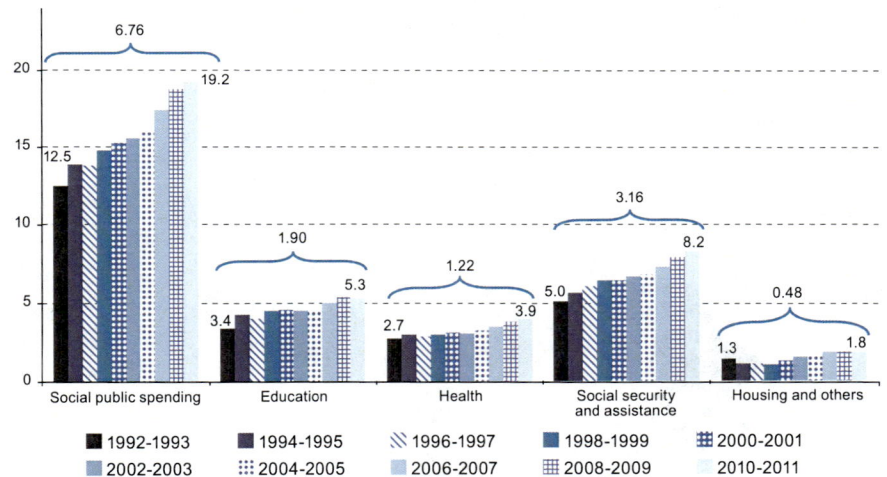

Source: Economic Commission for Latin America and the Caribbean (ECLAC), social expenditure database.
[a] Weighted average for the countries. The variation between the start and the end of the period under review is indicated above the column for each sector.

Another substantial jump over the past two decades, by 1.9 percentage points of regional GDP, was in social public spending in the education sector. This is associated with the expansion in coverage and access in the case of primary education in the poorest countries, and in the case of secondary education in the other countries (both spending on infrastructure and, above all, current expenditure, mainly on hiring more teachers). At the regional level the share of the education sector in social public spending held steady between 1992-1993 (27.2%) and 2010-2011 (27.5%), accounting for 28% of the increase in social spending between these two periods.

This trend came at the expense of social spending in the health sector, which saw its macroeconomic priority expand by less than the aforementioned sectors (1.2 percentage points of GDP between 1992-1993 and 2010-2011) and its share in social spending fall slightly, as examined in the following section.

Lastly, the sector that has been given the least priority in social public spending in the region is housing and others (which includes drinking water and sanitation, and more recently the environment), despite the fact that practically all countries, and especially major cities, still have pockets where marginal living conditions prevail. Spending in this sector increased by only 0.5 percentage points of GDP in 18 years and accounted for 9.5% of total social public spending at the end of the period under consideration. This makes it hard to develop programmes for upgrading slums (for the most part through sanitation programmes) or eradicating substandard dwellings, and it affects both the low-income population and, indirectly, the health sector, owing to considerable difficulties in controlling vectors of infectious and contagious diseases that spread easily in the absence of proper drinking-water, sewerage and waste-treatment systems. Scanty investment in this area has also hampered or slowed environmental conservation initiatives based on the creation of biodiversity conservation areas and on necessary measures for regulating human activity, in particular productive ventures, so as to prevent environmental degradation and pollution. There is a significant link between failing to implement such initiatives and poverty in some countries in the region, given the relative weight of these factors, as was discussed in relation to the multidimensional measurement of poverty in the first two chapters.

Box V.1

Updating social expenditure figures

To update social expenditure figures for this edition of *Social Panorama of Latin America*, data on the functional classification of public spending up to 2011 were obtained in accordance with the total and sectoral spending series published in previous editions. Information was gathered for 11 countries up to 2011 and for 8 up to 2012. The decision to publish these figures was based on the fact that it is important to have recent data, even if they are only provisional, approximate or partial. The figures were updated during the third quarter of 2013, and the exercise was finalized in early October.

In most cases, it was possible to collect data on central government budget execution, and in a number of countries figures for actual spending were obtained from agencies with budgetary autonomy, local governments and non-financial public enterprises. Although differences in institutional coverage make comparisons between countries difficult, it was decided to publish the most comprehensive data available for each country, except when they posed significant constraints for constructing a series for 1990-2011. This is because the primary interest of ECLAC is to cover as much information on social public spending as possible, in order to convey the effort being made by States in this area.

The following is a classification of the countries by institutional coverage of the social expenditure series used:
- Total public sector (NFPS + PFE): Costa Rica
- Non-financial public sector (GG + NFPE): Argentina, Brazil, Colombia, Panama and Peru
- General government (CG + LG): Cuba
- Central government (BCG + AA): Bolivarian Republic of Venezuela, Chile, Dominican Republic, Ecuador, El Salvador, Guatemala, Jamaica, Plurinational State of Bolivia, Trinidad and Tobago and Uruguay.
- Budgetary central government: Honduras, Mexico, Nicaragua and Paraguay

Where: AA, agencies with budgetary autonomy; BCG, budgetary central government; CG, central government; FPS, financial public sector; GG, general government; LG, local governments; NFPE, non-financial public enterprises; NFPS, non-financial public sector; PFE, public financial enterprises.

Considering that a number of countries only very recently adopted the classification system presented in the *Government Finance Statistics Manual 2001* of the International Monetary Fund (IMF) (which is harmonized with the 1993 System of National Accounts (SNA)), the 1990-2011 series is not always compatible at the subfunction or subgroup level. Most of the countries publish the functional classification in aggregated form and use classifications of their own.

Data continuity problems are shown in the lack of information for the full series or for certain years or functions in particular cases. For example, there are no data for the Plurinational State of Bolivia between 1990 and 1994. In the case of El Salvador, there are no data for 1990-1992 and the series for 2004-2009 are not strictly comparable with those for previous years owing to a change of methodology. There are no social security figures for Nicaragua as the Nicaraguan Social Security Institute is an autonomous entity. The series for Ecuador refers to the central government until 2006 and to the general State budget from 2007. For other countries it was not possible to construct the full series as the data on intermediate periods were lacking. Such is the case with the data for Jamaica and Trinidad and Tobago for 1997-1999. For Colombia, a methodological change and a switch in the basis for calculating GDP mean that the series for 1990-1999 and 2000-2012 are not comparable. The Dominican Republic has published two social public spending series, one for 1990-2002 and the other for 2003-2010, with methodological differences that mean that the two are not entirely consistent in regard to the social sectors, though they are in terms of general social public spending. The figures for Mexico relate to programmable spending of the budgetary public sector from the National Public Finance Account; however, available data on the highly decentralized spending execution in that country indicate that the figures should be read more carefully than in other cases because social spending may be substantially understated (for examples of centralized and decentralized execution of social spending, see ECLAC (2001)).

Like previous editions, *Social Panorama of Latin America 2013* uses biennial averages to present social spending data. The indicators published are for total social public spending and its component functions and sectors (education, health, social security and assistance, and housing, sanitation and other functions not included in the above categories) as a percentage of GDP, in dollars per capita, and as a percentage of total public spending. In the case of this last indicator, official information from the countries is used, but these figures may differ from those based on other classification systems (such as economic or administrative classifications of spending) because some include interest payments on the public debt and others do not, and because different methodologies are used to classify disbursements.

Box V.1 (concluded)

The 2013 edition, as with those for 2011 and 2012, includes the change made by ECLAC to set 2005 as the base year for calculating GDP in constant dollars. All social spending calculations in constant dollars are therefore expressed in dollars at constant 2005 prices.

The figures used to calculate percentages are in current prices for each year and each country. These proportions are then applied to the GDP series in dollars at 2005 prices to obtain per capita social spending, expressed in dollars. This may result in certain variations in relation to the data in constant currency reported by the countries, which depend on the degree of appreciation or depreciation implicit in the official parity of each country's currency in relation to 2005, and also on the demographic data on which the per capita calculations are based.

Figures at current prices on total and social public spending (and the sectoral breakdown of the latter) are official data provided by the corresponding government bodies. Depending on the country, these may be directorates, departments, sections or units for planning, budgeting or social policy within the ministries of the treasury, finance or economic affairs. In addition, information on budget execution was obtained from the countries' general accounting offices or treasury departments, and occasionally from central banks, national statistical institutes, and national social and economic information systems.

The figures for GDP in dollars at constant 2005 prices are official ECLAC statistics; the population figures come from projections by the Latin American and Caribbean Demographic Centre (CELADE)-Population Division of ECLAC.

Source: Economic Commission for Latin America and the Caribbean (ECLAC).

B. Trends in public spending on health

During the 1990s, public spending on health was affected by large fluctuations associated with highly volatile growth; however, subsequent increases in real terms offset those falls. Since the mid-2000s, coincident with a widespread push to increase social spending, public spending on health has been relatively shielded from economic swings and as a result has been more stable and inertial. Against the backdrop of the financial crisis, although social spending did not benefit from an injection of resources as part of an explicit countercyclical policy, it was protected to the extent that its share of both GDP and public spending increased.

This section examines both recent and long-term trends in public spending on health. The limited availability of information for the past few years imposes restrictions on measurement. The different degrees of data aggregation at the central government, general government and non-financial public sector level make it difficult to compare countries or groups of countries (see box V.1). Spending trends should therefore be considered illustrative, inasmuch as there may be considerable under-recording of resources targeting the health sector in central government reports, and even more so in the case of federal governments.[2]

Although public and private health-care systems coexist in the countries of the region, as do systems or subsystems within the sector with mixed financing, all of which usually involve either the full payment or at least the co-payment of services by the individual (private household expenditure), the lowest-income population tends to depend to a large extent on services provided by the public sector as the sole source of coverage in the area of health, funded with fiscal resources (ECLAC, 2008). Indirect evidence of this can be seen in the next section, which analyses out-of-pocket spending on health, highlighting the existence of repressed demand for health care among the low-income population. The significant levels of poverty and vulnerability in most of the countries of the region and, therefore, the high dependence of large sectors of the population on public health-care systems show the importance of analysing the trends in public expenditure in this area, taking into consideration that larger amounts do not necessarily reflect increases in coverage, the expansion of benefits or improvements in the quality of these services.

---

[2] The understatement of public resources devoted to health may vary among countries for the same level of government, depending on the degree to which State spending is decentralized, as well as the level of budgetary autonomy of health systems (including the level of co-payment for health services) and, therefore, the degree of institutional dependence on transfers from the central government and their own revenues.

During the 1990s, public spending on health, as with most components of social public spending —with the sole exception of spending on social security— was affected by large fluctuations associated with the highly volatile growth that characterized much of the decade. At the regional level, public expenditure on health swung widely during the 1990s, although the episodes of lower spending were followed by increases in real terms which broadly offset the downswings. In general, these variations occurred in conjunction, or with a one-year delay, with the variations in regional GDP (see figure V.6).

Figure V.6
Latin America and the Caribbean (21 countries): annual public spending on health and GDP, 1993-2012
(Percentages)

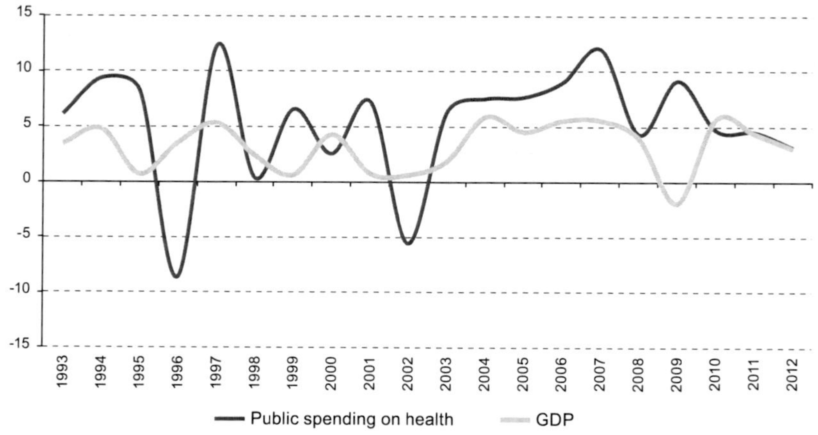

Source: Economic Commission for Latin America and the Caribbean (ECLAC), social expenditure database.

For a group of 21 countries in the region, one third of budget executions came in below the previous year's (45 episodes of spending decreases and 90 of absolute spending increases between 1993 and 2000); a good part of these fluctuations were associated with swings in the countries' economic cycles. During the 1990s, even where countries did not experience a drop in GDP, but rather a decrease in growth rate, health spending was nevertheless closely linked to the economic cycle. In specific terms, spending went down or stagnated as the sector tended to be used as an adjustment tool when faced with the need to rein in public spending, or it held steady in the face of real or projected drops in tax revenue. The cuts did not affect current spending (such as payroll or supplies) so much as the investment component (such as construction and maintenance of hospitals and clinics, and acquisition of new technology).

On balance for the 1990s, the macroeconomic priority of public spending on health in the region (that is, as a percentage of GDP) increased from 2.7% in 1992-1993 to 3.1% in 2000-2001. But 1996-1997, in particular, saw a sharp decline to 2.8% of GDP, down from the 3.0% of GDP recorded in 1994-1995 (see figure V.7).

These declines occurred even as total public spending held steady or grew, with health spending shrinking as a share of total spending (that is, its fiscal priority) on several occasions. These reductions in public health spending occurred even as other sectors saw higher social spending (education and pensions, for example), so health spending lost significant ground in terms of its share in social spending (see figure V.7).

Since the mid-2000s, coincident with a widespread push to increase social spending and protect it from economic swings, public spending on health has been gaining stability (becoming less procyclical) and becoming more inertial, mainly in countries with larger tax takes, higher total spending, and by extension, higher social spending. The average figures for 21 countries in the region show that resources for this sector increased systematically, at least until 2009, and even outpaced GDP growth, and that there was a sharp countercyclical spike in 2008 when regional GDP fell by almost 2%. The exception was a marked fall in 2002, which can be explained primarily by Argentina and Colombia reducing their health spending by over 20%[3] (see figure V.6).

---

[3] In 2003, other countries significantly tightened up the resources allocated to health (Panama, Paraguay and the Dominican Republic), but they account for only a small share of regional public expenditure earmarked for this sector.

Figure V.7
Latin America and the Caribbean (21 countries): public spending on health as a share of GDP,
of total public spending, and of social public spending, 1992-1993 to 2010-2011 [a]
(Percentages)

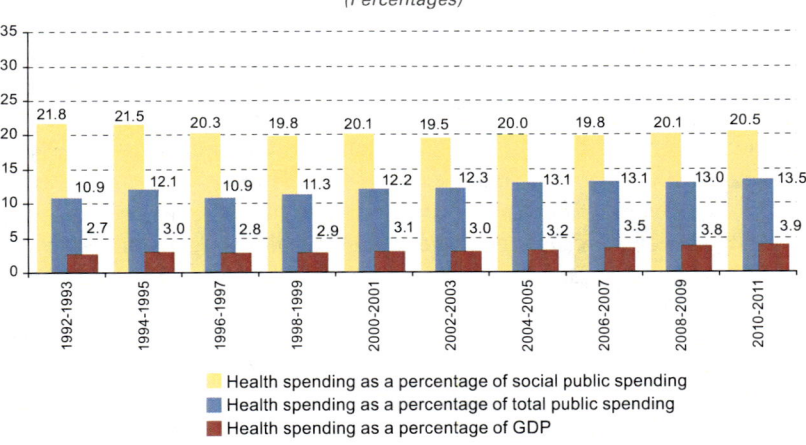

Health spending as a percentage of social public spending
Health spending as a percentage of total public spending
Health spending as a percentage of GDP

Source: Economic Commission for Latin America and the Caribbean (ECLAC), social expenditure database.

In a related trend, in the vast majority of countries the macroeconomic priority of health spending began to pick up at the beginning of the 2000s and reached 3.9% of GDP in 2010-2011. To some extent that increase has boosted the share of health spending in the total budget (that is, its fiscal priority) and in the social budget. According to the general trend observed in the countries over almost 20 years by comparing the macroeconomic priority of public spending on health in 1992-1993, 2000-2001 and 2010-2011, on balance over the past decade, only Colombia, Panama and the Bolivarian Republic of Venezuela have seen that priority decrease; Mexico was the only one to post a reduction in health spending as a percentage of GDP between 1992-1993 and 2010-2011, owing to adjustments that were made in the 1990s (see figure V.8).

Figure V.8
Latin America and the Caribbean (21 countries): public spending on health as a percentage of GDP,
1992-1993, 2000-2001 and 2010-2011 [a]
(Percentages)

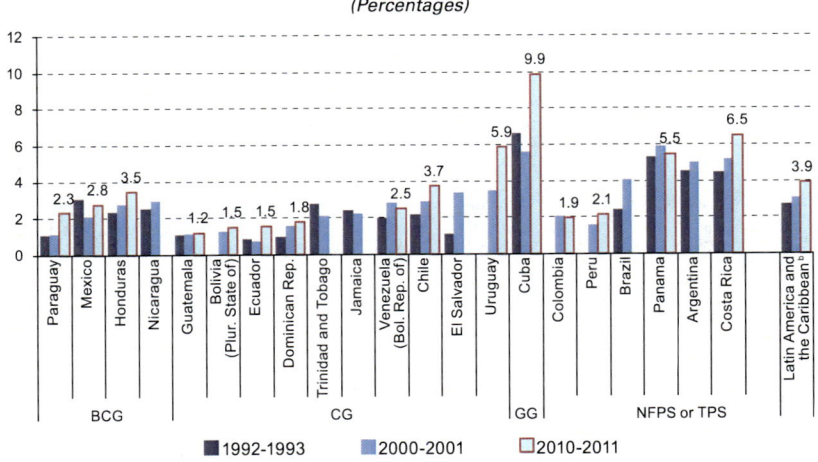

■ 1992-1993   ■ 2000-2001   □ 2010-2011

Source: Economic Commission for Latin America and the Caribbean (ECLAC), social expenditure database.
[a] The institutional coverage of countries' spending figures is as follows: BCG, budgetary central government; CG, central government (includes budgetary central government and agencies with budgetary autonomy); GG, general government (includes central government and local government); NFPS, non-financial public sector (includes general government and non-financial public enterprises); TPS, total public sector (includes non-financial public sector and public financial enterprises).
[b] Weighted average for the countries.

Against the backdrop of the financial crisis and its impact on the real economies of the region, the public health sector was not particularly hit (only 14 instances of budget cuts out of a total of 57 in the 21 countries between 2008 and the most recent data available). Although it did not benefit from an injection of resources as part of an explicit countercyclical policy (for example, job creation through increased investment spending), the sector was protected to the extent that it even increased its share of both GDP and public spending.

The shielding of public spending on health from the financial crisis is seen most clearly between 2008 and 2009, when regional GDP fell: 11 of the 21 countries analysed suffered a drop in GDP, yet just two countries (Colombia and the Bolivarian Republic of Venezuela) reduced their spending on health and only the latter did so procyclically (that is, associated with a fall in GDP). On other occasions, budget cuts were made irrespective of the GDP trajectory, but in general these were subsequently reversed. According to the information available, only Guatemala and the Bolivarian Republic of Venezuela recorded systematic cuts in their health budgets in recent years: a drop of 16.2% between 2009 and 2012 in the former and 44% between 2007 and 2010 in the latter. The 12% reduction in health spending in Cuba in 2011 is also worthy of note, since the subsequent 6.7% increase did not return it to the level seen in 2010 (see table V.1). However, it is estimated that the public health budget for the region as a whole increased by more than 20% in the period between 2008 and 2012.

Table V.1
Latin America and the Caribbean (21 countries): recent trends in public spending on health and GDP, 2008-2012
(Percentages)

Country	Level of government [a]	Annual variation in health spending					Annual variation in GDP				
		2008	2009	2010	2011	2012	2008	2009	2010	2011	2012
Argentina	NFPS	14.3	22.3	...	...	...	6.8	0.9	9.2	8.9	1.9
Bolivia (Plurinational State of)	CG	-17.8	24.8	5.1	2.9	-4.6	6.1	3.4	4.1	5.2	5.2
Brazil	NFPS	5.4	8.5	...	...	...	4.8	-0.3	6.9	2.7	0.9
Chile	CG	16.1	21.1	0.7	-1.9	9.7	3.7	-1.0	5.8	5.9	5.6
Colombia	NFPS	13.2	-2.3	8.8	3.6	6.3	3.5	1.7	4.0	6.6	4.0
Costa Rica	TPS	18.3	12.4	2.8	5.3	9.1	2.7	-1.0	5.0	4.4	5.1
Cuba	GG	8.4	11.2	-12.0	6.7	...	4.1	1.4	2.4	2.8	3.0
Dominican Republic	CG	-3.8	1.0	34.9	...	...	5.3	3.5	7.8	4.5	3.9
Ecuador	CG	34.5	5.5	2.9	3.3	27.5	6.4	0.6	2.8	7.4	5.0
El Salvador	CG	0.2	8.0	...	...	...	1.3	-3.1	1.4	2.0	1.6
Guatemala	CG	5.9	19.1	-5.2	-9.6	-2.2	3.3	0.5	2.9	4.2	3.0
Honduras	BCG	9.5	24.5	2.3	...	...	4.2	-2.4	3.7	3.7	3.3
Jamaica	CG	...	...	...	...	...	-0.8	-3.5	-1.5	1.3	-0.3
Mexico	BCG	-0.1	9.0	2.5	6.6	...	1.2	-6.0	5.3	3.9	3.9
Nicaragua	BCG	3.3	7.0	...	...	...	4.0	-2.2	3.6	5.4	5.2
Panama	NFPS	...	...	10.2	6.3	6.1	10.1	3.9	7.5	10.8	10.7
Paraguay	BCG	-10.7	54.6	13.1	...	...	6.4	-4.0	13.1	4.3	-1.2
Peru	NFPS	30.9	19.4	3.9	8.2	20.2	9.8	0.9	8.8	6.9	6.3
Trinidad and Tobago	CG	51.3	...	...	...	...	3.4	-4.4	0.2	-2.6	1.2
Uruguay	CG	30.9	10.6	18.4	13.1	...	7.2	2.2	8.9	6.5	3.9
Venezuela (Bolivarian Republic of)	CG	-28.3	-19.7	-3.3	...	...	5.3	-3.2	-1.5	4.2	5.5
Latin America and the Caribbean [b]		4.3	9.2	4.7	4.5	3.1	3.9	-1.9	5.7	4.3	3.0

Source: Economic Commission for Latin America and the Caribbean (ECLAC), social expenditure database.

[a] The levels of government are NFPS: non-financial public sector (includes general government and non-financial public enterprises); CG: central government (includes budgetary central government and agencies with budgetary autonomy); TPS: total public sector (includes non-financial public sector and public financial enterprises); GG: general government (includes central government and local government); and BCG: budgetary central government.
[b] Weighted average for the countries.

But the relatively broad and sustained increase in health spending in the 2000s should not mask the wide variation in spending levels from one country to another. In around 2011, average annual health spending was in the area of US$ 226 per capita for the region as a whole, but in countries with a high level of spending (more than US$ 300 per capita), such as Argentina, Chile, Costa Rica, Cuba, Panama, Trinidad and Tobago and Uruguay, it was as much as US$ 413. For countries with intermediate levels of spending (between US$ 100 per capita and US$ 300 per capita), such as the Bolivarian Republic of Venezuela, Brazil, El Salvador, Mexico and Peru, the per capita average was around US$ 175. Countries with low levels of spending (under US$ 100 per capita) allocated on average just US$ 55 per capita to health; they were Colombia, Dominican Republic, Ecuador, Guatemala, Honduras, Jamaica, Nicaragua, Paraguay and Plurinational State of Bolivia. While the group of countries with the lowest levels of per capita health expenditure increased their spending in this area by 4.1% annually between 2000 and 2011 and the intermediate group saw theirs go up by 4% annually, per capita health spending in the countries with the highest levels of spending jumped up by 7.4% annually. This resulted in a wider gap between the countries in terms of per capita public spending on health (see figure V.9).

Figure V.9
Latin America and the Caribbean (21 countries): per capita health spending
(Dollars at constant 2005 prices)

A. Per capita health spending by country grouping, 1992-2011

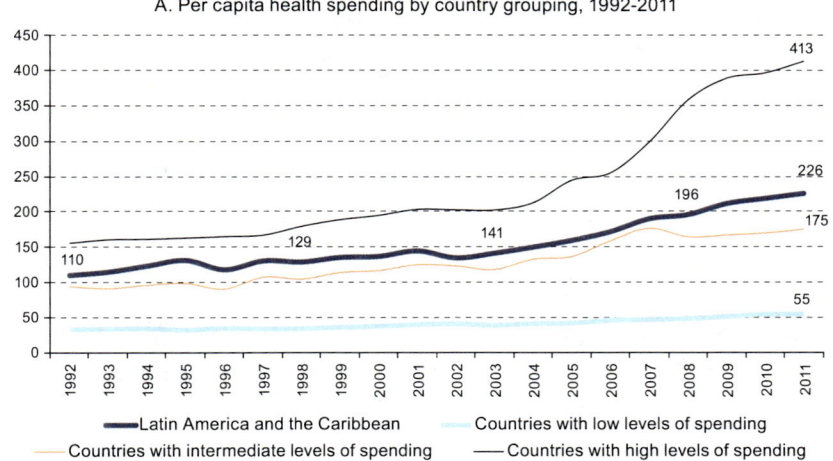

B. Per capita spending on health by country, latest year available[a]

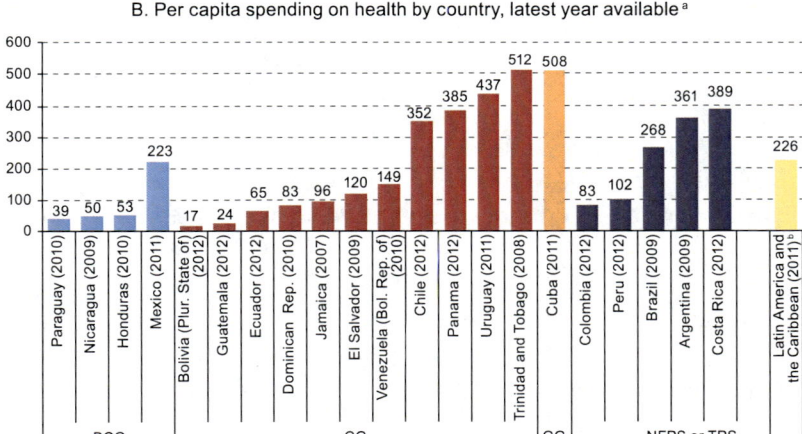

Source: Economic Commission for Latin America and the Caribbean (ECLAC), social expenditure database.
[a] The institutional coverage of countries' spending figures is as follows: BCG, budgetary central government; CG, central government (includes budgetary central government and agencies with budgetary autonomy); GG, general government (includes central government and local government); NFPS, non-financial public sector (includes general government and non-financial public enterprises); TPS, total public sector (includes non-financial public sector and public financial enterprises).
[b] Weighted average for the countries.

The countries which must make greater efforts to increase health spending are Guatemala, Honduras, Nicaragua, Paraguay and the Plurinational State of Bolivia, whose annual expenditure is below US$ 55 dollars per person. Although the macroeconomic priority of health spending is not low in Honduras, Nicaragua and Paraguay (3.5%, 4.1% and 2.3% of GDP, respectively), in the Plurinational State of Bolivia and Guatemala there is scope for increasing the resources allocated to it, which are equivalent to only 1.3% and 1.1% of GDP, respectively.

The next section analyses private household spending on health, in particular direct or out-of-pocket expenses in this area, either in payment or co-payment for services received.

C. Some features of out-of-pocket health spending in the region

Out-of-pocket health expenses are antithetical to the notion of shared responsibility or risk diversification. In addition to their related negative effects on well-being, in some cases they can also be potentially inefficient; for example, when they are the result of high prices for medicines and overpriced services in certain markets or the provision of unnecessary services. Therefore, reducing such costs represents a complex challenge to be tackled on the path towards achieving a more universal social safety net based on shared responsibility.

1. Definition and scope of out-of-pocket spending

Health-care goods and services have three main sources of financing whose weight varies from one country to another depending on the structure of each health system: general and specific taxes, social security contributions collected through payroll taxes, other taxes or contributions, and household outlays.

As defined by the Pan American Health Organization (PAHO, 2007), household spending on health services encompasses two types of expenditure. Direct expenditures, known as out-of-pocket health expenses, include household outlays on health-related items such as hospitalizations, outpatient procedures and medicines, and are net payments, that is, after any reimbursements that might be received from the health-care system or insurance. Indirect expenses are outlays for prepaid medical care plans, private medical insurance or contributions to public insurance.

A look at out-of-pocket health spending as a percentage of the household budget and its relative composition, as well as the comparisons between income groups, yields important information on the spending options of households and sheds light on what happens in countries with very different health systems. The analysis of how these spending patterns are related to the various forms of financing is still relatively unexplored terrain, and causal links cannot therefore be established.

Households make these direct payments as the need arises, generally to the service provider. This spending depends on each household's ability to pay and is thus antithetical to the notion of shared responsibility or risk diversification. It is therefore one of the least fair ways to finance health care. The population is vulnerable to varying degrees to incurring out-of-pocket health expenses that adversely affect their socioeconomic position. The degree of vulnerability is a function of both the magnitude of the out-of-pocket expense in question and household spending capacity (see table V.2).

In this type of analysis, spending capacity is defined as total household spending minus the value of the subsistence line allocated to food expenditure, which is the average amount spent on food by the group that allocates around 50% of its resources to this item (for more detail, see box V.2). The burden of out-of-pocket health expenses shows the ratio of these costs to disposable household spending capacity; threshold values can be set to determine the level at which costs become catastrophic (approximately 30% to 40% of spending capacity)[4] (see table V.3).

---

[4] The 40% threshold set by Xu (2005) and Murray and others (2007) was adopted in the analysis by ECLAC (2008). More recently, Knaul and others (2011) set it at 30%, thus expanding the universe of households whose spending falls into that category. The present analysis uses the 30% threshold, which improves the sample quality of the universe that can be analysed using the surveys; the findings are therefore not comparable with ECLAC (2008).

Table V.2
Latin America (18 countries): general indicators on out-of-pocket health spending
(Percentages)

| Country | Spending capacity as a percentage of total spending [a] | Out-of-pocket health expenditure | | Households without out-of-pocket health expenses | Households with out-of-pocket health expenses: share of spending capacity allocated to those expenses [a] |
		As a proportion of total spending	As a proportion of spending capacity [a]		
Argentina (2004/2005)	61.9	5.0	6.8	45.7	12.5
Bolivia (Plurinational State of) (2003/2004)	58.8	3.1	4.5	43.2	7.9
Brazil (2008/2009)	85.5	5.0	5.7	14.3	6.7
Chile (2006/2007)	68.3	4.3	5.6	34.5	8.6
Colombia (2007)	59.4	1.9	2.9	36.4	4.6
Costa Rica (2004)	73.2	2.1	2.6	36.5	4.1
Dominican Republic (2007)	42.6	6.4	11.9	18.6	14.6
Ecuador (2003/2004)	72.9	4.7	6.2	4.0	6.5
El Salvador (2006)	65.4	4.3	6.1	13.7	7.1
Guatemala (2006)	56.8	6.2	9.4	11.3	10.6
Honduras (2004)	59.2	11.2	16.4	19.4	20.3
Mexico (2006)	75.0	4.7	6.0	19.8	7.5
Nicaragua (2005)	42.7	6.6	12.6	17.2	15.2
Panama (2007)	72.2	2.4	3.1	10.1	3.5
Paraguay (1997)	43.5	3.6	7.2	7.7	7.8
Peru (2008)	61.7	7.0	10.4	7.5	11.2
Uruguay (2005/2006)	77.9	2.8	3.4	25.9	4.6
Venezuela (Bolivarian Republic of) (2008/2009)	53.5	3.1	4.4	60.4	11.1
Latin America [b]	62.8	4.7	7.0	23.7	9.1

Source: Economic Commission for Latin America and the Caribbean (ECLAC), on the basis of special tabulations of data from income and expenditure surveys conducted in the respective countries.

[a] Spending capacity is defined as total household spending minus subsistence expenditure (food expenses incurred by each household, calculated for each country). Xu (2005) defines a line of relative subsistence, which is estimated as the average food expenditure per capita for a family whose food expenditure as a share of total household expenditure is located between the 45th and 55th percentiles of the food share distribution (number of household members raised to the power of 0.56). See Ke Xu, "Distribution of health payments and catastrophic expenditures. Methodology", *Discussion Paper*, N° 2, Geneva, World Health Organization (WHO), 2005 [online] http://www.paho.org/chi/index.php?option=com_docman&task=doc_view&gid=149&Itemid=.
[b] Simple average for the countries.

Box V.2
Use of household income and expenditure surveys to analyse household out-of-pocket spending on health

In any given country, surveys of household income and expenditure are among the most important sources of information relating to the economic decisions of households and are usually part of integrated household survey systems and, more generally, national statistical systems. They are designed to obtain information on, and to analyse the structure of, household budgets, savings and debt, to define or update basic food baskets and the costs of satisfying other basic necessities, and to update and modify baskets and bases for consumer price indices.

The System of National Accounts (SNA) defines household spending on goods and services for individual consumption as part of household final consumption expenditure. Households also receive goods and services for individual consumption from non-profit institutions serving households (NPISH) or from government agencies. Under SNA, actual final consumption of households is the sum of final consumption expenditure plus the goods and services transferred to households by NPISH and the individual goods and services produced or purchased by the government but delivered to households (State subsidies or royalties). Households can therefore purchase goods and services for individual consumption directly from the producers of those items (enterprises, government entities, non-profit institutions, households or the rest of the world), produce a portion thereof on an own-account basis for their own consumption or obtain such items from other households.

Expenditure surveys or expenditure modules included in household surveys are used to measure current household expenditure. Current expenditure consists of final consumption expenditure (including, for example, payment for drivers' licences, automobile registration and similar expenses) and non-consumption expenditure (including income tax and wealth tax, social security contributions, insurance premiums, cash transfers to persons not belonging to the household and interest payments), and normally excludes goods and services granted by NPISH and government agencies as well as intermediate consumption expenditure (for example, goods and services for use in productive activities).

Survey modules on expenditure typically gather information on: (i) final consumption expenditure (food and non-alcoholic beverages; alcoholic beverages, tobacco and narcotic drugs; clothing and footwear; housing, water, electricity, gas and other fuels; furniture, articles for the home and regular maintenance; health; transport; communications; recreation and culture; education; restaurants and hotels; and various goods and services); and (ii) non-consumption expenditure (including interest payments; social security contributions; income tax; other taxes; and other current transfers).

Box V.2 (concluded)

Depending on the availability and breakdown of information organized according to the Classification of Individual Consumption According to Purpose (COICOP), the following items were classified as health expenses for the purposes of this chapter: consultations of physicians in general practice; medicines; consultations of physicians in specialist practice (including dentists); treatments; therapeutic equipment; laboratory services and testing; hospital services, related services (for example, ambulance services or nurses), and other items (such as injections and alternative or natural medicine). Health insurance was also included under the category of other goods and services.

Household spending on health services represents the health-care costs paid by families through direct payments (out-of-pocket expenses) that cover all of the aforementioned items, except for the last. Indirect expenses are outlays for prepaid medical care plans, private medical insurance or contributions to public insurance (PAHO, 2007).

Out-of-pocket health expenses are direct household outlays on health-related items such as hospitalizations, outpatient procedures and medications, and are net payments, that is, following the deduction of any reimbursements that might be received from the health-care system or insurance (from the surveys it is not possible to distinguish whether the reimbursement has already been deducted from the direct payment or, in other cases, how much the future reimbursement will be). The burden of out-of-pocket health expenses shows the magnitude of these costs with respect to household spending capacity, which in operational terms is calculated as total household spending minus subsistence expenditure.

Subsistence needs refer to the food expenses incurred by each household. The level of subsistence expenditure, that is, the amount needed by each household to adequately feed its members, should be estimated for each country. For determining poverty, as well as for measuring household subsistence expenditure, a food-share-based relative poverty line is used, according to which the line of relative subsistence is estimated as the average food expenditure per capita of a family located between percentiles 45 and 55 of the ratio of food to total consumption (Xu, 2005).

The surveys used are listed below together with an indication of the period when the different monthly subsamples were taken.

Surveys of income and expenditure

Country	Name of the survey	Period of implementation
Argentina	National Survey on Household Expenditure	October 2004 to December 2005
Bolivia (Plurinational State of)	Continuous Household Survey	November 2003 to November 2004
Brazil	Family Budget Survey	May 2008 to May 2009
Chile	Sixth Family Budgets Survey	November 2006 to October 2007
Colombia	National Income and Expenditure Survey	September 2006 to September 2007
Costa Rica	National Income and Expenditure Survey	April 2004 to April 2005
Dominican Republic	National Household Income and Expenditure Survey	December 2006 to December 2007
Ecuador	Urban Household Income and Expenditure Survey	2002-2003
El Salvador	National Household Income and Expenditure Survey	September 2005 to August 2006
Honduras	National Survey of Living Conditions	2004
Mexico	National Household Income and Expenditure Survey	Third quarter of 2006
Nicaragua	National Household Survey to Measure Standards of Living	July to October 2005
Panama	Household Income and Expenditure Survey	July 2007 to June 2008
Peru	National Survey of Living Conditions and Poverty	January to December 2008
Uruguay	National Household Income and Expenditure Survey	November 2005 to October 2006
Venezuela (Bolivarian Republic of)	Fourth National Family Budgets Survey	September 2008 to September 2009

Source: Economic Commission for Latin America and the Caribbean (ECLAC), Household Survey Data Bank (BADEHOG).

The PPP dollar conversion factors published in World Development Indicators of the World Bank were used to calculate expenses in dollars at constant 2005 prices; the rate of exchange used was the 2005 rf series. As it was not possible to obtain the specific exchange rates for all of the subsamples throughout the reference period for all countries, the indexing and calculation of local currencies with respect to the dollar at constant 2005 prices was based on the averages of the consumer price indexes for the whole period of implementation of the corresponding survey.

Source: Economic Commission for Latin America and the Caribbean (ECLAC), Household Survey Data Bank (BADEHOG); Michel Séruzier, *Medir la economía de los países según el sistema de cuentas nacionales*, Santiago, Chile, Economic Commission for Latin America and the Caribbean (ECLAC)/Alfaomega Colombiana S.A., 2003; Ecuador National Statistics and Census Institute, Resumen metodológico (aplicación de la Encuesta de Ingresos y Gastos de Hogares Urbanos de 2002-2003), no date; Darwin Cortés, "Análisis de los gastos de los hogares colombianos 2006–2007", National Administrative Department of Statistics (DANE)/Universidad del Rosario, 2009; informes metodológicos y de resultados de las encuestas de ingreso y gasto por países; Pan American Health Organization (PAHO), Health in the Americas, 2007, Washington, D.C., 2007; K. Xu, "Distribution of health payments and catastrophic expenditures. Methodology", *Discussion Paper*, No. 2, Geneva, 2005.

Income and expenditure surveys measure the impact of these expenses exclusively in the month that the survey is carried out but not their more enduring effects, such as the medium- and long-term potential for impoverishment triggered by a catastrophic health event. They do not capture the recurrence of expenses or the timing of their magnitude and intensity. Despite these limitations, surveys give an idea of the uneven capacity of households to meet expenses not covered by insurance in cases of acute or chronic morbidity.

Because out-of-pocket health expenses are antithetical to the notion of shared responsibility or risk diversification, detrimental to well-being and in some cases potentially inefficient (for example, the expense incurred as a result of high prices for medicines in certain markets, overpricing or the provision of unnecessary services), reducing such costs represents a complex challenge to be tackled on the path towards achieving a more universal social safety net based on shared responsibility.

Table V.3
Latin America (18 countries): indicators of impoverishment in relation to out-of-pocket health expenditure
(Percentages)

Country	Incidence of poverty			Households impoverished by out-of-pocket expenses	Households with catastrophic health expenses (accounting for 30% or more of spending capacity)		
	All households	Households without out-of-pocket expenses	Households with out-of-pocket expenses [a]		Percentage of households with catastrophic expenses	Incidence of poverty among households with catastrophic expenses [a]	Households impoverished by catastrophic out-of-pocket expenses
Argentina (2004/2005)	14.3	24.2	6.0	1.2	6.7	7.7	12.7
Bolivia (Plurinational State of) (2003/2004)	15.6	22.5	10.4	0.7	3.0	14.7	12.5
Brazil (2008/2009)	2.8	7.9	1.9	0.6	2.5	3.9	8.8
Chile (2006/2007)	8.2	17.7	3.2	0.5	3.7	4.8	8.6
Colombia (2007)	14.5	20.0	11.4	0.6	1.1	24.7	21.4
Costa Rica (2004)	7.6	15.4	3.1	0.3	0.5	5.4	13.3
Dominican Republic (2007)	16.0	23.1	14.4	3.4	11.9	26.1	19.8
Ecuador (2003/2004)	2.0	7.5	1.8	0.3	2.0	3.7	4.3
El Salvador (2006)	11.0	24.0	9.0	0.9	2.5	5.7	8.4
Guatemala (2006)	10.0	16.5	9.1	1.7	8.3	4.6	9.5
Honduras (2004)	18.8	24.9	17.3	4.7	20.0	12.4	18.9
Mexico (2006)	2.8	5.6	2.1	0.5	4.1	2.8	4.1
Nicaragua (2005)	22.1	28.3	20.8	3.2	12.7	21.7	15.6
Panama (2007)	3.1	8.2	2.5	0.2	0.9	0.3	2.2
Paraguay (1997)	20.7	34.7	19.5	1.6	4.1	38.6	12.1
Peru (2008)	10.8	32.0	9.0	1.5	6.4	14.3	10.7
Uruguay (2005/2006)	3.7	10.3	1.4	0.1	0.5	2.6	2.1
Venezuela (Bolivarian Republic of) (2008/2009)	16.6	23.4	6.1	1.0	4.0	10.5	17.3
Latin America [b]	11.1	19.2	8.3	1.3	5.3	11.4	11.2

Source: Economic Commission for Latin America and the Caribbean (ECLAC), on the basis of special tabulations of data from income and expenditure surveys conducted in the respective countries.
[a] Households living in poverty prior to incurring the out-of-pocket expense, whether catastrophic or not.
[b] Simple average for the countries.

2. Expenditure by level of income, impoverishment and repressed spending

As might be expected, the magnitude of out-of-pocket expenditure varies greatly depending on income distribution. The lower out-of-pocket spending of the poorest sectors may indicate that they are insured (which cannot be measured very accurately owing to the sample sizes involved and the differences in the level of detail recorded by the surveys and the variety of ways in which they codify expenditure) or, if not, that they are unable to incur such expenses. Figure V.10 shows the disparities in average out-of-pocket spending on health by income quintile in Latin America.

An analysis of out-of-pocket expenditure on health as a proportion of spending capacity disaggregated by income quintile does not reveal any clearly discernible patterns at the country level. Looking at the structure of expenditure, households in the lower income quintiles spend proportionally more on medicines, while the proportion spent on specialist care rises as income increases (see figure V.10). Among other information that this reveals about the costs borne by households, this could suggest that a lack of social protection pushes poorer groups to self-medicate during episodes of illness.

Figure V.10

Latin America (18 countries): average household monthly out-of-pocket health expenditure, and spending on medicines and specialist care as a share of out-of-pocket health expenditure by income quintile, around 2006

(2005 purchasing power parity (PPP) dollars and percentages)

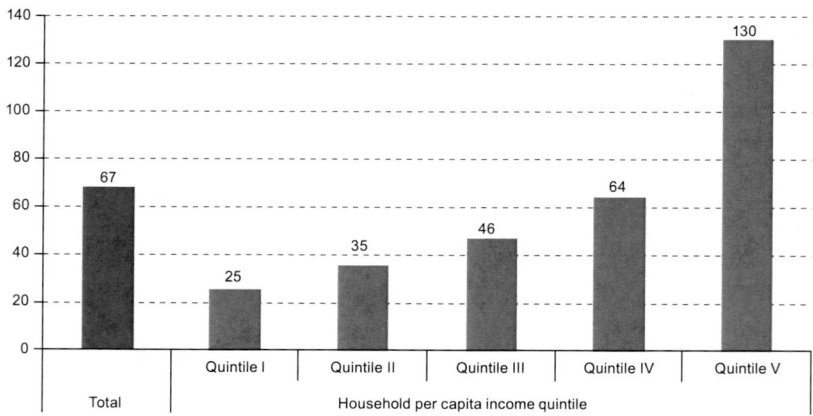

A. Simple average for 18 countries: household out-of-pocket expenditure on health

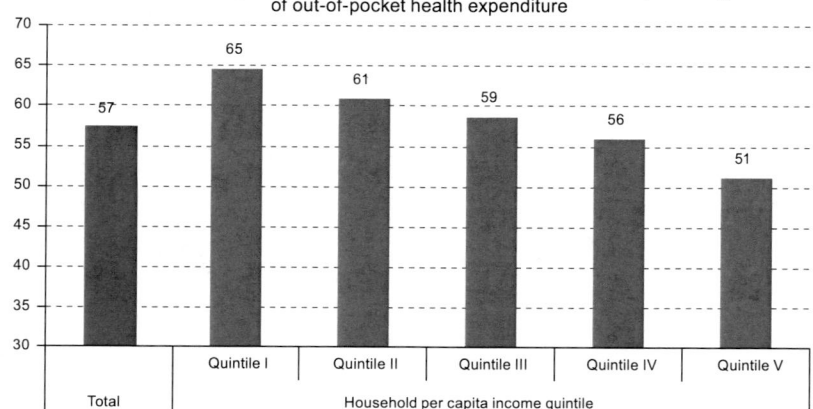

B. Simple average for 16 countries: spending on medicines as a percentage of out-of-pocket health expenditure

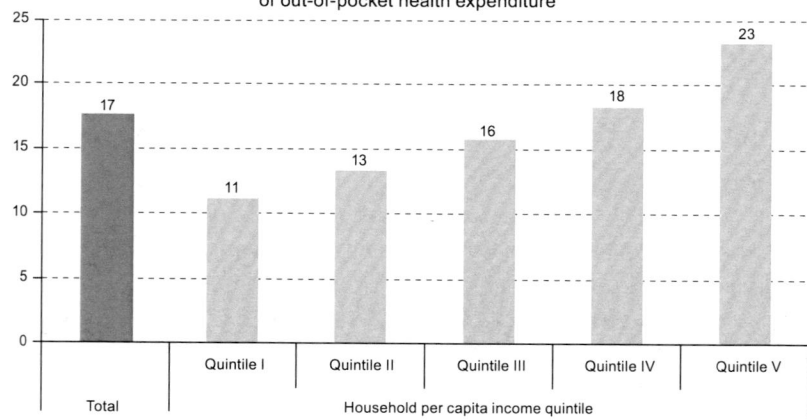

C. Simple average for 18 countries: spending on specialist care as a percentage of out-of-pocket health expenditure

Source: Economic Commission for Latin America and the Caribbean (ECLAC), on the basis of special tabulations of data from income and expenditure surveys conducted in the respective countries.

Out-of-pocket health spending can plunge households into poverty. To measure the phenomenon, first the percentage of households that sink into poverty among all households that incur out-of-pocket expenses is calculated; those figures are then added to the incidence of poverty calculated strictly on the basis of the subsistence line for food (see box V.2). Conducting this exercise in 18 countries of the region revealed the dramatic extent to which the incidence of relative poverty is rising in several countries in the region (see table V.3 and figure V.11).

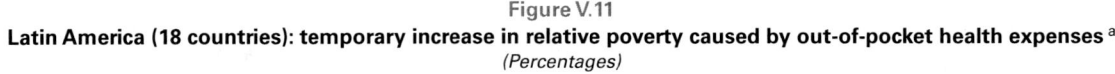

Figure V.11
Latin America (18 countries): temporary increase in relative poverty caused by out-of-pocket health expenses [a]
(Percentages)

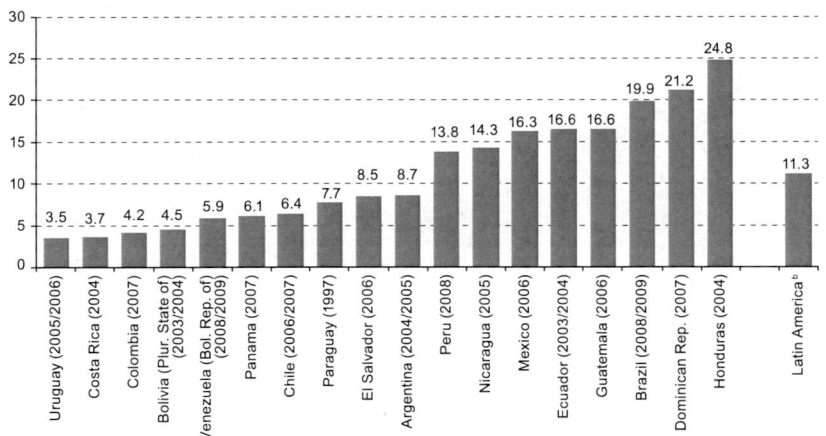

Source: Economic Commission for Latin America and the Caribbean (ECLAC), on the basis of special tabulations of data from income and expenditure surveys conducted in the respective countries.
[a] Greater details are available in box V.2.
[b] Simple average for the countries.

Some poor households are unable to make out-of-pocket health payments. There are many different reasons —positive and negative— why households might not spend on health: good health coverage through public or private systems; no morbidity events during the period in question; and precarious income or lack of access to credit. The last two prevent households from spending on health during episodes of morbidity when they do not have adequate coverage. If a household has limited spending options for these last two reasons (and thus does not incur that expense), there is no observable value that would indicate their actual need for health spending.

Figure V.12 shows that the incidence of out-of-pocket spending on health varies by income quintile. As a complementary indicator of inequality, there is an observable difference in the incidence between poor and non-poor households. It is striking, then, that the incidence of poverty (measured against the subsistence line) is higher among households without out-of-pocket spending, especially in countries with low health insurance coverage (see figure V.13).[5] Since the adverse socioeconomic conditions of those living in these households mean that they do not typically belong to a particularly healthy sector of the population or have good levels of insurance coverage, the lack of out-of-pocket health expenditure would seem to suggest a repressed capacity to incur out-of-pocket expenses among a certain contingent of the poor.

While catastrophic expenditure tends to be more closely associated with very high out-of-pocket expenses, those with a limited spending capacity are in fact unable to take on out-of-pocket health expenses, even when they are not insured (ECLAC, 2008).

---

[5]   Perticara (2008) was the first to draw attention to this.

Figure V.12

Latin America (simple average for 18 countries): households with out-of-pocket health expenses by income quintile, around 2006

(Percentages)

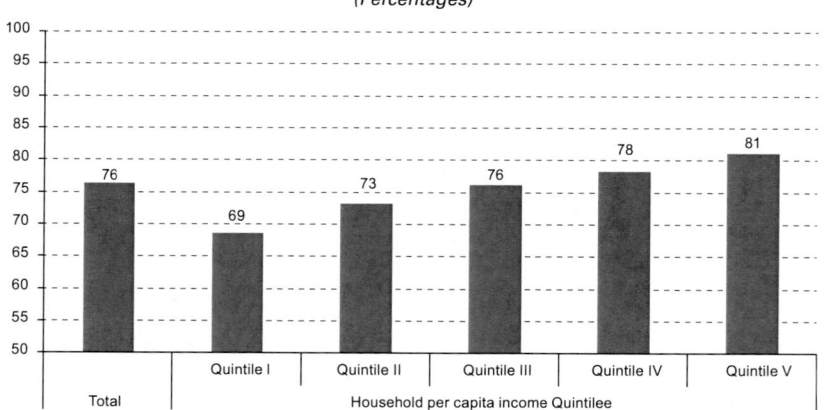

Source: Economic Commission for Latin America and the Caribbean (ECLAC), on the basis of special tabulations of data from income and expenditure surveys conducted in the respective countries.

Figure V.13

Latin America (18 countries): relative poverty rate among households with and without out-of-pocket spending [a]

(Percentages)

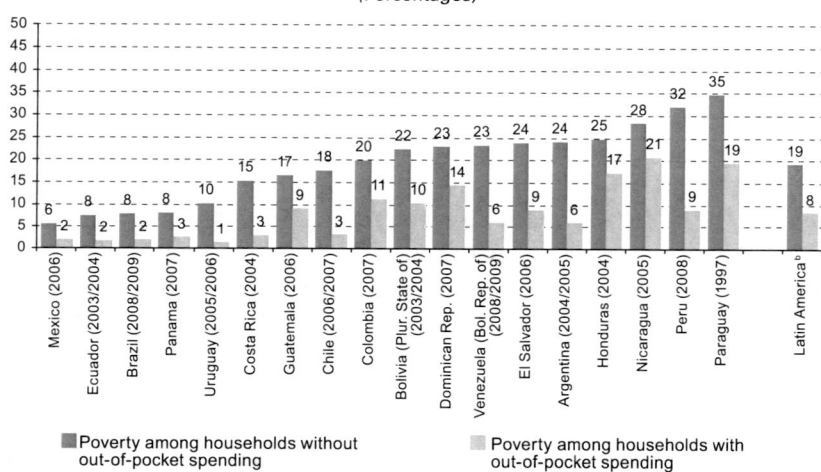

Source: Economic Commission for Latin America and the Caribbean (ECLAC), on the basis of special tabulations of data from income and expenditure surveys conducted in the respective countries.
[a] Greater details are available in box V.2.
[b] Simple average for the countries.

The concept of catastrophic health expenditure refers to the magnitude of these out-of-pocket expenses in relation to the general spending capacity of households. Such expenses constrict the capacity of households to cover other normal household expenses and can lead to debt or poverty. When the burden of out-of-pocket expenses surpasses a specific limit, they are considered catastrophic: usually the threshold is set at 40% of spending capacity (Xu, Evans and Aguilar, 2005).

In several countries in the region, catastrophic expenditure also affects a significant number of households that were already poor, regardless of the size of the expense. Among the countries where a considerable proportion of households face catastrophic out-of-pocket health expenses, their magnitude pushes the greatest number of households into poverty in Honduras, Nicaragua and the Dominican Republic (see table V.3).

D. A rapid and sustained increase in health spending: projections for Brazil, Chile and Mexico for 2010-2060

Short-term crises tend to dominate the headlines, public attention and national agendas, while revolutionary changes that happen gradually over several decades receive much less attention. Issues such as population ageing, growing rates of chronic diseases, global warming and inequality are either not considered pressing or are unfortunately relegated by the urgency of other events. This section highlights one such transformation that is relevant to the whole region: the possibility of a sustained and rapid increase in health spending over the coming decades, as a combined result of population ageing and economic growth.

1. A model for projecting health spending as a proportion of GDP

In the last century, national accounts were a key element in economic development activities, since they served as the basis for the adoption of measures pertaining to policies on international economic activity, the standardization of methodologies in order to facilitate comparisons between countries and the accurate definition of pertinent economic statistics to inform debates on public policy, providing the scientific basis for assessing economic and political theories. In this century, national transfer accounts are expected to be crucial to economic development efforts (Miller and Saad, 2012). They provide a complete and consistent assessment of economic relations between population groups (defined by age, sex and socioeconomic strata) within the framework of the national economy, in the same way that the national accounts measure the economic relations between sectors (households, production and government). Because national transfer accounts measure economic relations between groups in an economy (between men and women, rich and poor, young and old), they turn national accounts into a policy instrument for addressing inequality, population ageing and other challenges of this century, which is of vital importance not only in the region, but worldwide.

As part of this international data collection effort, information has been gathered on average annual health expenditure by age in 22 economies that are participating in a global project on national transfer accounts.[6] The findings are presented in figure V.14. Spending has been standardized across the different currencies and is expressed as a proportion of GDP per person of working age. To facilitate the interpretation of these statistics, in most of these economies GDP per working-age person is approximately equivalent to the average wage. Thus health spending can be seen as a percentage of the average annual wage. For example, expenditure equivalent to 5% of GDP per working-age person can also be considered equivalent to 5% of the average annual wage. In high-income economies, this is the percentage spent annually per child (see figure V.14). Expenditure on health in these economies declines after childhood and reaches its lowest point during adolescence, after which it begins to climb again until reaching its peak for the oldest age group. This pattern of health spending rising with age is shared by the high-income and middle-income economies. The high-income group spends a comparatively larger proportion of income on health care for all age groups, but especially for older adults. It seems logical to assume that as income grows —and the countries that are currently in the middle-income category edge towards the high-income level— spending on health care expands proportionally. This hypothesis underpins the projection model used here.

---

[6] These economies include high- and middle-income countries. The high-income economies are Austria, France, Germany, Japan, Republic of Korea, Slovenia, Spain, Sweden and the United States. The group of middle-income countries includes Brazil, Chile, China, Colombia, Costa Rica, India, Indonesia, Jamaica, Mexico, Peru, the Philippines, Thailand and Uruguay.

Figure V.14

Annual per capita health spending in high-income and middle-income countries by age [a]

(Percentages of GDP per working-age person)

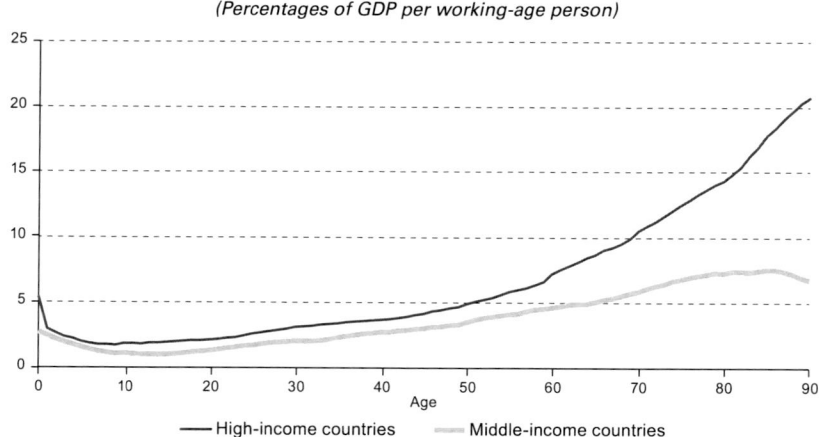

Source: Latin American and Caribbean Demographic Centre (CELADE)-Population Division of ECLAC, on the basis of information from the database of the global project on national transfer accounts.
[a] The high-income economies are Austria, France, Germany, Japan, Republic of Korea, Slovenia, Spain, Sweden and the United States. The middle-income economies are Brazil, Chile, China, Colombia, Costa Rica, India, Indonesia, Jamaica, Mexico, Peru, the Philippines, Thailand and Uruguay.

With a view to projecting future expenditure on health care, an analysis is conducted of the impact of two combined trends that most countries in the region will experience in the coming decades: population ageing and rapid economic growth. A simple two-component model was used to forecast health spending. The first component is demographic: the population in each age group from 2010 to 2060. This information was obtained from the population projections of the Latin American and Caribbean Demographic Centre (CELADE)-Population Division ECLAC and complemented with data from the United Nations *World Population Prospects* report for countries from outside the region. This demographic factor can be projected with a high degree of certainty. The second component is average annual health spending by age. Since this component is determined by technological, economic and policy factors it is much more difficult to project with certainty. According to the model, as economies grow, spending on health increases for all age groups, but especially in the oldest ones.[7] The trend towards higher spending as a percentage of per capita GDP is seen across all of the 22 economies participating in the global project on national transfer accounts and is proportional, in theory, to the variation in per capita GDP.

2. Population ageing, speed of economic growth and sustained increase in health-care spending

The combination of population ageing and rapid economic growth in the countries of Latin America and the Caribbean over the coming decades is likely to bring about a dramatic transformation in the economic and social fabric of the region. One of the major consequences of these changes will be a rapid and sustained increase in health spending. This section looks at three countries in the region (Brazil, Chile and Mexico), which were chosen because long-term projections of their per capita GDP are available (published by the Organization for Economic Cooperation and Development (OECD)). The analysis includes two European countries (Germany and Spain) as a reference.

Figure V.15 shows the impact of population ageing between 2010 and 2060 in the five countries selected. The population of older persons (aged 60 years and over) in the three Latin American countries is expected to grow

---

[7]   The Lee-Carter method was applied for modelling and projecting health expenditure, as follows: $\log(h(x,i)) = a(x) + k(i)*b(x) + f(x,i)$; where $h(x,i)$ represents annual average health spending for the age group x in country i; $a(x)$, $k(i)$ and $b(x)$ are the parameters of the model estimated using singular value decomposition; and $f(x,i)$ is the residual value. The projection assumes that $k(i)$ varies with per capita GDP according to the regression estimation $k(i) = c*d(i) + g(i)$; where k is the parameter estimated from the singular value decomposition and $d(i)$ is per capita GDP. It is assumed that the residual values $f(x,i)$ and $g(i)$ disappear linearly over the forecasting period (with weightings decreasing from 1.0 in 2010 to 0 in 2110). That is, the premise adopted here is that the residual values contain useful information only for the first 100 years of the forecast. See Mason and Miller (2013) for more detailed information on the model.

rapidly in the coming decades. In 2060, one in every three persons will be in this category. In Brazil, the proportion of older adults will more than triple from 10% of the total population in 2010 to 33% in 2060. A significant change is also expected in Chile (where this group will go from 13% of the population in 2010 to 34% in 2060) and Mexico (where it will go from 9% to 27% in the same period). The speed of this change is unprecedented. Owing to the rapid decline in fertility in these countries, the population will age much more quickly than it did in the European countries. Within 16 years, the proportion of older persons in Chile's population will match that of the current population in Spain; Brazil will reach that level within 25 years and Mexico within 30 years.

Figure V.15
Latin America and Europe (selected countries): projections for the proportion of the population aged 60 years and over, 2010-2060
(Percentages)

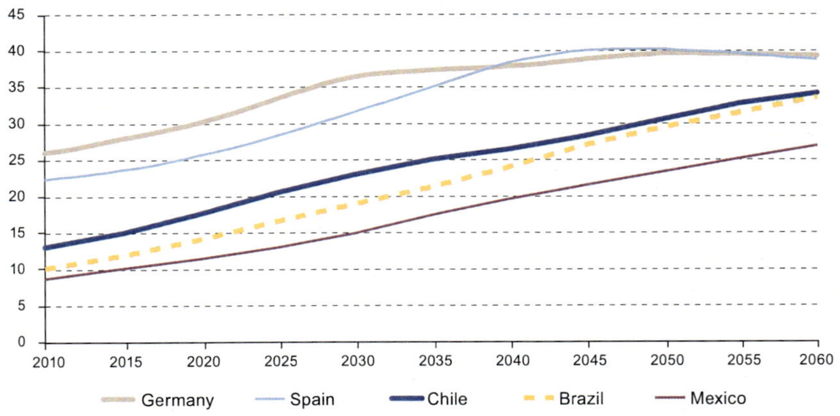

Source: Latin American and Caribbean Demographic Centre (CELADE)-Population Division of ECLAC, population estimates and projections: 2012 revision, and United Nations, *World Population Prospects: The 2012 Revision*, New York, 2012.

Although this transition is taking place much faster in the countries of Latin America than it did in Europe, it began earlier in Europe and is more advanced. As shown in figure V.15, the rate of population ageing is slowing in Spain and Germany, such that the percentage of older people should hold steady at between 35% and 40% of the total. Brazil, Chile and Mexico are expected to follow this trend, with the proportion of older persons in their populations stabilizing at between 35% and 40% of the total population in the final decades of the century.

The fact that older persons are becoming the predominant demographic group is a new phenomenon. To date, only Japan and some European countries have entered that demographic stage, and they have done so only in the past decade. Unless there is a dramatic reversal towards population rejuvenation, all countries will transition towards this demographic stage. For most of history, children have been the most numerous population group in all countries, with the under-20s making up the largest one. But the era of societies with a preponderance of children began drawing to a close in the late twentieth century. There followed a rapid increase in the working-age proportion of the population, which, growing at a faster rate than the dependent population, resulted in a demographic dividend. In future, older persons will eventually become the predominant demographic group in society, until a situation is reached in which two in five people will be older adults.

The demographic change described above will have major consequences. One of them is that these societies will allocate a substantial part of their revenue to health care since older people need such much more care than other age groups. As shown in figure V.14, in high-income economies a 90-year-old consumes on average six times more health-care resources than a person aged 20 years. In middle-income countries, this ratio is 3 to 1. Therefore, while it is true that health spending will increase as the population ages, the magnitude of that effect will depend largely on how close health spending in middle-income countries gets to that in the high-income countries.

The second of the two trends that will transform the region in the coming decades is related to the probability of rapid economic growth. Figure V.16 presents per capita GDP projections for Brazil, Chile and Mexico. The data come from a recent long-term forecast by OECD, which included these three countries from Latin America and the Caribbean along with others from different regions. The results are presented in dollars at constant 2005 prices, so that the trends observed reflect changes in real purchasing power. The data have been presented graphically using a logarithmic scale of per capita GDP, in order to highlight the convergence of the relative levels over time. The data for Germany and Spain are included as a reference.

Figure V.16
Latin America and Europe (selected countries): projections of per capita GDP, 2010-2060
(Thousands of dollars at constant 2005 prices)

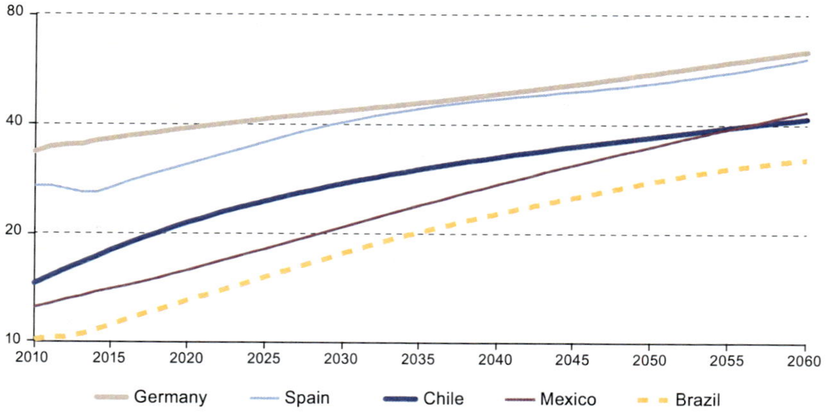

Legend: Germany — Spain — Chile — Mexico - - Brazil

Source: Economic Commission for Latin America and the Caribbean (ECLAC), on the basis of Organization for Economic Cooperation and Development (OECD), "Long-term baseline projections", *Economic Outlook*, No. 93, June 2013 [online] http://stats.oecd.org/Index.aspx?DataSetCode=EO93_LTB.

These Latin American economies, like other middle-income economies, are expected to grow at a faster pace in the coming decades than the high-income OECD economies, substantially reducing the income gap between them. Per capita income in Brazil is currently around US$ 10,000, about one third of that in Germany. However, Brazil is expected to see faster economic growth than Germany, so the OECD predicts that by 2060 per capita income in Brazil will be about half that of Germany. If, as expected, average income in Brazil triples in the coming decades, it will reach the current average level for OECD member countries. The projections also indicate that Chile and Mexico will follow a pattern of rapid economic growth in the coming decades: per capita GDP in Chile is expected to almost triple, and the pace of expansion of the Mexican economy could be even faster.

This surge in income can be expected to go hand in hand with a considerable increase in spending on health, since these middle-income economies are on track to match (and surpass) the current health spending patterns by age group in high-income countries. The analysis of the data relating to the health sector from the 22 countries participating in the global project on national transfer accounts indicates that rising income leads to proportionally larger increase in health spending, especially for older persons. The fact that spending on the health of older persons goes up more as per capita income increases is especially important because of the considerable expansion of this population group.

The impact of the twin trends of population ageing and economic growth is illustrated in figure V.17. As populations age, health spending increases since older persons require more medical care. As populations become wealthier, health expenditure also rises as higher per capita GDP comes with a proportionally larger expansion of health spending. The most probable result if these twin trends continue in Brazil, Chile and Mexico will be a sustained and unprecedented rise in health spending. Based on the forecast model used in this analysis, health spending could reach about 15% of GDP in these economies by 2060. For Brazil, Chile and Mexico, this represents a doubling of the size of the health sector relative to the economy.

The projected rapid growth in the health sector in these three Latin American countries means that they will surpass current German spending levels of about 11% of GDP within a few decades: by 2030 in the case of Brazil, by 2033 in Chile, and by 2048 in Mexico. Depending on the model, some European countries, such as Germany and Spain, will also see significant growth in the health sector (albeit at a slower rate than in Latin America) as their populations continue to age and to become wealthier. The demographic and economic convergence between these three Latin American countries and the two European ones (as evidenced in figures V.15 and V.16) is also reflected in the convergence in health spending as a percentage of GDP (see figure V.17). In 2011, there was a substantial gap between health spending in Mexico and in Germany —with Mexico (6.2% of GDP) spending about 45% less than Germany (11% of GDP). By 2060, this gap will have narrowed —with Mexico (13.8% of GDP) spending about 35% less than Germany (21% of GDP).

Figure V.17
Latin America and Europe (selected countries): projected health spending as a proportion of GDP, 2010-2060
(Percentages)

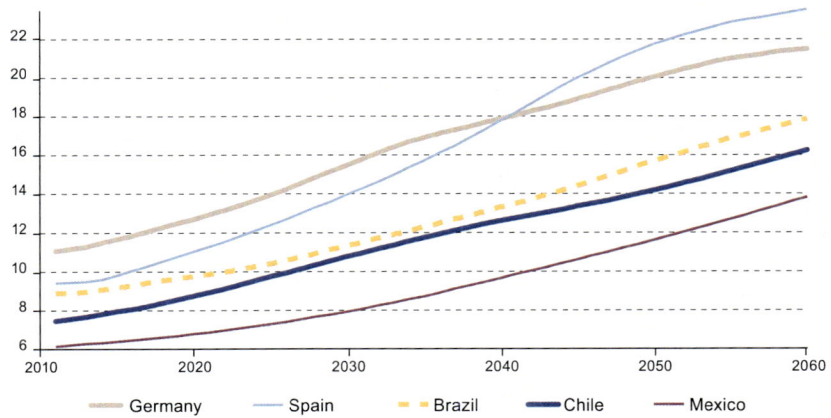

Source: Economic Commission for Latin America and the Caribbean (ECLAC), on the basis of the findings of the model constructed using the method developed by C. Mason and T. Miller, "Projecting health care expenditures for all NTA countries using a Lee-Carter approach", *NTA Working Paper*, 2013.

This dramatic change in the size of the health sector will be accompanied by an equally dramatic shift in the kinds of services being provided because of the different population that it will serve. Not only will the health sector be substantially larger, but it will be attending to very different needs to today's system. In present-day Chile, health spending on older persons accounts for about 30% of total health system spending, but by 2060, it is projected to account for 62% of the total. Even before then, by 2039, 1 out of every 2 pesos spent on health will be spent providing care to older persons. Similar trends are projected for Brazil and Mexico. This predicted shift in the population receiving the largest share of health sector services will profoundly transform the kinds of services the health system will offer: with rapidly increasing demand for health services targeting chronic diseases, such as heart disease, diabetes and cancer, as well as an important rise in the demand for long-term care. This will entail a fundamental restructuring of the health-care systems in these countries.

As the European countries are further along in the population ageing process, about half of their health sector is devoted to older persons (53% in Germany and 46% in Spain). The twin trends of continued population ageing and the shift towards greater spending on older persons as income increases are projected to lead to the domination of health-care spending by this age group: by 2060, older persons will account for 71% of health spending in Germany, and 69% in Spain.

3. Final considerations

On the basis of the analyses presented in this section on trends in population ageing and GDP growth and their combined impact on health care expenditure, the following conclusions can be drawn:

(i)   Applicability to other countries in the region

This analysis has focused on three Latin American countries (Brazil, Chile, and Mexico), owing to the availability of long-run forecasts of per capita GDP for these economies. The populations of these three countries are among the oldest in Latin America. However, the rapid and sustained increases in health spending forecast for these three countries are likely to occur in the other countries of the region as well, since all the countries in Latin America and the Caribbean will ultimately experience the twin trends of population ageing and rapid economic growth.

(ii) The expanding role of the State

States already bear most of the burden for financing health care for older persons. In addition, the catastrophic expenditures associated with many chronic illnesses and the enormous costs of long-term care are beyond the means of most individuals and families. Consequently, it is likely that financing health systems will emerge as a critical problem in Latin America and the Caribbean, requiring urgent government attention. A previous study on fiscal spending in the areas of health, pensions and education found that for many governments in the region, financing the health sector will probably pose a greater challenge than funding pensions (Miller, Mason and Holz, 2009).

(iii) Importance of prevention strategies

The illustrative projections presented confirm previous research (Miller, Mason and Holz, 2011; CELADE, 2010), showing that the impact of population ageing is likely to be as great in Latin America as in Europe. The magnitude of the growth in health care will bring about a major social transformation, as health care emerges as a key economic sector. Studies which have examined preventive care strategies, such as the recent OECD study on obesity (OECD, 2010), have concluded that prevention strategies will not result in significant cost savings for the health-care sector. If this holds true, then large increases in the size of the health sector in Latin America are unavoidable. As a result, countries will most likely have to choose between investing in preventive care or paying the consequences in terms of curative and palliative care. But both options involve an expansion of the health-care sector. Consequently, the decision to invest in broad-based preventive care strategies should not be based on presumed cost-savings, but rather on the improvement that these strategies are likely to make to the health of individuals and the health of economies.

Bibliography

CELADE (Latin American and Caribbean Demographic Centre-Population Division of ECLAC) (2010), "Illustrative projection of health care spending in Latin America and the Caribbean in the 2006-2040 period", *Population and Health in Latin America and the Caribbean: Outstanding Matters, New Challenges* (LC/L.3216(CEP.2010/3)), Santiago, Chile, ECLAC Ad Hoc Committee on Population and Development, May.

ECLAC (Economic Commission for Latin America and the Caribbean) (2008), *Millenium Development Goals. Progress Towards the Right to Health in Latin America and the Caribbean* (LC/G.2364/Rev.1), Santiago, Chile, November.

___ (2001), *Social Panorama of Latin America 2000-2001* (LC/G.2138-P), Santiago, Chile, October. United Nations publication, Sales No. E.01.II.G.141.

Johansson, Åsa and others (2012), "Looking to 2060: long-term global growth prospects", *OECD Economic Policy Paper*, No. 3, Paris, Organization for Economic Cooperation and Development (OECD).

Knaul, Felicia Marie and others (2011), "Household catastrophic health expenditures: a comparative analysis of twelve Latin American and Caribbean Countries", *Salud Pública de México*, No. 53, supplement 2, Cuernavaca, National Public Health Institute.

Lee, Ronald and Andrew Mason (eds.) (2011), *Population Aging and the Generational Economy: a Global Perspective*, Cheltenham, Edward Elgar Publishing.

Mason, Carl and Tim Miller (2013), "Projecting health care expenditures for all NTA countries using a Lee-Carter approach", *NTA Working Paper*.

Miller, Tim and Paulo Saad (2012), "Final technical report to IDRC on ageing and development: national transfer accounts in Latin America and the Caribbean", Santiago, Chile.

Miller, Tim, Carl Mason and Mauricio Holz (2011), "The fiscal impact of demographic change in ten Latin American countries: projecting public expenditures in education, health, and pensions", *Population Aging: Is Latin America Ready?*, Daniel Cotlear (ed.), Washington, D.C., World Bank.

Murray, Christopher and others (2003), "Assessing the distribution of household financial contributions to the health system: concepts and empirical application", *Health Systems Performance Assessment*, Geneva, World Health Organization (WHO), January.

OECD (Organization for Economic Cooperation and Development) (2013), "Long-term baseline projections", *Economic Outlook*, No. 93, June [online] http://stats.oecd.org/Index.aspx?DataSetCode=EO93_LTB.

___ (2010), *Obesity and the Economics of Prevention: Fit not Fat*, Paris.

PAHO (Pan American Health Organization) (2007), *Health in the Americas, 2007*, Washington, D.C.

Perticara, Marcela (2008), "Incidencia de los gastos de bolsillo en siete países latinoamericanos", *Políticas Sociales series*, No. 141 (LC/L.2879-P), Santiago, Chile, Economic Commission for Latin America and the Caribbean (ECLAC). United Nations publication, Sales No. S.08.II.G.18.

Xu, Ke (2005), "Distribution of health payments and catastrophic expenditures. Methodology", *Discussion Paper*, No. 2, Geneva, World Health Organization.

Xu, K., D. Evans and A. M. Aguilar Rivera (2005), "Designing health financing systems to reduce catastrophic health expenditure", *WHO Technical Briefs for Policy-Makers,* No. 2, Geneva, World Health Organization (WHO).

Publicaciones recientes de la CEPAL / *ECLAC recent publications*

Comisión Económica para América Latina y el Caribe / *Economic Commission for Latin America and the Caribbean*
Casilla 179-D, Santiago de Chile.

Véalas en: www.cepal.org/publicaciones
Publications may be accessed at: www.eclac.org

Contacto / Contact: publications@cepal.org

Informes periódicos / *Annual reports*

También disponibles para años anteriores / *Issues for previous years also available*

- *Balance Preliminar de las Economías de América Latina y el Caribe 2013*, 94 p.
  Preliminary Overview of the Economies of Latin America and the Caribbean 2013, 92 p.
- *Estudio Económico de América Latina y el Caribe 2013*, 222 p.
  Economic Survey of Latin America and the Caribbean 2013, 212 p.
- *Panorama de la Inserción Internacional de América Latina y el Caribe 2013*, 130 p.
  Latin America and the Caribbean in the World Economy 2013, 122 p.
- *Panorama Social de América Latina, 2013*, 228 p.
  Social Panorama of Latin America, 2013, 228 p.
- *La Inversión Extranjera Directa en América Latina y el Caribe 2013*, 154 p.
  Foreign Direct Investment in Latin America and the Caribbean 2012, 142 p.
- *Anuario Estadístico de América Latina y el Caribe 2013 / **Statistical Yearbook for Latin America and the Caribbean 2013**, 228 p.

Libros y documentos institucionales / *Institutional books and documents*

Prospectiva y desarrollo: el clima de la igualdad en América Latina y el Caribe a 2020, 2013, 72 p.
Comercio internacional y desarrollo inclusivo: construyendo sinergias, 2013, 210 p.
El Estado frente a la autonomía de las mujeres, 2012, 238 p.
Eslabones de la desigualdad: heterogeneidad estructural, empleo y protección social, 2012, 266 p.
Cambio estructural para la igualdad: una visión integrada del desarrollo, 2012, 330 p.
Structural Change for Equality: an integrated approach to development, 2012, 308 p.
La hora de la igualdad: brechas por cerrar, caminos por abrir, 2010, 290 p.
Time for Equality: closing gaps, opening trails, 2010, 270 p.
A Hora da Igualdade: Brechas por fechar, caminhos por abrir, 2010, 268 p.

Libros de la CEPAL / *ECLAC books*

120 *Broadband in Latin America: beyond connectivity*, **Valeria Jordán, Hernán Galperin and Wilson Peres (editors), 2013, 348 p.**
119 *La montaña rusa del financiamiento externo: el acceso de América Latina y el Caribe a los mercados internacionales de bonos desde la crisis de la deuda, 1982-2012, Inés Bustillo y Helvia Velloso, 2013, 150 p.*
119 *Debt financing rollercoaster: Latin American and Caribbean access to international bond markets since the debt crisis, 1982-2012,* **Inés Bustillo and Helvia Velloso, 2013, 135 p.**
118 *Sistemas de innovación en Centroamérica. Fortalecimiento a través de la integración regional, Ramón Padilla Pérez (ed.), 2013, 222 p.*
117 *Envejecimiento, solidaridad y protección social en América Latina y el Caribe. La hora de avanzar hacia la igualdad, Sandra Huenchuan, 2013. 190 p.*
117 *Ageing, solidarity and social protection in Latin America and the Caribbean Time for progress towards equality,* **Sandra Huenchuan, 2013, 176 p.**
116 Los *fundamentos de la planificación del desarrollo en América Latina y el Caribe. Textos seleccionados del ILPES (1962-1972), Ricardo Martner y Jorge Máttar (comps.), 2012, 196 p.*

115 *The changing nature of Asian-Latin American economic relations,* **German King, José Carlos Mattos, Nanno Mulder and Osvaldo Rosales (eds.), 2012, 196 p.**

114 *China y América Latina y el Caribe. Hacia una relación económica y comercial estratégica,* Osvaldo Rosales y Mikio Kuwayama, 2012, 258 p.

114 **China *and* Latin America and the Caribbean Building a strategic economic and trade relationship, Osvaldo Rosales y Mikio Kuwayama, 2012, 244 p.**

113 *Competitividad, sostenibilidad e inclusión social en la agricultura: Nuevas direcciones en el diseño de políticas en América Latina y el Caribe,* Octavio Sotomayor, Adrián Rodríguez y Mônica Rodrigues, 2012, 352 p.

Copublicaciones / *Co-publications*

Decentralization and Reform In Latin America. Improving Intergovernmental Relations, Giorgio Brosio and Juan P. Jiménez (eds.), ECLAC/Edward Elgar Publishing, United Kingdom, 2012.

Sentido de pertenencia en sociedades fragmentadas. América Latina desde una perspectiva global, Martín Hopenhayn y Ana Sojo (comps.), CEPAL/Siglo Veintiuno, Argentina, 2011.

Las clases medias en América Latina. Retrospectiva y nuevas tendencias, Rolando Franco, Martín Hopenhayn y Arturo León (eds.), CEPAL/Siglo XXI, México, 2010.

Innovation and Economic Development. The Impact of Information and Communication Technologies in Latin America, Mario Cimoli, André Hofman and Nanno Mulder, ECLAC/Edward Elgar Publishing, United Kingdom, 2010.

Sesenta años de la CEPAL. Textos seleccionados del decenio 1998-2008, Ricardo Bielschowsky (comp.), CEPAL/Siglo Veintiuno, Argentina, 2010.

El nuevo escenario laboral latinoamericano. Regulación, protección y políticas activas en los mercados de trabajo, Jürgen Weller (ed.), CEPAL/Siglo Veintiuno, Argentina, 2010.

Internacionalización y expansión de las empresas eléctricas españolas en América Latina, Patricio Rozas, CEPAL/Lom, Chile, 2009.

Coediciones / *Co-editions*

Perspectivas económicas de América Latina 2014: logística y competitividad para el desarrollo, CEPAL/OCDE, 2013.

Latin American Economic Outlook 2014: Logistics and Competitiveness for Development, ECLAC/OECD, 2013

Juventud y bono demográfico en Iberoamérica, Paulo Saad, Tim Miller, Ciro Martínez y Mauricio Holz, CEPAL/OIJ/UNFPA, 2012.

Perspectivas económicas de América Latina 2013. Políticas de Pymes para el Cambio Estructural, OCDE/CEPAL, 2012.

Latin American Economic Outlook 2013. SME Policies for Structural Change, OECD/ECLAC, 2012.

Perspectivas de la agricultura y del desarrollo rural en las Américas: una mirada hacia América Latina y el Caribe 2013, CEPAL/FAO/IICA, 2012.

Reforma fiscal en América Latina. ¿Qué fiscalidad para qué desarrollo?, Alicia Bárcena y Narcís Serra (eds.), CEPAL/SEGIB/CIDOB, 2012.

La sostenibilidad del desarrollo a 20 años de la Cumbre para la Tierra. Avances, brechas y lineamientos estratégicos para América Latina y el Caribe, CEPAL/ONU, 2012.

Sustainable development 20 years on from the Earth Summit. Progress, gaps and strategic guidelines for Latin America and the Caribbean, ECLAC/UN, 2012.

Perspectivas económicas de América Latina 2012.Transformación del Estado para el desarrollo, CEPAL/OCDE, 2011.

Latin America Outlook 2012. Transforming the State for Development, ECLAC/OECD, 2011.

Perspectives économiques de l'Amérique latine 2012. Transformation de l'État et Développement, CEPALC/OCDE, 2012.

Breeding Latin American Tigers. Operational principles for rehabilitating industrial policies, Robert Devlin and Graciela Moguillansky, ECLAC/World Bank, 2011.

Cuadernos de la CEPAL

101 *Redistribuir el cuidado: el desafío de las políticas,* Coral Calderón Magaña (coord.), 2013, 460 p.

101 **Redistributing care: the policy challenge, Coral Calderón Magaña (coord.), 2013, 420 p.**

100 *Construyendo autonomía. Compromiso e indicadores de género,* Karina Batthyáni Dighiero, 2012, 338 p.

99 *Si no se cuenta, no cuenta,* Diane Alméras y Coral Calderón Magaña (coords.), 2012, 394 p.

98 **Macroeconomic cooperation for uncertain times: The REDIMA experience, Rodrigo Cárcamo-Díaz, 2012,164 p.**

97 *El financiamiento de la infraestructura: Propuestas para el desarrollo sostenible de una política sectorial,* Patricio Rozas Balbontín, José Luis Bonifaz y Gustavo Guerra-García, 2012, 414 p.

96 *Una mirada a la crisis desde los márgenes,* Sonia Montaño (coord.), 2011, 102 p.

Cuadernos estadísticos de la CEPAL

41 *Los cuadros de oferta y utilización, las matrices de insumo-producto y las matrices de empleo. Solo disponible en CD,* 2013.

40 *América Latina y el Caribe: Índices de precios al consumidor. Serie enero de 1995 a junio de 2012. Solo disponible en CD,* 2012.

39 *América Latina y el Caribe: indicadores macroeconómicos del turismo. Solo disponible en CD,* 2010.

38 *Indicadores ambientales de América Latina y el Caribe, 2009. Solo disponible en CD,* 2010.

37 *América Latina y el Caribe: Series históricas de estadísticas económicas 1950-2008. Solo disponible en CD,* 2009.

Documentos de proyecto / *Project documents*

La economía del cambio climático en la Argentina: primera aproximación, 2014, 240 p.
La economía del cambio climático en el Ecuador 2012, 2012, 206 p.
Economía digital para el cambio estructural y la igualdad, 2013, 130 p
The digital economy for structural change and equality, 2014, 128 p.
Desarrollo de la telesalud en América Latina: aspectos conceptuales y estado actual, Alaneir de Fátima dos Santos y Andrés Fernández (editores), 2013, 614 p.
La integración de las tecnologías digitales en las escuelas de América Latina y el Caribe. Una mirada multidimensional, Guillermo Sunkel, Daniela Trucco, Andrés Espejo, 2013, 166 p.

Series de la CEPAL / *ECLAC Series*

Asuntos de Género / Comercio Internacional / Desarrollo Productivo / Desarrollo Territorial / Estudios Estadísticos / Estudios y Perspectivas (Bogotá, Brasilia, Buenos Aires, México, Montevideo) / **Studies and Perspectives** (The Caribbean, Washington) / *Financiamiento del Desarrollo / Gestión Pública / Informes y Estudios Especiales / Macroeconomía del Desarrollo / Manuales / Medio Ambiente y Desarrollo / Población y Desarrollo / Política Fiscal / Políticas Sociales / Recursos Naturales e Infraestructura / Reformas Económicas / Seminarios y Conferencias.*
Véase el listado completo en: www.cepal.org/publicaciones / *A complete listing is available at*: www.eclac.org/publications

Revista CEPAL / *CEPAL Review*

La Revista CEPAL se inició en 1976 como parte del Programa de Publicaciones de la Comisión Económica para América Latina y el Caribe, con el propósito de contribuir al examen de los problemas del desarrollo socioeconómico de la región. Las opiniones expresadas en los artículos firmados, incluidas las colaboraciones de los funcionarios de la Secretaría, son las de los autores y, por lo tanto, no reflejan necesariamente los puntos de vista de la Organización. La *Revista* CEPAL se publica en español e inglés tres veces por año.
CEPAL Review first appeared in 1976 as part of the Publications Programme of the Economic Commission for Latin America and the Caribbean, its aim being to make a contribution to the study of the economic and social development problems of the region. The views expressed in signed articles, including those by Secretariat staff members, are those of the authors and therefore do not necessarily reflect the point of view of the Organization. CEPAL Review is published in Spanish and English versions three times a year.

Observatorio demográfico / *Demographic Observatory*

Edición bilingüe (español e inglés) que proporciona información estadística actualizada, referente a estimaciones y proyecciones de población de los países de América Latina y el Caribe. Incluye también indicadores demográficos de interés, tales como tasas de natalidad, mortalidad, esperanza de vida al nacer, distribución de la población, etc. Desde 2013 el Observatorio aparece una vez al año.
Bilingual publication (Spanish and English) proving up-to-date estimates and projections of the populations of the Latin American and Caribbean countries. Also includes various demographic indicators of interest such as fertility and mortality rates, life expectancy, measures of population distribution, etc. Since 2013, the Observatory appears once a year.

Notas de población

Revista especializada que publica artículos e informes acerca de las investigaciones más recientes sobre la dinámica demográfica en la región, en español, con resúmenes en español e inglés. También incluye información sobre actividades científicas y profesionales en el campo de población.
La revista se publica desde 1973 y aparece dos veces al año, en junio y diciembre.
Specialized journal which publishes articles and reports on recent studies of demographic dynamics in the region, in Spanish with abstracts in Spanish and English. Also includes information on scientific and professional activities in the field of population.
Published since 1973, the journal appears twice a year in June and December.

Las publicaciones de las Naciones Unidas y de la Comisión Económica para América Latina y el Caribe (CEPAL) se pueden adquirir a través de:

Publicaciones de las Naciones Unidas
PO Box 960
Herndon VA 20172
Estados Unidos

Tel. 1-703-661-1571
Fax 1-703-996-1010
Contacto: publications@un.org
Pedidos: order@un.org

Publications of the United Nations and the Economic Commission for Latin America and the Caribbean (ECLAC) can be ordered through:

United Nations Publications
PO Box 960
Herndon VA 20172
USA

Tel. 1-703-661-1571
Fax 1-703-996-1010
Contact: publications@un.org
Orders: order@un.org

www.un.org/publications